ur between VII & VIII.

# THE BEST ALPINE START YOU CAN GET

Climbing packs the way we want them

For more than fifty years Mountain Equipment has been at the forefront of Himalayan and alpine climbing. We've now taken that experience, passion and opinion to the design of our new range of climbing packs. Lightweight, durable and highly weather resistant, the Tupilak series of packs have been developed specifically for climbers and mountaineers needing the very best in simple, functional design. Excelling on rock, ice and mixed ground, they provide uncompromising functionality for alpinism's leading edge.

## MOUNTAIN
### EQUIPMENT

mountain-equipment.co.uk

# THE
# ALPINE JOURNAL
## 2018

Glen Denny's stunning photograph of Royal Robbins on the epic, eight-day first ascent of the Half Dome route *Tis-sa-ack* (VI, 5.9, A4), climbed with Don Peterson in 1969.

# THE
# ALPINE JOURNAL
## 2018

## The Journal of the Alpine Club

A record of mountain adventure
and scientific observation

Editor: Ed Douglas

Production: Jane Beagley

Volume 122

Number 366

Supported by the
MOUNT EVEREST FOUNDATION

*Published by*
THE ALPINE CLUB

© 2018 by the Alpine Club

THE ALPINE JOURNAL 2018
Volume 122 No 366

www.alpine-club.org.uk

Address all editorial communication to the Hon Editor:
Alpine Club, 55 Charlotte Rd, London, EC2A 3QF
email: journal.editor@alpine-club.org.uk

Address all sales and distribution communications to:
Cordee, 11 Jacknell Rd, Dodwells Bridge Ind Est, Hinckley, LE10 3BS

Back numbers:
Apply to the Alpine Club, 55 Charlotte Rd, London, EC2A 3QF or, for
1969 to date, apply to Cordee, as above.

First published in 2018 by The Alpine Club
Typeset by Jane Beagley, Vertebrate Publishing
Printed and bound by Novoprint SA, Barcelona

A CIP catalogue record for this book is available from The British Library

ISBN 978-0-9569309-7-2

Front cover: Traversing towards the Grande Rocheuse. *(Ben Tibbetts)*

Endpapers
Front: One of the photographs from an album given to E O Shebbeare by
the 1929 German Kangchenjunga expedition, both of which feature in this
year's *Alpine Journal. (Sue Morton, DAV)*
Back: Micha Rinn on the summit ridge of Monarch Mountain after the
first ascent of *Game of Thrones*. The Waddington massif is on the left
skyline. *(Simon Richardson)*

# Foreword

On 7 August 1945, a day after the American air force dropped the atom bomb on Hiroshima, the *Manchester Guardian* ran this short paragraph on the inconsequential world of mountaineering: 'A British Mountaineering Council has been formed by the various mountaineering clubs of Britain. Its chief objects are to encourage the sport of mountaineering and to make it more widely known that it is by no means expensive; to give advice and help on clothes, equipment, bivouacking, food, and the best climbing centres; to put climbers in touch with local clubs and leading mountaineers; and to provide instructors for training leaders for recreational organisations, for whom there is already a considerable demand.'

Many readers will know that the BMC was formed in December 1944 and may wonder why the *Manchester Guardian* took eight months to report the news. One answer was the new organisation's stuttering progress. While the inaugural meeting was indeed held on 2 December 1944, the Scottish Mountaineering Club held its own annual general meeting that day and voted not to approve the new organisation's constitution, fearing excessive English influence. There was also a letter to the Club's president Leo Amery questioning how it was that the Alpine Club could breathe life into this new creature when the Committee hadn't discussed it and it hadn't been put to a general meeting. These issues were addressed, ruffled feathers smoothed, but it wasn't until 15 December 1945 that the BMC constitution was finally agreed. Considering the debate surrounding the BMC's latest constitutional reform one is tempted to quote the king of Jerusalem: there is nothing new under the sun.

Putting such vexed issues to one side, it's undeniably the case that the world of British mountaineering and rock climbing so familiar to Geoffrey Winthrop Young, the BMC's greatest champion, is utterly transformed. There are now tens of thousands of British climbers who don't ever go outside let alone anywhere near a mountain. Performance and all that implies dominates climbing in a way that it simply didn't 20 years ago, let alone 74. 'Trad' rock climbing is the exception rather than the rule in the rest of the world. Those of us with a passion for ethical alpinism must count ourselves a small minority in this brave new world.

Even worse, one of the fundamental joys of mountaineering, the freedom of the hills is increasingly mired in bureaucracy and even corruption, as Ian Wall's report from Nepal in this edition of the *Alpine Journal* makes clear. According to a government enquiry, 35% of helicopter rescues in Nepal were fraudulent, costing insurers $4m. Trekking staff members have even been spiking their clients' food with laxatives or baking soda to provoke illnesses that prompt helicopter rescues and a kickback that is worth more than the price the trekker paid for their holiday. Sometimes the trekkers have shared in the spoils themselves. If you want to know why your insurance premiums have risen steeply, there's your answer.

Sharp practice in the Himalaya isn't confined to spurious rescues. One guiding company was hauled in recently to explain to the tourism ministry how names could appear on an Everest permit when no monies had been paid to the relevant authority: the company has been fined $44,000. Then there is the issue of liaison officers, paid for by expeditions, who decide to trouser their fee and remain at home, or else far from where they might do some good. The very principle of peak fees for most mountains is questionable. Why is it that a mountaineer should pay hundreds, even thousands of dollars to go climbing when a trekker can access the Everest region for tens of dollars. Is their impact so much greater?

What would Geoffrey Winthrop Young make of all this? He would find interesting parallels, I'm sure, with the struggles the Alpine Club had with Chamonix guides in the late 19th century when sharp practice and low standards were challenged, as the historian Koen Van Loocke's work on the early guiding profession illustrates in recent editions of the *Alpine Journal*, including this one. Young himself was an advocate for guideless climbing and maintaining individual responsibility and self-reliance. He was also an advocate for trusting young people to get on with things. If there are problems for alpinism, then it's down to alpinists to advocate for change and pressure those with access to power to represent our case properly. No one else will do it for us.

After several years' service Susan Jensen has stepped down as associate editor in charge of Area Notes. I'd like to express the Club's thanks to her, and also to Rod Smith, who has taken over as associate editor with responsibility for the 'In Memoriam' section. I'd also like to offer my personal thanks to Peter Rowland and the Alpine Club Photo Library for their contribution. He was particularly helpful in tracking down images of those members of the Club who died in the First World War. Their sacrifice, so ably recorded by Peter Foster on page 105, puts the travails of climbers and climbing organisations into sharp perspective.

*Ed Douglas*

**Correction**
In last year's obituary for Ken Wilson, we misidentified the controversial 1960s rock climber Keith McCallum as Duncan McCallum. We apologise for the confusion.

# Contents

THE YOUTH OF TODAY

PAST TIMES

NORTH AMERICA

HIGH ASIA

THE GREAT WAR

SCIENCE & NATURE

ART & LITERATURE

HISTORY

AREA NOTES & MEF

This year's frontispiece illustrations feature members of the Alpine Club who died in the First World War to commemorate the centenary of the Armistice signed on 11 November 1918. For a more detailed account of their sacrifice, please see Peter Foster's article 'The Alpine Club at War: 1914-18' on page 105.

# The Youth of Today

Capt C F K Carfrae (1884-1915), 5th Battalion Oxford & Bucks,
killed near Ypres.

# Arjuna's Bow

The south-west pillar of Arjuna (6100m) in Kishtwar, climbed in 2017 by Ben Silvestre, Uisdean Hawthorn and Pete Graham. They called their route *Gandiva* (E3, M5, 1400m) after the bow given to the hero Arjuna, by the creator Brahma. 'We thought this a fitting name as the arête is bow shaped and faces towards the Brammah massif.' *(All photos courtesy of Uisdean Hawthorn and the team)*

*Arjuna in Kishtwar is a dramatic granite massif that has seen a small but significant number of ascents in the last few decades. A Polish group climbed Arjuna South via the south-east ridge in 1981. Two years later, a Polish expedition climbed two new routes, one up the west face of Arjuna South in alpine style, another up the central pillar of the west face to reach Arjuna's main summit, fixing the lower 500m of the climb. In 2017, a Slovenian team comprising Urban Novak, Marko Prezelj and Aleš Česen established another new line on Arjuna's west face, naming it All or Nothing (ED+, M7+, WI5+, A0, 1400m). It was the second ascent of the main summit and the first in alpine style.*

*Switched on to the peak's remaining potential by Mick Fowler, in September 2017 Ben Silvestre, Pete Graham and Uisdean Hawthorn left the road head near Gulabgarh on the Chenab river, two days' drive north-west of Manali and north-east of the town of Kishtwar. After an exciting river crossing via a wooden box suspended on steel wires, they spent three days trekking up the Kijai Nala to reach base camp, a lush meadow above a glacier, on 17 September. After a rest day, they spent two days finding a route to the bottom of the unclimbed west pillar of Arjuna South (6100m) where they stashed some equipment. This was a long 11km walk away,*

The memorable road from Udaipur to Gulabgarh in Kishtwar.

Pete Graham and Ben Silvestre at a shepherd's hut on the walk-in to base camp.

The initial ice gully at the start of the route.

*so they chose to acclimatise on an unnamed peak just above base camp (c5400m), walking first up to 5,000m and then returning with a tent. An attempt on the summit was curtailed because of poor rock but the climbers achieved their aim and now prepared for the main event.*

On our return to camp after a day of stashing gear on the upper glacier, there was a huge thunderstorm – the first bad weather of the trip – and we had to dig trenches to stop base camp from flooding. This continued for a couple of days, but as it cleared the forecasts indicated a weeklong high pressure, and it became clear that our time was approaching. Sadly Pete got ill, and we had to wait a couple of days, but this allowed the face to clear from the storm, and allowed Uisdean and I to sample the excellent bouldering around camp.

Finally it was time to go, and we left camp early with light bags, with most of our gear already at the base of the route, at 4,700m. We were fairly intimidated, so we brought a big rack in case we needed to aid sections, or rappel the route. We packed food for four days, and enough gas to melt water for six. Given the steepness of the rock and size of the packs, we chose to bring jumars for the seconds, the leader climbing on a single rope, with a tagline to haul his pack if necessary.

The following morning we left early and climbed some chossy ramps to access steep snow ramps, leading up to a notch at 5,000m. This gave the

Pete Graham leading one of the hard pitches on day one. The granite was solid and excellent.

start of the real rock climbing, and we were pleasantly surprised to find excellent, featured granite, leading up to the start of the arête. Six excellent pitches took us to a palatial bivy site at around 5,300m. Pete fixed another pitch to below a large corner whilst Uisdean cleared the ledge of stones.

A comfortable night spooning in the Rick Graham Sufferbag v3.0, [Editor's note: Pete is the son of the Lake District climber Rick Graham] left us feeling ready for what looked like the steepest, blankest section. I took the lead, and the corner provided an excellent technical exercise. From the next belay it seemed as though the cracks would not link up, but the appearance of 'chicken head' protrusions on the face made a continuation seem possible. A traverse around the arête gave access to another crack, which lead up and back round the arête to the base of an intimidating chimney. Thankfully, this was avoided by climbing chicken heads on the right wall, in a fairly run-out position, to gain a steep and strenuous hand crack. Above this, another traverse around the arête, in an extremely airy position, gave access to a full 60m pitch reminiscent of the *Strand* at Gogarth. We were all in disbelief at the quality of the climbing, though the seconds had to enjoy it in their imaginations, as they struggled with jumars and big bags. The 'Strand' pitch gained easier-angled ground and Uisdean led a few long pitches to a good bivy site near the top of the pillar at around 5,800m.

Happily, this bivy site was exposed to some wind, and we had to spoon with all our might to keep warm. We left camp slowly the following morning,

Graham leading the fourth pitch on day one.

Ben Silvestre leading the big roof on day two.

with Pete leading us to the top of the pillar in three pitches. From here we had to abseil 30m into a notch, and we wondered for a while whether to leave a rope fixed. Pete and I used this tactic in Alaska a couple of years ago, which reduces the commitment, but necessitates a descent by the same route. Eventually we decided that we could probably climb back up by aiding some thin cracks, if absolutely necessary, so we pulled the ropes and committed.

Above us a headwall loomed, with some roofs blocking our view to what lay above. I took over and did a 30m pitch on excellent chicken-heads to a short way below the roofs. There seemed to be a notch, which I aimed for, pulling through on huge holds, with all the exposure one could ask for. I stopped above to haul up my bag, change into my big boots, and catch my breath since we were passing the 6,000m mark, and then led up snow to belay a short way above. A long pitch on steep snow took us to a small, but sheltered bivy.

That night was a lot warmer, and our fatigue made the much-reduced size of the ledge seem fairly insignificant. We rose early and Uisdean did a couple of big traverse pitches to land us below the right-hand of two 'horns', which dominated the summit area of the mountain. A steep and extremely strenuous mixed step guarded entry to the gully, which gave great ice climbing up to the summit ridge, and then the summit, in a further three pitches. We stayed there an unusually long time, perhaps 20 minutes, and then began to descend off the back.

About 12 abseils down an obvious icy gully landed us on a glacier, which we walked down in the moonlight, until a steepening demanded a further five abseils. Arriving in a notch above a continuation gully, we stopped to

Pete leading off on day three.

Steep pitches out of a notch on day three were made manageable by more excellent rock, this time featuring large chicken heads.

The third bivouac.

Uisdean Hawthorn leading off on the fourth day.

brew up, eventually deciding that we were too tired to blindly stumble down the gully in the dark. We stopped for a short sleep, which turned out to be profoundly deep, and were woken neither by the dawn, nor the Nalgene bottle, which we failed to shut properly and soaked our sleeping bags.

We rose before the sun hit the gully, and after a further four abseils, and much gratitude in our decision to wait for light, we reached the snow cone we had ascended to begin with, and arrived straight back at our tent. A frenzy of eating, and extreme satisfaction in the balmy temperatures, allowed us to recuperate enough to carry our bags most of the way to base camp that evening. We decided to call the route *Gandiva* (5.11, or E3, M5, 1400m), which is the name of a bow given to Arjuna, hero of the *Mahabharata*, by the creator god Brahma. We thought this a fitting name as the arête is shaped like a bow and faces the Brammah massif.

There are many other possible objectives in the valley, from 300m rock routes on quality granite to 900m big walls, to more typically mixed alpine objectives, predominantly ridges of all difficulties. Arjuna itself is a very large mountain with a huge amount of potential, much like the north face of the Grandes Jorasses, and many more quality lines.

Pete Graham on the summit ridge.

Uisdean Hawthorn, Ben Silvestre and
Pete Graham on the summit of Arjuna.

Pete Graham back at base camp.

BEN TIBBETTS

# Aiguille du Jardin

The summit of the Aiguille Verte (4122m) with the Grande Rocheuse (4102m) and the Aiguille du Jardin (4035m) to the east or right. The *West Pillar Direct* (TD+, VII, 500m) takes an elegant line through the complex terrain of its south face. For a topo, see Alps & Dolomites on page 239. *(Ben Tibbetts)*

*The Aiguille du Jardin is among the more serious 4000ers to reach, more difficult than either of its illustrious neighbours the Aiguille Verte or Les Droites. From many aspects it appears, like the Grande Rocheuse, as a subsidiary summit on the east ridge of the Aiguille Verte. However as you approach the Couvercle refuge in summer you reach the lip of the Talèfre basin and the magnificent view opens up before you. For the final few hundred metres as you walk up the old moraine, the Aiguille du Jardin stands out proudly from the ridgeline directly ahead of you. From that angle it certainly appears as an independent summit, its imposing south face defended by magnificent buttresses of steep red granite. This collection of buttresses has remained barely explored, except perhaps by crystal hunters, despite being visible from the terrace of the refuge. Will Sim and Ben Tibbetts found a new line on the west pillar: a dozen pitches of sculpted granite grooves and strenuous cracks leading to easier mixed terrain and the summit.*

In 1911 the Austrian optician Karl Blodig became the first person to climb all the 4,000m peaks of the Alps. Two years later he discovered that the Aiguille du Jardin and Grand Rocheuse had been recognised as independent summits rather than mere subsidiaries of the Aiguille Verte. Thanks to the

11

Will Sim finishing up the cracks and grooves of pitch two on the *West Pillar Direct*. (Ben Tibbetts)

outbreak of war, it wasn't until 1931 that Blodig was able to attempt them. He climbed the *Whymper Couloir* with his son but at the Col de la Grand Rocheuse they were caught in a storm and had to retreat. Blodig returned in 1932, aged 72. Unaware that it had had its first ascent just five days earlier, he climbed the north-east couloir of the Col Armand Charlet solo. Having crossed the rimaye at 6.25am, Blodig reached the Col at 3.15pm, climbing, we should remember, with basic crampons that had no front points and on terrain approaching 60°.

'I was pleasantly surprised when the top was completely calm … though my fingers were so cold and stiff that I failed to open the tin of stewed peaches that I had been looking forward to for hours.' He continued upwards, but 'after the outrageous effort I put my old muscles through I only managed to advance at a snail's pace.' He reached the Grande Rocheuse summit at 5.55pm 'with strangely mixed feeling of unspeakable bliss and legitimate pride. I had longed for this moment for years, and many times doubted whether I would succeed.' He returned to the col to bivouac for the night before ascending the north-west ridge of the Aiguille du Jardin the following morning. He returned once more to the col, gathered up his tent and climbed back down the couloir and descended to Argentière. In his youth he had been proud of his achievements; 'today I've become small and modest because I know how often I barely controlled my fate and only a benevolent gesture of the mountain let me return unharmed.'[1]

1. K Blodig, 'Grande Rocheuse und Aiguille du Jardin', *Des Deutschen und Österreichischen Alpenvereins (Jahrbuch)*, Vol 64, Innsbruck/Munich, 1933, pp100-4.

Will Sim leading pitch four, behind the 'obelisk'. *(Ben Tibbetts)*

Working out the best line up mixed terrain to the summit. The Dent de Géant and Mont Blanc emerge from cloud in the background. *(Ben Tibbetts)*

## June 2018

I used to play the saxophone as a youth. I sometimes played by myself in churches or in wild outdoor spaces where I felt infinitely connected as the sound reverberated into infinity. In the last decade I have played irregularly and now am often disappointed with the incoherent sounds I make. I find rock climbing can be similar. When you are well-practised and attuned to the rock, no matter what your actual level, the sensations and connections can sometimes be powerful, even on the most modest cliffs or boulders. For several years my rock climbing has atrophied, as photography took up more and more of my energy. In a small town culture like Chamonix people talk endlessly of who climbed or skied which line and in what style. It nourishes a culture of performance. I sometimes wonder though if performance, and what seems like its natural corollary, ego, is not on some level the very opposite of creativity. I find one of the many joys of art and photography are their uncompetitive nature.

For my projects I see mountain skills like rock climbing or skiing not as ends in themselves but as tools to get to extraordinary places, both physical and psychological, where I can begin learning from the landscape. These, and the creative tools of drawing or photography, I see as ways of opening my consciousness to my surroundings. Once in a while it precipitates that gorgeous yet ephemeral experience: the hum and flow of synergy with the environment.

Halfway through June, having only just hung up my skis and barely climbed anything technical in six months, I wondered if I would actually be able to grapple my way up the routes I hoped to do during the summer. The winter season had left me with overgrown thighs and withered arms: like a T-Rex. The exigencies of writing, drawing and designing a book were keeping me surprisingly busy, and weak. Nevertheless the high-altitude rock was drying quickly and I wanted to try a line I had spotted on the Aiguille du Jardin before the desperate heat of mid-summer.

I had noticed the steep red pillars of the Jardin several times over the years, but they are in a wild location and there are plenty of excellent routes that are much easier to access. It was only when I was hunting for an interesting

Above: Will leading the devious traverse after pitch seven. *(Ben Tibbetts)*

Right: The beautifully textured wall on pitch five of the *West Pillar Direct.* *(Ben Tibbetts)*

route for my 4,000ers book project that I realised it could be better than the classic east ridge. I rang many climbers with an intimate know-ledge of the massif and it appeared there were only three routes on these buttresses, climbed in 1964 and 1967 and a further line, by a Scottish friend, Simon Richardson, climbed in 1995. Simon sent me some pho-tos of their ascent and confirmed the rock was clean, highly featured granite. Examining my own photos, taken from afar, it appeared there might be a direct line up the centre of the west pillar. I had no idea how hard the line might be, but realised that there was a strong chance it would stretch my capabilities.

Will Sim and I had planned to do a route together and he seemed like the perfect fit. We had trained together to become guides but had barely climbed in the subsequent four years. He is almost a decade younger than me, an exceptionally gifted mountaineer but all the while easy-going, gracious and unassuming. He has a humble and balanced temperament that is unusual in a gifted climber of his age, all this hiding behind a cheeky grin, full of mischief.

Will and I wandered up to the Couvercle refuge on a hot afternoon as the first cumulus were germinating and shifting around the highest peaks. As I sat on a boulder not far below the hut I spotted a young bearded vulture

turning on the thermals above. Since their reintroduction in Haute-Savoie in 1987 the fragile population of this beautiful endangered bird has been growing, their territories spreading slowly.[2] Though I had often spotted them in the nearby Aravis mountains, this was the first time I had seen one in the Mont Blanc massif.

The refuge was one of the first I visited in the Alps and it has hardly changed in nearly two decades: the edges have worn, the musty odours deepened and rubber clogs replaced with Crocs. The guardian, Christophe Lièvre, lent us his spotting scope, not for watching birds but for a closer

2. The bearded vulture reproduces very slowly. Having been eradicated from the Alps around the beginning of the 20th century, a program of captive breeding and release has managed to re-establish the population. There are now 15 pairs of bearded vulture in the French Alps and nearly 50 across the Alps.

inspection of the Aiguille du Jardin. Our initial plan was to attempt the 1964 route and perhaps come back for a new route. We sat on the massive Couvercle boulder and waited for brief clearings between the burgeoning clouds. At the first glimpse we revised our plan: we could see cracks and corners that almost linked up the centre of the pillar where I had envisaged the new line. We were very conscious though that through a telescope, or even quite close up for that matter, you can't get any idea of how hard the moves might be. Would we find a way up at 6a or would Will have to winch me up a pitch of 7b?

The refuge was peaceful; just a dozen folk murmured over their dinner.

After a short sleep Will and I set out at 2.45am, plodding slowly up the interminable glacier. A few other pairs of torches moved almost imperceptibly into other corners of the basin. It was the first fine weather in weeks but early in the season so the mountains were still quiet as the winter snows melted away. We crossed the rimaye up into the Armand Charlet couloir and then right across exposed snow to the base of the groove we had spotted. We kicked out a ledge in the snow, plugged some gear into a crack, and Will set off at 5.30am. The first hues of dawn soon began to glow on the Grandes Jorasses and Mont Blanc, but both the rock and air were cold and it was several hours before the sun crept round to meet us.

Within a few moves Will began making pleasing sounds, little grunts of delight, like a pig searching for truffles. He bridged delicately up the initial groove, across a band of quartzite, and sinuously wound his way up the cracks above. The rope crept out steadily. ('Ten metres! ... Four metres!') Once he had a belay I squeezed my feet, unaccustomed to such discomfort, into cold rock shoes. The rock was exceptionally clean and featured but I had never been so out shape. It seemed almost like a form of disrespect to come up here having not taken the time to train my body and mind. Though Will had climbed with the stealth of a gecko I could feel myself gripping hard on the holds. My feet felt wooden and uncoordinated, hunting for the largest holds. Though the moves were varied and delightful from the very start, with a heavy pack and a massive camera on my hip I could tell right away I would struggle on the steeper terrain above.

I joined Will, took the gear and set off, catapulting myself up with forced self-confidence. The pitch was mercifully easy, but the wide bulging cracks still felt wild and exposed. My fingers were still soft from a winter of wearing gloves and the sharp feldspar crystals soon took chunks out of my skin, a just reward for inelegant technique. It had snowed several days previously and both new and old snow was still lying in shady corners, making even easy cracks a little tenuous. After each pitch we marvelled at the variety of forms we encountered: chunky quartz veins, ripples and 'chicken heads'. At the fourth pitch our line crossed Richardson's route at a massive obelisk and a jammed block. Behind the tower was a tough-looking crack and I defaulted on my lead, assessing quickly that I might go overdrawn on my abilities. There was also a steep ramp of snow at the base of the crack that ensured cold wet shoes for the first brutal moves. As Will led up a new

Descending west from the summit of the Aiguille du Jardin. *(Ben Tibbetts)*

pattern of grunts and whistles suggested I had made the right choice. The sun began to creep round from the north-east to burn off the remaining moisture in the air and after struggling my way up behind him we finally arrived below a steep wall of incipient cracks: the crucial passage of our proposed line. Thirty metres beyond we could see an attractive groove, but the wall immediately above us looked like a different order of difficulty.

Will left his rucksack with me and set off to investigate. I relaxed in the sun and watched the story unfold, offering up the usual encouraging words. As the sequence became more mysterious I began to wonder how I would follow. The shallow cracks straight above looked rather desperate so Will climbed across the crest and out of sight to the right and then reappeared high above. To finally reach the groove he then climbed down another crack, balanced across a slab and arrived at a comfortable niche. We hadn't brought a haul line so I tied Will's pack onto the second rope and nursed it up beside me. A surprisingly elegant sequence of holds emerged one at a time from the blank looking wall but as I stretched up for a distant knobble my toe slipped and the crystals lacerated my index finger before spitting me off into space, ragged and bleeding.

A couple more corner pitches led us to the crest and a devious traverse finally brought us to a snowy saddle behind the first tower. The obvious chimney above, taken by the original 1964 route, was choked with ice so I crept up into a groove out right. I climbed easily for 20m until the cracks flared wider than our largest cam. They were icy and wet. My confidence faded quickly and I edged uncomfortably from side to side trying to work out what to do. As I sensed defeat the remaining energy and willpower drained from my arms. I could see the move was barely even difficult, but the moist rock scared me.

'Come on Ben, your not even trying,' Will called up in a withering tone. I looked again at the crack and tried the moves in my head. 'You bet I'm not even trying,' I thought. I could see myself flailing awkwardly in the crack. As my foot squirmed on a wet hold I imagined myself falling and smashing into the slab below. No phone reception here: rescue was unthinkable. My fears spun out of control and after a few minutes I retreated several metres to set up a belay. Will led through without even noticing the move.

A final pitch led us out to easier mixed terrain that was buried in deep saturated snow. I began grafting my way up but it was like climbing couscous. Some steps required several minutes' effort only for me to sink back up to my waist. It took nearly an hour to draw out one miserable rope length and I began to realise we might have to sleep the night on the ridge. Thankfully when we traversed round onto the east face the cooler snow led us more easily to the summit at around 5pm. With the sun already sinking in the west we scuttled down the north-west ridge, weaving around the various rocky towers and up onto the Grande Rocheuse as the afternoon clouds grew around us. We approached the precipitous west ridge of the Rocheuse and made several false starts before finally finding a rappel. Having assumed we would need to descend the complicated Moine ridge we were pleased to find that we were so late that the shaded slopes were already refreezing so we began the slow and meticulous business of descending the Whymper couloir, reaching the rimaye after dark and the refuge at 11pm.

As we stumbled back down the glacier I thought back over the day. Though I was immensely satisfied to have climbed the route and made it back down safely, I had found the experience mentally draining. I had just enough energy to drag myself up, and hardly any to open myself up to a more profound experience of the mountain environment. For many of the pitches I was stretched to the edge of my ability, with barely any margin to manage the delicate icy conditions. It reminded me that without a steady level of training it becomes difficult to climb in an open and calm state of mind. I wondered though: is the best climber the one pulling on the smallest holds, the one having the most fun, or the one having the most profound experience? Only rarely do these all seem to align. I knew for sure though that if I should have the good fortune to remain fit and survive that long I would be very grateful to be able to pursue my dreams aged 72 like Karl Blodig.

• An account of the first ascent of the *West Pillar Direct* (TD+, VII, 500m), Aiguille du Jardin. Ben Tibbetts' first book *Alpenglow*, featuring the finest 50 routes on all the 4,000ers is published next year.

LEO HOULDING

# The Spectre: An Antarctic Diary

Snow kiting with the expedition's objective Spectre, the tallest peak,
in the background. *(All photos courtesy of Berghaus)*

It's 20 November and we're in a Twin Otter heading south. My god this is
big country. The scale is overwhelming. Why do I choose to repeatedly
put myself through these epic trials? We just flew past the Pirrit Hills,
an impressive group of *nunataks*: rocky peaks protruding through the ice
about 160km from Union glacier. They were our plan B if we hadn't managed to raise enough money for the Spectre. The plan had been to ski in
from Union, climb and kite back. A similar trip to what we're now attempting but almost half the cost and about 10% of the distance.

Right now I'm wondering if we should have bitten off that smaller mouth-
ful, because it still looks pretty far. Spectre is 10 times that distance and our
trip will be 10 times as tough. Be careful what you wish for. I can't believe
people walk all that we are now flying over on their way to the South Pole.
It's so far and so featureless. It looks like an ocean: small waves of *sastrugi*
texture a surface that appears flat although it rises for 3,000m in altitude.

There are a fair few teams on their way from Hercules Inlet to the pole
right now, including my friend Carl Alvey, who is doing it for the fourth
time. The Ice Maidens, a British army team hoping to be the first all-female
to cross Antarctica, left Union last night and are currently on their way
to the Ross Sea. They have 1,700km to travel and no kites. Ben Saunders

Hard at work hauling a pulk. Most of
the polar travel was done with kites.
*(Berghaus)*

Leo Houlding, left, and Jean Burgun
head towards the summit of the
Spectre. *(Berghaus)*

is walking solo for a similar distance in the opposite direction. Their endeav-
ours give me confidence in our own. There's no way I'm psychologically
strong enough for such a long, monotonous walk. We are planning to haul
sleds with climbing gear to the foot of the Spectre, one of the most remote
mountains on earth, climb a new route and then complete a trans-continen-
tal trip using snow-kiting technology. It feels like a new kind of adventure.
The part I'm most concerned about is hauling sleds. Respect to all those
other polar travellers: we wish them the very best. Wind assistance will
make our journey far easier and faster, but then we have more than twice as
much stuff as those teams, and will be climbing a major objective en route.

My two companions are Jean Burgun from Haute Alp, an experienced
alpinist, big-wall climber and snow-kiter, part of the scene in the Alps that
is using kites to climb easy Alpine climbs in minutes. He and his wife are
custodians of a mountain hut in Val Louise. Mark Sedon is a mountain
guide and filmmaker. Born and raised in Christchurch, New Zealand,
he has led commercial teams to the summit of Everest as well as half a
dozen trips to Antarctica. The plane will drop us off at its maximum pay-
load range, known as the point of no return, but we have already past that
point. The time for fear and anxiety is behind us. There is no more preparation. It is time for confidence and cautious action. We have what we
have and must overcome every obstacle we face with the contents of these
pulks, our skills, cunning and experience.

No doubt there will be some fumbling in the first few days as we acclimatise to the altitude and cold and begin to figure out what clothing, gloves and
goggle set-ups work best and drill our camp, cooking and kiting systems. But
within a week, we'll be a tight unit. Time is on our side. Patience, caution
and wise decisions will be our closest allies as we head further beyond than
any of us have ever known. We are going to do this safely, successfully and
have the best of times on the way.

Drone photo of the team on the summit and a selfie in the same place: Mark Sedon, Jean Burgun and Leo Houlding. *(Berghaus)*

## First Camp

We're now in the tent, near as damn it to 88°S, 132°W: precisely where we wanted to be. It's sunny with a strong breeze and so really cold: pretty much what we expected and hoped for, although I must admit this cold is quite shocking. Our goggles steamed up and froze immediately exiting the aircraft. I had a buff around my neck and another over my face to protect my nose from the cold and that's why the goggles steamed up. I'm going to have to work out another system for tomorrow. Kiting blind across this bumpy, hard surface is not an option, but neither is leaving one's nose exposed.

We really are in the middle of nowhere and the magnitude of the journey we are about to undertake is utterly overwhelming. So we all ignore it and focus on the most immediate concerns: keeping warm and sorting gear. We must be some of the most isolated humans on the planet right now but spirits are high and we are ready. It's time to leave the past behind and focus on the here and now. Our loved ones will always fill our hearts but must be kept to the back of our minds. We need to concentrate on managing the cold, travelling and living as comfortably and healthily as we can out here.

## Base Camp

It's been relentless but we have completed the first leg of our journey. The spires of the Organ Pipe peaks tower above us; the Spectre is centre stage. It's 2 December and we've been travelling for almost two weeks. We started today at 5am, beached in the ugly centre of the Scott glacier. Surrounded by blue ice, pressure ridges and crevasses, it was not a pleasant place to start the day. After some discussion about the previous evening's travel arrangements, we decided it would be prudent to adopt a more conservative approach. We roped up and walked on our skis, dragging the pulks for 6km hoping to find more amenable and safer terrain towards the edge of the glacier. It was blustery and cold and we had to fight to keep our fingers warm.

Antarctic landscape from the Organ Pipes. *(Berghaus)*

Pulling the pulks across ice was surprisingly easy but it's extremely slippery and there were a few comedy moments as we took turns to crater: funny to watch but actually quite painful. We are all bruised. But our gamble paid off and we eventually picked up much safer, cleaner terrain, and were able to launch the kites. The wind had dropped to a gentle breeze, the sun was out, and for the first time since we were dropped off, it was pleasant out. For a moment it seemed like plain sailing for the final leg. It felt good to be underpowered, looping and spinning the kite to find maximum torque without worrying about the drastic consequences that just a twitch of the bar can make when overpowered.

Of course it couldn't last. The wind dropped to zero and our kites fell out of the sky. The silence was deafening. Patience is the key at these times. You have to be ready with a well laid-out kite to pounce on the slightest breath of wind. Once airborne, delicate but decisive movements can keep the kite flying in almost zero wind. But jump the gun and attempt to launch with insufficient breeze and the kite is a mess, requiring a full restart: anchoring the bar, walking the lines, laying out the kite, while others may be airborne waiting for all three to be ready. This time it took an hour or so but we managed it, all three catching a breeze and moving immediately into a horrendous crevasse field on *sastrugi*. Not a pleasant cocktail.

We veered into the centre of the Scott glacier to avoid it and were pleased to find sheets of white ice, not a kind surface but not a deadly one either and with more wind we scratched along until finally we caught our first glimpse of the Spectre before it disappeared behind Mount Harkness in

Leo Houlding and a solar phenomenon in the Antarctic. 'We've seen a few halos around the sun and a couple of sun-dogs but yesterday either somebody slipped something into our porridge or we were blessed to witness an utterly psychedelic, three-dimensional display of polar sun refraction and reflection.' *(Berghaus)*

the foreground. Shady and big, from far away our first impression was intimidating. But the Scott glacier is ever changing and requires too much concentration to linger long on the spectacular scenery.

Once again misled by Antarctic scale, it took several more hours of knee-wrecking ice kiting before a final technical descent through pressure ridges and crevasses led to a clear snowy run and the Spectre glacier. Mark went ahead over a kilometre to get set up for the money shot of our glorious arrival. Jean was a little ahead of me as we looped the again underpowered kites towards victory. Then suddenly I was yanked backwards. I tried to loop the kite to resist but it was useless: I was being dragged backwards across the snow. I looked round to find my pulk had vanished. Thankfully I stopped after about 10m and released the kite. I dug in a ski and wrapped myself around it. Then, no doubt sounding a little meek, requested assistance from Jean on the radio. True to form he came gallantly to the rescue and together we spent three hours retrieving the pulk from the crevasse. It was much like any other of the hundreds of holes we'd crossed in the last two days, but this one had swallowed my 150kg pulk whole just a kilometre from our destination. I limped down to Mark on skis looking rather bedraggled: not the glorious arrival I had planned. At least nothing was lost or damaged and apart from a terrific shock I was unscathed.

We camp and at 2am the Spectre briefly shows us her pretty side, basking in sunshine, flirting almost: she is a prize beauty. Such an immaculate massif, the rock looks outstanding and there are lines everywhere, as good for rock climbing as any granite spires I have seen. But then the cloud builds, the wind picks up and I remember where I am. The thought of being up there, even further away than we are here is too much. I think we need a day or three to acquaint ourselves with our new surroundings before committing to anything too tall. At least it is much warmer and less hostile down here than the beastly plateau. With kind weather, we have a chance. More harshness and we'll be looking for somewhere less steep.

Leo Houlding on Christmas Day, reflecting: 'We celebrated Christmas in style ... smoked salmon and egg brunch with 'Antarctic breeze' cocktails (vodka and electrolytes mix) and rum hot chocolate ... We exchanged small gifts, the best being set of zebra boxers from Jean to Mark, pulled crackers and listened to some cheesy Christmas classics.' *(Berghaus)*

**Route to the Top**

After a partial circumnavigation of the Spectre to check descent and ascent options we formulate a plan. Everything looks pretty hard, long and seriously committing. Climbing as a three and trying to photograph and film greatly reduces efficiency, and after much consideration we decided the wisest course of action is for all of us to attempt to summit by the route of least resistance. That would be to repeat the Mugs and Edmund Stump route on the north side of the Spectre. Though the north side is still a formidable peak, it lacks the aesthetic perfection of the south side. It is a complex maze of snow ramps, chimneys and steep buttress steps that do not form an obvious line to the summit.

We leave camp on 8 December in sunny, calm conditions at 8am with light loads and fairly minimal kit, nipping over the col we had inspected previously and are at the foot of the north side of the Spectre by 10am. A steep snow couloir offers easy access to the col that forms the left saddle of the Spectre when viewed from the spectacular south side. In the sun, without wind and on the move the temperature is balmy. But then we hit about 50m of shade in the couloir, and as Mark describes it, 'panic cold': 20°C colder than in the sun, where fingers freeze and muscles tighten within seconds. Thankfully we soon skip back into the light to survey the route and wait for its warming rays to rotate around onto the face we are about to climb.

Jean and I play the customary rock, paper, scissors to decide who will lead the first block. He wins. We enter the maze without too much anxiety as the weather is good and we figure even though we can't see an obvious line, there are so many features and options, surely we will find an easy way? That is our first mistake. We forget: nothing is easy out here. Very quickly, route finding became an issue. We're now playing snakes and ladders: Jean is faced with four ladders to climb leading in four very different directions, three of which lead to snakes and a slide back down. In situations like this, the best course of action is for the leader to try to have a decent look at every option before committing to one, as once committed if it turns out to be a dead end it is more time consuming to descend and try another.

We have no choice but to try our hardest to find a way through we can climb without too much risk, and this we do for several hours. Jean leads a particularly tough, scary pitch, quite low down. We convince ourselves that this was not the way Mugs and Ed would have gone, but for a few rope lengths above, the terrain looks okay, so we continue. We stumble across an old piton and sling abseil station from the Stumps. We zig and zag our way across the face, covering a fair amount of distance, over a great deal of time, without gaining much altitude. Gradually the cloud builds and the light flattens, and with it the intimidation increases. Our mood is subdued but we don't discuss retreat. Yet we are all thinking the same thing: 'if the wind picks up, this is a survival situation and we're out of here.' With the constant dead-ends and slow progress our grown-up game of snakes and ladders is becoming very committing. All the while the cloud thickens. Is this the front of a storm or just a band of moist air in the atmosphere?

It takes hours and hours to reach a false summit and then another. When we think we must be nearing the real top, we hit a 25m cliff-band. It's proper climbing but short enough that I'm sure I can get up it quickly but it proves wide, loose and hard. By the time we get to the top, still ages from the true summit, we are all starting to feel pretty strung out.

The level of commitment of being high on a steep, complex face out here at the end of the world is impossible to overstate. Away from the sanctuary of our camp, we are so very isolated, and so very exposed. If Antarctica snarls, it is very quickly a survival situation. Full of anxiety we push on to the summit, ready to turn and run at the first whiff of wind. But Antarctica smiles on us and eventually we can go no higher: the summit.

It is close to midnight, and in truth, it isn't a very joyous celebration: we are all anxious about the long complex descent. Seeing our camp so tiny and far below doesn't help matters. Jean leads fastidiously and efficiently and to our great relief the weather does not deteriorate further. We are back in the approach couloir within three hours and breathe a sigh of relief. Stumbling back into camp at 4.20am is a wonderful feeling. And almost immediately the wind begins to blow and as we lie down to sleep after a 24-hour session it gusts at over 30 knots. The gods have been kind to us.

**The Journey Home**
It's 24 December, Christmas Eve, and we have retraced our route back to where we were dropped off. Yesterday was our 'welcome back storm' in exactly the same spot as our 'welcome storm' a month ago. It was far less severe yesterday, but it was total whiteout with visibility less than five metres. There was no way to travel by kite in that, so we were tent-bound. It was surprisingly cold in the tent due to the lack of sun. At least that made our route choice easy. We are sticking with our original plan and won't be making a detour via the South Pole.

Leo Houlding in front and Jean Burgun ski kiting on the final day of the Spectre expedition. *(Berghaus)*

Today, as per the forecast, the sun is back and the wind has dropped. The wind is due to change tomorrow, giving us the six to 10 knots south-south-easterly we so desperately need. We could do with a minimum of 10 knots to send us on our way 350km to the Theil Mountains across terrain that has hardly ever been travelled and never traversed by kite. We then join the classic South Pole to Hercules Inlet kite route for 450km before venturing through the Sentinels back to Union glacier. The first 350km leg to Theil Mountains is the one we are most concerned about: we really need these south-easterlies or we're scuppered. Our entire expedition strategy was built on this wind pattern, but it is not what we have been experiencing.

We have been hearing that this is an exceptional weather year. Union glacier has experienced unusually high temperatures. Ben Saunders comments on his blog that in 17 years of Antarctic travel this has been the poorest weather he has experienced. So we must just hang in there with our strategy based on what we felt would be the most likely wind patterns. The good news is that with every kilometre we travel on this route, we are closer to more favourable wind flows as we approach Union glacier. That means, hopefully, the going should get easier.

**Fair Winds**
Yesterday, the day after Boxing Day, we were fully geared up on standby to leave all day. The wind direction and strength wouldn't allow us to go in the way we wanted. Twice we were fully packed and ready but within 100m it became clear it wasn't happening, so twice we re-pitched the tent in exactly the same place. Then the sky put on its mind-blowing rainbow show and we let go of the frustration and wondered at this place we are visiting.

After dinner I got into bed but right away Jean noticed the wind had changed direction. Sure enough it had swung around, if later than predicted, and we had a solid 10-12 knot south-easterly. Gearing up, we broke camp for the third time and set off at 11pm. Everything had come good and we were flying: a fully powered crosswind on a soft surface with clear, sunny weather. Our midnight run was as good as it gets: 101km in six hours. We called it a day at 5am but seven hours later were off again, tail end of the wind. We are halfway home in terms of kilometres.

**The Last Lap**

At 5am it was clear and very cold but within an hour we were ready to go. We began preparing the big kites, but the wind started to increase drastically so Mark and Jean launched the smallest kites and we got what we hoped for: some high-speed, solid-gold kite footage. Blasting along for 20km in less than an hour, we reached the end of Horseshoe valley. A maw of jagged peaks almost closed the path ahead of us but for a series of cols between the tooth-like peaks. We couldn't tell, from the line on our GPS, which col we were aiming for. As we climbed up to the mountains, the wind suddenly matched the terrain: turbulent, and uphill. Then it died and we were becalmed.

It took three hours to cover three kilometres before the gods flicked the switch and the wind came back on. We climbed the last steep section to the col in 10 minutes. The view was magnificent: the peaks of Horseshoe valley behind, and the great plateau beyond. In front, the snaking Henderson glacier, flanked by the painted rocky faces of sculpted mountains, spilled down into the vastness of the Ronnie ice shelf.

The wind funnelling through the col was a real hazard but distracted by the glorious vista I crashed my kite, which became hideously tangled. This was bad news on a steep windy col. Normally you anchor the kite and walk to it to untie the mess. That is mighty difficult in a precarious place with so much wind. Thankfully over the course of the last 50 days and thousand miles I had become extremely proficient at untangling kites.

About 500m later I caught up with the guys but as we crested the col to begin our descent the wind went nuts and we immediately all released our kites onto their safety lines resulting in an epic tangle. At the same time, Jean broke his toe binding just 20km from the now almost visible finish line. We popped up the tent and before Mark and I had finished our cheese and biscuits, Jean had located the spare and replaced the broken unit.

After lunch Mark, who spent years as a ski patroller, gave me a quick briefing on how to ski downhill with a heavy pulk. I was impressed how well it worked and we descended six kilometres of blue and red terrain with refreshingly little difficulty. When it flattened out we launched our mid-size kites and began once again to battle with erratic mountain airflows. After a frustrating hour it came good and we blasted the last few kilometres of the glacier and up the short steep hill to the Henderson col leading to Union glacier.

The finishing line. From left to right: Leo Houlding, Mark Sedon and Jean Burgun. *(Berghaus)*

We could now look down our final destination, the ALE Union glacier camp, visible six kilometres away. We regrouped, packed the kites and skied the last 100m to the glacier. Dangerous crevasses that had concerned us shrank into insignificance thanks to the snowmobile track and flags put out by ALE for their Antarctic marathon event a few weeks earlier and with the end in sight, a good hard surface and no wind, we took the hint and popped skins on our skis and began the victory lap. It was at least 15°C warmer than the morning and we were melting. A Twin Otter coming in to land spotted us and circled to wave his wings. Ten minutes later, Fred arrived on a snowmobile. With just two kilometres to go, we gave him the pulks to tow and skated without weight to the end.

# Looking to the Future

*Following the pattern in several mountaineering nations for mentoring schemes for young alpinists, there has been a debate in Britain over the last couple of years about whether something similar would be useful here and what it might look like. A number of organisations and individuals have been involved in this process, including the Alpine Club, the British Mountaineering Council and several leading alpinists, including the former editor of* Climb *magazine* **Ian Parnell**. *Here he talks to the editor of the Alpine Journal* **Ed Douglas** *about plans for the future and the state of British alpinism.*

**Can you tell me what's been achieved and how it came about?**
It started with Tom Livingstone approaching me and asking why there isn't a young alpine team in Britain, a mentored team, as there is in many places, like the one Steve House runs in the States, and Marko [Prezelj] does in Slovenia – and the French do, under Christian Trommsdorff. Tom approached me because I was on the BMC International Committee and so I raised it a bit at the meeting and then decided to try and get it kick-started. We put out a sort of call. It was on the BMC website but it was also a case of who we knew. Tom drew up a list of likely candidates. At that stage we weren't sure exactly who it was we were targeting: how talented, how young, how British they had to be. The reason it struck a chord with me is that I was thinking along similar lines. There seemed to be a bit of a gap between Tom's generation and my generation. There always have been gaps between generations but I felt we were seeing fewer young teams applying each year to the BMC for grants. Oddly, since we decided to do this, there's been a bit of a turnaround. It wasn't a scientific process but there was the sense it was the usual suspects and they were getting older and no one new was coming through. So Tom's desire for this chimed with me. We had an initial meeting in 2016 at the AC hut in the Lakes. We had got in touch with about 80 or 90 people and we tried to go a bit wider but that seemed enough to get started. We canvassed people's opinions to find out if there was a need for such a thing. The number who came along was just under 40 and the whole thing was free. The BMC put some money into that. And from that meeting and a meeting following it in early 2017 in north Wales and another at the Climbers' Club hut at Froggatt, we both had strong feelings about how such a system should go, and they were a bit different.

**How did they differ?**
My thought was that it didn't seem very British the way those young teams were run. It seemed to me they had a father figure in the middle of them

that was driving everything. The critical thing in alpinism is that you've got to make independent decisions in the mountains. That's the key to success. Not how hard you climb but being able to make sensible decisions. Not being driven by a guru. That slightly touchy-feely thing of what it is you really want. Is it worth the risk? Is it really me making those decisions or am I being driven by something else? So I didn't like that format. Also I felt that they were a really small group. The New Zealand scheme and Steve's scheme have a selection process and end up with half a dozen select individuals. I spoke to the NZ guys for an hour on Skype, and I spoke to Steve and I spoke to Marko, and they all did things slightly differently. But the common factor was that all the schemes focused on only a small group of alpinists, taking up a lot of resources. So we just felt that we had a chance to do something much broader. You want a pyramid-type structure anyway: you need to spread it out. Tom's vision was a kind of performance squad. You've got your competition for indoor climbing, and so for the mountains you'd have an alpine team. A set range of things organised for them. What I envisaged was a bit different.

**What challenges have you faced?**
One of the difficult things, inevitably, is that it's hard to get momentum going and even harder to keep it going. So you end up with one or two people putting effort in. It'll be up to full speed hopefully by the beginning of next year and the goal is that it will be self-sustaining, that the young alpinists themselves will be driving it. After the meetings, we had a few events and exchanges, which we'd organised with the help of the BMC or the AC, John Porter helped out, but we were thinking about what sort of structure we needed. We wanted youngsters running it, but also to rebuild connections between the older generation and the young generation.

**How have things changed since you were a young alpinist?**
In the past you'd go down the pub, and someone like Rab [Carrington] would be in the corner, and if you were going to Jannu, you'd go and buy him a pint and you'd learn a massive amount about Jannu. The scene is now much more diffused. There are WhatsApp groups, stuff like that. It seemed to me that the generational connection had been lost. My first breakthrough trip was Jules Cartwright asking me to go to Mt Hunter while we were in the pub. I hadn't even been to the Alps. I was climbing Scottish V. Jules had obviously worked down his list and arrived at me, but it was a transformative thing and that all happened because all sorts of people were mixing together.

**What kind of organisation has been agreed?**
So what we've landed on is a revitalisation of the Alpine Climbing Group (ACG). It still existed but was largely moribund. It was clearly the place for up-and-coming young climbers and was very significant in the 1960s, 1970s and 1980s but less so after that. It seemed like a natural home. The hope was

The young alpinist Alfie Maun belaying Karol Lejuszewski on the Polish-British exchange for young alpinists held in February and March 2018. *(Wadim Jablonski)*

that it would be an easy structure, which has that connection with the Alpine Club that I think is crucial. There's an enormous resource with the AC: grant support and brand, and the human resource is amazing: it's where leading alpinists go to retire. We've got Charles Stupart going through the structure in detail. I'd hoped it would be quick, but it's taking more time that I'd thought. But we're getting there. We're in the process of writing rules, not that the old ACG had any. We've got applications forms and criteria, which they feel are necessary, and that will go to the AC AGM. The frustrating thing is that it's now been a long time since we built up all that enthusiasm. I hope we haven't lost too much momentum. We've had sporadic events and are meeting soon for a big-wall workshop in Devon. What's missing is a proper home and the chance to say this is who we are. But we're getting there; we're close to lift-off.

**Once you've got that, do you see potential revenue schemes?**
Yes. I haven't thought too much about it. But there's a lot of good will from the BMC, the MEF and the AC, which have all pledged financial support. So that's great. At the moment it's helped a small group of people. Once it's going we can publicise it more widely and there will be people who want to join but aren't part of the scene.

**Have you seen big philosophical or ethical difference between Tom's generation and your own? Do you see big changes in British alpinism?**
I think it's difficult for one generation to assess another without getting all misty-eyed. Inevitably people think that their generation had it sorted and the new generation is doing it wrong. But it's pretty simple. We all just want to go climbing. There are some slightly different things in how alpinism works. In places like Chamonix, you've got such immediate information now that it's very easy to follow on the coattails of others. You wait until

someone does a particular route on the Jorasses and the next thing you know it's had a dozen ascents. These can be really high-end routes. For the younger generation there's a bit of that following going on. It makes perfect sense.

**There's a drift towards performance at the expense of exploration?**
There's a bit of that. That was my gut feeling, a prejudicial view if you like, that people weren't being ambitious in the way that at certain points other generations had been. It's quite a short thing, an alpinist's career, and maybe there's a good argument that you shouldn't encourage it. I'm very aware of that. I certainly don't want to be pushing people to do things they don't want to do. When we get together I go into that a lot, about how it's their responsibility. But people were going to Patagonia quite a bit, they were going to Canada quite a bit, and they're accessible things to do. You can focus on the climbing. As opposed to the Himalaya, where there's still enormous potential. It seems there's sometimes a block on how you might start engaging with the Himalaya. To me that was strange and again, it's the lack of mentoring. My mountaineering started when I went to the BMC. Roger Payne would have a month off where he'd go off on a big trip. I thought, if Roger can do it, then why can't I? It didn't immediately occur to me that he had 20 years of experience and that's why he was able to do it. But it removed a lot of the barriers for me. Initially, I had not gone to the Alps when my mates did because I thought it was too risky. Making those changes, you need mentors or wise heads, rather than inflammatory cheerleading.

**How do you see the strength of British alpinism?**
I think it's easy sometimes to look back and say it was so strong, there were loads of alpinists and so on. I'm not sure how true that was. When I was heavily involved, say 15 years ago, it was actually a really small group. We all knew each other, and it was probably only a dozen people. They were all at that peak time just before they got on the guides' scheme or got married. So you have these little thrusts, and perhaps inevitably they're quite short-lived. Very few people can keep up that level of intensity. Mick [Fowler] clearly can but he's unusual and very impressive. He has a sustainable model. One of the reasons I backed off was that I was suddenly going to Gasherbrum IV and then K2 and everything seemed to be going higher and harder. But the history of alpinism has most usually been a sequence of spikes of activity. When we arrived it felt like there'd been a bit of a gap. It's always felt it's been a bit more organised abroad.

**Alpinism is now proportionally a much smaller part of climbing?**
These days you mustn't assume that everyone will want to go alpine climbing. We do have to wave the flag a little bit. I'm not suggesting everyone should try but you have amazing experiences in the mountains. There are people out there with adventurous souls who would love to do this kind of thing but it's one of a number of choices, and if one particular choice is selling itself harder than another then people will go towards that. The

The exchange group and members of Krakow University Mountaineering Club.
(*Piotr Drozdz*)

things that are going on in Yosemite on El Cap – if you're a talented free
climber then you want to be involved with that. You can go to California
in the sunshine, hang out with beautiful people and have nice things to eat,
and there's this thing that old people used to do, something that is uncomfortable and hurts. There's also a bit of a myth on social media that alpinism
is something posh people used to do before the working classes discovered
how to rock climb properly and it fell out of fashion. But I still think it's the
most amazing thing you can do in climbing. As performance improves it's
a bit of a narrowing thing, because it takes longer to reach that standard
and it's more involved, and that can reduce the numbers involved: more
esoteric, if you will.

**What about gender?**
Alpinism is still very male. That's a battle and a very difficult one. There's a
lot of progress throughout society, removing limits from any kind of female
aspiration, which is brilliant. But in alpinism the battle certainly isn't won.
The perception is that it's a male thing. Having said that, there are quite
a few strong British female alpinists. They are a small group and they are
inevitably ambitious people; quite a few are on the guides' scheme or working as instructors up in Scotland during the winter. Rocio Siemens is a good
example. She's now based in Chamonix and has climbed Scottish VIII. She's
organising a meet in the Écrins and I'm hoping she'll be around for that as a
mentor. Female alpinists have their own channels, closed Facebook groups.
Out of our list of 80, about 15 are women, of whom two or three have been
involved in events. I'm not the person to reach out to them but Rebecca Coles
has been helpful. I've tried to create spaces on events that were for women
only but then had to fill them with men because no women wanted to fill
them. Part of that is my problem in communicating with the right people.
You really need a woman to pick that up and drive it. But once it gets going
and has some momentum then there's a great opportunity for someone.

# Past Times

Maj J B Corry (1874-1914), Royal Engineers,
the first member of the Alpine Club to die in the First World War,
from a shell-burst near Neuve Chapelle.

DENNIS GRAY

# Falak Ser: The Road To Heaven

Falak Ser (5918m), also Falak Sar, in Pakistan's Swat valley, from the south.

In life sometimes, one comes to realise, years after what was a signal event, both how lucky and also unaware you were that you were close to the edge of an adventure that might have led to a premature death. For me this is true of a solo journey I made to Pakistan in the early 1990s, an experience that remains the stuff of nightmares. By then I had visited the Himalaya several times, taking part in climbs and treks, and felt confident I could take off on my own to explore a relatively unpopular region, in terms of climbing history, on my own. I decided to travel to the Swat valley and explore the environs of its highest peak Falak Ser (5918m).

Before I explain what happened during that journey, some history and an explanation of Swat's place in Himalayan geography. It lies west of the Indus valley and east of Chitral, and its mountains are an extension of the Hindu Kush. It is widely known as the Switzerland of Pakistan. Historically it was a centre of Buddhism before the Muslim conquests, and in the Swat valley there are many reminders of this, including a large second century Buddha figure, subsequently badly damaged by the Taliban. The eighth-century tantric master Padmasambhava, whose influence on the development of Tibetan Buddhism is central, was born in Swat; he was the founder of the first monastery in Tibet, where he is also known as Guru Rinpoche, at Samye. He also founded the first of the four great schools of Tibetan Buddhism, the Nyingma-pa, or 'old ones', known for their red hats. Swat has also been visited by many other historical figures, including Alexander in 327BCE and before him Persian conquerors.

In terms of its modern story, the arrival of the fearsome Yusufzais, Pathans from Afghanistan who occupied Swat in 1515, is crucial. During the Raj, Swat was a Princely State, ruled by a wali, or leader, and remained so until 1969. (The Queen and Prince Philip stayed with the last Wali of Swat, Jahan Zeb, at his white marble palace at Merghazar in 1961.) During the Raj, the Yusufzais challenged British Raj forces on several occasions, including the Malakand uprising of 1897, an action made famous by Winston Churchill, then a second lieutenant in the cavalry writing despatches about the campaign for the *Daily Telegraph*. In events that mirrored the rise of the Taliban, a charismatic leader, Saidullah, drove the Pathans to a religious fervour and declared jihad against the British for imposing on them the Durand Line in 1893.

The Swat valley is wide and open at its southern end, but as you travel northward it slowly climbs from 1,000m to 2,900m and narrows as it does so. The valley is approached from the south by the Malakand pass and arriving at its base you realise why the 1897 campaign was so challenging and bloody. However once into the valley it is a fertile green sward to travel through, and in its lower reaches are orchards of apple and apricot; it was known in Buddhist times as Uddyana, meaning garden.

One reason I had chosen to visit Swat was because of pictures I had seen of its two highest mountains, Falak Ser (5918m) and Mankial (5726m) which showed them to be impressive peaks, despite their modest heights in Himalayan terms. Falak Ser was first climbed by New Zealanders W K A Berry and Cecil Tyndale-Biscoe in 1957; R L Holdsworth climbed Mankial as early as 1940.

My journey to Swat began in Rawalpindi where I caught a bus to Mingora. I spent a night there before travelling on to Kalam situated near the head of the valley. En route I had been surprised to encounter men dressed in Greek-style clothing, some of whom had blue eyes and light hair. Conjecture is that their antecedents arrived with Alexander, but once at Kalam I quickly realised I was in Pathan country, dominated by the fearsome Yusufzai. The Swat valley was as beautiful as I had expected, and in late summer its startling green hillsides and orchards were full of fruit. I stayed the night in Kalam in a cheap doss house and then set off laden with a heavy rucksack to climb the steep track that led up towards the Ushu valley. As I climbed the Falak Ser came into view. I could see that its huge south face would be beyond me on my own, but I entertained a crazy notion of attempting the bounding south-west ridge. The German climber and development aid worker Hermann Warth and the Sherpa Ang Choppal climbed the south face in 1990, overcoming 25 pitches of steep ice to reach the summit.

Ushu, situated on the Swat river with stunning views all around, appeared a restful place when I finally arrived there. Yet I began to feel uneasy moving around the village; its denizens did not appear to be too friendly. I could only surmise from their sullen looks that a lone climber was not only an unusual sight but also an unwelcome one. After a rest I shouldered my pack once more and walked on. I spent the night higher up the valley near Matiltan, sleeping in a rough shelter and cooking on a fire of wood taken from the plentiful supply left by its previous inhabitants. Early next morning, I was away swiftly to avoid the heat of the day, and for a few hours made good progress. Coming from a recent climb in the Karakoram I found no difficulty in the increasing altitude.

I was into rugged terrain by then, following an exposed rocky path along the steep sides of a gorge containing the Paloga river. Balancing along, I looked up ahead of me and noticed two tiny human figures a long distance away, but distinctly framed in the clear mountain air. Initially I guessed they were shepherds, but the closer they descended towards me, the more uneasy I became. They were losing altitude at such a pace that I realised they could not be with any animals. They must be chasing after something. Within a few moments, I realised that something was me. Panic set in. As they came closer I saw they were both armed with Kalashnikovs, so even if I dropped my pack and tried to run off downhill I would not escape them. Though scared witless I decided to keep walking towards them, trying to remember some Pashto. When they did reach me they were the two most frightening-looking characters I have ever met. Tall and bearded, they were dressed like the mujahideen I had met on the Afghan border the year before, except they were more ragged, being unwashed with rips in both their shalwar and kameez.

'Salaam aleikum,' I greeted them. Though surprised, they did not give way, and I realised I was now their prisoner. 'Hello,' I continued in English, gasping in fright whilst trying to smile at them. The two did not seem appeased. I froze with fear as one of the Pathans slung off his rifle, slipped its catch and pointed it at me. '*Ghar*,' I gasped, pointing at the mountains. 'I am going up into the mountains,' pointing up to where I thought Falak Ser must be. '*Ghar*,' I repeated. This brought the most unexpected response, for my two guards began to laugh loudly. Then one of them cried out '*Wonrrai!*' I nodded my head guessing they must think I was a hunter of some kind, but then I realised that this is what they were. They were not shepherds. They had been out looking for game to shoot.

I began to laugh hysterically in relief at this, and my mood carried over to the Pathans, who joined in with great shouts of mirth. The rifle that had been pointing at me was lowered and a hand extended. I have never been so relieved to grasp a hand in my life. Having shared some naan bread, we parted in good spirits, they to continue their descent down into the valley, I to climb up towards the base of Falak Ser. Some hours later, when I had reached high enough to see more clearly, I realised the approach to reach the peak's base and the face above were not challenges to attempt alone, at least not by me. Just before darkness I found shelter, below the snow level, and prepared for a long cold night.

I rose just before dawn to watch the rising sun strike the peak's southern aspect, which was impressive and challenging, an impression made all the more acute by being in such a remote place on my own. After cooking breakfast on some wood I had carried up with me from the valley, I repacked my rucksack and made ready to start back down the route to Ushu. I was worried what my reception might be on my return, for recent events had rather unnerved me. If I had known more about the tension in the whole Swat valley at that time and its future takeover by the Taliban I might have been even more disturbed.

Descending back down to Ushu I managed to cover in a day what had taken two on the way up, but apart from the two hunters I met no one else and with autumn setting in the mountains seemed deserted. Arriving in the valley, I was surprised to be met by a small group of local people. On this occasion they were friendly, unlike my last visit. Partly by sign language, partly because he could speak a little Urdu and English, I realised that the headman was inviting me to drink chai with him. Sitting in his hut he laughed long and hard about the fact that his nephews had nearly shot me. They had fought in Afghanistan during the Soviet invasion, as had many Swat Pathans, and some of their relations had died in the conflict. They had thought me to be connected to one of the Soviet supporting nations, some of whom had looked like me, and if I had not spoken to them in English they would have shot me. I realised how stupid I had been in not letting family and friends know about my plans to visit Swat, I could so easily have disappeared without trace, my body buried up in the mountains under a pile of rocks.

The Soviet-Afghan war changed everything not only in Afghanistan but also in Pakistan's North West Frontier. The involvement of the Americans and the Pakistan secret service in supporting and arming the mujahideen as a part of the wider Cold War conflict is still killing people in great numbers. It explains why in these areas so many of the denizens are armed; the year before my visit to Swat I was in Waziristan, and every male there seemed to be armed with an AK47.

In the 1990s Swat began a nightmarish descent into fundamentalism. A cleric called Sufi Muhammad split from mainstream politics and began to impose Sharia law on the peoples of the valley. His influence extended to Dir, close to Nanga Parbat, as well. He took his followers to Afghanistan to fight the Americans and was arrested on his return, but by then the Swat was in Taliban hands. One of their targets was a ski development in the lower Swat valley at Malam Jabba, a joint project with Austria. The Taliban declared skiing as un-Islamic, and decided to destroy it. Thanks to the Pakistan army's move into Swat to deal with the Pakistani Taliban it re-opened in the winter 2017.

There are approximately two million people living in the Swat valley, and in Mingora, its largest city, the Taliban committed their worst atrocities, with public hangings in its main square. This was the home town of a young schoolgirl called Malala Yousafzai, who the Taliban shot in the head for

The Shingardar stupa in the Swat valley, one of thousands of Buddhist remains, indicating the strength of the dharma in former times. The Tibetan saint Guru Rinpoche came from Swat. *(Shahid Khan/Alamy)*

advocating female education. The rest, as they say, is history. It's worth remembering that the Taliban was formed by Afghan Pashtuns who had studied in conservative Pakistan madrassas, like Mullah Omar and with the support of the Pakistani intelligence service ISI.

Such events often seem unrelated to our mountain ambitions. We just want to go about our activities peacefully, whilst respecting local peoples and their cultures appropriately. But events on Nanga Parbat (8125m) in June 2013 made us aware that we are not now immune to events taking place outside our own bubble. The area around Nanga Parbat has always been politically complex. Because of the depth and scale of the four access valleys set around the peak, people living there were isolated from one another. They each speak a different language, and seem distrustful of one another and outsiders.

This was brought into focus for me whilst leading a trip to the northern, Rakhiot side of the mountain, attempting to climb Julipar Peak (5500m) on the eastern flank of this huge face. Retreating in bad weather we crossed a pass by that name into the upper reaches of the Diamir to descend via the Patro valley, when we were halted on the screes below the summit of the pass by gun-toting locals. They wouldn't let us descend further unless we paid off our porters from Tato in the Rakhiot, employed them instead and paid a fee to camp in their valley. They were very aggressive, and it was obvious our Tato men were frightened. Fortunately, our sirdar Hussein could speak their language, Shina. In the end we had no choice: the weather was awful and the idea of retreating back over the Julipar pass was a no-no for our tired and dispirited trekkers. We did as we were told, paid off our Tato porters, and then handed over an amount of rupees in order to continue our descent.

Others can recount similar stories from the 1990s, including friends on the Rupal side of the mountain, but the events of the night of 22 June 2013 were unprecedented in the history of Karakoram mountaineering. Fortunately this notorious attack happened in a period of good weather. Most of the parties attempting the *Kinshofer* route were above base camp in the Diamir valley, when 16 militants dressed in the uniform of the Gilgit Scouts, guided there by a local, stormed the camp, and gathered the 11 climbers and two workers still in camp before them. They forced the climbers to hand over their valuables, money and mobile phones, which they smashed. They then made their prisoners kneel and began shooting them one by one in the head. One extraordinarily brave Chinese climber Zhang Jing Chuan broke free and ran into the night, followed by a hail of bullets, one of which grazed his skull, so that as he ran he was being blinded by blood running into his eyes. Fortunately, below camp is a ravine and he dived into this to escape. Ten climbers died that night, from five different countries, and one base-camp worker, who managed to convince the militants he was a good Muslim.

The militants left early next morning and the Chinese climber gingerly returned to base camp where he had hidden a mobile phone in his tent. He then climbed up towards camp one to alert climbers there as to what had happened. They managed to contact the Pakistani authorities, and shortly afterwards military helicopters arrived. Meanwhile climbers high on the *Kinshofer* decided to descend, and eventually all assembled safely in that place. Plans were made to walk out, but fears grew that the militants might still be in the area, and eventually everyone was airlifted to safety.

The massacre did predictably serious damage to Pakistan's trekking and climbing industry and begged serious questions in the Pakistani legislature. An official enquiry was established, and a three-man team made up of an army colonel, a captain and a police officer were sent to the area, but they met a gruesome fate, gunned down by the Taliban in Chilas on the Karakoram Highway, below Nanga Parbat. The climbers had erroneously claimed that they understood the attack was in retaliation for the killing of Osama Bin Laden, but the Taliban claimed responsibility, blaming a USA drone strike that had killed a local Taliban leader called Waliur Rehman. Before the enquiry team were killed they had managed to establish that the killers were local, 10 from Diamer district, three from Manshera, north of Islamabad, and three from Kohistan. Some of these were eventually tracked down and arrested under anti-terrorist legislation.

But questions remain. How could it be that the militants were dressed in Gilgit Scout uniforms? The British formed this irregular unit in the latter part of the 19th century from the Shia Hunzas of Gilgit, who were suited for that kind of soldiering. After Pakistan's independence the Scouts were

Pakistani soldiers on patrol in the Swat valley. The region has been a hotbed of Islamist insurgency. *(Shutterstock)*

melded into its new army and eventually became designated as the Gilgit Baltistan Scouts with the task of keeping the peace in the whole of that province, which includes the Karakoram. It seems to me that the attackers might really have been members of that outfit, for Kohistan is quite some way from the Chilas region, and how else would they know each other? And what of the local guides who helped the attackers reach base camp? Some reports said there were two of them, others one. Much remains obscure.

In climbing and trekking centres like Hushe, Skardu, Gilgit and Askole the locals were very critical of the Taliban action, for so many families had come to rely on this as their source of income. It has helped to raise standards of living and improved infrastructure throughout the whole region. More recently, climbers and now trekkers are returning with security bolstered by a special mountain unit of the Gilgit Baltistan Scouts. For areas like the southern flanks of Nanga Parbat they now accompany expeditions and remain in base camp.

The Karakoram has been a compelling destination for explorers and mountaineers for more than a century, a magical wonderland of peaks almost without parallel as challenges for climbers who won't readily stop going there. But all of us should remain aware of the terrorist threat because it isn't going away soon. Clashes between Sunni and Shia, attacks on Christians and renewed tension between India and Pakistan in Kashmir are all threats. We should keep a weather eye on these happenings before selecting an objective.

JIM GREGSON

# Jotunheimen:
# the Rough and the Smooth

Summer and winter in Norway's mountains

The smooth days of winter. Ski group on Skautflya below
the north side of Leirhøe. *(Jim Gregson)*

Skiing towards Kyrkjeglupen, with Kyrkja on the right. *(Jim Gregson)*

*Enten ru eller glatt, men fremfor alt, Jotunheimen.*[1]

*Norwegian proverb*

The Jotunheimen mountains of Norway hold the country's greatest concentration of peaks and summits that overtop the enticing altitude of 2,000m. If you choose a height difference of at least 100m between the nearest col and a summit, there are more than one hundred 2,000m peaks and at least the same number of secondary tops in the Jotunheimen region. More recent Norwegian mountain literature, which uses a much lower height differential, produces an even greater total of over 340 peaks and tops. And just as with 'Munro bagging' here in Britain, many Norwegian climbers and walkers follow their own quest to climb them all.

There are 2,000ers in other parts of Norway, but the largest cluster of higher summits lies in the area referred to on old maps as the Jotunfjeldene, a name was supplanted by that of Jotunheimen, the 'home of the giants', by the enthusiasm of poet Aasmund Olavsson Vinje, who in the late 1860s established first a rough stone shelter and then with friends a small wooden cabin at the western end of the large lake called Bygdin. Vinje coined the name 'Eidsbugarden' for this location and his cabin plus the ruins of the stone shelter can still be visited. In his distinctive verse Vinje extolled the virtues of the Jotunheimen landscape.

1. 'Either rough or smooth, but above all, Jotunheimen.'

South-west Jotunheimen panorama. Left to right: Hjelledalstind, Falketind and Stolsnøstind. *(Jim Gregson)*

In 1865 the so-called Golden Age of first ascents of major peaks of the Alps was coming to a close, but apart from ascents of a relatively few prominent peaks, such as Falketind in 1820, the mountains of Norway were little visited and largely unclimbed. Things began to change with the arrival of British visitors who hunted and fished, as related in the classic comic story by James A Lees and Walter J Clutterbuck *Three in Norway (by two of them)*, a book that inspired Jerome K Jerome's *Three Men in a Boat*. (Forgotten in Britain, it is still in print in Norway under the title *Tre i Norge ved to av dem*.)

More importantly the Norwegians themselves began to frequent their own mountains. In 1868 the banker Thomas Heftye and several of his city friends founded the Norwegian Hiking Association, better known as Den Norske Turistforening (DNT), which now has many thousands of members across many nationalities. The DNT began to promote and champion *friluftsliv*, the open-air life, as a philosophy, a movement that continues today as an important feature in the Norwegian attitude to landscape and nature.

Although early tourists had been able to find accommodation at scattered farmsteads and *sæters* (summer upland grazing locations) the development of hotels had followed more slowly. The DNT began a programme of acquisition and building of huts starting with the purchase of property at the

From left to right: Olavsbunuten and Mjølkedalstinden. *(Jim Gregson)*

west end of Gjende lake in 1870. Gjendeboden, now known as Gjendebu, is still one of DNT's most popular lodges. As more visitors – hunters, anglers, geologists and artists – began to frequent the mountains of Jotunheimen, the number of privately-owned huts and hotels increased and nowadays DNT itself operates a splendid network of more than 450 huts and lodges across Norway, all of them open to members and non-members alike. Thus Jotunheimen with its clutch of higher mountains and good accommodation grew in popularity.

Climbers and alpinists, certainly of Norwegian or Scandinavian origin, were slower to appear so more technical mountaineering was more of a later development than it had been in the Alps. Guides too, were not at first so evident but things would change. A catalyst was needed. Enter one William Cecil Slingsby, born 1849 into a family of Yorkshire textile factory owners. He explored his local hills as a youth but began to look higher and further afield after the first ascent of the Matterhorn in 1865 and the 1871 publication of Whymper's *Scrambles Amongst the Alps*. In 1872 Slingsby made his first visit to Norway. With one companion he set out to 'journey to the midnight sun' by ship, coastal ferries and overland. The impressive peaks of Romsdal captivated him and after reaching the city of Trondheim Slingsby and his friend turned inland and eventually reached Jotunheimen where he was even more impressed by the striking array of alpine mountains he saw, particularly in the Horungtinder group: modern Hurrungane.

After setting eyes on the very imposing Store Skagastølstind, thought unclimbable by many locals, Slingsby boldly declared that one day he would climb it. 'Storen', 'the big one', as it is familiarly known, was by some thought to be Norway's highest peak although later surveys proved it ranked at number three.

Ambition ignited, Slingsby returned to Norway in 1874 when he made the ascent of his first virgin summit, Vestre Memurutind. He also met the enthusiastic and experienced Norwegian mountaineer Emanuel Mohn with whom he was to share many more adventures in years to come. Linking up with Mohn again in 1876, Slingsby travelled to Bygdin in the south-west of Jotunheimen, guided by Knut Lykken. This particular trip 'lit the blue touch-paper' of Norwegian mountaineering with the completion of six very important first ascents, achieved over just six days with long and complex approaches over unexplored terrain.

On 21 July 1876, Slingsby, Mohn and Lykken left Vormeli and eventually reached the south-east side of Store Skagastølstind where they found a way up tortuous glacier slopes, at times following the fresh footprints of a bear through crevassed ground. They arrived, after a crevasse incident, at the high col later to be named as 'Mohns skard': here Mohn declared the mountain to be 'perfectly impossible'. Slingsby was not one for defeatism and continued alone with Yorkshire boldness: '... a tough piece of work... Three times I was all but beaten... I scraped away the ice and bit by bit got higher.... a knife-edged affair ... an overhang ... a loose rocky ledge ... in a few strides ... I gained the unsullied crown of the peerless Skagastølstind.' He erected a small cairn and wedged into it his handkerchief.

This historic solo first ascent was the vanguard for a wave of interest in the mountains of Norway by Norwegian and foreign mountaineers in the years following. Slingsby, smitten with these northerly peaks, made many more visits to Jotunheimen and to many other parts of Norway, succeeding in many more first ascents and repeats. He climbed with some of the best local guides and some prominent Norwegians, among them Ola Berge and Johannes Vigdal, and his parties included other British friends and often his wife. Another female companion was Therese Bertheau who in 1894 was the first woman to climb Storen, which she repeated with Slingsby in 1900. Slingsby himself climbed Storen a third time at the age of 59 via the long, exposed and complex ridge system running north to south. In 1921 he made his final 21st visit to his beloved Norway.

In 1904 Slingsby's classic, important book *Norway: the Northern Play-ground* was published, written after he had made fifteen visits. This work cemented his reputation as the father of Norwegian mountaineering bestowed on him by the Norsk Tinde Klub. It is still a good read today. His fame in Norway far outstrips any recognition he received at home, despite his participation in some important feats in the Alps and some contributions to British climbing. He was one of the first British mountaineers to develop any proficiency on skis, but regarded some Norwegians as less skilled in dealing with glaciers and ice, although he thought that there were very capable cragsmen among his companions.

Notwithstanding Slingsby's role in the development of mountaineering in Norway, more contemporary British climbers resort to places like Rjukan for winter ice-climbing, Lofoten for high-standard rock climbing or Lyngen for dramatic ski mountaineering. Despite the surge of interest in Roms-

The rough days of summer. Store Skagastølstind, aka Soren, Slingsby's most
famous first ascent, climbed in 1876
after a July snowfall. *(Jim Gregson)*

Below the rappel from Midtre
Tverråtinden. *(Jim Gregson)*

dal after the ascents of the Troll Wall it is probably true to say that only a
minority of British mountaineers pay much attention to the alpine climbing
available across the North Sea, and particularly the store of very attractive mountains in the various ranges of Jotunheimen. The very names of
the peaks should act like a magnet: Falketind, Glittertind, Galdhøpiggen,
Stolsnøstinden, Mjølkedalstinden, Store Skagastølstinden and on, many of
them first climbed by Slingsby. Don't care for crowds? Avoid the Alps in
high season and try Norway.

As well as having climbed extensively across the Alps and on many
expeditions to the Arctic in Greenland, my wife Sandra and I have over
many years developed our skills as telemark ski mountaineers, and we have
made numerous winter visits to the mountains of Jotunheimen where we
have made ascents and fabulous running descents of many of the peaks
which form Slingsby's legacy. This would be the 'smooth' of my title, for
winter's mantle of snow transforms these peaks into glittering castles. Travel
in winter, with the rhythms of uphill skinning, and sometimes a finish with
crampons and ice axe, is easier and wins the reward of superb swooping
downhill runs: off-piste skiing at its best, and most elegant when conditions favour the telemark turn. We remember the sharpness of Norwegian
cold, try to forget the ferocity of Norwegian wind, recall the vagaries of
Norwegian sastrugi and steer clear of immense Norwegian cornices. Our
photographs help us to relive some of those glorious days as we recall a

catalogue of ascents. Our skis have carried us to a host of high tops: Gald-høpiggen and Glittertind, rivals for crowning the height list, Storebjørn with its distinctive shape and steep glacier descent, Surtningssui famous for its panoramic summit outlook, the shark-fins of the Veotindane, the narrow crests of the Hellstugutindane, Trollsteineggje projecting like a spine from the surrounding glaciers, Uranostind and its satellite Slingsbytinden glittering with ice, the great bulk of Galdebergtinden glowing golden in sunset light, Bukkehøe protected by huge cornices and beetling cliffs. All of these we have done in the 'smooth, accommodating blanket of winter's snows.

In recent times we have travelled to Jotunheimen either in September or July, to further track Slingsby's footsteps. These trips have provided by contrast, experiences in the 'rough', for then the Jotunheimen wear a different garb. Approaches are longer and slower than on skiing days. River crossings are at times problematic. Gentle grassy paths are conspicuous by their paucity. Boulder fields and boilerplate rock slabs abound. Rock quality varies, from grippy gabbro to crumbling gravel. The ice ages and long winter frosts have left their mark. There is much and varied lichen growth. So-called *kartlav*, 'map lichen', makes for attractive green, black-speckled colouring. Less welcome is *skorpelav*, 'crust lichen', which grows profusely on certain rock types forming mats of jet-black encrustation. When damp or wet it becomes like soap and security of footing is lost. When it is fully dry it curls up and becomes very uncomfortable and prickly to handle, so expect sore fingertips after hours of rock climbing or scrambling.

Despite these factors, for general summer alpine mountaineering Jotunheimen has much to offer. You can choose from extensive scrambling above generally benign glaciers to awe-inducing exposure on traverses along airy arêtes and ridges. You have all the opportunities you want to bring into play the whole range of alpine climbing skills. Summertime daylight in Norway is so lengthy that starts and finishes in the dark are not usually part of the plan.

Peaks we have stared at over the course of many winters and decided that they would make better summer targets despite the vagaries of the 'rough' and have subsequently fallen under our boots have numbered among them lofty Mjølkedalstinden, the tricky 'ugly height' of Styggehøe in Visdalen, the intriguing and exposed Søregga south ridge of Uranostind, the narrow and airy scramble to get to Store Urdadalstind where groups of reindeer ran away from our descent line, the tiny summit rocks of Store Smorstabbtinden overlooking its neighbour Kniven, the crests of Store Austanbotntinden like camel humps, and the arduous rock and steep abseils needed to traverse the Tverråtindane, the complex and trying approaches needed to climb to Falketind, Hjelledalstind and Koldedalstind. We were, however, thwarted in our wish to attempt to repeat Slingsby's *bonne bouche* – just as we planned to try to climb Store Skagastølstind the weather dealt us a poor hand by plastering the peak with a lot of midsummer snow putting it firmly out of condition for the time we had available. This gives us a good reason to go back at least once more to the Hurrungane, Jotunheimen's most alpine massif.

The south ridge of Uranostind Søregga. *(Jim Gregson)*

The pictures help to tell the story. You want the smooth? Try winter, but don't be fooled by the lack of real altitude. Learn to ski, travel the mountains. Find out about the recently developed Høgruta i Jotunheimen, the Jotunheimen haute route, certainly not a pushover. Don't mind the rough? Use Slingsby as a signpost and buy a good map. Enjoy quiet days away from the masses. Get yourself onto high skylines and airy crests. Come down tired but safe. Delight in less-trodden ways. Jotunheimen awaits.

**Further reading**
J Baxter, *Hurrungane*, Scandinavian Publishing, Edinburgh, 2005.
W Clutterbuck, & J Lees, *Three in Norway (by two of them)*, London, 1882. (This is available in Norway in both English and Norwegian.)
A Dyer, J Baddeley & I Robertson, *Walks and Scrambles in Norway*, Ripping Yarns.com, 2006.
M and J Helgesen, *Norges Fjelltopper over 2000 Meter*, Glittertind Forlag, 2013.
S Hagen, *Høgruta i Jotunheimen*, Fri Flyt AS, 2015.
W Slingsby, *Norway: The Northern Playground*, Edinburgh, 1904.
*Klatrefører for Jotunheimen*, Norsk Tinde Klub, 2015.

**Useful websites**
Comprehensive coverage of 2,000m tops: *www.peakbook.org*.
DNT hut system and membership: *www.dntoslo.no*.
The Norwegian haute route and maps: *www.høgrutajotunheimen.no*.

# North America

Lt J R Dennistoun (1883-1916), Royal Flying Corps.
A New Zealander shot down by enemy aircraft,
he died several weeks later.

SIMON RICHARDSON

# Game of Thrones

The First Ascent of the South-West Pillar
of Monarch Mountain

The south-west face of Monarch Mountain in the Coast Range
of southern British Columbia. *(John Scurlock)*

'Whoah, that's big!' Jim skims over a low ridge and banks the helicopter in a tight left turn below a towering triangular wall that has suddenly come into view. We stare upwards humbled and awed by the scale of mountain above us. Helicopters move fast and we struggle to make sense of the blur of rock, ice and snow and take in the magnitude of Monarch's 1,300m-high south-west face.

'Hey Simon, there's our line!' Micha points through the plexi-glass towards a massive pillar of rock rising from the glacier all the way to the summit.

'Yeah that's right, it matches the photo.'

I speak confidently through the headphones and try and sound authoritative, but my primary emotion is fear. Can we really climb this thing? Yet in parallel I feel a sense of privilege: only a handful of climbers have ever seen this giant alpine wall and we are fortunate just to be here. We fly across a col and hover above the broad Empire Way glacier looking for somewhere safe to land. A couple of minutes later we sprawl over our bags to stop them blowing away as Jim takes off. Soon all is quiet and the helicopter is nothing more than a black dot in the sky.

How two climbers from Germany and Scotland came to know about one of the greatest unclimbed alpine challenges in western Canada requires some explanation. The story starts back in 1997 when Dave Hesleden and I first visited the Coast Range. This spectacular line of peaks lies between the Rockies and the Pacific Ocean and stretches for over 1,400km from the Canadian border to Alaska. On their western side, they rise straight out of the sea, with steep glaciated fjords penetrating tens of kilometres inland. This breaks the coastline up into dozens of islands and inlets where boat or plane is the only form of transport. The traditional approach to the mountains is a weeklong bushwhack from the coast, but most parties nowadays fly in by helicopter from the east.

Access may be difficult, but the Coast Range's first line of defence is the weather. Almost without exception, the many storms that track onto the west coast of North America hit these peaks first. Throughout the winter months snowfall levels are high, which sustain large ice fields next to lush rain forests. The main climbing season is July and August, but even then, the deciding factor between success and failure is nearly always the weather. Accounts of parties tent-bound for a week or more are all too common.

At 4,019m, Mount Waddington is the crown of the Coast Range and a real climber's peak. The high degree of precipitation and accompanying wind means its 250m summit-tower is almost permanently coated with ice and rime. It took more than a dozen attempts before the mountain was finally climbed in 1936 by a difficult and serious route on the south-west face by Fritz Wiessner and Bill House. At the time it was considered the hardest climb in North America. Most ascents of Waddington are now made from the Tiedemann glacier via the Bravo glacier route, which was pioneered by a Sierra Club team in 1950, but ascents are infrequent and the mountain is rarely climbed more than once or twice a year.

Simon Richardson climbing the north ridge of Pt2625m, on the north-south traverse of the peak, a warm-up for the south-west face of Monarch. The Sugarloaf (2620m) is the furthest left rock peak behind. *(Micha Rinn)*

Dave and I were attracted to the vast emptiness of the range and the scale of its major routes that dwarfed the alpine classics. Our prime objective was to climb Waddington but we surprised even ourselves, by reaching the summit on the third day of the trip. As expected it was wild and windy, so we adopted the Scottish trick of pulling our hoods on tight and pretending it was no different to a poor day on Ben Nevis. Two days later the weather settled, and our momentum carried us up the unclimbed south-east Ridge of Mount Asperity in a three-day 65-pitch outing. Unable to venture into the 1,400m descent gullies that were constantly avalanching, we made our way down by traversing the remote and jagged Serra Peaks. On the fourth day we were becoming concerned about the weather, and kept throwing furtive looks through the billowing clouds to the north-west where a single mountain stood head and shoulders above the surrounding summits. Miraculously the weather held and the Coast Range delivered one of the finest mountaineering outings of our lives.

On our way back through Vancouver, we had dinner with guidebook author Don Serl, the most active climber in the range. Don was very welcoming and explained that the south-east ridge of Asperity had been attempted several times, and the Serras were considered the most difficult summits in the area. They had only been traversed once before, so our outing was causing a little bit of a stir amongst the close band of Coast Range climbers. Don also revealed that the distant summit we had seen to the north was Monarch Mountain (3555m).

'It's the highest peak between Waddington and Mount Fairweather 1,000km up the coast,' Don enthused. 'But it's rarely visited and the weather is even poorer than the Waddington Range.' Despite Don's caution I was attracted by Monarch's isolation and dominance and a seed had been sown. Geographers call this singularity prominence, but for a mountaineer it was a more basic attraction: Monarch was simply a mountain that had to be climbed.

Monarch exerted a similar pull on the pioneers, and its first ascent by Henry Hall was a tour de force. Hall first attempted the peak in 1931 and made three further visits over the next five years, before finally succeeding on the glaciated east ridge with Hans Fuhrer in July 1936. The second ascent fell to John Dudra and Fips Broda in 1953 when they climbed the west face. Later Broda described their bold one-day ascent as 'a most exhilarating climb – in parts it was quite difficult and quite exposed.' These two routes are occasionally repeated, but the third route on the mountain has yet to see a second ascent. In August 1977, Dennis Mullen and Fred Beckey attempted the long south ridge, but were stopped by a deep notch at one-third height. After a bivouac and some creative abseil tactics to bypass the notch, Mullen carried on alone to the summit.

As it happened, Don also had a thing about Monarch. He was attracted to the long north ridge, one of the largest structural features of the range, and made five visits to the mountain before he was successful with Bruce Fairley and Bill Durtler in July 2000. Their three-day ascent, which traversed the north summit, the highest unclimbed subsidiary peak in the range, was one of the greatest routes of Don's sparkling Coast Range career. It looked like all the major lines had been climbed on this massive four-sided pyramid, but in 2001 Guy Edwards, Vance Culbert and John Millar made the first continuous ski traverse of the Coast mountains from Vancouver to Skagway. They saw countless peaks during their five-month journey, but Guy wrote afterwards in the *American Alpine Journal* that the scenic highlight was the view of the south side of Monarch. It was difficult to pick out any details from the grainy black and white photo that accompanied the report, but there was just the hint of a feature running up the south-west face.

By this time I had several Coast mountain trips under my belt. I'd explored the Septentrion Spires and Mount Zeus in the Pantheon Range, tip-toed up a perfect pillar of granite on Tiedemann's huge south face, kicked steps up a couloir on Mount Remote and experienced the out-there feeling of climbing lonely Mount Gilbert way to the south. Every time we had travelled new ground and the untouched beauty of the Coast Range had weaved their spell. So it was not a complete surprise when Guy invited me to go climbing with him the following summer. I hesitated, as Guy's ability and energy clearly outstripped mine, but then tragically he and John disappeared on the Devil's Thumb in April 2003. Under any normal circumstances this would have been the end to the story, but in April 2007

Micha Rinn on *Game of Thrones*, day two. The route's elegant line bypassed the face's lower spur to land at the bottom of its manage challenge, an upper spur climbed in 18 pitches. Despite improbable ground, the pair found an amenable that only added to its quality. *(Simon Richardson)*

Above: Micha Rinn and Simon
Richardson on summit Monarch
Mountain after first ascent of
*Game of Thrones. (Micha Rinn)*

Left: Micha Rinn on climbing the upper
spur on day two. *(Simon Richardson)*

mountain photographer John Scurlock made a remarkable flight around Monarch in his home-built aeroplane. His images revealed the south-west face in remarkable detail, and in common with his other mountain photos, he published them on the Internet.

Soon after I received an email from Don Serl. 'Hi Simon, have you seen Scurlock's photos of Monarch? OMG … look at that route up the south-west face!' I clicked on the link and there it was: the perfect line running up the centre of the 1,300m-high wall. It was a veritable *Walker Spur*: steep, logical and compelling, but most importantly, it appeared to be objectively safe.

We resolved to climb it together during the summer of 2008, but life got in the way, and our trip never progressed into the planning stage. Don attempted to pull another team together before retiring from serious climbing a few years later, but to no avail. Others showed an interest too. In 2004, Fred Beckey assembled a strong team on the glacier under the west face, but the weather was poor and they ended up climbing a new route on Princess Mountain instead.

My interest in Monarch was rekindled in August 2016 when Micha Rinn and I made the first ascent of the 1,600m-high *Diamond Ridge* on the Grandes Jorasses. It was a strong line, never too hard, but notable for being the third time the Tronchey Wall, the largest face in the Mont Blanc range, had ever been climbed. I had spent several years trying to persuade my climbing friends to attempt the route, but they had all graciously declined. Micha's strong technical skills complemented my wider experience, so when we were looking for a similar objective for 2017, John Scurlock's images of Monarch immediately came to mind. With the ideal partner raring to go, it was a case of now or never.

**Empire Way Glacier**
Our base camp is pleasantly situated on the broad col between Monarch and Page Mountain. The weather is initially poor, but on 30 July we cross the glacier and make a north-south traverse of Pt2925m. Our ascent follows a beautiful sinuous snow crest and we descend to the col separating the Empire Way glacier from the Monarch Icefield. There is a small cairn on the summit and we presume the peak had previously been climbed the col via the south ridge.

Two days later we climb Monarch by the *Dudra-Broda* route on the west face. It is a long and complex outing, with some exposed climbing on the 'hanging roof ice field' and a difficult mixed pitch leading to the summit ridge. We arrive back at the tent after a 16-hour day. The following afternoon we descend from the col to scope out the south-west face. The view from the west face across to our proposed line had been rather disheartening as the lower part is comprised of a series of vertical flat-topped towers separated by huge drops, similar to a set of skyscrapers standing in line.

This is the first time we have seen the face in full view and we study it for a long time. The wall can be divided into three sections. The lower two are defined by pronounced spurs: Scurlock's photos suggest we can link them with a horizontal traverse. The upper spur is the steeper of the two, and the *raison d'être* of the route, as it leads to the apex of the wall roughly level with the foot of the hanging roof ice field on the west face route. Above, the third section follows a lower-angled buttress leading directly to the summit.

We stare at the wall intently for several minutes until suddenly Micha breaks the silence. 'Hey Simon, rather than following the crest of the lower spur, how about climbing directly up to the foot of the upper spur and avoiding all the towers?' It's a brilliant suggestion. The beauty of Micha's line is that it is protected from stone fall by steep walls above and leads directly to the foot of the upper spur. We watch the face for over an hour and there are no falling rocks despite being exposed to the full heat of the afternoon sun. We name the features: the initial ramp; the hidden snowfield; the triangular snowfield; the great ice field. All are landmarks to guide us up this subtle and complex route.

Early next evening we are alongside the great ice field and at the foot of the upper spur. Micha's line has worked out perfectly but the climbing has become progressively more difficult through the day. The volcanic rock is solid, but the holds slope downwards and the cracks are flared which makes protection difficult to place. The upper spur is undercut at its base and we can't find a way through. We try a couple of different options with no success, and as a last resort we down climb a fault on the right to where it fades. The overhang is smaller here and we manage to pull through and fix a rope for the morning, before settling down to a comfortable bivouac.

A snowy Monarch Mountain illustrating the line of *Game of Thrones* with two bivouacs marked. *(John Scurlock)*

Next day we slowly pick our way up the upper spur. The rock climbing is steep and sometimes run out, and often when we think our options are closing down a single passage allows progress. Finally after 18 tense and absorbing pitches we emerge at the top of the upper spur where the angle abruptly eases. We move easily up broken ground to the summit buttress and an exposed bivouac above a huge drop overlooking the west face.

The weather is perfect and next morning we quickly climb a handful of mixed pitches to the top. The view from the summit is breathtaking. To the south-east Waddington stands out as a brilliant white wedge floating above a sea of cloud, and we can just make out Asperity and the Serra Peaks where the story began 20 years before. And to the north lie the intriguing summits of the Monarch Icefield beckoning further adventures for the future. It is tempting to linger, but instead we carefully descend the west face and reach base camp later that afternoon.

Two days later we tramp across the Empire Way glacier for a second time and traverse the long ridge running north from Pt2925m. We cross five summits and abseil a deep notch to reach the Sugarloaf (2620m), highest summit in the chain. As far as we know this shapely curved tower is unclimbed. We stand back and proudly admire Monarch towering high above us. Our adventure is finally complete.

**Summary**
Pt2625m, *North-South Traverse*, (PD), 30 July 2017. Monarch (3555m), *West Face* (D), 1 August 2017. Monarch (3555m), *Game of Thrones*, (ED2, 1250m), 4-6 August 2017. The Sugarloaf (2620m), (PD), 8 August 2017.

TOM LIVINGSTONE

# Alaska: Fun or Fear?

These images of the *Slovak Direct* (5.9, X, M6, WI6+, 2700m) that accompany
the first part of Tom Livingstone's article feature the ninth ascent of this
landmark Alaskan route, completed in 2018 in four days by Anne Gilbert Chase,
who appears in all of them, and Chantel Astorga, who took the photographs.
This was the first all-female ascent and the second female ascent of
an Alaskan route of this standard. *(Chantel Astorga)*

*In the spring of 2017,* **Tom Livingstone** *and* **Uisdean Hawthorn** *left for an
extended visit to Alaska with their goal the Father and Sons Wall of Denali.
Plagued with bad weather, they made an optimistic attempt on the Slovak Direct
instead which was shut down by worsening conditions. This spring they returned
to make a successful ascent of a new route, Fun or Fear?, on the east face of Jezebel
in the Revelation Mountains.*

Wednesday 3 May 2017. I lay in my tent, waiting. What was I waiting for? I didn't know. Expedition life seemed to have condensed
into eating, waiting or climbing. I couldn't tell if my sunburn was hospital-
grade, or whether it was just the funky light from the red fabric of the tent.
This was a borrowed Crux model, and it really stank in there. Sorry Crux.
Everything seemed off-colour; it was like the world's contrast had been
altered. Uisdean Hawthorn and I were resting, waiting for an opportunity
to climb Mt Hunter. The 1,400m north buttress tempted us from base camp,
so tantalisingly close. It stood proudly over the glacier, but when we hung

Right: Both women are former Denali guides. Astorga had previously reached the summit nine times and in 2010 skied from the summit down the west ridge. Chase had summited four times. Though they met on the peak eight years ago, their ascent of the *Slovak Direct* was only the third time they'd climbed together. The first time was their attempt in 2017, which Livingstone references in his article. The second time was the first ascent of *Obscured Perception* (VI, WI5, M6, A0, 70°, 1400m) on Nilkanth (6596m) in the Garhwal, featured in Area Notes. *(Chantel Astorga)*

Far right: Anne Gilbert Chase enjoying some easier ground on the *Slovak Direct*. Now a registered nurse, she lives in Bozeman, Montana with her husband Jason Thompson, who was the third member of their team on Nilkanth. Astorga is now an avalanche forecaster based in Idaho. *(Chantel Astorga)*

out with Colin Haley to 'chat shit', we realised climbing the north buttress is only two-thirds of the way to the summit. And reaching the summit, as we all know, is all that matters: everything else is just an attempt. Our egos insisted we'd never reach the cornice bivouac, the spot where you emerge from the buttress, and call it good. But I'm sure everyone says that until they get there.

By evening, the stove was roaring in the kitchen, more of a teepee tarp in reality. We'd pitched it wonky so it collapses often and then we bodge it again. We lost our washing-up liquid – it slowly melted into the snow on a warm day – so Uisdean has cleaned our pots and pans with hand soap. 'Soap is soap, right?' It did explain the odd coconut and jasmine aftertaste.

Monday 7 May. Yesterday morning we stumbled back onto the glacier after attempting the Moonflower route on Mt Hunter. We reached the final rock band after 17 hours of climbing, moving well and enjoying the continuously high quality. Our pace slowed as the evening shadows grew, but we still felt strong as we melted water.

I'd watched dark lenticular clouds cap Foraker and Denali during the afternoon, and wondered if the bad weather forecast for two days' time was arriving early. It wasn't a great surprise when the radio crackled at 8pm and Lisa, the Kahiltna base camp manager said, 'bad weather is due to arrive much earlier than expected.' Our hopes of climbing to the summit of Hunter suddenly stalled, and we talked of options. Of course, we could always

climb to the cornice bivy, but to what purpose? It seemed pointless to climb to an arbitrary point in the face of incoming bad weather; it would only protract our descent.

Soft, perfect snow crystals began to float through the air, landing on our jackets. 'I guess that settles it.' We began to rappel through the Alaskan night, back down the route, finally crossing back over the bergschrund 11 hours later on Sunday morning, exhausted. Apart from a few hours of dozing on Friday night, we'd been awake since Friday morning.

Sunday 14 May. Three weeks of our trip gone, one month left. I felt confident about that amount of time. It gave us a few weeks to acclimatise and a few weeks to wait for a weather window. All we really needed were four days of stable weather. How hard could that be? After our Moonflower attempt, we decided to focus on our main objective, Denali, and moved higher up the mountain. But we were now stuck at 11,000ft camp and it had been snowing hard since last night. The tent quickly became buried, and gusts of wind blew snow through the ventilation holes. Thin puffs of snow would funnel into our sleeping area, always finding a way in despite our best efforts.

We were grateful for the rest day, having hauled our enormous sleds the day before. We woke after 14 hours' sleep, ate porridge in our sleeping bags and then warmed the tent with the stove. The ceiling started to rain condensation and our sleeping bags became very damp. It was like being

The *Slovak Direct* is noted for its length: 2.7km of sustained climbed. Chase told *Climbing* magazine: 'it's extremely steep with a lot of mixed climbing and a bit of everything. There is a lot of water ice up to WI6 and difficult rock.' The pair spent three nights on the route, including one on a sloping ledge in bad weather wrapped in their tent. *(Chantel Astorga)*

in the tropical house at the zoo: 100% humidity and a light rain falling. I'm glad Uisdean had brought a hard drive filled with movies. We started *Band of Brothers*, still lying in our sleeping bags, waiting for evening. Then we could go to sleep for another 14 hours.

Later I pressed my head against the wet fabric of the tent, just to feel something. I'd been lying, trapped in this cocoon, for weeks. At least, that's what it felt like. The icy temperature seeped into my forehead. 'Ah yes,' I thought, recalling where I was: still in a tent, lying down. The wind eased outside and I wondered if the storm was passing. Then another gust slammed into the fabric and the tent rocked. Stale smells hovered around me. Dried sweat from t-shirts, worn for 14 days straight. Damp down, repeatedly soaked by condensation. Disgusting socks, worn continuously on multiday routes.

'Are our senses sharpened, or dulled?' I wondered. The contrast of pale snow against a deep blue sky seemed ethereal, hyper-bright. The white sunlight seemed almost to strobe. But in our storm-bound days, we felt the absence of temperature, fresh air and real colours.

Wednesday 17 May. 14,000ft camp. Breathe. Pause. Sit up. Pause. Breathe. Pause. Unzip sleeping bag. Breathe … The air felt thin, as though the oxygen had been wrung out of it. Lying in our red cocoons, breathing heavily, we waited until sun hit the tent. 'It'll be here any minute now,' I think, willing the warmth. I could see half the camp already lit up. A few people were standing outside their tents in enormous jackets, like penguins on the ice. They were either in the cold shade or suddenly basking in the morning light, flapping their arms.

My sleeping bag had a white layer of frost and ice where the condensation had frozen so I kept my head totally still, trying to avoid the shock of ice on skin. The temperature had dropped and the forecasts said -40°C. We would continue with our acclimatisation for the next few days. At least it was fresh.

During my 2012 trip to Denali with Tom Ripley, I'd learnt a lot about acclimatisation. We spent only two days above 14,000ft camp. There was a day trip to 17,000ft camp and then an attempt at the summit. I found it very hard to acclimatise, and didn't manage to walk to the summit via the West Buttress, unlike Ripley. On this trip with Uisdean, we spent much more time acclimatising, and I consequently felt much better at high altitude. On separate days, we go to 16,500ft, sleep at 17,000ft camp, go to 18,000ft, and then reach the summit. We also spend about a month at 14,000ft camp, which certainly helped.

Monday 5 June. After acclimatising, Uisdean and I had about three weeks. We felt fairly confident good weather would materialise. According to lore, there is often high pressure at the end of May or start of June, but it's important to note the weather in Alaska is notoriously unpredictable, unstable and poor. Forecasts are also often wrong. With only 15 days left before our flight, we still couldn't see any good weather on the horizon. The weather continued to be unsettled. Sunshine and snow mixed in an afternoon. We had snow at 14,000ft camp but it was calm at 17,000ft camp. High winds blasted the summit but it was eerily calm at 14,000ft.

We were lucky to be able to speak to Dougie, Rob's friend, who sent us detailed analyses of the forecasts. His accurate and thorough interpretations had been useful so far, but his predictions for Monday to Friday weren't looking stellar. The best we could see was: 'Tuesday and Wednesday will be less windy, less cloudy, and unlikely to precipitate.'

Our original objective had been the Father and Sons Wall but it was almost devoid of ice. The long period of good weather during March and April had probably melted a lot. This must have something to do with the relatively low altitude of the wall and its southern aspect. It had been a low snow and ice year in the mountains, and the Father and Sons Wall had suffered heavily. So we decided to launch for the *Slovak Direct*, on the south face of Denali. We planned for a day to approach and then hopefully three days on the route.

Neither of us felt much confidence in the weather. It wasn't forecast to be four days of high pressure, which is what you'd like for getting on one of the biggest alpine routes in North America. Our gut instincts were a mess, and I don't think either of us felt fully confident. We agreed that if we didn't have end-of-trip pressure, we wouldn't have launched with this forecast. Then again, if you don't try, you'll never know. Rob and Dougie both said: 'I wouldn't launch on this forecast.' So we tried to be like George Lowe, separating our ambitions from our situation in the mountains. But that didn't work and we went anyway.

The Wickwire ramp was a direct, fast and relatively safe way to approach the *Cassin Ridge*, taking only four hours. The climb up to the ridge and then the half dozen or so rappels and some down climbing were also relatively fine, depositing us near the base of the *Slovak*, in the East Fork of the Kahiltna. Total approach time was eight hours. In future, I'd consider approaching the Slovak on skis via the East Fork because you can leave all your food and kit at base camp and then acclimatise on the west buttress with the minimum necessary. This saves heavy sled hauling up to 14,000ft, which sucks. The East Fork is also a relatively relaxed approach when frozen, and takes around seven hours from 7,800ft camp.

Tuesday 6 June. Localised cloud had caused light snow to fall throughout the night. Although we could see patches of blue sky above, the dark clouds and sound of snow falling on the tent weren't encouraging. Lying on my mat, thinking of what lay above, we knew we were in for an adventure. We had seen the tracks from the women's team (Anne Gilbert Chase and Chantel Astorga on their 2017 attempt) approaching the route, which was a novelty: two teams on a route, which normally sees one ascent every five years.

Waking at 3am we reset the alarm until the snow and clouds cleared, which they did at 4.30am. We were quick to get ready, but spent the next hour debating whether to try. So much felt wrong: the poor forecast, the localised bad weather, the spindrift pouring down the route and the winds whipping at the ridge above. What if we got caught in a storm, high on the route? What if this wasn't a good weather window? What if we climbed too slowly because of the weather? We longed for a good forecast, but this window of 'less-shit' weather was all we had and time was running out. Despite our instincts, we decided to climb. We had to try; we'd come all this way.

The north face of Jezebel (2941m) in the Revelation Mountains, seen from the aircraft that flew Livingstone and Hawthorn in. The route follows the steep, narrow couloir. *(Tom Livingstone)*

The approach to the route's crux, a narrow, steep chimney, was sparsely protected névé *(Tom Livingstone)*

The chimney itself blocked further progress: serious and poorly protected. *(Tom Livingstone)*

After soloing the initial 350m, we put the rope on and I led the first M5 pitch. As I belayed Uisdean, Chantel appeared through the swirling spindrift along the ridge. It was pretty surreal to see these two. They were bailing, having climbed to 14,500ft, near the base of long ice corner pitches, before being forced to retreat due to spindrift and bad weather. They spent a day getting weather updates at the hanging glacier bivy. All forecasts had changed since we'd got ours two days before. The new prediction was for stronger winds and worse weather. Uisdean and I were psyched, but we have our limits. How badly did we want it? Not enough to climb into a storm, with the only way off being over the top of the highest mountain in North America. We know when to push it, but this route felt like we were trying to force it. When an experienced team with an updated weather forecast bails and you already feel like you're pushing, you have to accept reality. I began to re-lead the M5 traverse, this time back towards the ground.

Once back on the glacier of the East Fork with Gilbert and Chantel, the scant reward for seven weeks' effort was tough to bear. But that's the mountains. Sometimes we win, sometimes we lose, but it's always an adventure. Getting slammed by bad weather is better than falling off anyway. I hate bailing, but this was the right reason. The walk down from the East Fork was tiresome. It felt safer as a party of four, but the hot afternoon baked the snow and I broke trail for hours. I lost count of the number of times I fell into crevasses, sunk up to my chest or else swam through treacle snow. It felt like it went forever, but eventually we reached 7,800ft camp. Next day's walk to 14,000ft to collect our gear was equally long. It was a bitter end to our hopes for the *Slovak*, but at least we weren't fighting for our lives in a storm. Denali continued to be smashed by the weather. The following day we flew out of the mountains.

*

'Well.'

'Well!' Uisdean replied.

I'm sure the more climbing trips we go on, the less we need to say to each other. Our 2018 trip, to the Revelation Mountains in Alaska, seemed to feature very few words, most of them in the smattering of Spanish we'd learnt in Patagonia.

We sat beneath the steep and unclimbed north face of Mt Jezebel (2880m), gazing up at the possibilities. From a distance, the broad wall held many lines, but on closer inspection there was only one viable route. Giant seracs threatened everything except the 'chimney line'. The air was calm on the glacier, but we knew strong winds blasted the skyline ridge above. Large plumes of snow blew like streamers from the crest. Perpetually hanging in space, they were white smudges against a blue sky. The smudges eventually thinned, then vanished, blown far out from the mountain. Sparkling snow drifted slowly back to earth.

'Hmm. *Mucho viento!*' I said to Uisdean.

Our line was agreed. We thought the route might have three distinct sections. The first looked like steep snow; the middle was an enormous chimney, which swallowed everything falling from above. The final section looked like climbable black ice, but was perhaps threatened by moderate-sized cornices. There were so many unknowns with this potential route. We knew two teams had attempted a line to the right last year, although it looked pretty kamikaze. One party climbed a pitch then retreated due to

Having been shut down on the north face, Livingstone and Hawthorn switched to the east face, previously climbed by Pete Graham and Ben Silvestre via *Hoar of Babylon*. Livingstone and Hawthorn took the obvious ice goulotte to the right of the picture. *(Tom Livingstone)*

unprotectable vertical sugar snow. The other party bailed when the leader fell off and broke his leg. He was rescued a day later.

Clint Helander, local Alaskan and veteran of the 'Revs', had been in to attempt the north face three times but hadn't climbed a pitch. He was extremely helpful with providing info and I remembered his words: 'when it's safe, it's not really in condition. When it's in condition, it's not really safe.' Clint doesn't intend to return. 'I finally felt okay about letting it go.' But here we were, Uisdean and I. Like the guns we saw in the supermarket, our sights were set on the summit, ambitions aimed high. We were locked, loaded and ready to fire this route. The weather forecast was acceptable, although winds still blew on the ridge, a distant roar to remind us of its presence.

'Hmm. *Bueno?*'

'*Si.*'

We set our alarms for 4am. Then, having missed both of them, Uisdean and I started up the north face too late. 'Chopper Squadron' has a reputation to live up to, after all.

We started with hundreds of metres of steep névé and with each pitch the route became more interesting. Névé is that intoxicating mix of relatively easy climbing but often with no gear. It's all fun until you look down and realise you're 40 metres out, with no pro, and it's suddenly turned into steep snow. The second pitch had no gear in 60m. The third pitch was 75m, until I found a poor belay. The fourth was even longer. At least we were pleased not

to be on vertical sugar. In mid afternoon, we arrived at the biggest unknown factor of the route: the huge slot, which gave the route its name, was like a giant elevator shaft or chimney stack. It rose straight up for about 75m. We hadn't been able to see inside, wondering what lurked within until now.

The winds on the ridge above had obviously decided we were having too much fun, so unleashed hell. Between dark waves of spindrift washing down the cliff, we snatched upward glances. The chimney contained two overhanging mixed pitches of compact-looking black diorite, then a long overhanging pitch of snow, all capped with an enormous snow mushroom. The spindrift flew into space when it poured over the lip of the overhanging snow, and there were no cracks on the side walls we could use to aid around it.

'Huh.' I said.

'Huh.' Uisdean replied.

Above: The 10th pitch, known as 'The Gift'. Expecting hard mixed climbing, the ice continued as 'a long slither' that Hawthorn was able to climb quickly. *(Tom Livingstone)*

Left: Uisdean Hawthorn on pitch two of *Fun or Fear?* (AI6 R, M6+, 90°, 1200m), east face of Jezebel. *(Tom Livingstone)*

We've done enough to know when a pitch looks easy, hard, or really hard. And this chimney looked to be at least one level above really hard. We couldn't see a way: how do you climb overhanging sugar snow? This wasn't Cerro Torre, either. The two shorter pitches of overhanging diorite also didn't look good. I didn't want to say it, but in its current condition I wasn't sure if it was climbable. Perhaps one of my biggest weaknesses is I'm always psyched. If there's a chance, another option, one more try, I'll take it. But stood beneath this chimney as it unloaded heavy waves of spindrift, I couldn't see how we'd get up it and nor could Uisdean. Despite giving the route a good effort, we'd been totally shut down.

We began rappelling, one of my least favourite activities in the mountains. We lost a lot of wires but that's better than losing your head. A few years ago, the prospect of burning through racks worth of gear and many

metres of tat would've made me wince. Now I just accept it's part of the
deal with alpine climbing. I hacked at the nevé for ages to find anchors, and
by the time I found something, I didn't care that I'd only just got a new set
of wires. Easy come, easy go.

'Don't bounce on this one,' was all I said to Uisdean. When we finally
jumped over the berschrund, we looked back up at the chimney, and up at
the ridge.

'*Mucho viento! Poco loco!*'

Back at base camp, I thought over our experience. We didn't actually
climb any higher into the chimney proper to really see what the pitches
were like. We stood about 20m beneath and they sure as hell didn't look
good. But could we be absolutely certain? Maybe you could tunnel deep
into the sugar snow and find a crack in the back? Maybe it would form ice
after getting the summer sun? But after further thought, I agreed with Clint's
comments. The snow mushroom was too dangerous and the overhanging
sugar in the chimney wouldn't be consolidating any time soon. You could
drill your way up the sidewalls of the chimney, or there *might* be a crack,
but, for us, it wasn't climbing by fair, safe or rational means.

There weren't any other logical or safe lines on the rest of the north
face-proper, so we decided to focus our attention on the east face of Jezebel.
Fellow Brits Pete Graham and Ben Silvestre had first climbed this (See:
B Silvestre, 'The Trouble with Happiness', *AJ* 2016, pp64-9) but there were
plenty of amazing lines left. We decided on one that looked impressive and
with plenty of adventure. The start seemed to be the meat of the route, or so
we hoped, followed by plenty of climbing to the summit. The descent was
unknown, but we knew the weather looked good for a few days.

And so we started, under the cold cloak of night, our skis crunching
towards the east face of Jezebel. Uisdean fired the first pitch as night lifted
and dawn spilled onto the glacier. Technical and thought provoking, our
pitches often took time. Uisdean's 'pitch involved mixed climbing alongside
a vertical step of névé, then kicking onto it and quickly running for the sanctuary of easier ground above. Further pitches were steep, always long, and
often run out. We'd explored our comfort zones climbing run-out and steep
névé on our north face attempt, so this felt familiar.

After Uisdean's block, I led several long pitches up the couloir, chasing
the sunshine as it spread across the east face. In 10 minutes, Uisdean went
from freezing cold to boiling hot, then cold again as the shade returned
to his belay. A final crux pitch took me a long time when I discovered, to
my horror, that the steep wall of ice I aimed to climb was totally detached
from the rock. The sheet of ice hung five inches clear, like the skin of an
onion. I committed to it with a few high side-runners, then climbed higher
and further away, heading for the re-attached ice about five metres above.
I climbed carefully, meditatively, although I'm sure I was also making all
sorts of noises.

'Watch me here. *No bueno!*' I shouted down.

The onionskin of ice was so brittle I broke a 12-inch square hole into it

After a comfortable bivouac, the pair climbed the east ridge to the top.
*(Tom Livingstone)*

and put my arm inside as a better hold than my ice tools. I almost laughed when I looked into the hole and saw my ice pick poking into the inside of the onionskin, almost touching the rock underneath. Long stretches up a couloir took up most of the afternoon linked by a wonderful pitch we nicknamed 'The Gift'. Expecting more hard and involved climbing, we were delighted to find a long slither of thick ice. Uisdean raced up it, plugging in solid ice screws and pulling over the lip. A lucky break, I thought.

We met the east ridge of Jezebel towards the evening, thankfully moving together for most of it until we found a bivy platform that was flat and, crucially, faced east so we could welcome the morning sun. Except for a brief episode of fiery cramp, the night passed smoothly and when the sun popped over the horizon, it was like life being drawn back into lungs. The remainder of the route featured some 'classic alpine bullshit': traversing up and down, weaving left and right, avoiding towers and traversing snow slopes. We tried to judge when to pitch it and when to keep going. Finally, though, the northeast summit arrived at 12.30pm in clear, windless skies. It felt like a treat to be somewhere so special, after a rewarding experience, and with perfect weather. So many 'unknowns' had finally been answered. We could relax on the summit, lying down and soaking in the view of endless mountains. *Bueno.*

# High Asia

Lt H O S Gibson (1885-1917), 11th Battalion London Regiment,
a school-friend of George Mallory's, blown to pieces
during fighting at Gaza, Palestine.

## BRUCE NORMAND

# Gasherbrum IV

The south and east faces of Gasherbrum IV, both unclimbed. *(Bruce Normand)*

The Gasherbrum sub-range forms the very core of the Karakoram, the massif from which the Baltoro drains west, the Siachen south-east and the Shaksgam the north-east sides. Not for nothing is its highest point (Gasherbrum I, 8080m), tucked away at the end of 50km of ice and ringed by lesser summits, known as Hidden Peak. Although Gasherbrum I and Gasherbrum II both pass the magic 8,000m mark, and Gasherbrum II ranks as an 'easy 8,000er', their limelight is stolen quite definitively by Gasherbrum IV (7925m). The west face, known for good reason as the Shining Wall, rising unbroken for 2,500m directly to the summit, dominates the trekking nexus of the Pakistani Karakoram, Concordia. It is visible for days to all who set foot on the upper Baltoro.

The aesthetic fame of Gasherbrum IV among trekkers is more than equalled by its notoriety among mountaineers. While 'only' the 18th-highest peak on the planet, Gasherbrum IV is nevertheless the *ne plus ultra* of inaccessible mountain giants. It has indubitably the most execrable rock of any high peak where the climbing cannot stick to snow and ice: alternately badly fractured marble and impenetrably compact marble. Too high for freeze-thaw cycles to produce ice most of the surface area of Gasherbrum IV essentially takes no gear at all. Thus the mountain has no easy routes,

79

A map of the upper Baltoro glacier illustrating just how remote the Gasherbrum massif is. Camp one is marked as ABC and the correct height is 5,950m.
*(Central Karakoram National Park)*

has never been climbed in anything other than an epic, and has seen fewer pairs of feet (10) on its true summit than has walked on the moon (12). The footing on the moon is also a good deal less tenuous. Despite annual expeditions in the 1980s and 1990s, and sporadic efforts in this millennium, there remain no routes on the south, east or north faces of Gasherbrum IV and only two through the Shining Wall (*Kurtyka-Schauer* and *Central Rib*). The only route ever to have been repeated is the north-west ridge, which means that the route of first ascent, the north-east ridge, has not been repeated in the 60 years since it yielded to Bonatti and Mauri. The stories of the first ascent and the *Central Rib* are of bloody-minded persistence. The story of the *Kurtyka-Schauer* suggests a death wish is a handy thing to bring along.

In 2009, my eye for new and overlooked mountains led me to try Gasherbrum III. Not being nearly as brave as Geoff Cohen and Des Rubens, who made a very spirited attempt on the south-south-west ridge in 1985, we tried to get to the north-east ridge from the north, but were unable to get out of the cwm between Gasherbrum III and Gasherbrum IV. Taking a good look at the dark side of Gasherbrum IV from the cwm, the American Billy Pierson and I saw that one line on the centre left of the east face looked

Billy Pierson and Marcos Costa. *(Bruce Normand)*

Normand on the exit beside the final ice cliff. *(Billy Pierson)*

to be something of a straight shot up snowy gullies, with perhaps some short rock steps, depending on snow cover. This face offers the shortest possible technical route on the mountain, being 900m at 50°-55° from bergschrund to summit. The snow gully route would also lead directly to the main summit, rather than requiring the awkward traverse of the upper west face, which all existing routes must make. While the aim of the 2017 expedition was to put this fine theory to the test, we were not the first to have this idea: the east face was attempted in 1980 by Americans Craig McKibben and Steve Swenson, in 1993 by Yasushi Yamanoi of Japan, and in 1996 by a Korean team including the irrepressible Kim Chang-Ho. While Yamanoi did not get above the floor of the cwm, both the Americans and the Koreans were repelled low in the central gullies by spindrift and compact rock.

For our attempt on this project, Billy and I roped in the Brazilian Marcos Costa, as well as two other members who cancelled before the rubber hit

Costa leading the lower ice pitches from camp two to three. *(Billy Pierson)*

the road. Our team arrived in Pakistan in late May, flew immediately to Skardu and required only one day of formalities before setting out for Askole. All the new and onerous post-Nanga Parbat conditions, which we encountered in 2015, appear to have been rescinded or forgotten. Rising living standards in Askole can be measured from the many more porters smoking; several now own enough horses to do the majority of the heavy lifting. They also wanted to dispense with the usual rest day and evening party in Paiju, so we made the trek to Gasherbrum base camp (GBC) in six days. The Pakistani military has moved its own GBC a kilometre down-glacier since 2009, but in that time has succeeded in creating the most monumental eyesore, in the middle of the Central Karakoram National Park, with blackened rubbish of all conceivable sorts strewn over a 200m radius around the central huts.

Although the east face may be short, the approach is anything but. Our first task was to establish the seasonal trade route through the south Gasherbrum icefall to camp one (5900m) for the Gasherbrums I, II and IV. With a little foreknowledge and a few days of decent weather, we had found the route, shuttled two loads and occupied camp one by our fourth day beyond GBC, compared to 10 in 2009. We then continued north up depressingly flat glacier, ending with an even more depressingly soft slope, to camp two (6300m), beneath but sheltered from the icefall which breaks out of the cwm. Our problems started here. The 'straightforward' snow slopes on the

The business end of Gasherbrum IV's east face: technical climbing that the team did not reach. *(Bruce Normand)*

Costa setting out for the dead-end slab. *(Bruce Normand)*

right of the cwm icefall, which we had climbed un-roped in 2009, seemed to be in a permanent state of windblown crust and were essentially unusable. The left side turned out to require seven pitches of 50° ice, which we had to simul-climb for safety, followed by a long, deep traverse which turned out to be more stable than it looked, with the exception of its rotten and bottom-less final 100m. On our second weeklong stint above GBC, we managed to make two and a half trips up this route and to deposit most of our east face equipment in camp three (6900m), dug in at the base of a walk-in crevasse at the centre of the lower cwm.

By this time the somewhat stable weather periods we had enjoyed up to 20 June had started to lapse into generally unstable conditions which defeated any of our forecasts. Our first stay at camp three was shortened by a day due to incoming weather and the first week of July turned out to be very poor, although an alternative forecast did cause us a fruitless trip to camp two. Every foray we made beyond camp one required breaking a new trail. With our forecasts agreeing on an excellent weather window from 9 to 11 or 12 July, we set off on 6 July to camp one, 7 July to camp two, but were forced to declare 8 July a rest day while the copious snow of the day before stabilised. On 9 July we were back in our crevasse, digging out camp three while the afternoon weather deteriorated around us. On 10 July we pushed up snow slopes to 7,300m on the east face to deposit our rack and ropes

Two views of a dead-end. The blue line indicates the team's ascent, the red dot their high point. This second photograph was taken from camp two (6550m) on Gasherbrum II. *(Bruce Normand/Guillaume Vallot)*

and monitor the conditions: 50° snow over slabs of fractured marble with few useful surface features. The weather turned again to clouds and blowing snow which persisted for much of the night.

Our appointed summit day, 11 July, was clear and windy well before dawn. The first thing to go wrong was that our entire approach and climbing track from the previous day had been eliminated. Below the bergschrund was hard work and above it was very poorly consolidated. Back at our gear dump and thawing in the sunrise, we racked up with Costa leading, Pierson belaying in a snow hole and me casting around for any kind of protection. The best I could do was a centimetre of knife-blade in the only crack where the piton wasn't about to break the rock apart. At 25m out, Costa found a previously invisible compact white marble slab, only five metres long but entirely featureless. His efforts to find protection, or an alternative route, took some 40 minutes: across and right, up and left, lots of sweeping … but there was nothing. The slab was at minimum tenuous M8 and thus, in the absence of any form of gear or belay, the route was simply too dangerous to attempt. We cleaned the line and retreated to camp three before the lower face could become even more dangerous in the heat.

The afternoon brought clouds and wind again, which did little to temper the bitter disappointment. The completely un-forecast bad afternoon weather was doing nothing for the atrocious underfoot conditions in the cwm. We decided to use the last day of nominally good weather for a bid on 'G2.5', a 7,706m subsidiary peak at the edge of the long plateau between Gasherbrum II and Gasherbrum III. The hike up the cwm was a frigid post-holing nightmare, which caused Costa to retreat with frozen feet. Pierson and I reached the 45° snow gullies at the north-east end of the cwm, but were shut down yet again by bad weather: high winds and incoming clouds even before 11am. We almost had to re-break the track just to get back to camp three, and there was no doubt that it was time to descend before real weather arrived. We decided not to leave anything at camp three; the dangers of returning just to rescue some gear outweighed the chances we would be back for a lightweight bid on anything. Our descent beside the cwm icefall was made in spindrift so heavy it would have been comical had it not been so dangerous.

At base camp we needed a long rest. The weather was poor over the peaks

but not really on the glacier. Costa joined the neighbouring French team to summit Gasherbrum II. Pierson and I considered a bid on the 1958 route, but this was ruled out by Pierson falling ill, and in retrospect would not have worked due to inclement weather persisting through the window forecast to be good. While cleaning camps one and two, we made a final brief attempt on 'G4.5', a 6,950m peak on the ridge joining Gasherbrums IV and V, but had to stop at 6,700m due to dangerous snow conditions. We had to begin our walkout on 22 July and were in Askole on the day that the first stable weather period in five weeks arrived in the mountains.

With regard to the feasibility of the east face as a route on Gasherbrum IV, it is possible that, in a year with more winter snow or better winds, one might simply climb over some or all of its marble bands on unprotected snow. Our 2009 photos appeared to show only one serious rock obstacle, in a zone of fractured marble. As things stand, we suspect that the Americans in 1980 and the Koreans in 1996 were stopped by exactly the same compact slab as we were, and that more specificity in their reports could have assisted our decision-making. We observed that our compact slab might be avoided by following snowy streaks 50m to its right, although this may entail 100m-200m of climbing on rather thinly covered terrain. In 2017, we did not see much point in launching a bid on that variation in the extant conditions.

• The author would like to thank the Mount Everest Foundation, the British Mountaineering Council and the Montane Alpine Club Climbing Fund for their generous support of the Gasherbrum IV expedition.

# GEORGE CAVE

# Half a Route in Shimshal

Dawn breaks over the Hispar Muztagh range. *(George Cave)*

The porter was speaking fast and animatedly to our guide Karim. As the conversation went on, a small crease of concern crept across Karim's face. When he spoke, his mouth beamed with his characteristic smile, but the uncertainty in his voice was distinctly noticeable,

'We lost a donkey. He is dead. He fell into the river.'

Two thoughts formed in our minds: first the image of a flailing creature plunging down the side of the 100m gorge, its walls so steep we didn't see the river below for hours at a time. Second, we wondered which of our bags was on the donkey.

'It is the cooking tent. We lost the tent, and half of our fuel.'

We relaxed slightly, and then the morbid image in our minds shifted to include a donkey fireball.

Within the hour, our jovial band of porters and donkeys had joined us at Purian Sar for lunch; it was clear that today's gossip consisted of just one topic. At our camp the night before, we had drifted to sleep to the braying of a rather horny male donkey, pursuing his prize across the camp with limited success. It now transpired that earlier today he had spied the beautiful female ass on the switchback above him and unable to contain the urges that stirred inside, made straight for her up the scree. This was the donkey that had died: chasing what he loved.

We were the British Shimshal Expedition 2017, a rather grand title for what would better be described as four friends on a climbing holiday.

On the road to Shimshal, not for the faint-hearted. *(George Cave)*

Similarly matched in ambition and inability, we were travelling to Shimshal in north-west Pakistan on the advice of Karim Hayat, a local climber and guide whom I had met in Yosemite nearly one year before. Unlike some of my previous travels in central Asia, most of my friends and family had at least heard of Pakistan, even if their knowledge was shockingly limited, confined mostly to vague associations with terrorism and the Taliban. Undeterred, Ross, Clay, Steve and I put these concerns aside and came here with one purpose, to attempt some new routes on a small clutch of unclimbed mountains in the Shimshal valley.

Approaching the site of our base camp in the Gunj-e Tang valley involved a succession of transportation, each progressively less mechanised and more intimate with the environment than the last. From Islamabad we flew 45 minutes to Gilgit, soaring like birds past the fabled faces of Pakistan's 8,000m peaks which emerged just for a moment from a duvet of cloud to remind us of the heights to which we one day might aspire. From Gilgit we drove north towards Karimabad, pausing only when held up for an hour to admire the spectacle of the local police force's efforts to clear the road for the president's entourage. Like a what's what of 20th century weaponry, each policeman was armed in a different way; perhaps they had queued at the armoury that morning and been allocated equipment on a first come first served basis.

In Karimabad we changed vehicles, the much smaller, open-sided 4WD providing no protection from the raw realities of the road to Shimshal. Blasted horizontally across the cliffs, this single-lane track is just a few years old. It hugs a twisting waterway that shoots east towards Shimshal, welcoming visitors with a barrage of dust and a relentless buffeting made more absorbing by the formidable drop below. At every narrowing above the

While Shimshal is modernising, it has maintained its distinctive appeal, at least for now. *(George Cave)*

steep sided gorge I was thankful that I knew and trusted Karim to find us a driver and vehicle in a fit state to traverse this spectacular highway.

Shimshal was wonderful, a small oasis of tranquillity hidden high in the mountains near the Chinese border. Village life felt like a glimpse into 18th century rural England, with only the juxtaposition of solar panels and scythes, or farmland and Facebook adverts, providing any hint of the influence of the modern world on the inhabitants' way of life. We joined seemingly the entire male population in a high-altitude game of football where our excuses of clumsy approach shoes, a boulder-strewn field and noticeable oxygen deficiency covered for our shockingly poor technique.

Next morning we hired eighteen porters and eight donkeys for the final stage of our journey. Access to the mountain pastures beyond was possible only on foot. Our small procession threaded its way along the banks of the Pamir e-Tang river, the path no more than a delicate alignment of tree roots and boulders bonded magically to the sheer cliff walls. Irrespective of any climbing objectives, a trip to Shimshal for this hike would be a worthy objective in its own right. And then finally, after three days and the loss of one donkey, we reached the mountains.

Pakistan christened our new base camp with a dump of fresh snow. I thought to myself how beautiful it would look on Instagram, whilst wishing out loud that more favourable conditions would soon arrive. Along with Karim, who

On the three-day trek to base camp. *(George Cave)*

was really more friend than guide, we had retained the services of a cook and his assistant. Ensuring a plentiful supply of food that is both nutritious and tasty can be the crux for any expedition; with no time to shop for ourselves we had placed all our faith in Rahim and Sajad's culinary sensibilities.

On the first morning of the approach trek Rahim passed us all a small lunch bag. It turned out, upon later inspection, to consist of a boiled potato, boiled egg and a handful of nuts. Ross and I sat together that lunchtime, slowly chewing our partially cooked potatoes and silently fearing for our diet and sanity over the coming weeks. This sort of beginning didn't bode well.

We never quite understood if it had been a form of Pakistani culinary joke, but the change that followed couldn't have been more dramatic. Every day, Rahim and Sajad delivered a steaming succession of stunning concoctions, brought to life from the flickering flames of our two-ring gas hob on the floor of the mess tent: vegetable soups to start, gigantic dishes of rice and pasta, fresh melon, omelette and marmalade wraps, curries, breads and piles of French fries. Rahim was as good a cook as he was a boulderer and having

River crossing en route to base camp. *(George Cave)*

burned us off all of our improvised boulder problems on the approach trek that was quite a compliment. By the time we got to day four and he pulled out a great crème caramel for dessert he was definitely showing off.

Two weeks previously I had guided a friend up Mont Blanc, but any acclimatisation gained from that ascent had most certainly now abandoned me. Indeed, the crumbling rock ridge besides the Grand Couloir in Chamonix is grossly inadequate preparation for the disastrous moraine that welcomes and then ensnares any climber wishing to explore the depths of the glaciated regions of central Asia. Ross, Karim and I worked hard to earn the right to place our advanced base atop a cosy plateau at the base of the glacier. Below, caravan sized pieces of moraine wished nothing more than to tumble down to the valley beneath, cheese in a mousetrap awaiting the wayward foot of a climber. But above, beyond a small band of seracs, a long flat glacier, and a faint wisp of cloud, lay our prize: an isolated, regal, 6,000m peak and the objective for the expedition.

Ross had first spied the peak on Google Earth some nine months before. In base camp we had briefly considered joining Steve and Clay in a neighbouring valley where they were keen to climb, but after seeing our peak for the first time all considerations of alternative objectives fell away. It was the perfect combination of visual prominence, technical challenge and objective safety: a holy trinity of excitement that we wouldn't dare have contemplated from our bedrooms back in England. As planned our expedition split into two smaller parties and after eight days on the move we had both established our respective advance camps. All eyes were on the prizes above.

Above: Karim Hayat.

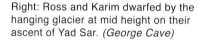
Right: Ross and Karim dwarfed by the hanging glacier at mid height on their ascent of Yad Sar. *(George Cave)*

For most expeditions to Asia, those first eight days could easily be eaten up in bureaucracy and sightseeing in a local town. Not us, sadly. Unable to afford the luxury of taking extended holidays from work, we were nonetheless unwilling to settle for a more conventional destination. The compromise was that our expedition was to be crammed into 19 days and already a third of that had been taken up simply getting to basecamp. Karim's dry wit reminded us of this from time to time, asking with a smile whether we felt the British Trekking Expedition was a success or not. The coming week was to be a race to climb, descend and return in time for our flights back to the office the following Monday.

At midnight on the morning of 5 September, Ross, Karim and I rose to the silence of a cloudless night. Crampons crunched comfortably on frozen snow and moonlight glinted like silver threads across the peaks behind us, a reminder of how perfectly the weather had fallen in tune with our plans. Our slow march towards the summit began.

Roped together we hopped across crevasses, following with ease tracks laid down the previous day. Before long an extensive bank of glacial ice lay above us. Our original intention had been to climb a route on the spectacular north face of the mountain, but as the realities of our tight timeline had hit home we'd switched our plans to the biggest line of weakness: a direct route up the middle of the south face. In high spirits and feeling confident, I had little idea quite how short a day's climbing it was to prove for me.

Absorbed in my own thoughts, I progressed silently up the slope behind the others. There is a rhythmic tranquillity that comes with ascending easy

Route on Yad Sar 6020m. *(Ross Davidson)*

Scottish I terrain, particularly on a windless morning just as dawn summons the courage to strike. A harmony of colours were spreading gracefully across the horizon like a heavenly parrot, spreading wings of purple, orange and yellow across a thousand distant summits. In that moment I felt perhaps the happiest I'd ever been in the mountains. It came, therefore, as something of a surprise to find myself violently retching just moments later, slumped over my axe, knees to the ice.

We continued on, trying to ignore it, but continued exertion wasn't proving the antidote I had hoped for. I was quite clearly not well, most likely succumbing to the altitude but still with another 500m of ascent left to complete. We deliberated for nearly an hour, for although deciding what I had to do took less than a minute coming to terms with it was far harder. Leaving the others to forge ahead, I descended alone and for the first time in the mountains found myself crying as I did. Dreams, plans and excitement rolled slowly off my cheeks, dripping into cracks in the ice beneath me. Half way up our first and only objective, my time climbing in Pakistan was over.

Ross and Karim summited the 6,015m peak that afternoon. Stretched out ahead of them was a knife-edge ridge of sugary snow, which looked spectacular but was completely incompatible with a long career as an alpinist. They made a wise choice and using abalakovs descended the hanging glacier that had formed the second half of the climb. Ecstatic and exhausted, they stumbled back into camp just before sunset to relieve me from John Grisham.

'This route is too long, it needs a camp one,' declared Karim, and promptly fell asleep.

In the adjacent valley, Steve and Clay had also seen success, climbing a new route the previous day on a peak attempted by a Japanese team in 2001. They had ploughed a long course through deep snow, thankful as the thick clouds rolled in that it presented only a few technical difficulties. 'I only made Clay rope up because I didn't want to carry the rope anymore,'

Karim heads up the final slopes to the summit ridgeline of Yad Sar.
*(Ross Davidson)*

Rahim Hayat, the admired cook.
*(George Cave)*

George Cave, poleaxed by the altitude sickness that ended his climb.

grinned Steve to us back in camp.

Climbing complete, only a heavy, painful load-carry separated us all from another of Rahim and Sajad's signature dishes. Rahim hadn't wasted any time in our absence, claiming most of our base camp boulder problems for himself by building great towering cairns on their rocky summits. Swap his sole-less shoes for some B3s and who knows what he could achieve. Karim promised us a treat of the rare snow peacock for dinner; our gullible minds were clearly addled after our brief time in the mountains for the meat looked suspiciously like chicken. It was time to go home.

Our return to Shimshal three days later coincided with the arrival of solar lighting in the town. To celebrate, it was quickly decided that for some reason I should commission a new solar lamppost for the village elders in front of the entire town. They listened politely to my rambling speech and didn't laugh at any of my jokes.

## RICHARD ZÖLLNER

# The Mountains of South-eastern Iran

Hezar and Kuh-e Hezar rising from the Iranian plain seen from the east.
*(Mojtaba Vasou)*

Trotting on along the road, I realised how I actually preferred this to finding another ride. Walking really is the only form of locomotion I have ever found adequate for human comprehension. Even riding a bicycle: how much there is we cannot take in any more. At the same time I was aware of our timetable: four days, two mountains 130km apart as the crow flies but 320km on the road we would most likely travel hitchhiking. I found comfort in the knowledge that even if we had to walk the last 20km to the base of our mountain in 40°C heat, we could still manage to climb up to the hut by about 9pm or 10pm. And then there was the beauty of the landscape: ochre volcanic hills radiating from the bulky mountainside ahead, wild rhubarb flowering in red and yellow, anthracite coloured lizards, flocks of sparrows as brown as the land and among these robust, earthy tones the otherworldly blue of the Eurasian roller (*Coracias garrulus*) and always the green, the inconceivable green of the irrigated fields in the valleys below.

Then, suddenly, a lorry ground to an abrupt halt beside us, having come around the last bend in the road seemingly without any sound whatsoever. The driver didn't even bother to look at us, but a large group of schoolboys in the open bed of the truck waved us on board. Climbing up, Mojtaba,

View W from the summit of Taftan shortly after sunrise. *(Richard Zöllner)*

At one of the active fumaroles on the summit of Taftan. *(Richard Zöllner)*

A brook with sulphurous water high on Taftan. *(Richard Zöllner)*

my Iranian friend, had soon found a little corner to squeeze in among them. I must have seemed hesitant, because I was motioned to what seemed like a large metal box, well suited for sitting on. In Iran visitors from other countries are treated with great respect and friendliness. Only this time my 'hosts' were boys aged 10, who must be the same all over the world. They were smiling in my face and were all well aware of my backside becoming quickly and uncomfortably hot from my seat, which turned out to be a saucepan filled with food, apparently having come straight from the fire.

Reaching Dare Gol (Flower Valley), the endpoint of the road and a popular picnic spot, I was so glad to disembark. Here we fell into the hands of a mullah organising a school holiday weekend for the boys. As is the custom, we were invited to eat with them. My experience of Iran told me that should we accept we would most definitely not reach the hut that day, so as politely as possible we excused ourselves. The mullah, a local of Khash, turned out to be a man of great learning and soon we were discussing Seneca and Marcus Aurelius, incurring substantial delay. As he insisted on showing us the way we set off together, still deep in conversation, followed by some of the boys, trying to sneak up on us to beat the mullah's bottom with a thorny twig; something he took with the fatherly dignity of somebody who has not forgotten that once he too had been young.

Over two hours later we parted. Encounters like these are one of many reasons I have fallen in love with Iran. A country full of an intelligent people grossly misrepresented in western media, full of hospitality and openness, eager to meet foreigners. For me, mountaineering is more than the rocks or the ice or the route or the top and more than the sum of these parts. It's these aspects of anthropology and natural geography that really drive me to seek out places like this. As human beings, how could we view the mountains isolated from the matrix of the world in which they rest, suspended like the clasts of a sedimentary breccia, poorly sorted, so much so that the matrix and clasts become one. This then is man and these are the mountains, and both are of interest for their interplay with each other.

Catching up for lost time we sped up, first along a brook and through a narrow valley, with some enjoyable scrambling in places, gaining height, leaving the gorge higher up for an easy path leading to the Sobah hut, reaching it as the sun sank low and the longer wavelengths started to dominate, while around us a sea of jagged volcanic peaks reached upwards as black as charcoal suspended in fire. Mojtaba had started making tea – what other occupation could be more quintessentially Iranian – but I had to call him over. I had identified Kuh-e Bazman's dark silhouette to the south-west, the great mysterious mountain nobody knew anything about. This was as we stood 3,100m up the active volcano Taftan (c3930m?). Next morning we would go to the summit, but all I could think of was this other volcano, the most alluring of peaks in all of Baluchistan.

An early start at 3am ensured we reached the lower active summit of Taftan, also known as Maddeh Kuh, before sunrise. The wind blew noxious smoke from the fumaroles along the summit ridge towards a flank of the mountain with 60m tall rock needles rising from unconsolidated tuff. Having seen and smelled enough here, a short, half-hour traverse over rocks and snowfields led to the higher inactive Nar Kuh summit, 3,930m according to my own measurements. (In older literature and maps the altitude for this mountain is often stated as exceeding 4,000m.) Looking down from the summit, one wonders how people could possibly eke out a living from this bareness, but, albeit in small densities, they do. Underground water pipes know as *qanats* provide the basis for this, often running for tens of kilometres from the mountains to the settlements on the plains.

Up on the summit, the fresh breeze and altitude provided an acceptable climate and only with reluctance did we manage to part from it, reaching Dare Gol at noon, where the celebrations of one of the numerous religious holidays in Iran were in full swing: plenty of tea, sweet soft drinks, dates, confectionery, kebab and watermelon everywhere. Young couples that had stolen away from the city for a day were strolling about, holding hands behind trees amidst the strewn rubbish. For a westerner this is hard to understand: how it could be romantic to linger among such a profusion of discarded plastic bottles and other garbage. But perceptions of these matters are different and the problem is only seen as such by some. During a visit in 2015, I collected 32 plastic bottles on the descent from the summit of Damavand alone.

Finding a ride away from Taftan back to the main road was less straight-

The Qaleh Hasan Ali crater near Rayen, a good example of the geological richness of this region. *(Richard Zöllner)*

forward than expected. Because of the holiday, everybody was travelling in the wrong direction. Eventually we managed to find somebody and later somebody else, making it all the way to the city of Iranshahr. Here the brutal heat of 44°C stifled one's every movement. Before leaving on this expedition I had managed to get hold of some contacts in a village not far from Bazman volcano but my phone had developed a peculiar fault. I could talk to whoever answered the phone but couldn't hear their replies. So we had no way of knowing if our arrival in the village would be welcome or even expected. By coincidence we ended up near a post of the Iranian Red Crescent and were taken in for cool water, tea and biscuits. Explaining our goal, we were soon made to watch several lengthy videos involving rope-work in emergency situations, such as abseiling from motorway bridges. Just when one of our hosts had donned his full kit for a live demonstration of these skills on a bridge nearby a bus pulled over and we were on our way again, this time for a ride westwards, to Bazman town.

Here further assistance from the same organisation ensured our onward progress over unsurfaced roads to our destination village. And then the moment came when we could finally see our mountain, in the last light of the day. Much to my dismay it was far from the pristine wilderness I had hoped for. Several large antennas crowned the summit, clearly visible as black silhouettes against the not yet black sky. Luckily we arrived shortly after and there was no more time for disappointment.

Our host had heard our telephone calls or else was ready anyway for guests, the latter being more likely. While Iranian hospitality undoubtedly ranks as among the best in the world, within Iran it is the Baluchi people who are regarded as being most generous. This, however, comes at a price. As a general rule of thumb, the more generous a people, the later dinner is served. In our case, this was at 11.30pm, which is not at all unusual in this region of the world, but which made our planned start of 2am impossible. The route I had envisioned, via the relatively steep east ridge of the mountain was out of the question as well. Instead, we were told we could, owing to the antennas, only go 'near the summit' and this only on a dirt track, which itself runs to within near the summit. A mountaineer's nightmare unfolded in front of me. The remote peak I had dreamed of reduced to an 18km slog 2,000m up a dirt track. Luckily I am not easily deterred and since I was already here, the first foreign visitor to the mountain for 40 years, or so I was told, it would be foolish not to go up.

At 4am next day we finally started, walking at great speed to cover as much ground as possible during the cool of darkness. At noon we reached a point 'near the summit', lunch offering a very welcome excuse to linger once more in the lower temperatures of higher altitude. Here at 3,450m it was a mere 30°C. It was 3pm when we finally convinced ourselves to begin the descent. If the landscape is generally similar in appearance to Taftan, the vegetation is markedly different. The lower slopes and moist ravines are covered in *baneh* trees (wild pistachios, *Pistacia atlantica*). The whole massif is a protected area, supporting among other animals a population of leopards. Later, in the first darkness, still with some 7km to go, we met a group of Basij, members of a paramilitary organisation, and were promptly invited for food. Unfortunately the kid-meat kebab served to us not only brought sustenance but also salmonella poisoning, which resulted in my hospitalisation in the city of Zabol a few days later.

After two weeks spent recovering from this misfortune and on other exploits, my path led me to Rayen, a small town situated at 2,200m on the slopes of Kuh-e Hezar and famous for its ruined medieval adobe castle. The wider area is of outstanding geological interest, boasting for example Iran's largest volcanic crater at Qaleh Hasan Ali, a 'maar', or broad, low-relief volcanic crater 300m deep and 1,200m in diameter. Having at that time spent three weeks constantly in the presence of others, some moments of solitude would be a welcome relief and what better opportunity than an ascent of Kuh-e Hezar, at 4,465m the highest mountain in Iran outside of the Alborz? From a well-known waterfall near the town, which I reached by hitchhiking, I made my way along the stream feeding this waterfall, first over a wide plateau, later through a narrow valley, necessitating several river crossings up to a small hut, where I was glad to be the only guest. Having reached this location at noon I set out, thinking I could reach the summit on the same day and return to the

A forest dormouse (*Dryomys nitedula*) in the shelter at Kuh-e Hezar *(Richard Zöllner)*

Sajad Ali Abadi and Mojtaba Vasou in the Qanatqestan gorge during the approach to Joupar mountain. *(Richard Zöllner)*

hut by torchlight but was turned around by a heavy thunderstorm at 4,000m.

The night was eventful insofar as soon after dark a large group of rodents started to scuttle about noisily. Nothing more that your average night in a bothy, I thought, and put in earplugs only to be woken an hour later by one of them sitting cosily on my forehead. Needless to say, this incident made further sleep rather difficult. Reminding myself that biology constitutes one of my main fields of interest, I set out to observe these animals, counting 11 at one time and soon identifying them as forest dormice (*Dryomys nitedula*). At 3am I had had my fill of this kind of entertainment and started for the summit, reaching it after fast progress up easy scrambling, already familiar from the day before, among large flocks of snow buntings (*Plectrophenax nivalis*). Hezar stands isolated on the vast Iranian plain. Further in the west Lalezar, another well-known mountain in this region, rose gently towards the sky. By way of contrast, to the north-east the Joupar massif stretched upwards in more abrupt steps.

After a week pursuing other interests, I reached the climax of my current Iranian mountain adventures. In Kerman I met up once again with Mojtaba as well as Sajad Ali Abadi, a well-known Iranian mountaineer who is famous for his knowledge of the area. As is often the case, Iranian mountaineers are eager to team up with their colleagues from other countries. Soon we were speeding along the motorway – I am yet to meet an Iranian who does not exceed the speed limit – south towards Kuh-e Joupar. This 60km chain of peaks constitutes one of the most famous arenas for technical mountain-eering outside of the Alborz and Zagros ranges.

Our aim was the highest summit: Seshak (4135m), or 'three horn'. For this we followed the Qanatqestan valley, a narrowing and deepening gorge

Mountain hut and resident donkey at Kuh-e Joupar. *(Richard Zöllner)*

through red sandstone. After some 8km a steep 100m ramp, about V Diff, is climbed to exit on a gently sloping plateau, which is traversed to a tiny mountain hut. Here the donkey in residence, living in the vicinity of the hut for as long as Sajad can remember, greeted us enthusiastically. The location of this building could not be more impressive, nesting in a cirque of the highest peaks, with Baluchi, second-highest summit in the range, apparently being the most technical, although it appeared gentle and easy angled from what I could see.

Next morning we started for our summit at 5am, first easily, but soon through a steep and loose couloir called Qife Mosibat, and later over steep snowfields and firm rock, mostly just Diff but up to HVS in places, to a gap in the ridgeline. The rest of the route runs on the western side of the mountain, passing a small emergency shelter constructed from the debris of a crashed aeroplane. After this, mostly easier ground led to the pointed summit cone, which we reached at 11am. To keep in line with another Iranian tradition, we took the last step onto the summit together holding hands. The whole ridge of this massif lay either side of us. The complete traverse ranks as one of the most highly prized achievements among Iranian mountaineers. With the snowfields having turned into bottomless slush, difficult down climbing alongside them was necessary. As no rope was carried this ensured some exhilarating situations. With the long walk out from the hut we did not reach the car until 9pm.

A turn in the weather the following day prevented our planned attempt on nearby Kuh-e Palvar and Mojtaba and I said goodbye to the mountains

The convoluted line of the Joupar ridge as seen when facing south from Seshakh summit. *(Richard Zöllner)*

with a 35km trek through high plateaus to the east of Kerman. We sat for a long time on one of the minor summits along the way. Still tired from our previous efforts, we had forgotten to take food and had to be content with what we found left over in our bags. This we supplemented with wild sage, eaten in huge bundles between what little sangak bread we had, like the *sabzi* or greens, which form such an integral part of Iranian cuisine. Our eyes gazed over the desert below. My time was up, my flight home in two days' time. In the last light of the day Sajad picked us up, waiting with a watermelon in a tiny mountain village. I once more realised what a special place this country is. The mountains of Iran impress with their endless variety of forms and sizes. Her people offer one of the richest, most engaging social tapestries over which journeys like these can be woven.

# The Great War

2nd Lt E D Murray (1884-1916), Black Watch,
died of wounds sustained at the battle of the Somme.

PETER FOSTER

# The Alpine Club
# at War: 1914-18

The Alpine Club's war memorial, which included three members omitted from
the roll of honour: they are Lt G A Arbuthnot, Capt H Duhamel and Capt T E
Goodeve. Maj H M Battye is the only member lacking a portrait in this edition
of the *Alpine Journal*. Some of Battye's letters are in the Imperial War Museum.

In 1915 a list of current members of the Alpine Club serving in the
armed forces was published in the *Alpine Journal*; supplementary lists
appeared in subsequent issues during the war. There are some omissions,
notably George Leigh Mallory, who joined the Royal Artillery, and Noel
Odell, who served in the Royal Engineers, and many future members of
the Club saw active service. The following account features some of the
108[1] men listed in the *Journal* and their experiences. At the outbreak of
war, 24 members were current or retired regular officers, half of them in
the Indian army; nine were officers in the Territorial Force. Amongst the
volunteers there were 15 doctors, eight lawyers, seven schoolmasters and

1. At the outbreak of war the Club's membership stood at 730.

seven company directors; the youngest was 24 and the oldest 62. With one exception[2], all the volunteers received commissions. Seventeen members were killed in action; three died on active service from illness and accident. Nine members were awarded the MC; the Rev E G Wells[3], of the Army Chaplain Service, received two bars. Six were awarded the DSO.

Capt E L Strutt (1895),[4] 2nd Battalion Royal Scots, was probably the first member of the Club to arrive in France with the British Expeditionary Force. He was certainly the Club's first casualty. Having fought at Mons and retreated to the Marne, his battalion was returning north in the 'Race to the Sea', when Strutt was severely wounded on 14 October. 'A bouquet of six shells burst low in quick succession,'[5] blowing him several yards, rendering him unconscious and temporarily paralysed. Three weeks later, the first member of the Club was killed. Maj J B Corry (1908), Royal Engineers, had arrived in Marseille from India in the last weeks of October and on 31 October entrained for the front. Four days later, whilst engaged in digging trenches near Neuve Chapelle, 'about 10pm three howitzer shells burst almost together; one of them landing right in the trench,'[6] instantly killing him and four others. Twenty miles to the north the first battle of Ypres had commenced and on 11 November the Prussian Guard attacked in an attempt to deliver the decisive stroke. Capt L C Oppenheim (1899), 2nd Battalion Highland Light Infantry, friend and climbing companion of Strutt on more than 80 Alpine expeditions, watched their advance but the Germans were stopped and driven back across the front of his battalion whose fire felled them 'in swathes'. Two days later, Oppenheim was wounded badly by shrapnel.

By now it had become clear that the war would not be over by Christmas. The Club's committee considered the propriety of holding the annual winter dinner, concluding that it should not take place, and it was suspended for the duration of the war. But the Club's regular meetings continued, the tradition of announcing the deaths of members at the beginning of each meeting highlighting the gradual loss of a younger generation. The Committee also deliberated on the position of ordinary and honorary members of the Club who were citizens of now enemy states. With regard to the former the problem was resolved by the fact that membership lapsed automatically on non-payment of the subscription; the question of honorary membership was more difficult but it was decided to expunge their names[7] from the list. However, the international bond of mountaineering was not severed completely and the deaths in battle of prominent German and Aus-

2. G E Howard (1907) was promoted company sergeant-major, the senior NCO, in the Artists' Rifles, a London-based territorial regiment whose principal role was to train officers.
3. E G Wells (1878-1952), elected to the AC in 1906. Curate of St Mary's Southampton, he was posted to the Italian front in 1915. The citation for the award of the first bar refers to carrying messages through 'heavy enemy barrage' and 'his cheerful devotion to duty'. The second bar was awarded for attending the wounded under the 'heaviest machine-gun fire.' (S Addington, *For Conspicuous Gallantry*, Leicester, Troubador, 2006, p280.)
4. The date in parentheses is the year of election to the Club.
5. *Alpine Journal* 28, p407
6. Ibid p397
7. Dr Paul Güssfeldt, who had made the first ascent of the Peuterey ridge via the Aiguille Blanche in 1893, and Prof Carl Diener, a former president of the Austrian Alpine Club.

Gen C G Rawling (1870-1917), Somerset Light Infantry, was awarded the Distinguished Service Order for his leadership at Passchendaele. Shortly afterwards, chatting with friends outside brigade headquarters, he was killed by German shellfire. Although never a member of the Alpine Club, he was the subject of an obituary in the *Alpine Journal*. He had explored widely in Tibet, including in the Everest region.

Capt H Duhamel (1853-1917), 28th Chasseurs Alpins, founded the Grenoble section of the Club Alpin Français, featured in the exploration of the Écrins, co-authoring the 1905 guidebook with W A B Coolidge, and was a major influence in the development of French skiing. He served as an instructor and died in a tragically banal accident, slipping on an icy courtyard at the army barracks at Bonne in Haute-Savoie.

trian climbers were noted respectfully in the pages of the *Alpine Journal*.

When the 1915 campaigning season began Britain was committed to offensive action in France and combined naval and military operations in the Dardanelles. In March the British army launched its first large-scale attack of the war at Neuve Chapelle. The 4th Battalion Black Watch, under its commander Lt Col Harry Walker (1906), played a prominent part in the battle. Walker, company director, territorial officer and vice-president of the Scottish Mountaineering Club, was mentioned in dispatches and gazetted CMG. Capt G T Ewen (1911), 1st Battalion Manchester Regiment, barrister and an original member of the Rucksack Club who had volunteered six months earlier, was awarded the Club's first MC for his actions in the battle. He joked that his climbing experience had enabled him to get out of his trench quickest.

On 25 April the first wave of the Mediterranean Expeditionary Force

Maj O E Todd (1879-1915), 5th Gurkha Rifles, killed in an accident in India.

Lt Col C Stonham (1858-1916), Royal Army Medical Corps, died from illness contracted in Egypt.

landed at Cape Helles on the western tip of the Gallipoli peninsula, and at Anzac Cove, some 13 miles away on the northern coast. Three days later the first member of the Club, Lt Col C G Bruce (1892), arrived with his battalion, 1/6th Gurkhas. 'I shall never forget,' he wrote, 'steaming into Helles in the early morning of a glorious spring day, and watching the bombardment of Achi Baba and the neighbouring hills by our fleet – the gorgeous colouring and tranquility of the sea and the masses of shipping and the great warships in action. Even as we steamed in we could see the earth rising from the sides of the hills where the shells broke.'[8] The next day, at a nearby beach, temporary sub-lieutenant L G Shadbolt (1910), who in 1911 had made the first continuous traverse of the Cuillin ridge, landed with the Hood battalion of the Royal Naval Division. Heaps of bodies were already piled on the beach; the battalion, soon under fire from Turkish guns, dug in. Two weeks after the landings little progress had been made. The majority of the troops were still on or near the beaches, pinned down by fire from Turkish positions on the cliffs and hills above.

The beaches at Cape Helles were dominated by a rounded, gently-sloping hill, 709ft high, called Achi Baba, and a major offensive to seize it was mounted. The attack began on 6 May, the Hood battalion leading

8. C G Bruce, *Himalayan Wanderer*, London, Alexander MacLehose & Co, 1934, p254.

the advance in the centre, but just over 48 hours later the battle had been fought to a standstill. A few days later Bruce's Gurkhas achieved a local success, capturing a bluff overlooking the beach from which Turkish machine-gunners had been wreaking havoc. Twelve of the enemy were decapitated. Bruce wrote proudly, 'my regiment had carried out a little duty which exactly suited the genius of the Gurkha.'[9]

The assault on Achi Baba was resumed on 4 June. Shadbolt, his arm shattered by a bullet, was evacuated to a hospital ship. Bruce, 'after a very unpleasant day' during which his battalion had been mauled, learned that he was to receive support from his former battalion, 1/5th Gurkhas, which had landed only the day before. His own officers either killed or wounded, Bruce 'was obliged to go down myself and do my best creeping out on the cliff faces to show the officers commanding companies of the 5th Gurkhas in turn the line of advance.' Knowing the officers and many of the men well, Bruce recalled movingly, 'I don't think I ever had a more unpleasant task given me in the whole of my life, knowing full well the most hazardous nature of their task ... and the practical certainty that I was saying good-bye to my best friends.'[10] Amongst them was Maj Hedley Battye (1914), 'a first rate climber', who was shot through the head leading his men forward. (The Battye family was filled with Indian army officers. Battye's father, Maj Legh Richmond Battye, also of the 5th Gurkha Rifles, was killed in the Hazara Expedition in what is now Pakistan in 1888, while his brother Richmond Moffat Battye, of the Bengal Cavalry, was killed in the Tirah campaign of 1897.) Bruce 'still remained one of the lucky ones,' but on 30 June 'got my little present which took me off the peninsula and sent me to England to hospital for a year or nearly so.'[11] Cut down by machine-gun fire he had been wounded in both legs.

During June and July, five pitched battles were fought at Cape Helles. All were frontal attacks of short duration, a day or two or even less; none succeeded in altering the front line by more than half a mile. Reinforcements were dispatched and plans made for a break out of the Anzac bridgehead, not much bigger than Regent's Park, supported by a new landing at Suvla Bay, immediately north of Anzac. The attack began on 6 August. Col A H Tubby (1894), Harley Street specialist and consulting surgeon to the British Mediterranean Expeditionary Force, who was on board a hospital ship off Cape Helles, recalled the events of the day from his perspective:

> 'So ended an eventful day of twenty-one hours, which commenced with five major operations; then, the ship in danger from shell fire, cries of "Ship on Fire", an alarm of "Submarines", the arrival of over 300 wounded, a view of a pitched battle at Cape Helles and the sound of another at Anzac.'[12]

---

9.  Ibid p256.
10. Ibid p258.
11. Idem.
12. A H Tubby, *A Consulting Surgeon in the Near East*, London, Christophers, 1920, pp48-9.

During that evening Capt R D Squires (1913), 9th Battalion Sherwood Foresters, a volunteer battalion raised in response to Kitchener's call, had landed without encountering any opposition at Suvla Bay. After two days of indecision and torpor, the battalion was ordered to advance at 4.45am, 9 August, and by 8am Squires was dead. On the same day at Anzac, Capt C J Reid (1909), 9th Royal Warwickshire regiment, a rugger blue and games-master at his old school Haileybury, reached the crest of one of the overlooking ridges, but the Turks counter-attacked, surrounding Reid and his company and all were killed. Meanwhile, back at the bay, Maj Bernard Head[13] came ashore with his territorial battalion, 1/5th Royal Welch Fusiliers, and three days later was killed during a piecemeal attack.

On the western front Capt C A Werner (1906), 2nd Battalion Rifle Brigade, schoolmaster at Harrow, had been killed in May, leading his company in the first line of the attack on Aubers ridge, carrying his ice axe, which he had decided would be a useful tool and weapon. In July Lt H E Tyndale (1909), 8th Battalion King's Royal Rifles, had been badly wounded in a pitiable action at Hooge. An officer in an adjoining battalion described the affair:

'The German trenches were to be attacked again that same afternoon. It is only charitable to assume that the staff from their position fifteen miles back were imperfectly informed of the real position. At 3 o'clock the four battalions duly went over the top and were swept out of existence by an enemy whose machine guns there had been no time to locate, and on whom our meagre artillery preparation had made no impression. Many of the men were caught on our own wire, and I believe that none got more than fifty yards beyond the edge of the wood.'[14]

In September Capt C F K Carfrae (1910), 5th Battalion Oxford & Bucks Light Infantry, was killed near Ypres and Lt Col Walker was mortally wounded during the battle of Loos, in which Maj L W Bird (1914), 1st Royal Berkshire Regiment, was wounded and awarded the DSO.

The medically qualified members of the Club served in various roles: as regimental medical officers, commanders of field ambulances, surgeons in casualty clearing stations, on the staff at base hospitals and as senior consultants to the expeditionary forces. Most were concerned with managing the wounded and conventional illnesses, but in 1915 the military authorities were faced with a novel and disabling condition: shellshock. Unsure about its nature, a 'brilliant band' of academic psychologists and doctors was recruited to investigate the phenomenon under the direction of Dr (and temporary major) R G Rows (1911), the newly appointed medical superintendent at Maghull Hospital near Liverpool. Their observations gave rise to the view that shellshock was primarily a psychological reaction to the stresses of war. It was at Maghull that W H Rivers began to experiment with

---

13. Head has the unfortunate record of probably the briefest ever membership of the Club. Elected in April 1915 he was killed four months later.
14. Quoted in M Gilbert, *First World War*, London, HarperCollins, 1994, p179.

Capt A M Slingsby (1885-1916), Rifles Frontier Force, Indian Army, shot through the heart during fighting at Kut.

the techniques of psychotherapy, which he would later employ at Craiglock-hart War Hospital, where he famously treated the poet Siegfried Sassoon, who described his experiences in his fictionalized memoir *Sherston's Progress*.

During the first months of 1916 several attempts had been made to relieve the British-Indian garrison besieged in the Mesopotamian city of Kut. On 8 March Capt Ewen, who had been transferred with the Manchesters from France, and Capt A M Slingsby (1912), 56th Rifles, Frontier Force, were killed in another unsuccessful effort. 'You will be thankful to hear that his death was instantaneous,' wrote Slingsby's commanding officer to the family in an attempt to soften the blow, 'he was shot through the heart, while most gallantly leading the final rush of the 56th.'[15] In the same battle Maj H D Minchinton (1909), 1st Gurkha Rifles, and Capt Kenneth Mason (1914), Royal Engineers, were awarded the MC. Slingsby, Minchinton and Mason were all career officers in the Indian army and had used their fur-loughs to explore the Himalaya. Slingsby had reached 23,350ft on Kamet in 1913. After the war, Mason would found the Himalayan Club.

Unsurprisingly, perhaps, but in marked contrast to the number of regular army officers in the Club, there was only one serving naval officer amongst the members at the outbreak of the war: Cdr J C Hodgson (1907). On 30 May 1916, he sailed from the Firth of Forth in command of HMS Moorsom, one of six destroyers deployed to act as a submarine screen for

15. *Alpine Journal* 30, p336.

the Second Battle Cruiser Squadron, to meet the German High Seas Fleet off Jutland. The enemy was sighted at 3.25pm, 31 May, and 'at 4.10pm destroyers were ordered to attack enemy with torpedoes.' Hodgson reported in his dispatch for the Admiralty:

> *'"Moorsom" attacked with the leading division of 13th Flotilla; but torpedoes were not then fired, as enemy destroyers attacked simultaneously, and to engage them made position for torpedo attack bad. When enemy destroyers had been driven off, Battle Cruisers had turned 16 points and enemy's Battle Fleet was coming up astern of their Battle Cruisers. Torpedo attack was made on van of Battle Fleet, two torpedoes being fired. Ship was shortly afterwards hit aft, but no immediate damage to fighting efficiency was done. A second torpedo attack on Battle Fleet was then carried out, two torpedoes being fired.'*[16]

The laconic style conceals the fact that the action had been 'hot' and merited the award of his DSO.

The story of the career of Lt J R Dennistoun (1912), who was one of the few members of the Club to serve in the Royal Flying Corps, is the stuff of the *Boy's Own Paper*. A New Zealander and sheep farmer, he had undertaken several exploratory expeditions in the Southern Alps, crossing new passes and making first ascents.[17] In 1912 he went to Antarctica as an unpaid volunteer on Terra Nova's voyage to supply Scott's polar expedition. Following the outbreak of the war Dennistoun travelled as a deckhand on a ship to England where he enlisted, and was later commissioned, in the fashionable yeomanry regiment, the North Irish Horse, favoured by the wealthy aristocracy and nick-named 'The Millionaires Own.' He arrived in France in November 1915. On 16 June 1916 he was seconded to the RFC. Ten days later, three enemy aircraft attacked the biplane piloted by his cousin, in which he was acting as observer and bomb-thrower. Both men were wounded and the main fuel tank was hit and caught fire. They crash-landed behind enemy lines and were captured. Dennistoun died from his wounds and injuries a few weeks later. He was 32.

Meanwhile, on the ground, the battle of the Somme had opened. On 20 July, Lt E D Murray (1910), Black Watch, died inconspicuously from his wounds received the day before and was buried at Corbie in the extension to the communal cemetery. The area originally set aside had already been filled with graves.

L S Amery (1899), a sitting MP, gazetted captain 14th Royal Warwickshire Regiment in October 1914, had been immediately posted to intelligence and at the end of 1916 was in Salonika, where with Strutt, recovered, promoted and appointed chief liaison officer to the commander of the allied forces in the Balkans, he planned to climb Mount Olympus, but nothing came of it.[18] Voyaging home in December, his ship was torpedoed. Amery

---

16. *http://www.dreadnoughtproject.org/tfs/index.php/Harwich_Force_at_the_Battle_of_Jutland*
17. His name has been given to a peak, a pass, and a glacier in New Zealand.
18. L Amery, *In the Rain and the Sun*, London, Hutchinson, 1946, p28.

opened his cabin door 'to see a regular cataract, created by the waterspout of the explosion, pouring down the companionway.'[19] Passengers and crew took to the boats and the ship sank soon after. As the flotilla of lifeboats got under way, he recalled,

> *'we saw the distant smoke of an approaching vessel. Saved already! A few minutes later she revealed herself as the submarine which had torpedoed us. We were all ordered to stop ...'* [20]

The Germans began to round up the officers. Amery hid, grimly humming 'Rule Britannia' to himself and evaded capture. As the submarine sailed off, he 'crawled out and cautiously cocked a farewell snook.'[21] Eventually he was rescued by a French hospital ship. When he reached England, Lloyd George had replaced Asquith as prime minister and included Lord Milner in his small war cabinet. Amery, a devotee of Milner, was appointed assistant secretary to the war cabinet and became involved in the conduct of the war at the highest level.

Friendship with Milner also resulted in John Buchan's (1906) appointment as director of the department of information, established to run government propaganda. Buchan, who had 'literally climbed into the Alpine Club,'[22] had been commissioned into the Intelligence Corps in 1915 and attached to the general staff, a period of which he wrote: 'I lead a life of most inglorious security.'[23] But whatever the challenges of his new post they were surely less colourful than those of Richard Hannay, his fictional hero of *The Thirty-Nine Steps, Greenmantle* and *Mr Standfast*, written between 1914 and 1918.

On 11 December 1916, Lord Justice Pickford, whose presidency had coincided with the years of war to date, gave his valedictory address to the Club. Reflecting on the progress of the war, he said:

> *'I wish I could feel as sure that there was an equally general and clear appreciation of the difficulties we have still to face, and the way to face them.'* [24]

The year 1917 proved to be more of the same: huge effort and accompanying casualties on the western front and continuing operations in the Middle East which drained men through battle and disease. In March, 2nd Lt N S Done (1912), Royal Fusiliers, was killed on the Somme, joining the ranks of the missing. He is one of 70,000 men with no known burial place whose names are remembered on the astonishing Thiepval Memorial, 'a structure of pure form, intimidating in its size, admonitory in its grandeur and implacable in its intelligence.'[25] During the April battle for Gaza in Palestine,

19.  Ibid p30
20.  Ibid p31
21.  Idem
22.  S Gillon, *Dictionary of National Biography 1931-1940*, OUP, 1949, p112
23.  J Adam Smith, *John Buchan: A Biography*, OUP, 1985 p198
24.  *Alpine Journal 31*, p4.
25.  D Crane, *Empires of the Dead*, London, William Collins, 2013, p214.

Left: Capt T E Goodeve, Royal Engineers, was a railway engineer who served in Palestine and died in a train accident in 1919.

Middle: Maj B Head (d1915), 1/5th Royal Welch Fusiliers, killed at Gallipoli just four months after being elected a member of the Club. *(Auckland War Memorial Museum)*

*Right:* Capt C Inglis Clark (1888-1918), Army Service Corps, Indian Cavalry, was serving in Mesopotamia when he was shot by a sniper. He is buried in Baghdad. The hut built in his memory under Ben Nevis is the closest thing the UK has to an alpine hut.

Lt H O S Gibson (1911), 11th Battalion London Regiment, a school-friend of Mallory, was 'blown to pieces by a shell.'[26] In the largely forgotten campaign in east Africa, A F Wollaston (1908), naturalist, explorer and medically qualified, who had been appointed temporary surgeon RN, was in charge of a small steamer on the Rufiji river, bringing out sick and wounded. After 18 months as a ship's surgeon he had been despatched to Africa 'because some idiot told the Admiralty that I knew all about the country and its diseases.'[27] For his work in Africa he was awarded the DSC. On learning of the award he wrote self-deprecatingly: 'For what I cannot imagine unless it is a prize for being the oldest naval surgeon.'[28]

In the spring of 1918 the Mesopotamian campaign was fizzling out, although not before claiming the life of Capt C Inglis Clark (1911), Army Service Corps, but it was a critical period on the western front. In March the Germans had launched a powerful offensive that had the Allies reeling and in April they attacked near Ypres, where the fighting was desperate and Sir Douglas Haig issued his 'backs to the wall'[29] order. Capt R E Thompson (1902), 2nd Battalion Hampshire Regiment, and Lt C A Hartree (1912), Royal Garrison Artillery, were killed.

In August 1918 the weather and conditions in the mountains around

26. *Alpine Journal* 32, p114.
27. N Wollaston, *My Father, Sandy*, London, Short Books, 2003 p121.
28. Ibid p126.
29. 'With our backs to the wall and believing in the justice of our cause each one of us must fight to the end.' According to A J P Taylor: 'In England this sentence was ranked with Nelson's last message. At the front, the prospect of staff officers fighting with their backs to the walls of their luxurious chateaux had less effect.' (*English History 1914-1945*, OUP, 1965, p102)

Lt G A Arbuthnot (1872-1916),
Grenadier Guards, killed in action,
aged 43. Briefly a Conservative
member of parliament for Burnley,
Arbuthnot is buried at the Citadel
New Military Cemetery, Fricourt.

Col B Hopkinson (1874-1918), Royal
Engineers, killed in a flying accident in
England testing new weapons.

Zermatt were especially fine and, surprisingly, Maj A C Morrison-Bell
(1908), Scots Guards, was able to take advantage. Morrison-Bell, MP for
a Devonshire constituency, had been captured in 1915 in an action that he
described for his local paper:

> '*Suddenly an inferno began. A mine exploded a few yards from where I stood
> ... Tons of stuff seemed to come my way ... It knocked me down but I was
> not buried ... The explosion was the signal to the Germans, who were not
> a hundred yards off, to rush our trenches ... The whole thing was over in a
> quarter of an hour ... I realised suddenly I was alone ... Two men jumped
> down and covered me with revolvers.*' [30]

Following three years' internment in Germany, 'that very disagreeable
country with its everlasting turnip diet,'[31] he had been transferred on parole
to Switzerland and was given a month's leave to go to Zermatt. Amongst
other peaks, he climbed the Matterhorn, 'or Cervin (as all our pro-Entente

30. *Alpine Journal* 29, p203.
31. *Alpine Journal* 32, p293.

party were obliged to call it under penalty of being fined a franc for each infraction).'[32]

Just three months before the armistice Col Bertram Hopkinson (1897), Royal Engineers, was killed in a flying accident, the last member of the Club to die on active service.[33] In 1915 Hopkinson, professor of engineering at Cambridge had been placed in charge of a unit concerned with developing armaments for the RFC. Piloting himself in a Bristol fighter, he crashed in bad weather en route for London.

For the survivors there was promotion and honours for some, others were faced with lengthy recovery from their wounds and the rest were left to ponder the 'sheer mystery' of their survival. Older members who had not served mourned the loss of sons. In 1922 Norman Collie, president of the Club, reflecting on the aftermath of the war, wrote:

> *'It is true that the hills are still the same ... but in human affairs ... the old days unfortunately cannot come back. We are years older than we were before the war; the old order has been rudely broken; but in spite of these evil days we can show that we are still capable of outbursts of great mountaineering energy.'* [34]

---

32. Ibid p296.
33. Lt Col Charles Stonham (1890), RAMC, had died in 1916 from illness contracted in Egypt and Major O E Todd (1910), 1/5th Gurkhas, had also died in the same year following an accident in India.
34. *Alpine Journal* 35, p1.

TARQUIN COOPER

# Forgotten Frontier

## The Alps in the First World War

The Tre Cime di Lavaredo Peaks from a cave post
excavated in the First World War. *(Shutterstock)*

*Salvaci dal gelo implacabile, dai vortici della tormenta, dall'impeto della valanga;
fa che il nostro piede posi sicuro su le creste vertiginose: su le diritte pareti, oltre
i crepacci insidiosi ...*[1]

*Prayer of the Alpino*

The Somme, Passchendaele, Ypres; they are carved on our national consciousness like the lines of a Wilfred Owen poem. A centenary on from
the end of the First World War, it's the trenches, mud and barbed wire of the
western front that spring to mind. Yet the Alps witnessed arguably an even
worse carnage. A century on it seems timely to revisit this forgotten frontier.

The war in the Alps was one of several lesser-known theatres: the eastern
front against Russia, the Balkan front and the wars across the disintegrating

---

1. 'God Almighty, who govern all elements, save your soldiers armed with faith and love; save us from relentless cold and swirling blizzards, from the strength of avalanches; help our feet set a safe pace on dizzy peaks,
and on the steep slopes, beyond treacherous crevasses ... '

Ottoman empire that stretched from north Africa to present-day Iraq, including Gallipoli. In the mountains there was fighting in both the Caucasus and Carpathians, both of which were to witness some of the most futile and catastrophic losses of life in the war. In the Caucasus, Enver Pasha lost at least 30,000 men (perhaps as many as 90,000) in an entirely futile frontal assault against the Russians in the winter of 1914-15. Most died from hypothermia. Not to be outdone, the following month Austria's chief of the general staff, Conrad von Hötzendorf, launched a disastrous offensive against the Russians in the Carpathians. Soldiers were woefully unprepared, going into winter battle armed with cardboard soled shoes and summer uniforms. Many simply froze to death. There were 800,000 casualties.

The front that's perhaps of most interest to alpinists is that across the Eastern Alps. It stretched for over 600km between Italy and the Austro-Hungarian empire. It weaved from jagged spire to jagged spire, from the Stelvio pass to Lake Garda, across the Dolomites, Carnic and Julian Alps, before following the Isonzo[2] river all the way to the Adriatic between Venice and Trieste. Between 1915 and 1918 this was the frontline between imperial Austria and the relatively new nation state of Italy. It was the scene of some of the fiercest fighting of the war, all of it almost entirely futile: the front barely moved at all.

At the outbreak of war in 1914 Italy was neutral and for a year remained on the fence as both sides wooed her like a prospective bride. Austria-Hungary reminded Italy of the 1882 Triple Alliance with Germany to which she was a signatory, and made some half-hearted territorial offers. Britain and France were completely shameless and promised the earth, agreeing to support Italy's territorial claims to the Tyrol and large swathes of land along the Adriatic. The result of this slightly dubious act of bribery was that Italy joined Britain and France, eager to assert her new sense of national pride. Both the Germans and Austrians were horrified by Italy's betrayal; obituary notices appeared announcing her death. One ran: 'The passing resulted from a breach of faith, megalomania and an incurable greed for territory. The funeral will take place on the newest battlefield.' That battlefield was the Alps.

Like British generals a year earlier, the Italian general staff thought it would all be over quickly, and they'd be in Vienna by Christmas. They underestimated the challenge of getting through the mountains. In the weeks after Italy declared war on Austria on 23 May 1915, the Alpini rushed to seize strategic peaks. Formed in 1872, the Alpini was the first dedicated mountain warfare unit. By contrast, Austria's defence was left to the Standesschützen, a home guard of men too young or old to fight in the regular army, but with a strong ethos of upholding local religious and family traditions. It numbered 30,000 men. One of then was Sepp Innerkofler, a noted ibex hunter and mountain guide who put up more than 50 routes in the Dolomites. He was to lead one of the most daring and futile assaults of the war, one

---

2. Isonzo was the Italian name for the river and the name given to the 12 battles in this sector. Today the river is part of Slovenia and called the Soča.

Paying respects to Italian soldiers killed in the Dolomites during the First World War whose bodies were recovered from their Alpine graves, outside the Madonna della Difesa church in Cortina d'Ampezzo in 1921. *(Alamy)*

that characterised the fighting in the high mountains where chivalry still played a part.

Like many, he would have felt personally moved to protect his hills from foreign invaders; the frontline went through his beloved Drei Zinnen hut, opposite the Tre Cime, which was destroyed by Italian artillery. (This part of present day northern Italy, extending as far south as Lake Garda, was then part of the Austrian Tyrol, which is why today it's still German speaking and the Tyrol remains an emotive subject). In those opening weeks, Innerkofler was busy. A week after the first shots were fired on 24 May 1915 he saw his first action atop Cima Undici, Elferkofel, repelling a party of Italian climbers. Over the next six weeks he'd take part in 17 patrols. On 18 June he and his son Gottfried fought side by side in a violent duel with the Alpini to hold an observation post atop Cima Uno, Einserkofel.

On 4 July he led the ascent up Paternkofel, following the route up the north-north-west ridge he opened in 1886, today a grade IV climb. With five men, armed with rifles and grenades, he attempted to take the Italian position in a surprise dawn raid. Accounts vary on what exactly happened. One has it that he was shot, in another he was struck by an Italian throwing rocks down the face: not the first time rocks would be used as weapons in this way and certainly not the last. Either way, Innerkofler did not survive the day. Afterwards, at great risk, the Italians lowered down to retrieve his body. Immediately recognising him as the famous Austrian guide, they buried him on the summit with a simple cross that read: 'Sepp Innerkofler Guida'.

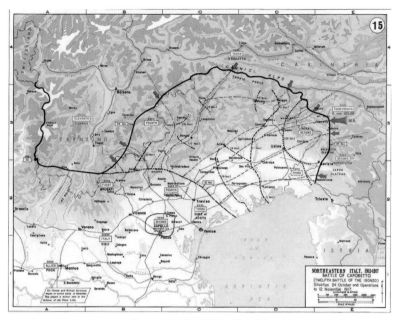

A cartographic representation of the twelfth battle of the Isonzo, which became known as the Battle of Caporetto, and saw the Italian army in full retreat.

After the war Innerkofler was re-buried in the family burial plot in Sexten. Another alpinist who joined up was the young Karl Prusik, inventor of the knot. In the Carnic Alps he was celebrated for capturing 'a small rock on the Wolyerkopf', apparently only a few metres from the enemy. After the war he saw alpinism as a way of preparing German youth for the next one: he served in the Waffen-SS in the Second World War.

Mountain ranges have always formed borders and armies have always sought to capture and hold the high ground, but the First World War was the first time in history that actual summits would be fought over, when mountaineers would be called upon to lead assaults up steep climbs and engineers would tunnel underneath to blow up summit positions, disfiguring the landscape for ever.

Caporetto, now in Slovenia, the 12th battle of Isonzo, was the largest mountain battlefield in history, the Italian collapse recorded by Ernest Hemingway. The Adamello witnessed the first recorded incident of fighting on a glacier. It was a war that saw ingenious engineering come to the fore: roads had to be built, hundreds of kilometres of trenches blasted in rock and tunnels excavated. At the Col de Lana, nicknamed 'blood mountain', Italian sappers tunnelled to within five metres of Austrian positions, lay five tonnes of nitro-glycerine and blew the Austrians – and the summit – to smithereens. There was also mine warfare at Lagazuoi. Underneath the Marmolada glacier, enterprising Austrians built their positions within the ice to escape enemy fire, only to discover a new enemy: death from carbon monoxide poisoning. The glacier still regularly spits out detritus from the war, a process that is accelerating as the climate warms.

It's easy to assume the Alpine front was just a sideshow but it was every bit as significant as the western front. Had the Germans captured Venice – and they very nearly did – the war might have ended differently. Arguably troops had to contend with far greater elemental dangers than on the western front. Casualty figures for Italy and Austria-Hungary are staggering: some 4.5 million were killed, missing or wounded, compared with Britain's 2.5 million killed and injured and the vast majority were along the Isonzo sector. In the high Alps, some 60,000 were killed in combat and an additional 60,000 would succumb to the elements via hypothermia, hunger and exhaustion. But it's the number who died in avalanches that is truly mind-boggling: up to 60,000 were killed by 'the white death' during the two winters of 1915-16 and 1917-18.

In January 1916 a young Austrian Karl Mayr, who'd only signed up because it promised a ticket to university, witnessed the aftermath of a slide that killed 250 men on the Raukogel. 'It was a dreadful sight which brought tears to the eyes of even the most hardened men,' he wrote. The worst month for avalanches occurred in December 1916, when as many as 10,000 died. Heavy snow, as much as four metres, fell during one 48-hour period, followed by a warm *föhn*, creating optimal slide conditions. On 13 December, an estimated one million cubic metres avalanched onto the Austrian barracks on the Gran Poz of Marmolada, burying over 300 men.

'We uncovered dead and more dead, a great many of them were our glorious youth,' Lt Col Viktor Scherf recalled. They managed to save just 45 men while 270 died. 'We saw a confusion of beams, boards, arms, bodies and heads. In front a man danced and sang ghoulishly for he had gone mad,' wrote survivor Josef Strohmaier. Incredibly, four days after the avalanche, five men appeared out of the rubble. They were in a hut that had been torn from its position and somehow managed to dig their way out. In a war of horrors it received barely a footnote.

As a result of both sides fighting an enemy even greater than themselves it's perhaps not unsurprising that there are many recorded instances where opposing troops made informal agreements. The Christmas Day truce on the western front is well known but in the Alps, such comradeship between enemies was not uncommon.

At the Stelvio pass, where things were generally quieter, patrols were led by Alpine guides on both sides who often knew each other. In one incident early in the war, rival patrols met on a mountaintop and shared lunch. Many similar acts are recorded: on Monte Cristallo, an imperial Austrian officer apparently asked the Alpini to ensure his troops were less exposed as his command had asked why he was not shooting at such easy targets. At the Plöckenpass in the Carnic Alps, the two sides, at great risk of courts martial, exchanged tobacco for food to survive. The Austrians generally had a ready supply of cigarettes but were low on food while the Italians had more to eat, as well as the obligatory quarter litre daily ration of wine and coffee, but were always running short of tobacco.[3] Thus the two sides would occasionally meet in the middle and come to an arrangement.[4]

Some of us might feel that there could be worse things than a posting to the Dolomites. Indeed, it was a sentiment shared by some soldiers who'd never seen mountains before, such as those who made up the newly formed German Alpenkorps that was sent to bolster the Austro-Hungarian line in 1915. 'As a mountain tourist, I'm sending you the best greetings,' wrote Lance-Corporal Brunken of the Hanoverian Reserve in a postcard to a friend. 'We have already made a considerable mountain climb that went up into the clouds. Deep snow was found up there that doesn't go away during the summer. It's very romantic.'[5]

Yet, for the most part, conditions in the mountains were grim. You only have to look at the thin woollen clothing on display in many of the region's First World War museums to wonder how anyone survived. German Alpine troops were theoretically issued with hobnailed boots, wore woollen putties up to the knees and a single-layer woollen jacket over a rough under-layer with dubious thermal qualities. They carried rope, a torch on their chest, snow goggles, a walking stick and in some cases an ice axe. But less than half the troops were issued with mountain kit: the rest had to make do with regular leather boots. These weren't up to the task: 'They are not waterproof and not suitable for snow,' complained a machine-gun detachment of the German Alpenkorps. 'They are fitted with thin soles so that the nails do not hold and must be hammered back into place daily.' German troops also complained about the unsuitability of their headwear, whether the spiked helmet or peaked caps which became too warm or water logged, much preferring the felt hats worn by the Italian Alpini.

Rations were also thin, the bread stale, vegetables non-existent. 'To perform the strenuous duty, breakfast and evening meal portions of bacon, sausage and cheese must be delivered,' demanded the 2nd Jäger regiment in a 1915 report. The results of poor equipment and food were predictable. After a 79-hour patrol in the Tofana mountains Lt Denzel complains that the number of his men to drop out in his approximately 80-strong commando unit rose from 14 to 44 as they tried to carry out their work in temperatures as low as -10°C with little food or shelter. 'The illnesses were without exception weakness of the heart, rheumatism, stomach complaints and intestinal trouble,' he wrote. The replacements he was given fared worse. They came from Silesia and East Prussia and had not seen mountains before. 'They were insufficiently equipped: without ice axes, ice cleats, climbing shoes, overcoats and many without a knapsack. The results of this soon be-

3. Austrian soldiers on the Carnic front were entitled to 250g of bread, 100g of pasta and 80g of meat per day compared to the average Italian's daily allowance of 600g of bread and 100g of meat and pasta. However, there's a big difference between 'entitlement' and what they actually got. Because food was cooked far away, it usually arrived cold and sometimes frozen.
4. A slightly different exchange of goods occurred at Gallipoli. An Australian NCO was demonstrating grenade throwing technique and lobbed a tin of bully beef into a Turkish trench. A few minutes later some Turkish cigarettes came back with a note in French thanking them for the beef.
5. The following recollections of German troops are taken from Immanuel Voigt's The Alpine Corps on the Dolomite Front, 1915.

Public interest in the sacrifice by Italian troops in the Dolomites remains high; this re-enactment is from a 2005 commemoration. *(Shutterstock)*

came evident. The physical robustness of these replacements was very low.'

However, the Dolomite theatre was a relative picnic compared to the brutality and wholesale slaughter of the Isonzo front. During the first of the 12 battles, Virgilio Bonamore, an Italian officer of the 21st battalion of the Bersaglieri, wrote in his diary for 2 August 1915 of the grim reality.

*'In these days I experienced the saddest horrors of the most dreadful war. It did not stop raining even for a moment. It was so cold that 50 men from the entire battalion had to descend from the mountain due to frozen feet. On 29 July I was staying in a trench for the whole 24 hours, crouching among dead bodies: ours and those of the enemy. The stink was unbearable, and to top it all, we had to resist a fierce attack from the enemy, which we repelled ...*

*The rations were scarce, consisting mainly of bread, cold boiled meat of lean taste and some cans. Water is brought in skins; it is very scarce and stinking. I did not eat or drink for two days. The stinking corpses, the cold, the undrinkable water, the lack of sleep because of constant alarms – all this drove me into a very miserable state. On 30 July I descended to the glacier to collect a bag of snow. An hour of descent and two hours of ascent among the rocks and very dangerous abysses. On my way I saw a great number of our poor dead soldiers who had fallen from the height.'*

Italian 'Alpini' in action in 1915.

The loss of life was mostly futile. At the end of the war the frontline was in almost the same place as it was at the start. The one notable breakthrough was on the Isonzo. It had witnessed 11 bloody battles reminiscent of the western front by the time the Germans decided to launch a co-ordinated attack in October 1917. The Germans smashed through Italian positions and had them on the run as far as the outskirts of Venice, some 100km to the west.

One of the most extraordinary breakthroughs was under the leadership of an ambitious young German lieutenant by the name of Erwin Rommel. In the first three days he captured 15 miles of the Kolovrat ridge, including Mt Matajur, and took 9,000 Italians prisoner with just 200 men, at the lost of just six dead and 30 wounded. Over the next three weeks he and his men kept up this relentless advance over hill country, often hiking up to 1,000m of ascent at a time, carrying heavy weapons and packs, fighting difficult skirmishes in the hills and towns on minimal sleep. They didn't stop until they reached Longarone on the banks of the river Piave, where they took another 10,000 Italians prisoner. Whatever one's feelings of warfare, it's impossible not to admire the relentless energy, endurance and mountain fitness of Rommel and his men.

The battle became known as the disaster of Caporetto, now the Slovenian municipality of Kobarid. To respond, the Italians withdrew from all their high mountain positions, which they had fought so hard to protect, sending their men to stem the rout. Ultimately it was the arrival of 200,000 French

The Dolomite front has become a focus for tourism in recent years. The Alpe-Adria long-distance trail officially opened in 2012. From the Grossglockner in Austria to the Adriatic Sea, this huge route passes through Italy, Austria and Slovenia in 46 stages. From this, three separate peace trails have been developed in these three countries: the Itinerari di Pace sul Carso della Grande Guerra in Italy, the Pot Miru in Slovenia, and the Karnischer Höhenweg. Cicerone publishes a useful guidebook. *(Alamy)*

and British troops that stopped the advance and saved Venice. The following year the Germans and Austrians retreated back to the Isonzo.

Rommel is not the only celebrated character who ended up in this sector. The Isonzo would be a formative experience for two men volunteering in separate ambulance units. One was a 19-year-old American called Ernest Hemingway, whose experience would be fictionalised in *A Farewell to Arms*. The other was our very own Geoffrey Winthrop Young, celebrated alpinist and later Club president. He lost a leg during an artillery explosion and was then caught up in the mad and dangerous retreat following Caporetto. In Hemingway's *Farewell to Arms*, the protagonist finds himself in the pandemonium of retreat, accused of being a spy and only saves himself from being shot by jumping into a river. Although fictionalised, such scenes would have been common. Winthrop Young faced a similar nightmare, only for real. During the retreat, an Italian captain tried to commandeer his ambulance at gunpoint. Winthrop Young gives a lively account of what happened next in his autobiography *The Grace of Forgetting*. 'I ordered the car to drive on; calling his attention, among other things, to my superior rank and the order forbidding us to carry combatants. He drew a revolver and held it to the young driver's head.' Winthrop Young then did something extraordinary for someone whose leg had been amputated less than two months previously. 'Quick action seemed to be indicated. I vaulted forward on an arm-swing over the bonnet of my car, caught the captain's wrist and discharged my most throaty Florentine curses in counterblast to his abusive yelps. He wrestled to bring his arm down to shoot. The position grew unstable. I was holding him with one hand while balancing on one leg, and with my other hand I was steadying myself against the radiator behind. I suppose my next movement would have been to fling both arms round him and overwhelm him with *avoirdupois* [weight]. Fortunately at that point an Italian orderly appeared and managed to cool the situation.'

Winthrop Young had founded his ambulance unit on the western front and witnessed the destruction of Ypres. His experiences of the war ultimately led him to campaign for peace in the 1930s, travelling frequently to Berlin to meet with prominent opponents of the Nazis, many of whom were later murdered, and on one occasion attempted, unsuccessfully, to hand deliver a message of peace to Hitler. Another combatant to turn his experience into a rich literary output was the writer and filmmaker Luis Trenker, the author of 23 books, whose vast filmography includes 1931's *Berge in Flammen*, worth watching for the spectacular mountain and skiing scenes alone.

Today, one of the most remarkable aspects of the frontline is that so much of it is still there to see. Almost the entire frontline across the Alps has been preserved in some form or another, unlike the western front, where the passage of time has all but erased the signs of fighting. Partly because trenches carved in rock have a natural longevity to them, partly thanks to those unsightly metal ladders being reinvented into the 'sport' of via ferrata but mostly thanks to the efforts of Prof Walther Schaumann, a retired Austrian colonel and historian of this sector of the First World War.[6] In 1972, he took it upon himself to raise a small army of volunteers to restore the trails, tunnels and trenches. Hundreds of volunteers signed up from across Europe. The result is a 500km sign-posted high mountain trail from the Adamello to the Sexten Dolomites via the northern shores of Lake Garda. The trail then continues across the Carnic Alps and then south for another 100km over the Julian Alps to the Adriatic. Its name is the Sientero della Pace, or Path of Peace.

One hundred years on, it's tempting to look back at the events of the First World War and imagine that these things could never happen again but if man is capable of anything, it's amnesia. You only have to recall the shooting of Tibetan refugees on the Nangpa La a few years back or Google the Siachen and Sino-Indian conflicts to know that mountain wars are still an issue for our times – and even closer to home, look at the simmering tensions in the Balkans. In today's febrile Europe, it seems we can't take anything for granted.

---

6. Prof Schaumann also set up the excellent First World War museum in Kötschach-Mauthen below the Plöckenpass near Lienz. Its free 84-chapter podcast in English on the many aspects of the war offers a good introduction to the conflict.

Shortly before he was killed in 1915, 2nd Lt Alexander Douglas Gillespie wrote requesting that France and Britain build a pathway after the war on the western front. His wish was ultimately not granted. But with the Sientero della Pace, the Alpine countries have done a better job of remembering. It serves as a reminder of the horror and futility of this conflict. It also offers some of the most spectacular high mountain trails and scrambles of the Alps.

**Further Reading**

H Dalton, *With British Guns in Italy*, London, Methuen, 1919.

E Hemingway, *A Farewell to Arms*, New York, Scribner, 1929.

T Koren, *The Walk of Peace from the Alps to the Adriatic*, Ustanova Fundacija Poti miru v Posocju, 2015.

M Thompson, *The White War: Life and Death on the Italian Front*, 1915-1919, London, Faber & Faber, 2009.

I Voigt, *The Alpine Corps on the Dolomite Front*, 1915: Myth and Reality, Athesia, 2015.

M Wachtler, *The First World War in the Alps*, Athesia Spectrum, 2006.

J & E Wilks, *Rommel & Caporetto*, Pen and Sword Military, 2012.

G W Young, *The Grace of Forgetting*, Country Life, 1953.

**Acknowledgements**

With thanks also to Hugo Reider, the Drei Zinnen hut guardian and author of *Krieg um Sexten* and to Indy Neidell, whose excellent First World War podcasts on YouTube have provided additional material.

# Science & Nature

Lt Col H Walker (1869-1915), 4th Battalion Black Watch,
killed at the battle of Loos.

# The Mind Has Mountains

Malcolm Bass and Paul Figg celebrate reaching
the summit of Janhukot in 2018. *(Guy Buckingham)*

*O the mind, mind has mountains; cliffs of fall*
*Frightful, sheer, no-man-fathomed. Hold them cheap*
*May who ne'er hung there.*

*Gerard Manley Hopkins*

It had been a difficult day and I was tired. Part of me was hoping that
my last patient, here for his first appointment, wouldn't turn up. Lots of
people don't turn up for their first appointment, and the free slot would
give me a chance to catch up on the day's notes. But dead on the hour the
receptionist rings to say that he is in the waiting room. I poke my head
round the door, say his name, and a tall, slim man in dark chinos and open
necked shirt stands up.

I smile at him.

'Hello, we're just down here.'

He says nothing, but smiles back and I lead him down the short corridor to the consulting room. I go in first, hold the door open and he walks in.

'Sit wherever you like.'

He chooses the chair near the door, and I sit in the one by the window. We both settle. I smile at him again.

'So Mr Albright, what brings you here?'

He looks away from me up to the top corner of the window, pauses, then looks back at me and says: 'I think I need some help with my climbing.'

*

I qualified as a clinical psychologist in 1991 and found a permanent job in the NHS almost immediately. This was not due to any particular expertise on my part: trained psychologists were still a rare breed back then. By 1992 my financial position was secure enough, after years of poorly paid, short-term jobs taken en route to qualification, to go on my first Himalayan trip. Many more followed. I am still climbing in the Himalaya and I am still practising as a clinical psychologist.

After I submitted a particularly psychological trip report to the *Alpine Journal*, the editor gently suggested it might be better to write trip reports about climbing, and to corral the psychology into a dedicated article based on my overlapping experiences as a clinician and an alpinist. So I am going to attempt to describe how a clinical psychologist might think about alpine climbing.

I should start by defining those terms. 'Clinical psychologist' is a legally protected title and refers to practitioners who have completed a psychology degree and then a doctorate in clinical psychology, both at universities approved by the British Psychological Society. The majority of clinical psychologists (just 'psychologists' from here on) are employed in the NHS in mental health or disability services; others work in local authority social service departments, private healthcare, or are self-employed. The details of the work they do and the people they seek to help are determined largely by their employing organisation, but their broad purpose is to use the science and technology of psychology to understand and alleviate distress and promote mental wellbeing. The sort of alpine climbing I discuss here is that which involves pitches of technical climbing at altitude on big snowy mountains in glaciated regions.

Alpine climbing has a rich literature, as well as vigorous oral and visual storytelling traditions. Compared to these ways of thinking and communicating about alpinism, psychology is a relatively quiet newcomer to the scene, and I make no claim that it gives any greater depth of insight. But I hope I can show that a psychological approach to the subject offers an interesting perspective. And the psychological approach I will be using here is broadly positivist and materialist: crudely that there is an external world

The south-west buttress of Janhukot. *(Hamish Frost)*

out there, and we can learn how it works through observation and experiment. This is in contrast with the post-modern idea that what we think of as reality is constructed in our minds from concepts our culture teaches us, and that unbiased observation is impossible, or even meaningless. Psychology needs both approaches: we are physical beings of flesh, blood, bone and fluids, each experiencing the world in a unique way that has only the most tentative connection with reality.

I am always brought up short when I show people who aren't alpinists photographs of my potential beautiful new route. They don't see it. They just see a mountain. Because in reality there are an infinite number of possible lines up a mountain and that is what non-climbers see when they look at the photograph. They don't see the 'magic line' that leaps off the page at me: this only reveals itself to the fully indoctrinated alpinist. Our alpine-climbing culture has taught us what to see. Score one for the post-modernists. But when we are five days up that route, sleep deprived from sitting bivouacs, and we fully believe our judgment is as good as it was on day one, we will be wrong: our mental faculties will have declined in measurable ways (Killgore, 2010). That levels the score for the materialists.

Back to the punctual Mr Albright: how might I, as a clinical psychologist, begin to think about his request for some help with his climbing? I will start by referring to him here as 'A' in the classic Freudian tradition, although let me reassure you that Freud will now be restricted to cameo appearances.

It doesn't take long to establish that A feels torn. None of his last three, long and costly trips to the Pakistan Karakoram have resulted in a summit. His most recent collapsed in a welter of interpersonal and financial disputes, which are still rumbling on months later. A large part of him just wants to give it all up but he senses that this won't be easy. And, confusingly for him, another part of him wants to go the other way: to give up his job, train harder, plan better, aim higher and 'give up this renaissance man, dilettante bullshit of doing a lot of different things (and none of them very well by real standards).' (Twight, 2000). He either wants to stop, or to get better.

Ambivalence is a universal human experience, and often very painful. Psychologists approach it using a simple technique known as motivational interviewing (Miller, 2013) in which the person is helped to explore all the pros and cons of continuing with, or stopping, certain behaviour. The psychologist doesn't advise, instead they guide the discussion so that the person becomes aware of all the actual and potential consequences of each course of action, both wanted and unwanted. Commonly used with people struggling with drugs or alcohol, the approach encourages frankness about the joys they bring the person, as well as a lingering over the costs. A and I will need to talk about all the good things that alpinism brings him, but we will also need to talk about death.

I have a lot of communication with active alpinists. We often talk about attempts on new routes on peaks over 6,000m, but we very rarely talk about the risk of getting killed. And if we do it is usually by way of a joke. Yet the risk of getting killed is high, perhaps very high. One estimate of the lifetime risk for 'elite' alpinists of getting killed in the mountains puts it at just over 20%. The risk is less for women at 12% but not statistically significantly less, although there were far fewer women in the sample. (Weinbruch and Nordby, 2010). Liz Hawley's records (Windsor et al, 2009) suggest that at least one in every hundred people going above base camp on peaks over 7,000m in Nepal will die there. (Peaks below 7,000m seem much less risky.) And of the 14 alpinists I met at the 2011 Piolets d'Or two have since been killed in the mountains (Bjorn Evind Årtun and Kyle Dempster) and one of the nominees I never met as he died in a crevasse fall before the event (Max Belleville).[1]

Is A aware of these figures? And have they really hit home? Perhaps, like his psychologist, he has created what he hopes is a valid argument why they don't apply to him: he only climbs steep buttresses and ridges with minimal objective danger and he only goes to glaciated mountains once a year.

1. In reality A would never get to see an NHS psychologist merely because he is ambivalent about future alpine climbing. The demands on mental health services are such that most psychology time is devoted to helping people at risk of suicide. But if Weinbruch and Nordby's figures are anything to go on, then elite alpinists are more likely to die in the mountains than people with serious mental health problems are to die by suicide. However, to be rigorous, given the vast differences in methodologies and sample sizes between the studies, this comparison should be given very little weight.

Maybe he's right and those behaviours do reduce the risk. Or maybe his risk assessment is subject to one of the many biases that experimental psychology has shown to undermine the quality of our decision making (Lebowitz and Lee, 2015). The choice supportive bias, where we exaggerate the positive attributes of choices we have already selected, might be at play here.

And that tentative statement 'might be at play here' brings us to one of the big problems of psychology. Many of psychology's findings are based on the study of large groups in an attempt to reveal universal principles that apply to all human beings. Yet this method smoothes out the differences between people. So while it is now clear from experiments there is a general tendency for most people to display a choice supportive bias, to overrate the positive attributes of choices they have already made, within that group there will be outliers, people who already hate the choice they've made. The general findings, useful as they are at the population level, may not apply to the person sitting in front of you now. People vary. Clinical psychologists attempt to solve this problem by drawing up an individual formulation with each person. Psychological findings pertinent to the issue at hand are advanced tentatively, as hypotheses, to see whether they chime with the person's experience. If not, they are laid aside. But if they do ring true they become part of the formulation, part of the shared understanding of what is going on.

Psychology is often pilloried for that familiar offence of 'stating the bleeding obvious'. One of Feldman's Everest findings could be seen as a prime example: he and his colleagues found that people who experienced high anxiety levels on the mountain had less chance of reaching the summit than those who felt less anxious. So maybe A experiences intolerable levels of anxiety when high above the Batura glacier, and it is these that turn him back prematurely? But it turns out that A's experience is rather the opposite; he feels a sense of calm, of being in his element, quite different to being at work. Hypothesis rejected, we need to do more work to formulate why he turns back, but another interesting door has opened.

The great variability of human beings, and the problems with trying to apply general findings to specific individuals, means that readers may find that some of the ideas in this article don't resonate with their own experience. But they might be true for people that you climb with. It is easy to fall into the trap of assuming that others experience the world just as we do, or, conversely, to deny any commonality of experience: people are generally not very good at guessing what is going on in other people's heads (Ickes, 2003). Our guesses are likely to reveal more about our own mental state than about the other person's. So if you really want to know it's best to ask (Epley et al, 2017). But only do so if you have the mental energy and will to respond to what you hear: sometimes it's best not to know. When tired and pushing hard on a big climb I often don't care where my partners' heads are at as long as they appear vaguely functional.

The applicability problem is more pronounced for women. Unless researchers are trying to investigate something specific about the psychology of either men or women, current best practice is to have equal numbers

Malcolm Bass and Paul Figg descending from the summit of Janhukot.
*(Guy Buckingham)*

of each gender in your study groups, and to report whether and how gender influenced the results. This is harder if you are studying alpinists because of the gender imbalance in the activity. The studies cited here range from those that have no women in the study group (e.g. Van Yperen, 2009), through those that have a good balance but don't report on any differences (e.g. Woodman et al, 2009) to those that report on the gender differences they found (Weinbruch and Nordby, 2009). So it is less likely, but still quite possible that the concepts described here will ring true for women.

However, once again, we have neatly stepped away from thinking about death. Human beings seem to struggle to give ideas that provoke deep anxiety, like death, disease, infection and child abuse the right amount of attention. We seem either to worry about things excessively and fruitlessly, or to gloss over them. We struggle to hold them in mind effectively. This can be helpful, even protective; thinking about difficult things all the time is exhausting and ultimately disabling. Denial, blocking painful facts from awareness, is one of the classical defence mechanisms that Freud stated we use to protect our psyche (McLeod, 2009).

The culture of the group we belong to has an enormous influence on most of us. In modern western society most of us belong to multiple communities, each with their own distinct culture. Alpinism seems to me to be a strong culture. Its members are keen to identify as alpinists (or maybe alpine climbers or, more rarely now, mountaineers), and identifying as such influ-

Paul Figg and Malcolm Bass under the west face of Vasuki Parbat in 2010.

ences our behaviour. We have all read many of the same books and admire many of the same historical figures. We cherish alpine style, don't know how to prusik properly and like Scotland. And maybe we unconsciously glorify death in the mountains. I can't provide any hard evidence for this claim; I sense it more than see it. I sense it in our rush to talk about recent climbing deaths, in the words of some obituaries, in our celebration of lethal climbs, and in our veneration of the dead. This is maybe because I have been particularly sensitised to the issue: from ages seven to 12 I went to a private boarding school, a preparatory school for the famous public schools, and there absorbed the idea that if you'd missed your chance to die gloriously being torn apart by machine gun bullets as you led your men over the top, then expiring near either pole, up a mountain or at sea was a reasonable substitute. I escaped that system at 12 and went on to a school run by the strictly pacifist Society of Friends: the Quakers. I was taught to hear the call to glory and then given the tools to question it.

Back to the clinic: A is not in denial about the risks. One of the reasons he is thinking about quitting is that each climb is another roll of the dice. He doesn't need motivational interviewing to become aware of the risk of death, nor of the impact that would have on those close to him. He is clear-eyed too about the things that he loses by climbing as he does. It takes a lot of time and attention to plan, and execute these big trips; time that he could spend with the people that he loves, or working on something useful.

Some of the other drawbacks are a bit harder to pin down. A tells me how, when he is actually on an expedition, he is sometimes ambushed by powerful negative feelings about the whole enterprise that seem to leap out of nowhere: terror of getting killed; crushing guilt about the risks he is taking with the future happiness of the people who love him; boredom and a sense of futility. Granted that altitude sickness, gut problems, bad weather, a virus or some awful combination of all these is often the harbinger of these miserable states of mind, but A wonders why they are both surprising and, at the same time, very familiar.

A Freudian would point to another defence mechanism, repression, sometimes known as motivated forgetting, which explains it well enough: A has had exactly the same feelings on previous trips and then forgotten all about them. There is also a huge experimental literature that shows how people are not very good at predicting how they will feel in any given future situation, or at remembering how they felt last time they were in that situation. We tend to overestimate how happy events will make us feel and for how long. And we remember previous mood states most accurately when we are once again in that same mood state: the vicious downward spiral in depression. If A wants to get an accurate picture of how he really feels on expeditions he will need to keep a journal and read it when he is thinking about his next trip. And despite his doubts, part of him has already started thinking about his next big trip. Why?

We have finally arrived at the 'why' question. We were always going to end up here but even so, it is with some trepidation that I begin.

The human mind seems prone to a couple of tendencies when thinking about causation. First we have a preference for single-factor answers: the apple falls because of gravity. And second we like to set up rival plausible hypotheses in competition with one another: is the increase in adolescent mental health problems caused by social media or the fear of not being able to find a job and buy a house? But human behaviour is influenced by an almost infinite array of factors, each of which, on their own, seem to make a disappointingly small contribution from a psychologist's point of view.

As Niall Grimes begins a conversation with Steve McClure for his Jam Crack podcast he half jokes that his task is to find out 'what is your major malfunction numb nuts?' (It's a quote from the Stanley Kubrick film *Full Metal Jacket*.) This quest, to find the unresolved childhood hurt that drives the hero, has its roots in psychoanalytic theory, and has become so influential and widely practiced in biography, especially concerning alpinists, that we scarcely notice its presence. We feel satisfied when the account is properly resolved, when we understand what exactly is wrong with the star. There might be something in this: for instance Van Yperen in 2009 found that parental divorce rates were much higher in those adolescents who went on to make a professional career in soccer than those who didn't. But we need to be cautious about it becoming the only sort of answer we are looking for. The influential positive psychology movement has encouraged us to look just as hard for the positive characteristics, strengths and habits of

The New Zealand alpinist Pat Deavoll on Bekka Brakai Chhok in 2008.
*(Malcolm Bass)*

successful, happy and fulfilled people (Carr, 2003).

We know that any behaviour (and for all its complexity and culture, many psychologists would think of alpine climbing as a behaviour) that persists over time will be maintained by a wide variety of factors, will offer many rewards. In the jargon the behaviour will be maintained by many functions. This is what leads to its persistence. The reason the 'why' question is so engaging and so hard to answer, is that alpine climbing offers so many rewards. I find it helpful to resist the temptation to ask 'yes, but what is the real reason?' I ask instead 'what are the important rewards for this person (maybe ourselves) at this time?' And this is what I would do with A, because whether he ultimately decides to keep climbing, or to stop, understanding what he gets from it will be helpful. If he decides to stop it will help him in planning a different lifestyle, one that meets these needs in other ways; and if he goes on it will help him focus on attaining what matters to him.

We would start back at the beginning, with his early days on rock or in the hills. Long-lived behaviours typically shift function over time and what motivated our first steps may not be what we are after today. The archetypes of this are the Himalayan superstars who find freedom, camaraderie and beauty in the mountains in their youth, only to end up competing with one another for fame to the point of death.

In a very readable article Jim Lester (2004) described his findings from reviewing a great swathe of climbing literature in search of 'passionate climbers' describing the meaning they found in the activity. He categorised the main themes thus:

A sense of freedom
A sense of power, energy and vitality
Contact with a better self
Assertion of self
Conquest of self
Escape from self
Contact with a higher power
Unity

These are mostly self-explanatory, but it may help to add that Lester's 'contact with a higher power' includes both religious experiences and also new-age contact-with-the-universe or dissolution-of-self type experiences. (As you can maybe tell, I don't get either.) Unity is a sense of wholeness or integration: 'I feel completely and wholly myself'.

Lester's list provide a useful set of prompts for A and I as we explore the functions of alpinism in his life. And as we think about whether he experiences any sense of asserting himself, I am reminded of something A said earlier in our conversation, that he felt calm and in his element when on the mountain. He is not alone in this.

In the most sophisticated series of empirical studies on the psychology of mountaineering to be published to date, Tim Woodman and colleagues from Bangor University (Barlow et al, 2013) may have identified two related specific motivations for very many mountaineers (to use their term). These are the desires to experience emotion regulation and agency. Emotion regulation is the ability to 'influence which emotions we have, when we have them, and how we experience and express them' (Gross, 2002) and agency is the sense that we can influence what happens in our lives. These motivations are specific in that they are more present in mountaineers than in other high-risk sports people (sky divers, extreme skiers and rock climbers) and 'normal' controls. Mountaineers appear to have a stronger desire to experience emotion regulation and agency than other people, possibly because they don't feel they have them in day-to-day life. And, these studies suggest, mountaineering delivers the experience of emotion regulation and agency that its adherents are looking for, and that these effects persist and go with the climber back into their day-to-day life. The theory just about manages to avoid the 'damaged alpinist' trope by suggesting that mountaineers have a relatively high expectation of achieving effective emotion regulation in their day-to-day lives, not that we are poor at emotion regulation.

This idea certainly strikes a chord with A. Although he is doing pretty well in the 'real world' – he is in a loving relationship, is doing well enough at work – he lives with a constant buzz of low-level anxiety. Sometimes this seems to be about money, sometimes about his health, sometimes about his family; nothing is ever really very clear, he's never quite sure what he should be doing next: it's worrying and exhausting. On the hill things are much clearer. He is frightened of things that might kill him, and he can act to avoid them. He feels the urge to stop, to just sit down and rest when breaking trail up the snow field, but he knows how to push on through. Things are both simpler and harder, he knows what has to be done, and often he knows how to do it.

But as A and I discuss the pros and cons of him committing to another few years at the sharp end we both notice something missing from both Lester's list and the agent plus emotion regulation account: other people. This doesn't mean that these ideas aren't valid, they just represent a different level of analysis, the intrapersonal (within the person) rather than the interpersonal.

Now we're going to leave A and my clinical psychologist self as we sit in the consulting room discussing how his climbing friends, because he really only has climbing friends, and the memories, plans, and rituals they share bind him to the activity. I don't know what he will decide, and perhaps it doesn't really matter: if we rule out more extreme events such as life-changing injuries or illness, major trauma, or migration, we find that for most of us our happiness levels remain about the same whatever we do: the 'happiness set point', explained in Carr, 2003. If he decides to carry on with his Karakoram adventures, and if he decides that summits matter, then he has some work to do to find out what, if anything, is holding him back. He might just have been unlucky so far: the stars do need to align to let us get up these sorts of routes. If so, the persistence he has shown so far will serve him well. But perhaps it's something else? Maybe he aims too high? Or climbs with the wrong people? Or turns round too early? Whatever it is I hope maybe that a concept from psychology, more likely sports psychology than the clinical sort, will help him to the summit and safely home again.

And now, to finish, I'm going to say a bit of what I know of my own psychology. In the course of my work I have been subject to multiple personality assessments. Psychologists define personality as the relatively enduring aspects of the way a person thinks, feels and behaves, those features of a person that are apparent across a wide range of situations. The personalities of climbers and mountaineers have been much studied (e.g. Gray, 1968, in this journal). This is at least partly because it is an easy thing to study; ask each participant to fill in a questionnaire and the research is done. I have found it hard to draw any conclusions from this literature, partly because the researchers have used so many different classification systems, and maybe because there isn't a standard alpinist personality type.

In an attempt to get round the problems caused by multiple classification systems many personality researchers are rallying round a system called 'The Big Five'. The Big Five have been derived mathematically rather than conceptually: factor analysis has been used to look at the responses to thousands of personality assessments of many different types, and the answers have found to coalesce into five broad clusters. These are: conscientiousness, agreeableness, neuroticism, openness to experience and extraversion. CANOE is the mnemonic. It's also referred to as OCEAN.

Through my work I have been assessed numerous times, and find that my personality is pretty average on extraversion and agreeableness, but high on

Malcolm Bass on the 2014 attempt on Janhukot. *(Simon Yearsley)*

openness to experience, conscientiousness, and neuroticism. Openness to experience is about curiosity, exploration, the search for new experiences, and the drive to learn new things. It was that trait, reinforced by a family and school culture that valued adventure, which first drew me to the outdoors. If I saw a picture of someone climbing a mountain I wanted to try that. When I looked at my dad's caving photographs I wanted to go underground. At first I pretended to have adventures, and then I started to have real ones. And it still underpins a lot of my motivation; if I see a picture of a half decent mountain in a part of the world I haven't been to my pulse quickens and I just want to go there. Hatching a plan with a friend to go there is even better, especially if the trip is some time away and the trip shimmers in a much discussed shared future.

Let's get that neuroticism out of the way; it is the tendency to feel negative emotion, to feel anxious, to worry, to get frustrated and angry, to take things to heart. It is being the opposite of being a calm, phlegmatic person. This could be my major malfunction. It is certainly true that I live on a bit of an emotional roller coaster. Fear (of dying) and guilt (about leaving and maybe dying) undermined several of my early attempts in the Himalaya and Karakoram. But on the other hand anger helped me up my hardest climb, the west face of Vasuki Parbat (6780m) in the Indian Garwhal Himalaya with Paul Figg in 2010. In the run up to this trip I had been treated unfairly at work by a more senior psychiatric colleague in ways that had cost me money and status. I felt the righteous fury of the wronged and silenced.

I reverted to adolescence and trained manically to a soundtrack of raucous, worryingly self-destructive punk. I was really going to show them. Sports psychology research suggests that John Lydon (previously Johnny Rotten) was right: anger is an energy (Woodman et al, 2009 ) and it drove me up that face. But sadly I don't think many of those psychiatrists saw the trip report on UKClimbing or read the *Alpine Journal*.

I don't like climbing like that now. It has a slightly out of control feeling, and it leads to mistakes, several of which we made but got away with. I am more comfortable with fear now too, partly through familiarity, and partly through a deliberate effort, mostly through mindful meditation, to reduce my emotional reactivity across all aspects of my life, the conscientious side of my nature being useful for holding me to such long-term programmes. My neuroticism should make me an ideal candidate to benefit from the experience of more effective emotion regulation on the hill. But sadly, because I am a fan of Woodman and colleagues' elegant programme of research, I find that my ability to regulate my emotions is about the same on a mountain as it is at work. So what do I get from alpine climbing?

I like Lester's list, but for me it misses out both the natural world, and the social element of alpine climbing. Spending time in nature, in woods, near streams, by the sea, and yes, sometimes on mountains (but only some mountains) is a great source of joy to me. On Scottish hills I tend to feel a pretty reliable mixture of happiness and awe. I feel that I belong in the landscape, warm towards it, and to some extent embraced by it. It's totally different in foreign, glaciated mountains: here I sometimes feel repugnance or disgust towards the mountains, sometimes a shiver of fear. I get the urge to zip up the tent and shut them out. What they seem to offer me is challenge: something strengthening, but not in the least consoling. There is a lot for me to think about here, and it is a rich area too for research psychologists who are just getting to grips with how our relationship with nature, and our physical activities within it, effect our emotional state (e.g. Lawton et al, 2017).

One last psychological theory now to bring in the social element of alpinism: Ryan and Decci's self-determination theory (2000). This is an ambitious project: an attempt to describe, in a parsimonious way, core human psychological needs. Their theory suggests three such needs: competence, relatedness, and autonomy. How well then does alpine climbing meet all core human needs? Pretty well in my case, which is probably why I am still doing it. I feel very free when I am in the mountains. Free from duties and responsibilities that I don't value, free from rules I don't respect, free to move around, and free to be myself: I feel a sense of autonomy, a sense of freedom, and some of what Lester calls unity.

I think that competence has now become my major driver. I feel a great sense of personal pride in having acquired the skills to plan and execute trips to climb new routes on big mountains: it seems to have taken me a very long time. But as much as I enjoy using the skills I have learnt, it is the real prospect of doing things better next time that I find so compelling. Expeditionary climbing is a complex process, and the Himalaya is a complex environment:

there is a vast amount to learn about both. I am writing this just a month after coming back from climbing Janhukot (6810m) in India with Paul Figg and Guy Buckingham, and the list of improvements that I want to make on my next trip is growing fast. And it's not just my own sense of competence that appeals, I am aware that I enjoy being seen by others as competent in this sort of climbing. It offsets to some extent how I appear at Kilnsey.

Feeling part of a small national and international community of alpinists involved in the same sort of endeavour matters to me too, and that sense of belonging, of being known, takes us into the outer edges of Ryan and Decci's concept of relatedness, the need to be close to other people. This style of climbing favours small, self-contained expeditions, typically five or six people at a remote base camp and even smaller climbing teams; there are only ever two or three of us on the mountain. We climbers will know each very well from years of travelling and climbing together in these environments. And we will be together, working towards a challenging mutual goal, in relative isolation, for a matter of weeks: classical conditions for the development of a strong team spirit, which I find enormously rewarding to share.

That it is rewarding to be part of a small, trusted group working together to learn how to live in and explore a challenging, novel environment: I wonder if an evolutionary psychologist would have anything to say about that?

## References

M Barlow, T Woodman, T Hardy, 'Great Expectations: Different High-Risk Activities Satisfy Different Motives', *Journal of Personality and Social Psychology*, 2013, 105(3), pp458-75.

E Barrett & P Martin, *Extreme: Why Some People Thrive at the Limits*, Oxford University Press, 2014.

A Carr, *Positive Psychology: The Science of Happiness and Human Strengths*, Hove, Brunner-Routledge, 2003.

P Elbert & S Robertson, 'A Plea for Risk', *Royal Institute of Philosophy Supplements*, 2013, 73, pp45-64.

T Epley, N Eyal & M Steffel, 'Perspective Mistaking: Accurately Understanding the Mind of Another Requires Getting Perspective, Not Taking Perspective', *Journal of Personality and Social Psychology*, 2017, 114:4, pp547–571.

G Feldman, C Zayfert, L Sandoval, E Dunn & J Cartreine, 'Reward Responsiveness and Anxiety Predict Performance of Mount Everest Climbers', *Journal of Research in Personality*, 2013, 47, pp111-15.

D Gray, 'Personality and Climbing', *Alpine Journal* 1968, pp167-172.

J Gross, 'Emotion Regulation: Affective, Cognitive, and Social Consequences', *Psychophysiology*, 2002, 39, pp281–91.

W Ickes, *Everyday Mind Reading: Understanding What People Think and Feel*, New York, Prometheus Books, 2003.

J Kerr & S Mackenzie (2012) 'Multiple Motives for Participating in Adventure Sports', *Psychology of Sport and Exerise*, 2012, 13(5), pp649-57.

W Killgore, 'Effects of Sleep Deprivation on Cognition', Progress in Brain Research 2010, 185, pp105-29.

Simon Yearsley on Dunlung Kangri in 2012. *(Malcolm Bass)*

E Lawton, E Brymer, P Clough, & A Denovan, 'The Relationship Between Physical Activity Environment, Nature Relatedness, Anxiety, and Psychological Well-being Benefits of Regular Exercisers' *Frontiers in Psychology*, 2017, 8.

S Lebowitz & S Lee, '20 Cognitive Biases that Screw up your Decisions', Business Insider UK, (retrieved online from *http://uk.businessinsider.com*), 2015.

J Lester, 'Spirit, Identity, and Self in Mountaineering', *Journal of Humanistic Psychology*, 2004, 44, p86.

W Miller & S Rollnick, *Motivational Interviewing: Preparing People to Change*, Guildford Press, 2002.

S McLeod, 'Defense Mechanisms', *www.simplypsychology.org*, 2009.

R Ryan & E Deci, 'Self Determination Theory and the Facilitation of Intrinsic Motivation, Social Development, and Well-being', *American Psychologist*, 2000, 55:1, pp68-78.

M Twight, 'Twitching with Twight', *Kiss or Kill*, Seattle, The Mountaineers Books, 2001.

N Van Yperen, 'Why Some Make It and Others Do Not: Identifying Psychological Factors That Predict Career Success in Professional Adult Soccer', *Sport Psychologist*, 2009, 23.

S Weinbruch & K-C Nordby, 'Fatal Accidents among Elite Mountaineers: A Historical Perspective from the European Alps', *High Altitude Medicine and Biology*, 2010, 11 (2), pp147-51.

J Windsor P Firth, M Grocott, G Rodway & H Montgomery, 'Mountain Mortality: A Review of Deaths that Occur During Recreational Activities in the Mountains', *Postgrad Medical Journal*, 2009, 85, pp316-21.

T Woodman, P Davis, L Hardy, N Callow, I Glasscock, & J Yuill-Proctor, 'Emotions and Sport Performance: An Exploration of Happiness, Hope, and Anger', *Journal of Sports and Exercise Psychology*, 2009, 31, pp169-88.

MIKE SEARLE

# The Nepal Earthquake

## Causes, Effects and Rebuilding a Himalayan Village

*Figure 1* A satellite image of the Himalaya illustrating the location of the April 2015 earthquake in Nepal that killed at least 9,000 and its aftershocks. *(USGS)*

A t 11.56am Nepal time on 25 April 2015 an earthquake of magnitude 7.8 struck the central Nepal Himalaya with its epicentre beneath the district of Gorkha (*Figure 1, 2*). The epicentre of the earthquake was approximately 34km east-south-east of Lamjung, 77km west-north-west of Kathmandu and 73km east of Pokhara. The hypocentre, the point within the earth where an earthquake starts and below the surface epicentre, was at the relatively shallow depth of 15km. The earthquake focal mechanism shows that it occurred along a compressional thrust fault termed the Main Himalayan Thrust that ruptured the Nepal Himalaya for over 150km eastwards from Gorkha. This earthquake was the latest in a series of similar earthquakes that have built the Himalaya, as the Indian plate converges with Asia and under-thrusts the Himalaya.

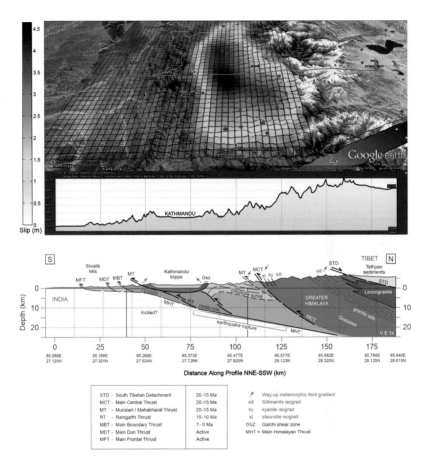

*Figure 2* A diagram illustrating the depth, spread and scale of the earthquake. The map and cross-section shows the Kathmandu-Ganesh Himal area showing the area uplifted by the Gorkha earthquake and the section of the Main Himalayan Thrust that ruptured, after Elliott et al (2016); Searle et al (2017).

Earthquake aftershocks show that the rupture occurred only in one direction, eastwards from the epicentre. Rocks beneath the Kathmandu valley moved by up to 4.5m horizontally as the Indian plate slid beneath the Himalaya. Synthetic Aperture Radar Interferometry (InSAR) recorded the post-earthquake ground motions around the area from the European Sentinal-1a satellite, comparing the imagery before and after the earthquake. Each colour contour on the 'interferogram' shows 2.8cm of ground movement with respect to the satellite (*Figure 3*). The data shows that an area approximately 120km by 50km around Kathmandu lifted up by at least one metre in less than one minute. The high peaks to the north including Mount Everest actually subsided very slightly as the whole Himalayan slab tilted towards the north.

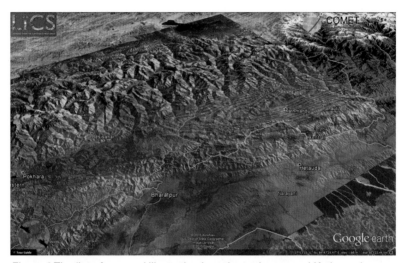

*Figure 3* The 'interferogram' illustrating how the region around Kathmandu was raised in altitude by as much as a metre over the course of roughly a minute. *(John Elliott, COMET, University of Oxford)*

Unusually, the fault did not rupture all the way to the surface as would be expected. None of the active thrust faults along the southern margin of the Himalaya in the Terai recorded any rupture. This worrying fact means that the stresses causing the earthquake are retained at depth, buried beneath the southern Himalaya, and this area remains under imminent danger of a further earthquake at any time.

The following day, 26 April, several aftershocks with magnitudes up to 6.7 occurred as the plates readjusted. Aftershocks continued long after the main earthquake with the main damage recorded from the Gorkha region east across the Ganesh, Langtang, Jugal Himalaya and the Kathmandu valley. The largest aftershock was the 7.2 earthquake that occurred on 12 May, 120km east of the Gorkha earthquake epicentre, south of Mount Everest.

This earthquake resulted in much more intense shaking, and triggered many huge rock and ice avalanches, the most devastating of which occurred in the Langtang valley north of Kathmandu (*Figure 4*). A massive slab of rock 500m high and 400m wide fell down the south face of Langtang Lirung completely destroying the village of Langtang where three-storey houses were totally buried. The entire population of more than 450 people were killed. Twenty-five years ago, I was part of an expedition to climb the south face of Langtang Lirung and the lower part of our route was the exact path of the avalanche. On Everest, 21 climbers were killed and many others were stranded above the icefall when huge avalanches crashed down from Lingtren and the Lho La pass on the Tibet border, wiping out the route through the Khumbu icefall above Everest Base Camp.

The Gorkha earthquake resulted in at least 9,000 deaths. More than 500,000 houses were destroyed and approximately three million people

*Figure 4* The most devastating single incident occurred in the 7.2 aftershock that occurred in May. A vast block of rock half a kilometre wide fell off Langtang Lirung burying the village of Langtang below and all its inhabitants. (a) South face of Langtang Lirung; (b) view from camp two south face showing the landslide section; (c) scar of the landslide and the debris covering Langtang village; (d) path of landslide in Langtang. *(Thompson-Reuters)*

were made homeless. In Kathmandu several world heritage sites including ancient temples such as the Trailokya Mohan and the Kasthamandap temple in Kathmandu's Durbar Square collapsed, as did the famous landmark the Dharahara tower, causing many fatalities (*Figure 5*). The ancient city of Patan suffered extensive damage with numerous buildings and old temples collapsing. Bhaktapur suffered even worse with several ancient temples around its Durbar Square and many of the old houses near the river bank reduced to rubble. The famous stupa at Boudhanath toppled over. The World Bank estimated that over $6.66bn was needed to rebuild the country. Villages along the Budhi Gandaki valley north of Gorkha around the epicentre were affected particularly badly. Several villages, notably Laprak and Barpak, had almost all houses flattened by the quake. Landslides blocked the Budhi Gandaki hindering access, and it was days after that the first relief parties managed to trek into these remote villages.

For over 10 years myself and my students at Oxford University Earth Sciences department had been working on the geology of the Nepal Himalaya and we employed porters and sirdars from the village of Yarsa, one of three villages that make up Kashigaon on the east bank of the Budhi

*Figure 5* After the earth stopped shaking: (a) Earthquake damage in Kathmandu; (b) Patan's Durbar Square; (c) the collapsed Dharahara Tower; (d) the fallen Boudhanath stupa. (e) Widespread destruction in Baprak village right above the epicentre in Gorkha district. (f) Aerial photo Laprak village.

Gandaki river in the Gorkha Himalaya. They were always hard working, happy and proud and many became good friends. Kashigaon, like many hundreds, even thousands of hill villages in rural Nepal, was badly affected by the earthquake, and located right above the epicentre (*Figure 6*). Several houses collapsed completely, killing people inside, and the remaining houses were all badly cracked and unsafe. Many of their buffalo and other animals were killed, and several of their terraced fields slid into the Budhi Gandaki valley. Two huge scars in the cliffs beneath the village marked enormous landslides. The villagers were frightened of aftershocks that continued for months afterwards, so slept out in the open fields.

I was due to fly to Kathmandu one week after the earthquake to trek to Annapurna Base Camp with a group. Of course, we had to cancel, but when I found out about the level of destruction throughout central Nepal I was horrified. We immediately set up a fund in the Department of Earth

*Figure 6* Remote villages, still the norm in Nepal rather than the exception were often left to cope on their own with limited government help: (a) Collapsed houses Yarsa village, Kashigaon district after the earthquake; (b) Locals clearing land; (c) Building the new school. (d) Completed new school at Yarsa. (e) Yarsa, Kashigaon school at the opening ceremony 20 May 2016. (f) Yarsa village with the new school (brown building on left) above cliffs showing scars from landslides.

Sciences at Oxford University, Worcester College, Oxford, and our local Himalayan pub, the Rose and Crown in North Parade. In three weeks we raised over £8,000, which was sent directly out to the Kashigaon village bank account in Pokhara.

Local sirdars, headed by Suka Ghale and Ash Bahadur Ghale, managed to buy food, tents, tarpaulins, tin roofs and basic building material in Pokhara and made several trips trekking up to the village to distribute these. Suka and Ash Bahadur even managed to commandeer an Indian army rescue helicopter to drop supplies by air, although the ground was too steep for the helicopter to land. The village is one long days' walk from the end of the road at Arughat Bazar up steep mountain paths on the Ganesh side of the Budhi Gandaki valley. The local villagers received little help from the government which had more pressing needs in Kathmandu and Langtang, so we decided to 'adopt' Kashigaon and Yarsa villages and help with whatever funds we could raise.

One year after the earthquake we managed to raise over £31,000, which was channelled through Doug Scott's Community Action Nepal (CAN), a registered UK charity. After adding the government's gift aid, CAN transferred all funds directly to the village bank account in Pokhara. The village committee decided how to spend the money on reconstruction, building an entirely new school to replace the collapsed one. Every penny of money raised went directly to the Kashigaon account and from there to the village reconstruction. We provided the funds for building materials and engineers and the villagers themselves provided all the labour. On 20 May 2016 the new school for 150 kids in Yarsa was officially opened. We are continuing to help these hard-working and wonderful Nepali villagers and are now trying to raise more money for building a clinic in the village.

Seismologists and geodesists have long predicted that the Main Himalayan Thrust could rupture along this part of the Himalaya. Global position system data shows that convergence between India and south Tibet occurs at a rate of $17.8 \pm 0.5$ mm/year in central and east Nepal and 20.5 mm/year in western Nepal. The last major earthquake along the Himalayan front was the 1934 Bihar-Nepal of magnitude 8.1 that destroyed much of Kathmandu and eastern Nepal. The largest known Himalayan earthquake was the 1950 Assam earthquake of magnitude 8.6. In western Nepal, the 1505 earthquake ruptured the far west of Nepal segment, but central Nepal, centred on Kathmandu, was in a seismic strain shadow where an earthquake was expected. We can now predict, using past earthquakes, GPS and InSAR satellite geodesy, roughly where along the Himalaya the strain is building up and an earthquake can be expected, but the precise timing of the earthquake cannot be predicted.

Despite the devastation of the Gorkha earthquake, Nepal was lucky in some respects. The earthquake happened on a Saturday afternoon, so most villagers were outside in the fields, and the schoolrooms were empty. If the earthquake occurred at night or when schools were full, as happened in the 2005 Pakistan earthquake, the death toll would have been much greater. The earthquake did not occur during the monsoon. If it had the rains would have caused many more landslides and misery for homeless victims. The outside world was remarkably generous in relief aid and donations but the hold-ups in getting this aid to the remote villagers were immense. The one international airport at Tribhuvan was quickly over-flowing, the appallingly bad road network out of the Kathmandu valley has always been one long traffic jam. The only way in to the remote mountain villages was by helicopter and government bureaucracy refused to allow some larger helicopters to fly.

The most worrying factor is that the Gorkha earthquake did not cause a surface rupture and thus the strain built up remains at depth. The likelihood of another earthquake is great, either to the south of Kathmandu where the

Main Boundary Thrust reaches the surface, or to the west of the epicentre, west of Gorkha where the fault did not rupture and remains locked – or both. There will definitely be more earthquakes like Gorkha in the future, possibly much larger ones. We just do not know precisely when.

• Nepal remains in need of aid following the Gorkha earthquake. Donations can be made to Community Action Nepal (*www.canepal.org.uk*).

## References

T Ader, J-P Avouac et al, 'Convergence Rate across the Nepal Himalaya and Interseismic Coupling on the Main Himalayan Thrust: Implications for Seismic Hazard', *Journal of Geophysical Research*, vol 117, 2012, B04403, doi:10.1029/2011JB009071.

R Bilham et al, 'GPS Measurements of Present-day Convergence across the Nepal Himalaya', *Nature*, v. 386, 1997, pp61-4.

J Elliott et al, 'Himalayan Megathrust Geometry and Relation to Topography Revealed by the Gorkha Earthquake', *Nature Geoscience*, 2016, doi: 10.1038/NGEO2623.

M Searle, J-P Avouac, J Elliott, and B Dyke, 'Ductile Shearing to Brittle Thrusting along the Nepal Himalaya: Linking Miocene Channel Flow and Critical Wedge Tectonics to the 25 April 2015 Gorkha eEarthquake', *Tectonophysics*, 2017, pp714-5, pp117-124, doi:10.1016/j.tecto.2016.08.003.

MARK CAREY & RODNEY GARRARD

# Lessons from the Andes

## A Call to Reconnect Mountaineers and Science

A contemporary picture of Lake Palcacocha in the Cordillera Blanca.
*(Shutterstock)*

In the late summer of 1939, Dr Hans Kinzl and his German Alpine Club (DAV) companions were attempting Mount Huaytapallana (5572m), also called Lasontay, meaning 'smoking ice'. It was his third expedition to the Andes. By then, he'd climbed more than a dozen 6,000m peaks in the Cordillera Blanca and the Cordillera Huayhuash. He'd made the first ascent of Peru's highest peak, Huascarán (6768m), in 1932 and of Siula (6344m). As a University of Innsbruck glaciologist and geographer, however, he was interested in something more than setting records. He produced some of the first maps of the Andean ranges, studied the flora and fauna, evaluated the causes and consequences of a glacial lake outburst flood and, long before the general public started paying attention to climate change, he analysed the dynamics of glacier retreat. Tragically, an avalanche engulfed the group: three of his fellow climbers died, but Kinzl survived.

Three days later, Kinzl learned that the German army had invaded Poland. The government of Peru immediately broke ties with Germany and Kinzl became an exile. He spent a year trying to escape Peru and return to his wife in Innsbruck, at last slipping onto a Japanese freighter, taking only the gear, photographs and scientific records that he could carry with him.

Lake Palcacocha in 1939, a year before Hans Kinzl warned in an academic article published in Spanish that a glacial lake outburst (GLOF) was likely. A year after that, Lake Palcacocha burst out of its bed, generating a tsunami-like flood that killed at least 1,800 people in the city of Huaraz. *(Hanz Kinzl)*

After travelling across China, he snuck onto the Trans-Siberian Railway. In the spring of 1941, he arrived home. After the war, a denazification panel scrutinised whether his Andean mountaineering and scientific studies had been an arm of Nazi expansion. He was cleared of any wrongdoing but the implications of his work would go unheeded, at the cost of hundreds of lives.

Kinzl was part of that long tradition of mountaineer-scientists dating back to the beginnings of both modern alpinism and glaciology in the 18th century. His predecessors included the great Swiss mountaineer and natural scientist of the Alps, Horace-Bénédict de Saussure, famous for his obsession with Mont Blanc. In 1787, a year after paying the promised reward to the first ascensionists, de Saussure climbed the mountain himself, accompanied by 18 guides who transported lavish provisions and bulky scientific equipment to the summit, among which was a helio-thermometer, a large box lined with black cork whose cover consisted of three layers of glass separated by air spaces, with a thermometer inside. He used this to measure the power of sunlight at different elevations for nearly two weeks on the Col du Géant, in the Mont Blanc massif. De Saussure published his observations of the region's glaciers and geology in *Voyages dans les Alpes* (1779-96). The book contributed to his reputation as the 'father of alpinism' and also made Mont Blanc an enticing location for the study of glaciers.

From the end of the 18th century until the middle of the 19th century, Swiss, Italian and French scientists dominated mountaineering in Europe.

In 1840 the Swiss-born biologist and geologist Louis Agassiz, who later emigrated to the US to teach at Harvard, set up a camp on the Unteraar glacier in Switzerland, building a hut next to some overhanging slabs of rock. Known as the Hôtel des Neuchâtelois, the shelter became Agassiz's summer research residence, attracting a stream of visiting scientists. He and his group of guides and porters hauled scientific instruments to his 'hotel' to study the glacier and measure its motion. He bored holes into the ice to test flow at various depths, and pounded wooden stakes in different regions of the glacier to record its pace. After two years, he noted that the hut had moved 486ft downhill. His work contributed to ideas about the Ice Age. He also proved that breakthroughs in glaciology arose from personal interactions with ice and snow, from time at high elevation and from expertise in mountaineering. An example of scientists taking real risks in and around mountains with a strong connection to the Alpine Club is John Tyndall, who slept on the summit of Mont Blanc, surrounded by thermometers he placed in the snow.

Those first ascents of Mont Blanc, and the broader link between mountaineering and glaciology, were inextricably linked to the political climate of the time and the struggle over sovereignty in Chamonix and Geneva. Mountaineering and science were part of the process of political control. Knowledge acquired by mountaineer-scientists facilitated understanding of, for example, glaciology, made the landscape legible and consequently governable and exploitable. Glaciers formed natural resources to be traversed, explored and exploited as part of a particular view of citizenship and state power. Ventures into the Alps, or beyond Europe, ended up extending the sphere of states, thereby facilitating European government control not only over the Alps, but also the Himalaya, Andes, Rwenzori, Arctic and elsewhere. The marriage of mountaineering and glaciology has not always been a benign link, free of politics and power.

This is the tradition that Kinzl stepped into on his first journey to Peru. Kinzl was born in 1898 in the small town of Sankt Florian, 10 miles from Linz. From his home, he could gaze out at the jagged, snowy line of the Alps on the horizon, a view that lingered in his mind, drawing him to high mountains for the rest of his life. That fascination with landscapes and rural places only increased after he joined the army. On Christmas Eve, 1917, Kinzl's troop was ambushed and he was hit by gunshot fire in the right hand. He never recovered fully, having to hold a pen in his middle fingers and greet people with his left hand: one can assume this also affected his climbing. After the war, Kinzl was able to combine his passion for mountains and intellectual rigor through graduate work in geography.

In 1930, while he was a professor at the University of Heidelberg, Kinzl received a letter from the DAV asking if he wanted to join an Andean expedition. 'Of course,' he replied, thrilled to explore what he considered some of 'the most beautiful high mountains in the world.' Kinzl argued that being in the mountains for extended periods, often with a need to assess ice conditions to stay alive, yielded important observations and tremendous knowledge about mountain processes. 'A great number of scholars, especially

The glaciologist Dr Hans Kinzl, seated right, and his German Alpine Club (DAV) companions, who attempted Huaytapallana (5572m) in 1939.

geologists, have become famous for being researchers of the natural world and also as mountaineers,' he wrote, 'in this way representing living symbols of the fundamental ideals of mountaineering [where] we find this intimate union between mountaineering and science.'[1] In 1940, in an article printed in Spanish, he noted that 'glacial lakes represent certain dangers for the Cordillera [Blanca] valleys and the people directly at the foot of the mountain range.'[2] A year later, Lake Palcacocha burst out of its bed, generating a tsunami-like flood that killed at least 1,800 people in the city of Huaraz. Kinzl had predicted that such floods would be rare. Believing that the only way to protect nearby populations would be to construct enormous retaining walls, he had concluded that the 'economic value' of the upper valleys was not 'sufficiently large to justify such high costs' of disaster mitigation, and that people should move. Nonetheless, residents protested that the authorities had ignored Kinzl's warnings.

Local newspaper journalists praised Kinzl for his willingness to get to know the Andean landscape in ways that non-mountaineering scientists never did. Not only did he publish in Spanish, he learned some Quechua, the regional indigenous language, gave lectures in Huaraz and Lima and

1. H Kinzl, 'Las Tres Expediciones del Deutscher Alpenverein a las Cordilleras Peruanas,' *Boletín del Museo de Historia Natural 'Javier Prado'* IV, no 12, p4.
2. H Kinzl, 'La Ruptura del Lago Glacial en la Quebrada de Ulta en el Año 1938,' *Boletín del Museo de Historia Natural 'Javier Prado'* Año IV, no 13, 1940, p164.

even planted Peruvian flags on summits as a sign of respect. In 1945 a Huaraz resident complained about the government's neglect of glacial lake flood prevention programs: 'It is important to remember that more than ten years ago a German scientific commission – the most extensive and capable that has ever been in the region – lived in and explored the entire Cordillera Blanca of Ancash for a year.'[3] A decade later, the Innsbruck professor received the Peruvian Order 'al Mérito' for his distinguished services to the country.

NASA's ASTER satellite image of Lake Palcacocha, April 2003. Note the supposed 'crack' in the glacier above Palcacocha at the centre of the image. (NASA)

In the years after the Second World War, universities and research centres extended their control of mountain science while climbing boomed without any scientific justification or, increasingly, political aspirations either. This had surprising consequences. For example, in 1962, US mountaineer-scientists David Bernays and Charles Sawyer spent several weeks analysing rock-ice instability on Huascarán, seven months after part of Glacier 511 had slid off the mountain, triggering an avalanche that killed 4,000 people. When they reported the imminent threat of the severely fissured glacier, the Peruvian government authorities forced them out of the region, telling residents to 'return to your homes with your faith placed in God,' threatening anyone who spoke in favour of the Americans' conclusions to be charged under the penal code for 'disrupting public tranquillity.' Eight years later, a rock-ice slide from Huascarán killed nearly 10,000 people.

The sharp separation between climbing and scientific studies only grew stronger in subsequent decades, not just in Peru, but worldwide. By the 1970s, mountaineers did not need to rely on science for credibility, justification or prestige. At the same time, satellites, remote sensing, and GIS were gaining momentum and influence, which put glaciologists in front of computers instead of out in the field analysing ice. The Ohio State University glaciologist Lonnie Thompson recently lamented about how difficult it has been to find glaciology graduate students who want to spend their time in the mountains. While these technological advancements have massively increased understanding of mountain glaciers and alpine regions, they also have significant limitations: if the images are not coupled with first-hand fieldwork analysis of environmental conditions, they can lead to misinterpretations.

In April 2003, NASA issued a press release warning about an 'ominous crack' in the glacier above Lake Palcacocha: 'Should the large glacier chunk break off and fall into the lake, the ensuing flood could hurtle down the Cojup valley into the Rio Santa valley below, reaching Huaraz and its

---

3. G Alejandro and F Roél, 'La catástrofe de Chavín,' *El Comercio*, 21 Jan 1945, p 11.

Palcaraju glacier and Lake Palcacocha in 2013, with siphons removing water to reduce the possibility of a GLOF. *(Paribesch Pradhan, National Snow and Ice Data Center)*

population of 60,000 in less than 15 minutes.' Worried residents demanded details about their fate, and visitors cancelled plans to travel to Huaraz. The lost tourism revenue alone was estimated at $20m. But NASA based its analysis on a satellite image, not the kind of eyewitness account that a mountaineer-scientist could have offered. And the report was stunningly wrong: when Peruvian scientists arrived on the glacier, they discovered the supposed crack was a rock.

University of Arizona glaciologist Jeffrey Kargel, among others, explains that satellite image analysis, ground and aerial observations, and ground-based instruments all combined together provide the most comprehensive glacier hazard monitoring.[4] In recent years, amid a rise of so-called citizen science and calls to diversify environmental knowledge, researchers and organizations have called for a resurgence of climber-scientist programs. Some groups such as Adventure Scientists engage mountaineers in collecting scientific data. Others, like the Office de Haute Montagne in Chamonix, focus on studying glacier and avalanche hazards that threaten not only climbers but also alpine villagers.

Those who spend time on the world's glaciers – mountaineers, guides, porters and local residents – possess tremendous knowledge of changing glaciers, but their observations often don't get into scientists' hands or computers. A tighter link between mountaineering and glaciology could help

4.  J Kargel, R Furfaro, G Kaser, G Leonard, W Fink, C Huggel, A Kääb, B Raup, J Reynolds, D Wolfe, and M Zapata, 'ASTER Imaging and Analysis of Glacier Hazards,' in *Land Remote Sensing and Global Environmental Change, Remote Sensing and Digital Image Processing 11*, (ed) B Ramachandran, C Justice, and M Abrams, New York, Springer, 2011), p325-73.

A 2003 photo of Lake Palcacocha's security dam that was partially destroyed when a landslide fell into the lake, creating waves that overtopped the strucutre. *(Mark Carey)*

uncover dynamic mountain conditions, understand and chronicle glacier change, and provide timely reports about hazards to protect people and help climate change adaptation. Increased collaboration could also change perceptions of climbing. Historians have often linked alpinism to a legacy of colonialism and exploitation of natural resources, characterizing it as a pursuit for wealthy, urban-based, generally white, outsiders, often undertaken at the expense of local people and diminishing their control over their own mountains. But mountaineering doesn't have to be just a race to bag peaks, set speed records or establish hard routes and go home again climbing can also be an intimate experience with a mountain: with increasingly active and ever-changing landscapes that scientists and societies are struggling to understand, especially amid the impacts of climate change.

One way to overcome the imperial tradition of dominating mountains and extracting experiences is to give back some of the knowledge and experience gained on the mountainside. Climbers can play key roles in a rapidly transforming alpine world, reporting on changes that affect their routes and alter the landscapes they've come to know so well. This information could be helpful, not only to scientists and policymakers but also to local residents living within those changing mountain landscapes crumbling mountains.

Without the mountain skills of climbers, glacier research would be much harder and much more expensive. And without their spirit of exploration, scientists would be more confined to the same old places. Mountaineering and science need a reconnection that can transcend their shared legacy in colonialist expeditions of the past and look to the future. As glaciologist Lonnie Thompson declared, 'There are a lot of words in the world of science and everyday affairs, but words don't work on mountains; you have to experience them.'

• A version of this article first appeared in *Revista de Glaciares y Ecosistemas de Montaña* (2016). For more information about Adventure Scientists see: *http://www.adventurescientists.org.*

VICTOR SAUNDERS

# The Peltzman Effect

Ski tourers approaching the Col du Berard above Chamonix. *(Ben Tibbetts)*

What has the automotive industry got to do with climbing? Well, quite a lot as it turns out. I have recently been spending quite a bit of time thinking about risk, climbing and skiing. Shortly after Christmas my friend and fellow Alpine Club member Ben Tibbetts was lucky to survive an avalanche on a mountain directly in front of my house. He had of course all the usual safety equipment and a huge amount of knowledge about avalanche, and yet he barely escaped with his life. The escapade led to bracing cups of tea, since Ben doesn't drink beer, and long conversations about the level of risk we accept in the mountains.

When I was a student there was a popular theory in climbing circles. The idea was you always accepted the same level of risk. There's a name for this hypothesis: risk homeostasis. I didn't think much about it at the time; it seemed pretty obvious to a climber. You would only do a climb if the level of protection were appropriate to the difficulty. What I didn't realise at the time was that this idea came out of the automotive industry.

In the 1970s, Sam Peltzman, now an emeritus professor at the University of Chicago, was working on a novel idea. His working theory was all about the unintended consequences of the clever safety features newly available for cars being advertised. He believed they prompted an increase in

161

risky driver behaviour. Drivers were in effect compensating for these new safety features by driving faster, effectively eliminating their benefit. It was obvious to Peltzman that for safety features to work they had to be invisible to the driver.

In the ensuing decades new ideas about risk homeostasis, for and against, where it couldn't be demonstrated and where it could, came tumbling out. The ideas were controversial and often heavily criticised. Essentially, people were in denial that their behaviour could eliminate the benefits of safety equipment.

While it would be cynical to think the main objections to these hypotheses came from the safety industry, it did seem probable that the main beneficiaries of expensive and visible safety features were going to be commercial entities, whereas the main beneficiaries of hidden safety features were going to be car drivers. ABS, for example, only encourages you to drive faster on slippery roads. If you don't believe me, try switching it off.

After Peltzman, it was shown that a clear example of safety misconception was that car seatbelts reduced road deaths. John Adams, in his seminal book *Risk and Freedom: Record of Road Safety Regulation* (Brefi Press, 1985) argued that the opposite was in fact the case. If confounding factors were stripped out, the reduction in road deaths was mainly due to imposed speed control. Once that speed was taken out, seatbelts actually increased road deaths. How so? Because while the lives of car drivers were saved, more pedestrians died. Car drivers, with the psychological security of a seatbelt, drove more quickly, killing more pedestrians along the way. The driver's behaviour had eliminated the benefits of the belts to wider society if not to themselves.

The great and hugely influential Sir David Spiegelhalter, Winton Professor of the Public Understanding of Risk in the Statistical Laboratory at the University of Cambridge, quotes Adams: 'if you really want to reduce road deaths, take away the seatbelts and put a dagger on the steering wheel pointing at the driver's heart.'

Hang on a minute, I hear you say. This business of transferring risk to innocent pedestrians: that seems singularly unfair, doesn't it? This sort of unfair behaviour is sometimes called 'moral hazard', a term that originated in the 17th century to mean an 'obviously bad thing' and by the 19th century had been adopted by economists to mean, essentially, inefficiencies in an economic system. I guess that's economics for you. There should be better name for it: 'unconscious selfishness' perhaps.

Either way, I cannot help thinking there is an element of moral hazard in wearing ski helmets while piste skiing. There is persuasive evidence that shows helmet-wearers ski faster than non-wearers. On a piste that means putting other skiers at risk. Here is a little test that demonstrates the hazard. All the helmet-wearers I've asked offer the same contradictory response. Asked if they ski more dangerously when wearing a helmet, they all say: 'no'. But ask them how they behave if they forget their helmets, they say something like: 'I would look around and ski a bit more slowly because of the idiots on the slopes.' The formula clearly works both ways. If they ski more carefully without helmets, it also means they ski more dangerously when wearing helmets. Yet most skiers I have asked are simply in denial that their behaviour changes with safety features.

I think this denial is less apparent with climbers. They know that added protection means they will climb harder routes. With poor protection they climb easier routes. There is a straightforward calculation: chances of falling off against the consequences thereof. The level of accepted risk remains at the same level: it is largely homeostatic. If you are an E1 climber, you can climb an exposed E1 5a just as well as a safe but difficult E1 5c. Your homeostatic level of risk is based around your understanding that you can always climb E1. Taking the helmet away from skiers doesn't mean they understand they will ski safer lines; they just slip into denial. I find this strange, but it does perhaps go some way to explaining why ski helmets do not appear to have contributed to greater safety on the slopes.

There is some evidence that the advantages of cycling helmets are similarly emasculated by behaviour. But for cyclists there is worse news: not only do helmets affect a cyclist's behaviour, they also negatively affect car-driver behaviour as well. Tim Gamble and Ian Walker of Bath University published a brilliant paper in 2016[1] showing that motorists pass closer to helmeted cyclists, and also closer to cyclists who 'owned the road' by taking the lane, as they are entitled to do, in the UK at least.

Many cycling authorities and governments around the world recommend wearing cycling helmets and in Australia it's mandatory. The reality is we should always ask what the evidence is and who is giving it to us. And why. Walker's experiment showed that cyclists, around Bath at least, would be safer if they abandoned their helmets and donned long blond wigs. I won't go into the detail here, but I advise you to read Gamble and Walker's work. It's also worth noting that when helmets were introduced to American Football the number of serious brain injuries went up until rules restricting tackling behaviour where changed.

All these examples were in the forefront of the discussions I had with Ben after his avalanche experience. I wondered if compensatory behaviour could nullify safety advice in this context. That is, by having knowledge of avalanche safety advice we would think we are protected by being expert and consequently compensate by acting more dangerously.

For example, we are variously told that avalanche victims should swim, or roll or cover their mouths, yet there is no ethical way of testing any of these ideas, and in fact most people caught in avalanche surf have little or no control of their limbs. Giving people the idea that they can alter the outcome of an avalanche could be fallacious and give skiers unreasonable confidence.

If piste skiers wear helmets, ski tourers use avalanche safety equipment. I think there is some analogy here and seems especially true of avalanche airbags. They work by making the victim float to the surface, thereby avoiding burial. The bags will make little difference if the avalanche occurs in terrain

1. T Gamble and I Walker, 'Wearing a Bicycle Helmet Can Increase Risk Taking and Sensation Seeking in Adults', *Psychological Science*, vol 27, 2, 2016, pp289-294.

traps, over cliffs and into trees, or in the case of trauma. Worse, there is evidence that a number of victims fail to trigger the bags.

About 10% of avalanche fatalities result from burial depending on which country you draw the statistics from. The airbags would be very effective in those cases, but most airbag wearers do not know that the extra safety is for 10% of the avalanche fatalities. They commonly believe instead that the bag will save them in most avalanches. This year the *Daily Telegraph* ran a story with the strapline: 'Research shows wearing an avalanche airbag backpack when skiing off piste save lives – is it time to buy one?' It's not in the manufacturer's interest to point out that nine times out of 10 the bags will not affect their future one way or the other. Thus if bag wearers over-compensate by more than 10%, which is entirely plausible, skiing slopes they wouldn't without bags, the bags will make their lives shorter not longer.

Like ski-helmet wearers, most bag wearers seem to hold contradictory statements as true. One: the bags don't affect behaviour. Two: there are slopes they would never ski without bags. Again and again we run into denial in the ski world. They practise unconscious risk compensation.

On the theme of moral hazard, climbers wear helmets ice climbing, alpine climbing and where they feel there is overhead objective danger. There are climbs they wouldn't dream of going on without a helmet. This is part of risk homeostasis. Climbers know they are going into more dangerous zones and add helmets to compensate.

But in these cases there is only the team of two, the consenting adults, at risk. Climbers don't generally put others in danger by climbing these routes. Similarly, wearing helmets while ski touring does not, I assume, make life more dangerous for others even if it doesn't make it safer for the wearer. Not much moral hazard or unconscious selfishness there, we thought. Somewhere in that winter afternoon, huddled around my little wood-burning stove, Ben and I talked about helmets and children without reaching any firm conclusions.

One thing we did agree on: as far as risk homeostasis is concerned, there is little to compare to our own grading system. If you are British, a VS climber or an E5 climber, you know exactly what level of risk you are prepared to take. Americans and French climbers take note: the British rock-grading system is a jewel. It offers the perfect expression of risk homeostasis.

# Art & Literature

Capt C A Werner (1877-1915), 2nd Battalion Rifle Brigade,
carried his ice axe into his last battle at Aubers Ridge,
an action rendered futile by poor artillery fire.

DONALD M ORR

# The Mountain Landscapes
# of Ferdinand Hodler

'View of the Lake of Thun from Breitlauenen' (1906),
oil on canvas, 65cm x 95cm. *(Kunstmuseum Basel)*

Ferdinand Hodler (1853-1918) was born in Bern where his childhood was
marred by poverty, illness and misunderstanding. He was the eldest of
six children but by the time he was eight years old he had lost his father
and two brothers to tuberculosis. At the age of nine he was assisting his
stepfather in painting signs and commercial artwork. Later as a student
he analysed and explored landscape and figure painting under Barthélemy
Menn, an admirer of Corot and the French Barbizon School; parallel to
these studies he was also influenced by medieval painting and the work of
Holbein. A brief stay in Paris in 1891 saw a maturity develop in his realism
and decorative abstraction whereby he was linked to the French Symbolists
and as his work expanded his 'style proved exciting to the publics other than
those in Switzerland.'[1] By 1900 he was closely associated with the avant-
garde style of Germany and Austria and regarded as part of the Secessionist
Movement in Vienna alongside Klimt and Schiele. As the century proceeded

---

1.  G H Hamilton, *Painting and Sculpture in Europe 1880-1940*, Harmondsworth, Penguin, 1967, p78.

'The Jungfrau Seen from Isenfluh'
(1902), oil on canvase, 75cm x 56cm.
*(Kunstmuseum Basel)*

'Self-Portrait' (1912), oil on canvas,
38.4cm x 29.5cm. *(Kunstmuseum
Basel)*

he came under the influence of the Fauvist movement in France and the German Expressionist painters with their European disciples.

This short paper will consider his mountain landscapes and, to a degree, how the great Symbolist friezes, the many self-portraits, the succession of drawings and paintings have concealed him as a major Alpine landscape painter.

In his late landscapes of the mountains around Lake Geneva he examined what he saw as the mystery of the Alpine landscape 'in spare lines and a few vivid colours, comparable to the best Fauve work.'[2] For Hodler the formal elements of the landscape were of themselves expressive and his insistence on heightened colour based on observation at varying times of the day and season, recording differing light and atmospheric effects allowed a vast range of experimental canvases, which in turn motivated many painters in Switzerland to understand the modern movements, and encouraged the transition from Impressionism to Symbolism. He scarcely left Geneva but became influential far beyond the frontier of Switzerland, becoming a prominent pulse in the work of Emile Nolde and the Die Brücke group in Germany. Kandinsky visited him in Geneva in 1906 and left strengthened by his expressionist colour and linear distortion and of Hodler's transcendental aesthetics. Towards the close of his life he 'had overcome the mistrust, and in the end became something of a national institution.'[3]

2. Ibid, p78.
3. Ibid, p70.

'Depicting the beauty, size and monumentality of the Alps was a project Hodler pursued nearly his entire life.'[4] Photographs show him at work in the open air on a large canvas beside the Grindelwald glacier in 1912 and reveal his continuing attempt to articulate the laws of nature, and thereby the world, through a series of closely examined studies of specific locations in the Alps that he returned to many times. The 'Eiger, Mönch and Jungfrau in Morning Sun' of 1908 is one of his earliest of the Jungfrau massif which was painted often whether as a group or individually and ranged from large canvases of the peaks to small studies of cliffs, snowfields and major features of the mountains. A series of canvases of the Dents du Midi were produced annually from 1911 from differing viewpoints as were various studies of the Breithorn, again from around 1911 onwards.

Landscape painting became an increasingly important activity towards the end of his life. Two paintings entitled 'The Jungfrau Massif from Mürren', both dated 1914[5], deal in detail with the vertical structure of planes and angles across this huge face where in one the bulk of the mountain is unfolded before us as it tapers to its summit and may indicate an awareness of the Cubist movement, while the other presents a tortured mass of abstracted rock and ice forming an impregnable series of ramparts that narrow as we ascend.

The colour variations of Alpine meadows also caught his eye in 'The Etangs Longs Near Montana' of 1915[6] allowing the use of his expressionistic colour scheme yet retaining a natural feel for distance, light and mountain structure. The following year detail and movement were principal features and two studies reminiscent of the Jungfrau series were produced at Champéry[7] where the force of the cascade flooding down is rendered in a naturalistic style but is still evocative of the rock and ice structures viewed from Mürren. Canvases of 'The Dents du Midi from Champéry' and 'The Dents Blanches at Champéry in the Morning Sun' also dominated his easel. 1917 saw Le Grammont featuring in several canvases along with 'The Dents du Midi from Caux' and the start of the long horizontal studies across Lake Geneva to Mont Blanc.

As his health deteriorated he seldom left his apartment and concentrated on the views of Mont Blanc and Lake Geneva at differing times and conditions, trying to render that aspect of infinity that fascinated him. In what was to be the last year of his life, Hodler focussed on the slim rectangular canvases depicting the mountain range across Lake Geneva produced, probably from his apartment at 29 Quai du Mont Blanc, Geneva. The dark of the mountain range, the heat of the new day rising beyond and both colour elements captured in the waters of the lake was recorded and rerecorded many times, allowing stark and stylish treatments from his Fauvist palette in numerous combinations but invariably outlined in blue: 'blue truly is the most important colour of Hodler's final years.'[8] His studies of this panorama

---

4. J Lloyd & U Küster (eds), *Ferdinand Hodler: View to Infinity*, Ostfildern, Hatje & Cantzl Verlag, 2013, p16.
5. The Jungfrau Massif from Mürren' (1904). Both oil on canvas, both 63 x 86cm. One is at the Musee d'Art et Histoire Ville de Genève. The other is at Fondation Saner, Stiftung für Schweitzer Kunst, Studen.
6. 'The Etangs Longs Near Montana' (1915). Oil on Canvas, 65.5 x 80cm. Private Collection.
7. 'Mountain Stream at Champéry' (1916). Both oil on canvas, the first, 83 x 98cm is at the Bünder Kuntsmuseum, Chur, the other, 69 x 87.5cm is at the Kuntsmuseum, Basel.
8. Lloyd & Küster, p20.

'Mount Niesen seen from Heustrich' (1910), oil on canvas, 83cm x 105.5cm.
*(Kunstmuseum Basel)*

were not limited to the early morning: 'Lake Geneva with Mont Blanc in the Afternoon, March 1918'[9] reveals a highly coloured but more naturalistic treatment of the subject where the high sun illuminates the snowy range and divides the mountains into snow and shadow against a pale blue sky, again echoed in the lake. Constantly seeking to express the eternity he saw everyday he was aware of his failing health and this prospect may well be reflected in 'Lake Geneva with Mont Blanc in the Mist, 1918'.[10] He died on 19 May 1918 in his Geneva apartment aged 65.

Hodler's international reputation has rested until recently on his major public works, often large-scale murals. On his return from France his work in the Symbolist style was polished and competent and was greatly enhanced by his adoption of a bright expressionistic palette. The demand for large scale Symbolic art in public buildings concentrated his efforts and made him famous in Switzerland, Austria and Germany. Such works as the 'March of the German Students into the War of Liberation of 1813'[11] 'The Night'[12]

9. 'Lake Geneva with Mont Blanc in the Afternoon, March 1918' (1918). Oil on canvas, 64 x 104cm. Private collection, Switzerland.
10. 'Lake Geneva with Mont Blanc in the Mist, 1918' (1918). Oil on canvas, 60 x 80cm. Private collection, Switzerland.
11. 'March of the German Students into the War of Liberation of 1813' (1908-09). Oil on canvas. Kustodie, Freidrich-Schiller-Universität Jena.
12. 'The Night'Painted (1889-90). Oil on canvas. Kunstmuseum, Berne.

'The Dents du Midi seen from Chesières' (1912), oil on canvas, 65.7cm x 88.3cm. *(Kunstmuseum Basel)*

and the more spiritually based 'The Chosen One' and 'Sacred Hour'[13] reveal the power of his figure painting, his ability to control large areas of colour, and his interest in thematic approaches to his subjects, never more so than in the colossal mural for the new town hall in Hanover: 'Unanimity'.[14] It may well be that on the strength of works like these he was commissioned by the National Bank of Switzerland to produce subjects for new bank notes. The resulting 'The Woodcutter' and 'The Mower' produced in 1907 were utilised by the bank but Hodler himself was never happy with their implementation and it must be noted that 'the history paintings intended to be specifically Swiss represent just a small part of his oeuvre.'[15]

It was in his largest, most expansive series that he ventured towards the notion of infinity. The number of individual figure studies, group sketches and final versions of 'View to Infinity' is quite colossal. Studies are held in Geneva, Stuttgart, Dallas, Zurich, Bern and Basel. The series was realised between 1907 and 1918; five versions of differing sizes exist, and these proved to be the last figure compositions that he would work on.

While much of his symbolic figure painting was based on the notion of 'parallelism', meaning the repetition of the similar, to produce an order, the same

13. 'The Chosen One' (1893-4) and 'Sacred Hour' (1907). Both oil on canvas. Berne and Zürich respectively.
14. 'Unanimity' (1911). Oil on canvas. Neues Rathaus, Hannover.
15. Lloyd & Küster, p11.

'Thunersee with Blüemlisalp and Niesen' (1912), oil on canvas, 27cm x 37cm.
*(Kunstmuseum Basel)*

method of construction is reflected in his many studies of the same mountain massif over the years most notably the views of the Alps from Geneva.

It would appear that the large public works and institutional honours bestowed on him have coloured the way successive art historians have regarded and written about Hodler. Generally, he is firmly placed as a European artist of the Fauvist-Expressionist movement heavily influenced by the French Symbolist movement. Yet it is through his interest in the spiritual aspects of life and his attempts to capture an essence of infinity through figurative renditions that he came to realise that human properties were simply breaths that go forth and that a greater, more enduring image faced him across Lake Geneva. It is uncertain when he seriously turned to landscape painting but by 1895 he was heavily involved in recording the structures, light and colour of the Alps. In the summer of 1917 he vowed he would not accept any further commissions and would commit himself to pursuing the infinite in what he referred to as 'paysages planétaires': planetary landscapes.

Looking at his work now, the public murals and Symbolist canvases appear very dated and firmly located in the art historical past. His serious self-portraits still stand the test of time but by far his most impressive work, still retaining a timeless element, is found in the many landscapes he produced throughout his native country. He stands alone as the one artist in European art history who continuously explored the mountain environ-

'The Dents Blanches at Champéry in the Morning Sun' (1916), oil on canvas, 64cm x 90cm. *(Kunstmuseum Basel)*

ment in all its aspects from mountain streams, rock formations, snowfields and glaciers. While his mountain colour schemes are dominated by the Fauve-Expressionistic palette he adopted, his compositions varied greatly in size and structure, many painted from a considerable height or, in the case of the views across Lake Geneva, at a distance allowing an entire range of mountains to be recorded. His 'ability to capture the essence of that mountainous country'[16] and his many attempts to encapsulate the ethereal nature of the mountain expanse and vastness, and the timelessness of sunlight upon the high peaks, place his work in a unique category only touched on occasionally by a few who would take on that restless realism and the quest for an essence of infinity.

Paintings are never merely about their subject matter; mountain landscapes have the capacity to take us beyond the simple view depicted on canvas towards that sense of infinity and the eternal that many intuit in colour and illusionistic depth. This is 'mountain scenery as leading the mind beyond what the eye sees.'[17] The summit experience is unique to each of us. Something distinctive happens at that exclusive spot between the viewer and the viewed, between the climber and the climbed that is personal and special to the mountaineer. In the same way, mountain imagery, depicted or textual,

16.  Lloyd & Küster, p9.
17.  S Schama, *Landscape and Memory*, London, Fontana, 1995, p473.

'Lake Geneva with Jura Hills' (1911), oil on canvas, 68cm x 90.5cm.
*(Kunstmuseum Basel)*

has a profound impact on the individual imagination, whether painter, poet or climber. The poem 'Mont Blanc' 'begins and ends in the caverns of Shelley's own mind.'[18]

Hodler intensified the scene before him through the limitlessness of blue tones to give a sense of unending landscape within a simple two-dimensional plane. His articulation of the infinite, attempting to evoke the idea of eternity by means of a contemplation into the vastness of the distance from his studio window, is a unique form of expression. There are no symbols of transience in his late landscapes despite his concentration on the evanescence of the lake or the ephemeral nature of the mountain light. The abstract, expansive horizontality of the landscape elements is made more forceful in their simplicity, imbuing his images with a soothing expressive power. Life is seen against the backdrop of eternity; a timelessness awaiting us articulated in the limpid austerity of the scene, a reflection of his own peace of mind at that time: open, calm, and stretching off to the horizon. Hodler's persistence in the refinement of his mountain images, his vision of eternity, and the effortlessness of his colour usage in his panoramas viewed across Lake Geneva show nothing so clearly as a vision of infinity we may crave, the potential scenery of our inner selves. In these canvases Hodler not only indicates direction of the serenity we require but can also reveal our point of departure.

18. Ibid, p489.

TERRY GIFFORD

# Mountaineering Literature as Dark Pastoral

We were a 70-year-old father and a 40-year-old son on our annual May Day climbing trip to Scotland from Somerset and Lincolnshire respectively. We had just avoided a rock climb in these inauspicious conditions and had turned away from the darkness of a dangerous uncertainty. Now we could enjoy the pastoral view with a mixture of relief and relaxed delight. Not that our unroped 'walk' to reach this point had been without its dark moments; we had negotiated an undercut diagonal ramp of heather, rock and woodrush grass below the mountain's summit rock wall. Even the rock-climbing guide advised that 'great care should be exercised when ascending Ledge 3 as it involves exposed moves on dubious combinations of heather and crumbling rock.' But now, as we leaned back on our heavy rucksacks of unused climbing gear in the sodden heather, we could zip up tight against the wind and watch the lightshow of sea and mist and sun in contention below.

It had begun with the familiar narrative of following a burn up over a boulder-strewn lip into a high corrie. In his book *At The Sharp End* (1988) Paul Nunn described this experience of walking into a mountain valley for a mountaineer as one of warm recognition: 'one feels that one is coming home.' He probably knew that he was echoing John Muir who wrote of late 19th century Americans discovering their first national parks, that 'going to the mountains is going home.' But Nunn was also aware that these were dangerous environments, referring enigmatically to an 'inescapable foreboding in Llanberis or Glencoe'. Writing about walking on the approach to climbs in the Himalaya under seracs he knew that at this stage of the mountaineering narrative death was not far away: 'One day soon some must fall. Oh, that we will not be there!' On 6 August 1995, walking down from the summit of Haramosh II (6666m) in the Karakoram range, close to his base camp Paul Nunn was killed by a falling serac. An experienced and respected figure in world mountaineering, whose caution had resulted in a succession of expeditions on which he had turned back before the summit, Paul is still greatly missed by those of us in the Sheffield climbing community who benefitted from his generous and lively friendship.

In *Reconnecting with John Muir* (2006) I argued that the literature of mountaineering, at its best, could be read as post-pastoral: enacting the classic pastoral movement of retreat and return, but all too aware of the dangers of idealisation in an unforgiving and unstable environment. Discussing the amazing variety, quantity and quality of mountaineering literature I wrote that 'the earliest British alpinists were scholars of English literature who

Terry Gifford's ideas about mountain literature being a form of 'dark pastoralism' are illustrated by the work of an artist whose work at least echoes that idea. Paul Evans was an outstanding sport climber and boulderer in the 1980s and 1990s living in Sheffield, and his insight as a climber undoubtedly informs this sequence of paintings of gritstone edges near the city. Evans is known for his cooperation with the academic world and creative writers and the focus of his work is nature, although more from the biological perspective than the Romantic. He wants his paintings to move viewers 'in the experience of both body and mind', and quotes James Elkins, who saw painting as 'liquid thinking'. 'In the final analysis,' Evans writes, 'my aim is to achieve something of a fragile balance between order and entropy. So, when successful, the paintings signify (for me at least) something of the fragile, yet sublime, beauty of nature in all its forms.' For more information on Evans and his work, see *www.pkevans.co.uk*. This first painting is 'Burbage South', oil and mixed media on canvas, 113cm x 70cm. *(All paintings reproduced with permission of the artist.)*

wrote about their new sport as an escape from their professional business of writing about other people's writing'. This tradition has continued from Leslie Stephen, the Victorian literary critic and author of *The Playground of Europe* (1871), to the journalist, poet and writer Geoffrey Winthrop Young, to the adult education university lecturer in English literature George Mallory, to the languages teacher Wilfrid Noyce, author of *Scholar Mountaineers* (1950), to Al Alvarez, kingmaker of poets in the 1950s and 1960s as literary editor of the *Observer*, and on to the *Guardian* writer and editor of the *Alpine Journal* Ed Douglas.

Women mountaineers, although fewer in number, have been equally talented writers, from the prolific American Himalayan explorer Fanny Bullock Workman, author of seven books published around the opening of the 20th century, to Dorothy Pilley, wife of the critic I A Richards and author of *Climbing Days* (1935), to Janet Adam Smith, literary editor of the *New Statesman* (1952-60) and biographer of John Buchan, to Katie Ives, current editor of the American journal *Alpinist*.

Anthologies of the best of this literary tradition abound, including *The Winding Trail: A Selection of Articles and Essays for Walkers and Backpackers* (1981), which retains a definitive status. Actually, an anthology for walkers titled *The Open Road: A Little Book for Wayfarers* (1899) was a set text for D H Lawrence at Nottingham University College when he took his teacher's certificate examinations. Of course, Lawrence was a keen walker, having heard of the outbreak of the First World War only when he descended from a walking tour in the Lake District. He famously crossing the Alps with Frieda in what served as a rather trying honeymoon during which they occasionally lost their way on mountain passes.

When Heather I Sullivan coined the term 'dark pastoral' in 2016 she did not have in mind the mountaineering experience or its vast and varied literature. Her conception was a larger one that could characterise literature in a pastoral mode that engaged with the paradoxes of the Anthropocene in a strategic 'doubled movement closer towards and away from green fantasies.' By 'refusing to separate our green dreams from the material manifestations of the new toxic nature' dark pastoral 'enacts the Anthropocene's vivid extremes.'[1] Might the 'green dreams' of a mountaineer's apparently feeling 'at home' in an environment that is not untouched by the consequences of the Anthropocene be read in the frame of dark pastoral? Wherever the mountaineer looks there is evidence of the Anthropocene and a growing sense of culpability, from the micro-level of plant disturbance by the 'gardening' of cracks by rock climbers documented by Paula Wright in *Alpinist*[2] to the macro-level of the problems presented to the mountaineer by glacial retreat in the Anthropocene reported in the *Alpine Journal*.[3] What mountain walkers refer to as the daily 'conditions' is, of course, the micro-evidence of the Anthropocene. A walker on Ben Nevis on 21 August 2017 would find no snow patches anywhere on the mountain that day. She might not know that this is the first day for eleven years that this has been the case, but she is most likely observing climate change at work. Walkers in mountains, who by definition must have 'green dreams' of a certain kind, are also only too aware of the agency of their environment and judging that agency is, of course, what is happening when mountaineers and hill-walkers 'assess the conditions', as my son and I were doing, to avoid dangerous choices.

So there is clearly a relationship between a literal sense of dark pastoral as an experience of personal danger in a beautiful and often idealised mountain environment, and the human culpability in contributing to the larger forces of climate as weather, or climate change as rock fall, or global warming as glacial retreat. As Sullivan puts it, 'dark pastoral is [also] a means of thinking in terms of material ecocriticism's emphasis on flows and non-human agency together with human agency.' So might Sullivan's notion of dark pastoral offer a sharper, more nuanced way of reading mountaineering

1. H Sullivan, 'The Dark Pastoral: Goethe and Atwood', *Green Letters*, 20(1), 2016, p48.
2. P Wright, 'Refuge', *Alpinist* 58, 2017, pp105-10.
3. W Haeberli, 'The Alps without Ice?', *Alpine Journal* 2008, pp201-2 and J Bamber, R Alley and D Lunt 'The Response of Glaciers to Climate Change', *Alpine Journal*, 2017, pp143-54.

literature? What might be highlighted and what might be overlooked in applying this frame to reading this body of work? Indeed, what might be considered to be lacking in the literature if it is read as 'dark pastoral' in Sullivan's sense of 'green fantasies' shadowed by the Anthropocene? In order to provide a current sample of the genre one might consider the five very different books shortlisted for the Boardman Tasker Award for Mountain Literature in 2016 for which the current author was one of the three judges.

Alex Honnold's book *Alone on the Wall*, written with David Roberts, describes the life of an un-roped solo climber as its sensational subject. Its cover shows Honnold walking across the thank-god ledge high on the north-west face of Half Dome at the head of Yosemite Valley. Honnold has his back to the wall and below his toes there is a vast drop as he edges sideways along the exposed ledge that is going to get narrower than his foot before he reaches a vertical crack. This is mountain climbing at its most simple and committing. But it is the quality of Honnold's articulation of his approach to this purest of pursuits that engages the reader, together with his honesty about the personal costs of his lifestyle and amazing achievements. He is philosophical when his girlfriend finally decided that, not only could she no longer watch his moving up, and then down, unroped, as he found the way to succeed on difficult moves, but that her own career could no longer be sacrificed to Honnold's nomadic lifestyle. On the other hand, Honnold's lifestyle led to his creation of the Honnold Foundation. After five years of living out of a van, the twenty-six year old was earning enough to have surplus income to donate to projects that make environmentally low impact, sustainable, alleviations of poverty worldwide. 'I'm deeply worried about the future of the world in the face of climate change, the unbridled use of fossil fuels, and so on. It's this passion, as much as anything, that led to the idea of the Honnald Foundation.' At the end of the book, Honnold, still in his twenties, writes: 'With my Honnold Foundation, what I really hope to do in the coming years is to improve the lives of the most vulnerable people in the world in a way that helps the environment. To support projects that both help the earth and lift people out of poverty.' Honnold's ability to control his fear and have complete faith in the techniques of his body to read rock in situations that define the sublime might provide one sense of dark pastoral. But his choosing to use his skill of bodily attunement to material nature to alleviate the consequences of the Anthropocene for some vulnerable groups of people completes a 'double movement' – in Sullivan's terms – of both horrific personal risk and environmental generosity.

More indirectly perhaps, this is also the case with Mark Vallance's memoir *Wild Country: the Man who Made Friends*. Following a traditional mentorship as a schoolboy by his head-teacher Robin Hodgkin and Sir Jack Longland, the father of his best friend, Vallance committed to the cold pastoral of Antarctica where he was base commander of the UK's most southerly scientific station at Halley Bay. It was here that the first of a succession of difficult decisions in his life tested his personal judgement and integrity. But his crucial life-changing decision followed his meeting, whilst climbing in

'Curbar', oil and mixed media on canvas, 113cm x 70cm. 'By applying paint in both upright and horizontal planes,' Evans says, 'I aim to exploit the drying, dripping and sedimentary processes to the full. Flooding the canvas on the floor allows beautiful tidemarks to appear as the paint dries. When the canvas is in the vertical plane, drips create a gravity-driven dynamic. Although there is a great deal of risk in this process, the results – with their direct correlation to processes that occur in nature – are often meditative in effect.' *(Paul Evans)*

America, with Ray Jardine who had invented what became known as 'the Friends'. They had too many parts to be judged commercially viable by US manufacturers, so Vallance came home to Derbyshire to take the financial risk and construct Friends himself on his kitchen table, with a welcome boost from his appearance on the TV show *Tomorrow's World*. Thus was his business Wild Country formed and as it prospered Vallance established the Wild Country Foundation, writing, 'I wanted to make a forceful statement to the climbing world that a company was willing to take a stand in favour of certain values to do with sustainability and strong ethics, much as Patagonia does now in the United States.' The explicit aims were 'the promotion of adventure in climbing and the preservation of the climbing environment'. Eight years down the line, when he found that his business partner wanted to make and sell military equipment, Vallance made a bold decision to sell out to him, although in the end it was his partner who sold to Vallance. Meanwhile, expecting to lose Wild Country, Vallance had committed to opening an imaginatively designed outdoor store in the countryside of the Peak District called Outside, the success of which led to the building of the first modern climbing gym in Britain, the Foundry, in Sheffield.

   Five years of working for the Peak District National Park on return from the Antarctic informed six years on the board of the national park board as

'Curbar', oil and mixed media on canvas, 113cm x 70cm. In contrast to the dynamic effect of drips, this perspective of Curbar is about accretion with the depth of paint on the main part of the crag fissuring in a way that dominates the viewer's attention. *(Paul Evans)*

a nominee of the BMC where Vallance had been founding secretary of the Access and Conservation Committee, organising a mountain conservation symposium in 1977. So it was no surprise when he became president of the BMC in 2002, although there was a darker reason for his decision. He had been diagnosed with Parkinson's disease, but wanted to keep 'involved in the mountaineering world': 'I like to think of my loss as the BMC's gain, but not everyone would agree with that.' Part of the reason for the success of *Wild Country* is the way in which it demonstrates that the spirit brought to bear on friendships, climbs, tough business dilemmas and BMC management, can ultimately be harnessed to deal with the onset of Parkinson's disease. But at its heart is an appreciation of upland pastoral landscapes and their vulnerability, especially for walkers and climbers in Britain, Vallance's version of Sullivan's 'double movement'.

That an apprenticeship on British uplands can lead to dark experiences on snowy mountains is illustrated in Simon McCartney's book, *The Bond*, although the reader might be left feeling that his personal survival is most in doubt in McCartney's account of two climbs in Alaska. The title is the theme of his book: the bond between climbers upon which he increasingly comes to rely in his accounts of two epic new routes in Alaska in 1978 and 1980 that demonstrate a remarkable self-awareness verging upon hubris, as he readily admits. It would be easy to say of this book that it is mostly dark with very little pastoral in that McCartney survives these two climbs only through a combination of luck and the generosity of other climbers.

The beautiful mountains that he chose to climb happen to be the most dangerous and the realisation after the second of these epics that both his skills and his psyche could not and must not be tested to such a degree ever again leads to his giving up mountaineering altogether. For a mountaineering audience such qualities resulted in this book, written with the hindsight of thirty years, winning the Boardman Tasker Award for 2016. From an eco-critical perspective perhaps the most telling image in the book is captioned 'The lighting of Studio City Macau is typical of our company's design build activity in Asia – calculated risks all.' Now living between Australia and Hong Kong McCartney makes his living from designing architectural lighting projects. In the Anthropocene such light offers an image of a very dark urban pastoral.

Also short-listed in 2016 was the biography of an Australian who travelled in the opposite direction and made his life in Britain. Robert Wainwright's biography of the Australian rebel George Finch, *The Maverick Mountaineer: The Remarkable Life of George Ingle Finch: Climber, Scientist, Inventor*, who demonstrated the value of oxygen in reaching almost 27,000ft on Everest in 1922, reveals an eccentric scientist and inventor with a complicated personal life. As a 13-year-old boy he was inspired to become a mountaineer by a view from a hill over the New South Wales bush in the spring of 1901: 'The picture was beautiful; precise and accurate as the work of a draughtsman's pen, but fuller of meaning than any map.' Although conceived as an artifice, this view was embedded with 'meaning' as well as 'accuracy'. 'I had made up my mind to see the world; to see it from above, from the tops of mountains whence I could get that wide and comprehensive view which is denied to those who observe things from their own plane.' George and his brother Max found themselves living in Paris with their bohemian mother and they began a traditional Alpine education by employing guides. Eventually one of the best climbers in Europe, George Finch also excelled academically and devoted himself initially to researching the development of chemical technology at Imperial College, London. Finch's research and personal experiments led him to controversially advocate the use of oxygen in early Everest expeditions, much against the views of the establishment and the cynicism of fellow climbers. But Finch's research back at Imperial College on his return from Everest came to earn him an international scientific reputation: he became a fellow of the Royal Society and a member of the panel awarding the Nobel Prize for physics. That research ranged widely in exploring various modes of fuel efficiency that had industrial applications taken up in a variety of worldwide industries. Quite clearly Finch was a mountaineer who was engaged with the Anthropocene in a practical scientific contribution before the Anthropocene was announced. So, without intending to, Wainwright's book exemplifies several dimensions of dark pastoral.

Finally, and by way of complete contrast, the shortlist of the Boardman Tasker Award included American science writer Steve Olson's book about a mountain event, *Eruption: The Untold Story of Mount St. Helens* (2016). When a smoking Mount St Helens actually erupted at 8.30 on the spring Sunday morning of 18 May 1980, 57 people were killed. Olson not only tells their personal stories, he also turns the tension between the science and the cultural assumptions at play on that day into a tragic thriller. Olson intends his book as a kind of allegory about our attitudes towards our planet in the Anthropocene, 'thinking the risk was small'. The mountain had been smoking for almost two months and the Forest Service had not closed off the areas where those camping out that weekend chose to pitch their tents and tarps. Olson carefully untangles the conflicting positions of the scientists, commercial logging interests, the Forest Service, politicians of different levels, conservationists, forest cabin owners and the recreational users of the mountain. It is a case study in the mismanagement of a natural event in which economic interests guided policymaking that put hikers and others at risk. That more people did not die was a matter of luck. If it had been a weekday hundreds of loggers would have been killed. On the Saturday or the Sunday afternoons there would have been day hikers. Only the weekend before, the Mount St Helens Protective Association had led a group of twenty local people on a hike up the Green River to show supporters the old growth trees that they wanted to save from the loggers. The Forest Service gave them the all clear, but an elderly mountaineer in the party, who had climbed Mount St Helens twenty times, became increasingly uncomfortable and returned to his car. Actually, ash fell three feet thick up to 20 miles north of the mountain. Downwind to the east two inches of ash fell from a black cloud 150 miles away. Olson reports that, 'students at Washington State University in Pullman, on the border with Idaho, made emergency runs to the convenience store to stock up on beer.'

In his epilogue, Olson points out the allegorical significance of this story as 'everyone on earth faces the certainty of higher temperatures, more intense storms, degraded ecosystems, and higher sea levels as we continue to pump more carbon dioxide into the atmosphere. In many ways we are all like the people camping northwest of Mount St Helens in the weeks and days before the volcano's eruption, blissfully unaware of the risks we face.' *Eruption* represents the epitome of the dark pastoral: walkers drawn by the direct experience of pastoral awe, many of them having an intimate knowledge of this mountain, had underestimated its dark potential for life-threatening instability, having been left exposed by the compromises and complacency of the politicians and land managers. If 'going to the mountains is going home', this is a home about which many things are still to be understood, including our best relationship with it.

One evening, from our camp at Lochranza below the mountains on the Isle of Arran, Tom and I took a walk back into the history of geological knowledge. From our sea level campsite we walked along the raised beach to round Newton Point under increasingly high former sea cliffs to search for Hutton's Unconformity. Tom had a degree in geology and hopping across rocks on the shoreline he found it first, explaining that, at this point the grey Precambrian schists sloping one way were overlaid by the sedimentary red sandstone sloping the other way. It was precisely here in 1787

'Derwent Edge', oil and mixed media on canvas, 113cm x 70cm. *(Paul Evans)*

that James Hutton first began his deductions that undermined the biblical view of the single-moment creation of the earth by showing that its formation came from processes that are still continuously at work, as indeed, the raised beach on which we camped demonstrated. Hutton's paper of 1788 concluded: 'The result, therefore, of our present enquiry is, that we find no vestige of a beginning, no prospect of an end.'[4] It was at this very spot on Arran that the modern science of geology began, and it is due to be changed again by the continuing, indeed accelerated, processes of the Anthropocene as the sea rises to cover our campsite. Both short and long-term 'darknesses' are at work on this pastoral mountainous island. Awareness of this lends a certain frisson to the psychogeography of walking on Arran, just as it does to reading contemporary mountaineering literature.

Yet, since we walkers and wanders in mountains are also wonderers, I could not help feeling that there was something missing from this notion of dark pastoral, something prompted by walking beside my son and wondering about his daughters, strong walkers and wonderers already. What exactly is this need to walk where we do not live and work, and to walk on mountains in sight of a sea that will eventually submerge our homes in Somerset and Lincolnshire? What do we take back from this archipelagic pastoral momentum of retreat and return between periphery and centre? Perhaps it is a higher hope that can engage with the darknesses, for all the unsatisfactory and paradoxically unsustainable costs of our journeys of retreat.

Perhaps it is a belief that the fundamental power of awe will inform our

4.  J Hutton, 'Theory of the Earth', *Transactions of the Royal Society of Edinburgh* 1, 1788, p304.

anxieties, that awe and anxiety will heighten each other as, back in our home places, we negotiate our daily dilemmas carrying these precious memories as core values, which, in turn, are why we contemplate a notion like the dark pastoral itself. Indeed, the challenge in negotiating this 'double movement' towards and away from our 'green dreams' is to avoid the darkness overwhelming the pastoral. It is certain that we must not only accept losses of biodiversity and losses in recalibrating what counts as quality of human life, but accept losses in our lives in order to have any long-term hope. But how much loss for how much hope? Perhaps we should all take a walk and talk that through.

### 'Tidemark', 75m, Severe, Cíoch na h-Oighe, Isle of Arran, 1 May 2017

Is it dry?

    The grey rock is dry.

But we have to cross those two
wet patches of weeping moss.

    Wet feet onto dry rock.

Is the wind a problem round the arête?

    We'll not hear each other.

Is that mist rising or falling?

    Hard to tell in this wind.

Well, we've pushed it to get here
traversing those wet rock moves in big boots.

    I took a different line
    but it was still dodgy.

Are these twa corbies
telling us something?

    Perhaps they have.

Shall we wait awhile?

    We are.

Have we made a decision?

    I think we have.

Do you see that shaft of light on the sea?

    It's changing by the second.

What a place to be.

    Two hours from the car
    and up that wet heather ramp.

Shall we go to the summit?

    Let's wait a bit longer.

We are.

    Look at that sea
    Shining back the sunlight.

Now there's the ferry.

    What a place to be.

Let's wait a bit longer.

JONNY DRY

# Challenging the Mountaineer's Gaze

## A Sixty-Year Education on Kangchenjunga

There are many spellings of the name 'Kangchenjunga' and many meanings too: 'Five Treasures of the Snow'[1]; 'Five Treasure Houses of the Great Snow'[2]; 'Five Treasure Houses *in* the Snow'[3]; and on and on. Laurence Waddell's ungainly 'Five Repositories of the Great Glaciers' illustrates what a fundamentally inadequate process it can be trying to represent someone else's culture: an unfortunate but perhaps inevitable consequence of translation.[4] A greater concern is how the name has become a sort of brand name, or slogan, shorthand for how Kangchenjunga and its local communities are perceived. The complexity of the region, its communities and their beliefs, are somehow bundled into a single neat package, turning complex and sometimes contrasting perspectives into a malleable commodity, to be side-lined or incorporated into the mountaineer's own culture. As Michael Hutt wrote about James Hilton's fictional creation Shangri-La, 'the continued perception of the Himalayan countries as magical realms also feeds back into political and social processes.' In preferring cultural constructs to reality, the Himalayan traveller can miss a great deal.[5]

The boundary Kangchenjunga straddles isn't just geographical: it's cultural and religious too. It illustrates the distinctions between Sikkim and Nepal, and indigenous groups: Lepcha and Lhopo. Reading mountaineering literature against such a backdrop, it becomes clear that while climbing writers learned significantly from the communities around Kangchenjunga, they also co-opted beliefs and attitudes that are infinitely more nuanced and complex than can ever be truthfully displayed on the page.

In 1883 William Woodman Graham travelled to Dzongri in Sikkim, among the very first alpinists to climb in the Himalaya. After an encouraging start that spring, climbing a 5,000m peak on the Singalila Ridge, he sat out the monsoon and then set off for the Kabru range, climbing three more peaks including a claimed ascent of Kabru itself. Yet when he returned to Britain, Martin Conway and anonymous voices in the Survey of India, poured scorn on his claim, a judgement shared later by the American

1. F Smythe, *The Kangchenjunga Adventure*, London, Hodder & Stoughton, 1946, p15.
2. J Tasker, *Savage Arena*, London, Methuen, 1982, p161.
3. C Bremer-Kamp, *Living on the Edge*, Utah, Peregrine Smith Book, 1987, p42.
4. S Pierse, 'Kangchenjunga: Imaging a Himalayan Mountain', ResearchGate, 2005.
5. M Hutt, 'Looking for Shangri-La: From Hilton to Lamichhane', in *Eloquent Hills: Essays on Nepali Literature*, Nepal, Martin Chautari, 2012, p83.

Tenchaddar praying

Mountain of Destiny: Kanchenjunga 1929
The illustrations for this article are taken from a new exhibition of photographs from the 1929 German Kangchenjunga expedition presented to E O Shebbeare and paintings of Kangchenjunga by the landscape artist Julian Cooper. They are reproduced with kind permission of the German Alpine Club and Sue Morton. The exhibition was curated by Dr Jonathan Westaway, University of Central Lancashire. See right for details.

William Workman, both of them rival claimants to Graham's altitude record. Graham published no accounts of his exploits and disappeared from the mountaineering world after being rejected by the Alpine Club, reappearing later in life in Mexico, as British vice-consul in Durango. [Editor's Note: For a reappraisal of Graham's adventure, see W Blaser & G Hughes, 'Kabru 1883: A Reassessment', *Alpine Journal*, 2009, pp219-28.]

Although no literature exists of Graham's first mountaineering foray to Sikkim, it captures something of the mysticism Kangchenjunga holds in the western imagination. It also reveals a paradox at the heart of mountain literature, because climbers also usually put the summit first and everything else sits in relation to it. That is a problem in a location like Kangchenjunga, which is a sacred space for the people who live near it. Summits don't mean much at all to them.

The community there is complex and diverse: Lepcha, Lhopo and Nepali groups occupy the Sikkim and Mechi regions on the flanks of Kangchenjunga. Lepcha are the indigenous people; Lhopo are essentially ethnic Tibetans with a longstanding presence in Sikkim. The influence of Nyingma Buddhist traditions on Lepcha and Lhopo culture is deep. Buddhist tradition teaches that Guru Rinpoche, known in Sanskrit as Padmasambhava,

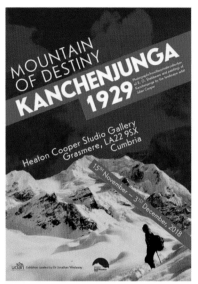

In 1929 the modern state of Germany launched its first Himalayan mountaineering expedition under the leadership of Paul Bauer. Its goals were explicitly nationalistic, motivated by a desire to rebuild faith in German manhood and leave behind the defeat and humiliation of the First World War. Bauer's various accounts of the Kangchenjunga expeditions in 1929 and 1931 are shot through with military metaphors and the language of struggle. His celebration of mountaineering comradeship harks back to the camaraderie of the trenches. Underpinning it all was a sense of German national destiny expressed in the language of racial theory.

But if the expedition's goal was to establish German mountaineers on the world stage it also brought them into contact with the multi-ethnic world of the Himalaya. The photographs taken by Bauer and his colleagues Julius Brenner and Dr Eugen Allwein exhibit a strong ethnographic sensibility, sensitive to the ethnic diversity of Sikkim and the wider region. Sherpa and Bhotia high-altitude workers are accorded special attention. They featured in group photographs and individual portraits. One remarkable photograph features the expedition cook Tenchaddar, seated outside a tent, praying in the half lotus position. It's a sublime image but underlines the fact that European mountaineers often ignored or belittled the spiritual practices of the expeditionary labour force they relied on.

This collection is unique, being annotated by E O Shebbeare, the British transport officer on the 1929 Kangchenjunga expedition. A forestry official and founder member of the Himalayan Club, Shebbeare was able to name most of the Sherpas featured in the photographs, preserving for us their individuality. In one tender portrait a group of seven Sherpas lies in the grass, smiling at the camera, twirling Edelweiss in their hands. The flowers, a symbolic link with the Germans' own Bavarian homeland, signal a tranquil moment before the fruitless struggle on the north-east ridge.

*Mountain of Destiny: Kanchenjunga 1929* captures a unique moment in German Himalayan mountaineering before the deadly focus on Nanga Parbat consumed so many mountaineering lives and before German and Austrian mountaineering organisations became subsumed into the Nazi Reich.

*Mountain of Destiny is at the Heaton Cooper Studio Gallery, Grasmere, Cumbria, from 15 November 2018, part of the Kendal Mountain Festival 2018.*
*https://www.heatoncooper.co.uk/*

E O Shebbeare's remarkable album takes care to identify workers employed on the 1929 Kangchenjunga expedition. *(All images with kind permission of the German Alpine Club (DAV) and Sue Morton)*

hid secret treasure texts in the Himalaya in the eighth century but narratives change from village to village.[6] Migration from what is now the modern state of Nepal dates back to long before the early 19th century and the East Indian Company's war with Nepal and the British military's 1888 action against Sikkim. But it was British hegemony that transformed the demographics of Sikkim, where the majority is now Nepali.[7] You can see how the anthropological tapestry surrounding Kangchenjunga is woven with a myriad of strands.[8]

The problem with mountain literature is that it often fails to communicate this complexity. There are always 'many layers of meditation between the world as it really is, and the world as it is subsequently rendered in travel writing.'[9] There is sometimes a clear preference for aesthetic style over objective accuracy. More often, portrayals of local people reveal unconscious assumptions in the writer and, indeed, the reader.[10] In mountain literature, such assumptions take the form of reaching the summit and fulfilling personal and cultural expectations. This cannot not, in itself, be considered a criticism. Mountaineering has long been documented as the pursuit of one's personal desires: 'Have we vanquished an enemy?' asks George Mallory.

6. A Denjongpa, 'Kangchendzönga: Secular and Buddhist Perceptions of the Mountain Deity of Sikkim among the Lhopos', *Bulletin of Tibetology*, 2002, Vol 38 No 2, pp5-37, p7.
7. M Hutt, 'Going to Mugalan: Nepali Literary Representations of Migration to India and Bhutan', *Eloquent Hills: Essays on Nepali Literature*, Nepal, Martin Chautari, 2012, pp99-101.
8. C Scheid, 'Hidden Land and Changing Landscape: Narratives about Mount Khangchendzonga among the Lepcha and Lhopo', *Journal of the Irish Society for the Academic Study of Religions*, 2014, Vol 1 No 1, pp66-89, p71.
9. C Thompson, *Travel Writing*, Abingdon, Routledge, 2011, p62.
10. Ibid, p133-4.

'None but ourselves.'[11] Or as Robert MacFarlane's wide ranging *Mountains of the Mind* (2003) makes apparent, the history of mountaineering 'isn't really a history of mountaineering at all [...] but a history of the imagination'. One may raise a question as to the broader value of mountaineering and its narcissistic drive, as well as both its environmental and cultural impact, particularly in a consumerist world, something rarely acknowledged.

Taking a broad 60-year sweep of literature on Kangchenjunga, from Frank Smythe's *The Kangchenjunga Adventure* (1930), to Joe Tasker's *Savage Arena* (1982) and Cherie Bremer-Kamp's *Living on the Edge* (1987), we are shown repeatedly the visceral power of the mountain as a mystical peak. As so often with mountain literature, self-absorbed with its own motivations, there is a failure to acknowledge properly the origins of an appropriated mysticism among the very communities that live and work at its foot. Although there are distinctions to be made between the three, particularly when considering the colonial shadow which hangs over Smythe, there is in all of them a tension common in mountain literature, one which simultaneously idealises the spiritual – co-opting it to the broader romanticised narrative of mountaineering – but misses local spiritual beliefs that are a key element to that narrative.

Mountain literature is rarely innovative, following a predictable arc that often starts with the origins of a personal story. Yet these origins are essential for understanding how a writer approaches any form of difference.[12] Geoffrey Winthrop Young noted that even as a young boy 'it was the fact of hills' that attracted him, 'their provoking mystery, and [...] their wilfulness in trying to go up where everything else was content to lie along.'[13] Smythe, writing later, developed this further, equating the feeling of mountains rising ever higher with 'promotion to the top of the form, where for a short time I remained, basking in the sun of the Geography Master's approval.'[14] The west, Robert Macfarlane suggests, has an inherent desire to ascend ever higher, quoting from Gaston Bachelard's 'Air and Dreams' that 'a human being in his youth [...] wants to rise up from the earth.' For early writers, Kangchenjunga, as with the wider Himalaya, was the natural progression for such ambitions, seeded in youth: 'to some the British hills are an end in themselves, and to others the Alps, but the "Journey's End" of the mountaineer is the summit of Everest.'[15] Whilst less explicit, both Tasker and Bremer-Kamp are caught up in that same 'beckoning silence of great height', as Joe Simpson called it, motivated by a desire to go ever higher and harder. If mountaineering in the 1970s and 1980s had progressed somewhat from simply attaining the summit to reaching it in a cleaner style by harder routes, the underlying motivators remain the same.

11. G Mallory, 'Mont Blanc from the Col du Géant by the Eastern Buttress of Mont Maudit', *Alpine Journal*, 1918, Vol XXXII, pp148-62, p162.
12. Thompson, 2011, pp16-7.
13. G Young, *On High Hills*, London, Methuen, 1947, p2.
14. Smythe, 1946, p11.
15. Ibid.

An informal portrait of seven of the team's Sherpas and other ethnic high-altitude workers. *(DAV, Morton)*

Lewa. *(DAV, Morton)*

Tenchaddar in more conventional climbing garb. *(DAV, Morton)*

*I was beginning to see that my whole life was dependent upon the pursuit of a most difficult and unlikely goal – the climbing of mountains by their hardest route. All my hopes and aspirations seemed to have become linked with that objective, and I no longer knew if I wanted that sort of life.*[16]

These motivations for climbing, whether looking to early Romantics who describe the revealed panorama of 'earth, and air, and earth-embracing sea' seen from the summit, or the more established genre of mountain literature, is the beguiling notion of utopia that mountains elicit. The very act of a journey is 'utopian because it is driven by hopeful expectation in one form or another.'[17] Utopias, however, are often specific to an individual or community. In mountain literature, whether writing with the self-awareness of Tasker or in the loose framework of colonialism we associate with Smythe, it is clear that the pursued ideal is to occupy that space. Smythe talks of 'attack'. Bremer-Kamp rejects such notions of conquest in favour of 'developing a rapport with the mountain to see what she might give us in return.'[18] The feminised language of Bremer-Kamp is a notable distinction to make between these writers, indicative of her broader concern with engaging with her surroundings. Smythe wants merely to triumph over a monster:

*like a two-headed giant [...] this face, which overlooks the Yalung Glacier, is savage and cruel. Even as I watched, there came a distant roar, the snowy lips of the giant writhed back, and an avalanche was spat out from between its teeth.*[19]

This is a conscious attempt to imagine creatively the ferocity of his surroundings, but such language creates an antagonism between man and nature. Bremer-Kamp's description, tinged with the same aesthetic drive to describe her surroundings with 'snarling, gaping jaws', tempers this with a heightened awareness; she knows 'by heart every rock and stone, ice gully and rivulet. They were part of me, I was part of them.'[20]

Despite their differences, the potential on Kangchenjunga to inhabit a psychological utopia is deeply attractive to all three climbers. The mountain had 'wormed its way into my subconscious', writes Tasker, 'it had been a thing of beauty beyond our reach. [...] For days it had hovered on the edge of my vision and when I returned home it re-emerged on the periphery of my imagination.'[21] Smythe writes in similarly heightened language 'the distant lightning became desultory and wan. The clouds were withdrawn from Kangchenjunga. Far up in the awakened stars something white gleamed steadfastly – the summit.'[22] The reality that lies there of course is

---

16. Tasker, 1982, p160.
17. B Ashcroft, 'Travel and Utopia', *New Directions in Travel Writing Studies*, ed J Kuehn and P Smethurst, Basingstoke, Palgrave Macmillan, 2015, pp249-62, p249.
18. Smythe, 1946, pp23-9; Bremer-Kamp, 1987, p21.
19. Smythe, 1946, p121.
20. Bremer-Kamp, 1987, pp102-3.
21. Tasker, 1982, p91.
22. Smythe, 1946, p64.

exhaustion, starvation, sickness and possibly death. However, the strength of the imagination to romanticise the 'distant lightning' or the danger of the 'beyond' is the very thing that draws the mountaineer ever higher, the allure of a utopia 'is not in its discovery but in its possibility, the fact that it remains beyond the horizon, beckoning to the traveller.'[23] In fact Kangchenjunga is the preeminent example of this since it can 'be seen by anyone who cares to visit the hill town of Darjeeling' where its prominence invites the mountaineer's gaze, yet its remoteness keeps it maddeningly out of reach.[24]

Kangchenjunga in the imagination is the idea to develop. What Tasker in particular has foregrounded is how such utopian ideals begin and end in the mountaineer's mind. As MacFarlane explains, mountains 'do not kill deliberately; nor do they deliberately please: any emotional properties which they possess are vested in them by human imagination.'[25] In 1914 George Mallory wrote a piece entitled 'The Mountaineer as Artist', suggesting that the lines climbers trace up mountains are a product of the mountaineer's imagination.[26] Michel Foucault describes 'heterotopias', environments where echoes of one's familiar society can be found and simultaneously challenged. They exist as much as a mirror to the individual as they do a newly discovered land:

> *The mirror is, after all, a utopia, since it is a placeless place. In the mirror I see myself there where I am not, in an unreal, virtual space that opens up behind the surface [...] from the ground of this virtual space that is on the other side of the glass, I come back toward myself; I begin again to direct my eyes toward myself and to reconstitute myself.[27]*

From the perspective of Foucault's mirror, the mountaineer's relationship with Kangchenjunga and its communities alter over the decades. This is the crux point: the power of both, but more importantly Kangchenjunga's communities, have gradually influenced and challenged the summit fever of foreign climbers. And whilst an important caveat must be made as to how mountain literature often reductively incorporates these beliefs, it nonetheless shows how, over time, the mountaineering gaze is learning as well as consuming.

*

Isolated in the extreme east of Nepal, Kangchenjunga is an independent range that stands apart from the rest of the Himalaya. Unlike Everest, it dominates the view: its five peaks proud against the skyline. It doesn't matter whether you're from the west, Nepal or anywhere: it has an intrinsic mystical otherness born from its inhuman scale. What we should analyse is not the presence of such mystery, but the way that it is approached, appro-

23. Ashcroft, 2015, p252.
24. Smythe, 1946, p13.
25. R Macfarlane, *Mountains of the Mind: A History of a Fascination*, London, Granta, 2004, p19.
26. G Mallory, 'The Mountaineer as Artist', *Climbers Club Journal*, 1914, Vol 53, pp28-40.
27. M Foucault, 'Of Other Spaces', *Diacritics*, 1986, Vol 16 No 1, pp22-7.

By 1929, the Himalayan Club had become central to providing climbing Sherpas and other staff for the growing number of expeditions. Few left Darjeeling or elsewhere without some involvement from E O Shebbeare: see p205 for an account of this remarkable man. *(DAV, Morton)*

priated or, in the case of mountaineers, triumphed over. There are a 'range of physical, emotional and spiritual experiences' that mountains can elicit, and whilst it may be easy to argue for the universal transcendence of a mountain, what is harder to account for is how such transcendence is understood in distinct cultures, or even within individuals.[28]

The response within communities around Sikkim and Mechi is one of deep religious significance. For both Lepcha and Lhopo communities, Kangchenjunga 'functions as the shared location for two distinct "hidden land" narrative constructs.'[29] The influences of Buddhism, as mentioned earlier, are a key commonality between the two and each has had historical influences on the other. Anna Balicki Denjongpa notes in her analysis of a Lhopo community in Tingchim village that differences in 'procedures, terminology and other aspects of culture' can be significant even between villages; this same attitude applies to the anthropological dynamic as a whole.'[30]

Despite increased migration of Nepalis into Sikkim and Darjeeling in the 19th century, the Lepcha people are widely held to be the earliest inhabitants of the area surrounding Kangchenjunga, notably Sikkim in northeastern India, Mechi in far eastern Nepal and areas of Bhutan and Tibet.[31] For the Lepcha, the peaks that surround them are a 'supreme paradise, from where immortal beings provide all the necessary cereals and good health. But these peaks are inhabited by gods (*rum*) and demons (*mung*), which must be constantly tamed and pacified.'[32]

Kangchenjunga is where the very first humans came from: it is a guardian, a source of good fortune and peace, and the literal head of all nature.[33] Their belief in a hidden land is encompassed by Máyel Lyáng, often associated with 'animals, […] agriculture, salt, the number seven and time cycles', a 'concealed utopia' near Kangchenjunga.[34] Yet it is also just as much a location of internal focus and purity. From both perspectives, Máyel Lyáng is directly affected by changes in contemporary society.[35]

For the Lhopo, the region is a land of riches and treasure known as Beyul Dremojong, *beyul* being hidden valleys blessed by Padmasambhava, and Kangchenjunga is the store house for these, specifically: salt, gold and precious stones, sacred scriptures, ammunition and medicine, a close correlation to the translations I quoted above.[36] Nonetheless this spiritual entity is generally understood to be reached by attaining a purity of mind, something that becomes more difficult to achieve as the area becomes increasingly urban-

28. S Bainbridge, 'Mountains', Routledge Companion to Travel Writing, ed Carl Thompson, Abingdon, Routledge, 2015, pp500-10, p504.
29. Scheid, 2014, p67.
30. Denjongpa, 2002, p7.
31. T Subba, 'Dynamics of a Hill Society: A Case Study of the Lepchas', available from DSpace Repository, p.117.
32. B Steinmann, 'Mountain Deities, the Invisible Body of the Society: A Comparative Study of the Representations of Mountains by the Tamang and Thami of Nepal, the Lepcha and Bhotia of Sikkim', *Reflections of the Mountain: Essays on the History and Social Meaning of the Mountain Cult in Tibet and the Himalaya*, ed A-M Blondeau and E Steinkellner, Vienna, Osterreichische Akademie der Wissenchaftenthe Himalaya, 1996, pp179-218, p179.
33. Scheid, 2014, p70.
34. Ibid, p72.
35. Ibid, pp74-6.
36. Ibid, p78.

ised and a rise in commercialisation pollutes the Lhopo's internal condition.[37] In April 2000, a campaign group called Concerned Citizens of Sikkim wrote to an Austrian expedition who had obtained a permit to climb Kangchenjunga: 'To us the mountain itself is a shrine and just as you would not climb on a statue of Jesus or Buddha or leave oxygen canisters or trash in its lap we do not believe in trampling on Kangchenjunga.'[38]

Such complex beliefs are often dismissed in early mountaineering literature and even when heard contribute to the overall reduction of Kangchenjunga as a 'mystical peak'. We see in Smythe's account an early reaction from mountaineers to the spiritual presence of the mountain:

> *The most rationally minded of men cannot gaze [...] upon Kanchenjunga without experiencing something of the same emotions of the simpler-minded Sherpas and Lepchas who dwell in the valleys below.*[39]

Even whilst conceding that mountains provoke a distinct feeling of transcendence, Smythe dismisses the very values of the communities that lie closer to this essential quality as being born from 'simpler' minds. Such tension continues throughout Smythe's writing, responding with contempt for local customs that, 'judged by European standards, [were] completely tuneless and unintelligible.'[40] Yet despite such ridicule, the music of the Pemayangtse monastery exerts its own power on Smythe, dragging him away 'from the twentieth century, [...] into the very heart of this mystic land, where time and space are limitless, and man is re-incarnated through eternity.'[41] Such moments however are fleeting and sit in a broader framework of 'othering', whereby porters are cast in three broad categories: dogs that must be wormed; children that must be nurtured; or 'Tigers' that triumph over adversity.[42] Whilst some of these portrayals are more positive than others, all three fail to present the people Smythe encounters in their true complexity. To liken porters to dogs and children is obviously demeaning. Even the apparently more positive category of Tiger deserves closer reading. It contains a contradiction, of skill and strength against an animalistic primitiveness, both of which romanticise the role of porter.[43] These characteristics have little to do with Smythe's subject and more to do with a feeling of lack or even loss that the European in Sikkim feels in relation to his own culture.[44]

> *We were back in a medieval land, caring nothing for progress, a land fiercely jealous of its ancient rights, its conservatism, looking askance upon modernity and the outer world. Perhaps it is happier so.*[45]

37. Ibid, p80.
38. Email sent to expedition sponsor by CCS in 2000.
39. Smythe, 1946, p61.
40. Ibid, p90.
41. Ibid.
42. Ibid, p67; p135; p144.
43. V Adams, *Tigers of the Snow and Other Virtual Sherpas: An Ethnography of Himalayan Encounters*, New Jersey, Princeton University Press, 1996, pp14-5.
44. J Fisher, 'Tourists and Sherpas', *Contributions to Nepalese Studies*, 1986, Vol 14 No. 1, pp37-61, pp46-7.
45. Smythe, 1946, p133.

Smythe's initial focus is on attack and conquest. He details logistics, the qualities of the team and the geographical and meteorological challenges that must be overcome in order to achieve the ultimate goal of western mountaineers: the summit. Yet as he begins to grapple with diametrically opposed perspectives, his descriptions fluctuate between the 'coldly hostile,' or 'cruel' mountains and the unexpectedly rich spiritual encounters he experiences:

> One of the curses of being a mountaineer is that an analytical mind [...] tends to detract from aesthetic enjoyment. [...] But here was a scene so magnificent as to submerge the sharp, ugly rocks of analysis [...] beneath the smooth rollers of pure contemplation. [...] The thought of how these peaks might be climbed did not intrude. I did not see couloir or ridge, did not endeavour to win a theoretical way to a summit.[46]

Smythe's response is undoubtedly provoked by his physical surroundings but the impact of his cultural encounters with Lepcha and Lhopo is plain to see. The very language Smythe uses closely mirrors that of his experience in Pemayangtse monastery. In both instances time becomes a fluid entity, the language rhapsodic and Smythe himself becomes less a voyeur trying 'to take some photographs' and more a part of the mountain's very fabric.[47]

Tasker's writing demonstrates a maturing of such responses. Gone is the explicit hierarchy of Smythe and racial slurs as 'coolies'; the picture is more nuanced.[48] Comparisons can certainly be drawn between the ways Kangchenjunga itself is perceived, as well as the more internal focus that Tasker describes in Doug Scott who tended 'to make his own pace, [...] preferring to walk alone with his own thoughts, reading and writing at every stop [...] in his search for insights into the mystery of life.'[49] There is a more notable meditative quality to Tasker's writing, its focus much closer to the broad themes of the Lhopo. Tasker and Smythe both mistake the mountain for a cloud rising above the land, their language closely mirroring each other:

> Above the village, in the sky, hovering white and unobtrusive in the distance so I thought it was a cloud, was the mountain.[50]
> I saw, between a gap in the nearer mists, the crest of a great cloud high up in the sky [...] But was it a cloud? [...] It was no cloud, but a snowy mountain.[51]

This is how popular notions of Kangchenjunga become fixed in the western imagination over time, Kangchenjunga 'as an ethereal realm, disembodied from the world and periodically revealed in the same manner as a vision.'[52] Such idealism is mirrored in the people these climbers

46. Ibid, p128.
47. Ibid, p85.
48. Ibid, p108.
49. Tasker, 1982, p165.
50. Ibid, p167.
51. Smythe, 1946, p85.
52. Pierse, 2015, p3.

encounter, 'among them [...] a young girl, the prettiest we had seen among the mountain people,' an idealised construction of the communities in the Kangchenjunga region.[53] Just as Shangri-La is 'an invented pseudo-Tibetan place-name' that alludes to a utopian ideal apparently lacking in the travellers' own culture, so too do the twin 'others' approached by the mountaineer – 'ethereal' summit and 'spiritual' communities – work to creating the same bias.[54] The effect is insulation from the poverty of the region or from cultural difference, while displaying a certain attraction towards the other.

Despite Tasker's doubts about the 'climbing of mountains by their hardest route', he nonetheless learns to 'relax, to leave the ordering of events to our trusted men of the hills [...] and begin to re-focus on the mountain ahead.'[55] There is here the same fixation on the summit, and something of Smythe's 'simpler-minded Sherpas and Lepchas who dwell in the valleys below' which suggests an ideological dynamic to the hierarchy: it's the 'men of the hills' that get the simpler tasks.[56]

The mere presence of an alternative perspective that reveres Kangchenjunga should place a significant barrier to achieving the summit the climber so strongly desires. (Joe Brown and George Band famously did not stand on the summit during the first ascent in deference to that perspective.) Yet an order of value is laid out in which the mountaineer ascends both literally and culturally to a higher plane, sidestepping the issue of conflicting values to claim the prize. Even the incorporation of individuals as porters is an ideological step as well as a logistical one. Porters, suggests Smythe, possess 'a born instinct for adventure', implying that adventure, a core trait of mountaineering, is in fact innate in the porters too.[57] Joe Tasker offers an alternative view of porters as those who 'showed neither pleasure nor displeasure, as if resigned to an existence which was always hard work.'[58] In relation to Sherpas, their 'engagement with mountaineering was as much an engagement with their own culture [...] games defined by their own history, their own politics, their own culturally shaped desires.' Much the same can be said in relation to the Lepcha and Lhopo.[59] Such variety allows only one conclusion: Kangchenjunga, indeed any mountain, elicits an array of reactions that have often been missed in conventional climbing narratives.

It is this shifting combination of culture, landscape and individual motivation that Bremer-Kamp aspires to describe. Whilst still 'blind to everything' but the north face of Kangchenjunga and writing from the perspective of the mountain as 'a mirror through which we could view ourselves', Bremer-Kamp nonetheless displays a noteworthy sensitivity in portraying the individuals she encounters.[60] Prompted by the environment around her, she reflects on the 'media exposure' that led to the 1978 K2 expedition

53. Tasker, 1982, p170.
54. Hutt, 2012, p87.
55. Tasker, 1982, p165.
56. Smythe, 1946, p61.
57. Ibid, p68.
58. Tasker, 1982, p171.
59. S Ortner, *Life and Death on Mt. Everest*, New Jersey, Princeton University Press, 1999, p248.
60. Bremer-Kamp, 1987, p74; p22.

Left: Expedition leader Paul Bauer. A member of the various Frei Korps after the First World War, he saw direct links between German militarism and alpinism. He became a member of the NSDAP in 1933 when Hitler came to power, at least in part to protect his position as a Himalayan expedition leader and founded the Deutschen Himalaya-Stiftung. *(DAV, Morton)*

Right: An unidentified local Lepcha man. The German photographers seemed attuned to the complex ethnic diversity they encountered on Kangchenjunga. *(DAV, Morton)*

she was a part of 'assuming the role of conqueror and adopting language that the advertising world and general public could easily relate to.'[61] She has forgone such large scale exploits, convinced 'that small is beautiful', undertaking a more intimate expedition to climb Kangchenjunga in winter.[62] Bremer-Kamp is however guilty of desiring the cultural construct of an unspoiled landscape. The reality is that the growth of the Himalayan tourist industry has left a 'thick suffocation of diesel fumes' that is a long way from the 'magical kingdom, devoid of foreign influence'.[63] Bremer-Kamp is shocked at the 'materialism and greed that had crept into a once naïve and innocent people' that appear to be motivated by 'Levi jeans and Nike running shoes'.[64] Bremer-Kamp's concern for the utopia that mountaineering has constructed fails to allow for the fact that to argue solely for 'the deterioration of Sherpa culture under the onslaught of modernization' is in fact too reductive.[65] The reality is that these communities have for centuries 'absorbed new ideas with enthusiasm' and just as some aspects of culture can be eroded, so too can modernity bring increased prosperity; one will be able to find advocates of both as well as opponents.[66]

Despite this, Bremer-Kamp offers a deeper insight into the lives of local people compared to Smythe, who rarely identifies the porters with a name, or even Tasker, who gives us Ang Phurba and Nima Tensing and liaison officer Mohan Bahadur Thapa. Bremer-Kamp offers not only names but also complex characters. What this reveals is somewhat shattering for the 'utopia' that mountaineering has tried to construct, and the modern day 'dystopia' that has supposedly eroded it. What we see instead is the multiplicity of humanity: Kusang is dismissed after stealing supplies; Sanglai experiences vivid inner turmoil as he chooses between 'traditional loyalties to his countrymen and the inner loyalties toward his Buddhist principles'; and Mongol becomes paralysed with fear after Bremer-Kamp's partner Chris dies at 7,500m.[67]

We see the skill of Sanglai running over moraine in cumbersome footwear carrying heavy loads to camp one. Then, to the climbers' surprise, he decides to quit. 'We asked Sanglai why he was descending: "Too cold? Don't like the food? Don't like the work?" and the only thing he said was, "I only small boy."'[68] Neither utopia nor dystopia exists, neither Tiger nor child. What does exist is the physicality of Kangchenjunga and a myriad of human responses to it. Despite all the caveats of travel writing as a whole, how inevitably it is an act of 'othering', Bremer-Kamp nonetheless presents welcome complexity when describing local individuals.[69]

One might argue that you are 'damned if you do and damned if you don't,' that one cannot seemingly hold any form of opinion for fear of undermining or misjudging communities and cultures. This is to an extent the point, since in approaching any issue western literature has the effect of fixing representation on the page in hyperrealist black and white. The oral tradition of Kangchenjunga's local communities is much more fluid, constantly changing and often not heard. The point though is to take as wide a view as possible. Mountaineering has for the most part failed in this regard, so focused is it on the summit. The Romantic view of mountains in the west has driven a Romantic view of local communities, leading to simplistic renderings.

The anthropologist Sherry Ortner suggests the objective of any writing, regardless of genre, should not be to argue 'one way or another, but rather try to counter any one-sided representation,' instead seeing individuals 'as real people, with complex lives and intentions of their own.'[70] It is clear from the timeline of Smythe's writing in 1946 to Bremer-Kamp in 1987 that mountaineering has indeed learnt; not simply how to more sensitively approach difference, but also how its own historical belief in the summit is only part of the picture, in fact simply being in the presence of mountains is valuable in itself, something that the communities of Kangchenjunga have upheld for centuries.

66. E Douglas, 'Upwardly Mobile, Geographical, 2003, Vol 75 No 5, pp86-94, p93.
67. Bremer-Kamp, 1987, pp75-6; p183.
68. Ibid, p79; p84.
69. Thompson, 2011, p133.
70. Ortner, 1999, p24.

# History

2nd Lt C A Hartree (1879-1918) Royal Garrison Artillery,
killed during the devastating German offensive of spring 1918.

JONATHAN WESTAWAY

# Thinking Like a Mountain

## The Life and Career of E O Shebbeare

Bengt Berg's warm portrait of E O Shebbeare, taken during the
early 1930s. Shebbeare facilitated Berg's pioneering camera-trap expedition
to photograph the wildlife of Bengal. All the pictures of Shebbeare that
accompany this article are reproduced with the kind permission of
Sue Morton, Shebbeare's granddaughter. Berg was a Swedish ornithologist
and one of the first natural history filmmakers.

Near the start of Percy Wyn-Harris's official documentary film of the 1933 British Everest Expedition, members gather around a table in Darjeeling.[1] Each one is profiled, their name appearing in intertitles. Most of us would be hard pressed to name any of the expedition members today, let alone identify them from the archive footage. One face in particular remains deep in shadow beneath a broad-brimmed tropical hat, the title announcing 'E O Shebbeare'. The deputy leader and transport officer for the 1933 expedition, Shebbeare appears again 12 minutes into the film in footage shot in Phari, Tibet, smiling and talking to the camera, supervising porters, posing with the other expedition members for a group portrait, the scenes intercut with shots of snow streaming from the sacred summit of Chomolhari.

A founder member in 1928 of the Himalayan Club[2], Edward Oswald Shebbeare had been the transport officer on the 1924 Everest expedition. He was subsequently transport officer for the Germans on Kangchenjunga in 1929 and 1931. His knowledge of Sikkim and of the indigenous peoples of the region and their languages was central to the logistical success of this and other expeditions. Despite this, his contribution has largely been downplayed and ignored by historians of Everest and Himalayan mountaineering, in part because practical knowledge in a colonial context formed no part of the contemporary archetype of the mountaineering hero. Lacking a degree or any university education, Shebbeare had joined the Indian Forest Service in 1906, eventually becoming chief conservator of forests for Bengal. Class and colonial experience differentiated him from most of the mountaineers selected by the Mount Everest Committee.

Look at any British mountaineering or expeditionary photograph from the period. A small group of sahibs stares impassively back at us. Out of shot a vast army of indigenous labour toils on the mountain: high-altitude workers, porters, cooks, mail runners. Indigenous expeditionary labour was seldom accorded due recognition in subsequent expeditionary accounts, published and unpublished. In sharp contrast, E O Shebbeare's recognition of indigenous autonomy and agency was exemplary for the period, a sympathy derived from his long experience of the subcontinent and his innovative approaches to forest management. In both his 1924 Everest diary held at the Alpine Club and in the two albums of photographs from the 1929 German expedition gifted to him by Paul Bauer [Editor's note: see p189 in this edition of the *Alpine Journal*] and now in a private family collection, Shebbeare has annotated every photograph of Sherpas, recording their names. Few of his contemporaries could have named more than a handful of the indigenous workers they encountered on the way to the mountain; very few bothered to systematically record them. Exploring Shebbeare's life and career shows us the hidden histories of mountaineering and exploration, highlighting the colonial official's role in traversing imperial and indigenous cultures, framing colonial encounters, mediating the culture shock experienced by

1. P Wyn-Harris, *Fourth Everest Expedition*, https://player.bfi.org.uk/free/film/watch-fourth-everest-expedition-1933-online
2. G Corbett, 'The Founding of the Himalayan Club', *Himalayan Journal*, Vol 1, 1929.

Shebbeare acted as transport officer for Paul Bauer's Kangchenjunga expeditions and also for the British on Everest in 1933, where he surprised Shipton, seen here on horseback, by reaching the North Col. As a seminal member of the Himalayan Club, few expeditions in this period made it into the field without his help.

mountaineers from Britain and making expeditionary knowledge possible.

Shebbeare's relative obscurity is, in part, related to the nature of the British imperial obsession with Everest and its symbolic importance, particularly in post-war reconstruction of imperial masculinity and British rule in India.[3] The Everest expeditions of the 1920s and 1930s were high-profile events designed to create enduring archetypes. The subsequent focus on a few individuals, in particular George Mallory and his mythopoeic disappearance, has left a legacy of hypertrophied heroism and endlessly repeated, highly simplified stories. As Charles Lind observed in the notes to his poem *An Afterclap of Fate*, 'Mallory has taken on an almost mythic status in our time,' doomed to the incurious attentions of 'the reverential monument builders & the debunking demolition squad' alike.[4] All too often, the history of mountaineering has become 'monumental history', Nietzsche's term for the history of outstanding individuals imagined as a series of isolated mountain peaks.[5] Monumental history was a reaffirmation of Carlyle's 'Great Man'

3. W Davis, *Into the Silence: The Great War, Mallory and the Conquest of Everest*, London, The Bodley Head, 2011.
4. C Lind, *An Afterclap of Fate: Mallory on Everest*, The Ernest Press, 2006, p120.
5. P Hansen *The Summits of Modern Man: Mountaineering After the Enlightenment*. Cambridge, Mass, Harvard University Press, 2013. J Westaway, review of 'The Summits of Modern Man: Mountaineering After the Enlightenment', *International Journal of the History of Sport*, Vol 32, 2, 2015, pp393-5. DOI:10.1080/09523367.2014.963960

theory of history, intentionally aristocratic and rhetorically reinforced by the cultural capital of idealised mountain landscapes and the power of mountains as metaphor; what historians call 'history from above'. Postcolonial perspectives on Empire have enabled us to begin to undertake a 'history from below' approach to Himalayan mountaineering and expeditions. Felix Driver's work on the hidden histories of exploration brings into focus the importance of indigenous knowledge and agency in exploration.[6]

As well as issues of race, ethnicity and the subaltern, the influence of class in a colonial expeditionary context has also been an under-examined area. The Mount Everest Committee in the 1920s clearly thought character and class every bit as important a mountaineering ability in its selection process, the 'Everest Mountaineering Archetype' being well attested to: public school, university degree, medical degree, army officer, middle-class professional, sportsman. Take a good look at those expeditionary photographs again. The figures in the photographs share many affinities as a ruling imperial class but can be divided on the basis of their experience of the Indian subcontinent. Most of the sahibs in those photographs only visited India, Sikkim and Tibet briefly, returning to Britain or elsewhere in the empire. There has been very little research undertaken on the lives of colonial officials involved in Himalayan mountaineering: the British political agents in Sikkim, Bhutan and Tibet who negotiated diplomatic access to the mountain, the Gurkha officers and NCOs, Survey of India officers, Indian Forest Service officials, acting as transport and liaison officers. Few have analysed the importance of colonial knowledge and expertise to the Everest expeditions, where success depended on a vast logistical pyramid of indigenous labour that demanded language skills, intercultural understanding and sympathy, good working relationships, command structures, and the deployment of geographical, political and diplomatic knowledge and authority to succeed.

Shebbeare was undoubtedly part of the Raj, the white colonial ruling class in British India but at the same time he was far removed from the 'Everest Mountaineering Archetype'. Whilst most historians treat him as a footnote to the Everest expeditions, he developed a legendary reputation amongst south-east Asian conservationists.[7] In the mountains, jungles and forests of the Himalaya, E O Shebbeare became a pioneering naturalist and forest conservationist, eventually becoming chief conservator of wildlife for Malaya. Captured by the Japanese in 1942 as part of F Spencer Chapman's first 'stay behind' party, he was interned in Singapore, retiring to Oxfordshire in 1947. As well as significant contributions to the scholarly literature on the flora and fauna of south-east Asia, in his retirement he wrote *Soondar Mooni: The Story of an Indian Elephant* (Gollancz, 1958), a book that explores non-human subjectivities and agency, providing us with evidence of Shebbeare's deep sensibility for the natural world and the non-human lifeforms we share

6.  F Driver, *Hidden Histories of Exploration: Researching the RGS-IBG Collections*. London, RGS & Royal Holloway, 2009.
7.  'A rare combination of outdoor ruggedness ... with an aptitude for scholarly observations of fauna and flora, Shebbeare became almost a legendary figure in eastern Asia.' E P Gee, 'Edward O. Shebbeare', *Oryx: The International Journal of Conservation*, Vol 7, 6, December, 1964, p274.

SOONDAR
MOONI

The story of an Indian elephant
*illustrated by the author*

E. O. SHEBBEARE
GOLLANCZ

Shebbeare and friend, India. He spent 32 years in the Indian Forest Service. Though known to climbers for his exploration, he would more accurately be described as a deep ecologist.

The cover of Shebbeare's remarkable natural history work *Soondar Mooni: The Story of an Indian Elephant*, published by Gollancz in 1958.

it with. Despite this, there is an almost complete lack of accessible biographical information about him. This is in large part because Shebbeare was notoriously diffident and self-effacing.[8] He never sought out fame and his experience on Everest and Kangchenjunga was only ever a small part of a life devoted to the imperial forestry service and wildlife conservation.

Shebbeare was born in 1884, the son of the Rev C H Shebbeare, vicar of Wykham, Yorkshire.[9] He was educated at Charterhouse and then the Royal Indian Engineering College at Cooper's Hill near Egham in Surrey 1903-06. Set up by the India Office to train engineers for the Indian Public Works Department, a forestry school was established in 1885.[10] Shebbeare spent the next 32 years (1906-38) in the Indian Forest Service, eventually becoming chief conservator of forests for Bengal in 1925.[11] His application to become a member of the Royal Anthropological Institute in 1940 indicates quite how extensive his experience of the Indian subcontinent was: he records

8. H Champion, 'Mr. E. O. Shebbeare', *The Times*, 19 August 1964, p12.
9. 'Obituary: Mr. E. O. Shebbeare', *The Times*, 14 August 1964, p10.
10. *https://en.wikipedia.org/wiki/Royal_Indian_Engineering_College*
Secretary of State for India, *The India List and India Office List for 1905*, London, Harrison, 1905. 'Compiled from official records by direction of the Secretary of State for India in Council', 'Royal Indian Engineering College, Session 1904-05, Forest Students, Second Year, Shebbeare, E. O.', 5.
11. H Champion & F Osmaston (eds), *The Forests of India, Volume 4: Being the History from 1925 to 1947 of the Forests Now in Burma, India and Pakistan*, Oxford, Oxford University Press, 1962, p287.

30 years in the 'E. Himalayas and hill tracts (Bengal and Assam)', 'W. Himalayas (U.P.) 1 year', 'Madras, Ceylon – brief visits. Burma, 3 or 4 short visits'. He claimed

> 'to have got to know the Eastern Himalayas and their peoples fairly well from Tibet to the Terai and Duars (roughly Nepal to Kamrup) and the Chittagong Hill Tracts, Khasi Hills and Lower Bengal less well.'

Under 'linguistic knowledge', he indicates he can read, write and speak Bengali and Nepali, has fair Hindustani, rusty German and very poor Tibetan. Of degrees awarded, university education and 'other theoretical training' Shebbeare records: 'Nil'.[12] It was exactly this practical knowledge won over decades on the Indian subcontinent that secured Shebbeare the deputy leadership of the 1933 Everest expedition. Col Eugene St J Birnie, the other transport officer on the 1933 expedition, recalled:

> 'Dealing with the rough mountain men of Thibet, who supplied us with our yaks and donkeys, was a task which needed immense patience and good humour. Any sign of irritation could be disastrous. Shebbeare surmounted all these difficulties with ease. His sense of humour captivated these tough hillmen and ensured the safe passage of the expedition to the Base Camp.' [13]

His humour was mixed with legendary toughness. On 3 June 1933 and against expedition leader Hugh Ruttledge's express orders, Shebbeare reached the North Col on Everest, Birnie commenting that Shebbeare:

> 'had his tea and a pipe, looked at the magnificent panorama of mountain scenery, and returned safely down those precipitous ice slopes, achieving an ambition of years! The North Col is 23,000ft in height and this was a superb effort for a man of 49 years of age.' [14]

Raymond Greene in his memoirs, *Moments of Being*, called Shebbeare 'the most loveable, imperturbable and knowledgeable of men'[15] and continued to visit him in his retirement after 1947 at his home near Banbury, Oxfordshire.[16] It is probably fair to say that all the major expeditions undertaken through Sikkim between 1924 and 1938 benefited from Shebbeare's expertise, either directly or indirectly via the Himalayan Club's role in marshalling porters, Sherpas and Bhotias and managing their pay, welfare and lading. Shebbeare was also assistant editor of the *Himalayan Journal* 1930-3, vice president of the Himalayan Club from 1933-4 and committee

---

12. Shebbeare's membership application, 19 July 1940, MS A71-336, Royal Anthropological Institute.
13. Anon, 'Shebbeare', *The Carthusian*, December 1964, p101.
14. Anon, 'Shebbeare', *The Carthusian*, December 1964, p101.
15. R Greene, *Moments of Being: The Random Recollections of Raymond Greene*, London, William Heinemann Ltd, 1974, p155.
16. E Birnie, R Greene, K. Biswas 'Obituary: Edward Oswald Shebbeare (1884-1964)', *Himalayan Journal*, Vol 26, 1965.

member 1936-8.[17] Paul Bauer records that in 1931, Shebbeare 'sacrificed his whole year's furlough to our undertaking and led the first body of porters a fourteen days' march to the Zemu glacier.'[18]

We can perhaps characterise Shebbeare's mountaineering as a mixture of the voluntary and the semi-official, all travel in Sikkim and Tibet requiring political clearance and assurances on behalf of indigenous communities and labour. Shebbeare was particularly trusted by indigenous communities, partly because he had instigated a revolution in Indian forestry by success-fully introducing the Taungya system, a traditional system of agroforestry originating in Burma that utilised intercropping to improve forest regener-ation, an experimental programme that had already been widely adopted when he summarised it's benefits in the *Empire Forestry Journal* in July 1932.[19] 'He advocated combining this with the tribal swidden cultivation and bringing the indigenous people back into the forests' and managing regrowth through the application of fire regeneration, and is now the model for 'almost every agro-forestry system in the tropics.'[20] Seow, writing in the journal *Malaysian Naturalist*, recorded that 'anthropologists working with hill peoples of India noted that the names of Shebbeare and some other officers have entered the oral histories of these people who praised them for their management of forests and stopping illegal logging.'[21] Sir Harry Champion, professor of forestry at Oxford, writing to *The Times* in 1964, indicated that under Shebbeare, the Forest Department in Bengal developed

*'a high reputation for its technical progress, fostered by an exceptional cama-raderie among its officers which was equally due to him. His deep and wide knowledge of the forest and forest life made him a valuable critic, ... The tough-ness, which a few who did not know him well thought he deliberately exaggerated as a pose, was an inherent part of a man than whom it would be hard to find a better companion, however difficult or uncomfortable the circumstances.'* [22]

As conservator of forests for Bengal, Shebbeare also pioneered both botanical and game reserves.[23] His work was already being acknowledged in 1932 when the Swedish naturalist Bengt Berg chose to dedicate his book on the Indian one-horned rhino and the Indian elephant to Shebbeare.[24] His obituary in *Oryx: The International Journal of Conservation*, records that 'it was due to his untiring pioneer efforts that legislation was passed for the protection of the Indian rhinoceros.'[25] Due to Shebbeare's representations, 'the Rhinoceros

17. E Birnie, R Greene, K. Biswas 'Obituary: Edward Oswald Shebbeare (1884-1964)', *Himalayan Journal*, Vol 26, 1965.
18. P Bauer, *Himalayan Campaign: The German Attack on Kanchenjunga, the Second Highest Mountain in the World*, Oxford, Basil Blackwell, 1937, p118.
19. E Shebbeare, 'The Sal Tangyas in Bengal', *Empire Forestry Journal*, Vol 11, 1, July 1932, pp18-33.
H Blandford, 'Assam: Progress Report of Forest Administration for the Years 1940-41', *Empire Forestry Journal*, Shillong, Government Press, Vol 21, 1942, pp72-3.
20. A Seow, 'Shebbeare: On the Shoulders of Giants', *Malaysian Naturalist*, September 2010, pp34-6.
21. Seow, 'Shebbeare', p36.
22. Anon, 'Shebbeare', *The Carthusian*, December 1964, p101.
23. Anon, 'Shebbeare', *The Carthusian*, December 1964, p101.
24. Bengt Berg, *Meine Jagd Nach Dem Einhorn*, (Frankfurt: Rütten & Loening Verlag, 1933).
25. E. P. Gee, (1964) 'Edward O. Shebbeare', *Oryx: The International Journal of Conservation*, Vol.7, issue 6

Preservation Act came into being and the Jaldapara Game Sanctuary, in the Duars, was declared a special Reserve for the preservation of the Rhinoceros.'[26] Section 4a of the Bengal Rhinoceros Preservation Act of 1932 made it illegal to kill rhinos and trade in their body parts.[27] It was this legislation, as well as the outbreak of the Sino-Japanese War in 1937 that cut off the illegal demand for horn, securing the survival of the rhino in India.[28]

In 1938 Shebbeare accepted the post of as chief game warden of the newly established King George V (subsequently the Taman Negara) National Park in Malaya, the only substantial national park in Malaysia for the next 64 years and therefore hugely important for conservation purposes on the peninsula.[29] Shebbeare became both a founder and president of the Malayan Nature Society (1940-2) and founding editor of the *Malayan Nature Journal*. He established a strong working relationship as a field naturalist working with Frederick Chasen, the director of the Raffles Museum in Singapore and supported 'Chasen's efforts to get the remaining wild areas of Singapore declared a wildlife preserve.'[30] All of this work was cut short by the Japanese advance through Asia in World War Two. In January 1941 Shebbeare, on his own initiative, raised a special secret unit of the 1st (Perak) Battalion of the Federated Malay States Volunteer Forces (FMSVF) to improve intelligence and mapping in Upper Perak on the Siamese frontier.[31] Known as Frontier Patrol 'it consisted of five Europeans with jungle experience, who were each given a section of the frontier for which they were responsible.'[32] Shebbeare's command included

> *Herbert Deane 'Pat' Noone, govt. ethnologist, protector of Sakais; with brother Richard (temporary at Perak Public Health Dept. he was formally under G2(I) – intelligence – 3rd Indian Corps, mapping), with own Temiar aborigines and Malays … Richard's patrol operated from Kroh. Pat from Grik area with elephants.*[33]

Shebbeare's command involved training in jungle warfare, running intelligence networks on the border and making forays into Siam to assess the Japanese military build-up and to develop cross-border supply routes in

December, 274, notes that the legislation 'resulted in the creation of Jaldapara as a sanctuary in northern Bengal in 1941'.

26. E Shebbeare, A Roy, H Tyndale, 'The Great One-horned Rhinoceros (Rhinocerus Unicornis L.)', *Journal of the Bengal Natural History Society*, Vol 22, 1948, pp88-91.

27. *Bengal Act VIII of 1932: The Bengal Rhinoceros Preservation Act of 1932.*

28. E O Shebbeare, 'The Bengal Rhinoceros Sanctuary', *Journal of the Society for the Preservation of the Fauna of Empire*, Vol 56, 1948, pp33-5.

29. Seow, 'Shebbeare', 36. E Shebbeare, 'Malaya. Annual Report of the Game Department, Federated Malay States, for the Year 1938', *Journal of the Society for the Preservation of the Fauna of the Empire*, Vol 38, 1939, pp32-5. J MacKenzie, *The Empire of Nature: Hunting, Conservation and British Imperialism*, Manchester, Manchester University Press, 1988, p278.

30. B Luyt, 'Collectors and Collecting for the Raffles Museum in Singapore: 1920-1940', *Library and Information History*, Vol 26, 3, September 2010, pp189-90.
http://www.maneyonline.com/doi/pdfplus/10.1179/175834810X12731358995235

31. B Farrell, 'High Command, Irregular Forces, and Defending Malaya, 1941-1942', *Global War Studies*, Vol 8, 2, 2011, p58.

32. D Holman, *Noone of the Ulu*, Singapore, Oxford University Press, 1984, p80.

33. Audrey Holmes McCormick http://www.malayanvolunteersgroup.org.uk/node/58

preparation for the defence of Malaya.[34] Frontier Patrol seems to have been disbanded late in 1941, its members being called up for regular deployment in the FMSVF and regular army units. In January 1942 Shebbeare was part of F Spencer Chapman's first ill-fated 'stay-behind party'[35] cut off by the rapid Japanese advance; he spent the remainder of the war interned in Changi prison, Singapore. Amongst the horrors of Changi he embarked on a lecture programme with other Malayan Nature Society members and contributed to the first edition of *An Introduction to the Birds of Malaya*.[36] Chapman later found Shebbeare's 'bungalow ransacked and both Shebbeare's scientific papers and the Society's early records were destroyed.'[37] Chapman did find 'several copies of the *Himalayan Journal* and one of his 1924 Everest diaries'[38] which he rescued and is now in the Alpine Club Library in London.

Upon his release from internment, Shebbeare returned to England via Bengal where he organized a tiger hunt for Richard Casey, governor of the Presidency of Bengal 1944-6, still sporting the rawhide boots he had commandeered from his Japanese prison guard. He re-established the system of game wardens in the King George V/Taman Negara National Park[39] but by 1947, with India on the brink of independence and Malaya destabilized by communist insurgents, Shebbeare retired. In May 1947 he paid one last visit to Jaldapara, 'the Rhino sanctuary near Nilpara, in Northern Bengal'[40], before settling into retirement near Banbury, Oxfordshire, devoting his remaining years to his family, his writing and bee keeping. In retirement he attended the annual meetings of the Empire Forestry Association.[41] He was a council member of the Fauna Preservation Society between 1954 and 1958 and again from 1959 until just before his death in 1964,[42] with many of his articles appearing in the society's journal *Oryx*. Amongst conservationists he was perhaps best known for a 1953 article in *Oryx* on the 'Status of the Three Asiatic Rhinoceros'.[43] He achieved a small measure of wider fame in 1958 with the publication of his book *Soondar Mooni: The Story of an Indian Elephant*, a book that explores non-human subjectivities and agency, providing us with evidence of Shebbeare's deep sensibility for what some scholars have termed the 'more-than-human' world. In the words of one

34. M Shennan, *Out In the Midday Sun: The British in Malaya 1880-1960*, London, John Murray, 2000, pp215-6. D Holman, Chapter Seven: 'The Frontier Patrol', *Noone of the Ulu*, Singapore, Oxford University Press, 1984, pp80-9.

35. B Hembry, *Malayan Spymaster: Memoirs of a Rubber Planter, Bandit Fighter and Spy*, Singapore, Monsoon Books, 2011, p131. F Spencer Chapman, *The Jungle is Neutral*. London, The Reprint Society, 1950, p49.

36. *http://myrepositori.pnm.gov.my/bitstream/123456789/2339/1/JB1899_ITMB.pdf*

37. Seow, Shebbeare, p36. '... the *Malayan Nature Journal* about 1940. Unfortunately, all spare copies of this publication, together with most privately owned copies, were probably lost during the Japanese occupation.' See E Shebbeare, 'The Senoi of Malaya', *Man*, Vol 47, 168, November 1947, p152.

38. F Spencer Chapman, *The Jungle is Neutral*. London, The Reprint Society, 1950, p94. See also 53.

39. J MacKenzie, *The Empire of Nature: Hunting, Conservation and British Imperialism*, Manchester, Manchester University Press, 1988, p280.

40. E Shebbeare, 'The Bengal Rhinoceros Sanctuary', *Journal of the Society for the Preservation of the Wild Fauna of the Empire*, Vol.56, 1948, p33.

41. Lord Milverton, 'Report of the Thirty-Second Annual Meeting of the Empire Forestry Association, held at the Assembly Hall, Royal Empire Society, Northumberland Avenue, London WC2, on Friday, 24 Sptember, 1954', *Empire Forestry Review*, Vol 33, 4, December 1954, pp352-61.

42. E Gee, 'Edward O. Shebbeare', *Oryx: The International Journal of Conservation*, Vol 7, 6 December 1964, p274.

43. E Shebbeare, 'Status of the Three Asiatic Rhinoceros', *Oryx: The International Journal of Conservation*, Vol 2, 3, November 1953, pp141-9.

reviewer, Shebbeare:

> '*describes most of the life history of an individual female elephant of northeast India. He thus lays on record a vast amount of valuable, first-hand, authentic information on elephants in their wild state, how they react to various natural and man-made events, and how they submit to capture, training, and working for man. The story is mostly told through the eyes and mind of the elephant, and the author appears to have what is probably a very accurate idea of the real thoughts of an elephant-without any undue tendency to an anthropomorphic approach to the subject.*' [44]

Richard Casey, governor of the Presidency of Bengal 1944-46 and subsequently Australian minister for External Affairs, in his foreword to *Soondar Mooni*, described Shebbeare as 'an unusual and rather remarkable man. He has spent the greater part of his life in jungles. He'd be lost and unhappy in a big city, but he is completely happy and at home in the jungle.' [45] The very last published piece Shebbeare wrote, a review of P D Stracey's book *Elephant Gold*, published in *Oryx* in August 1964 confirms Shebbeare's deep affiliation with the jungle biome:

> '*I enjoyed this book, partly because its author, like myself, acquired his taste for elephants against a background of undeveloped parts of Assam. Here the jungle got into his blood, as earlier it had into mine, and made him feel that days spent on game-paths through wild country, and nights in grass huts with the smell of wood smoke were the only life for him.*' [46]

Dr K Biswas, editor of the *Himalayan Journal*, described the virtue of Shebbeare's jungle affinity: 'His was a character by itself – fearless but amiable, enduring all who came into contact with him, simple due to his constant association with natural surroundings of the forest.' [47] *The Times* obituary of Shebbeare reiterates this:

> '*In a varied life in the east his name became a byword. He would disappear for periods into the forests he loved and the results would appear in technical papers on forestry, on the fishes of northern Bengal, on botany, and on zoology.*' [48]

Shebbeare, it seems to me, understood that to affiliate with nature first requires that we must occasionally disappear, encountering nature and immersing ourselves in the wilderness. His mountaineering expeditions

44. 'E P G', 'Soondar Mooni. By E. O. Shebbeare', *Oryx: The International Journal of Conservation*, Vol 4, 6, December 1958, pp385-6.
45. E Shebbeare, *Soondar Mooni: The Story of an Indian Elephant*, Illustrated by the author, London, Gollancz, 1958, p5.
46. E Shebbeare, 'Elephant Gold. By P. D. Stracey'. *Oryx: The International Journal of Conservation*, Vol 7, 5, August 1964, p262.
47. E Birnie, R Greene, K. Biswas 'Obituary: Edward Oswald Shebbeare (1884-1964)', *Himalayan Journal*, Vol 26, 1965.
48. Anon, 'Shebbeare', *The Carthusian*, December 1964, p101.

were in part driven by his enthusiasm for natural history. His short films shot on the 1933 Everest expedition are remarkable for their focus on the wildlife of the Tibetan plateau, particularly the bird life, featuring shots of alpine chough, Tibetan blue rock dove, brown accentor, Adams' mountain finch and the ubiquitous raven.[49] In retirement he corresponded with the pioneering animal behaviourist Konrad Lorenz and met and corresponded with the Scottish naturalist Seton Gordon, writing an article on the 'Birds of Everest' for *The Field* in 1959-60.[50] His granddaughter still has a letter from Smart's Circus in Oxfordshire granting him permission to visit their elephants any time he chose to.

Shebbeare's life exemplified a profound biophilia, the term coined by the evolutionary biologist E O Wilson. Wilson defined biophilia as the 'urge to affiliate with other forms of life'[51]. Let me illustrate my point by outlining a journey Shebbeare undertook, one that seems to challenge the assertion made by many environmental historians that, during the 20th century, imperial forestry officials increasingly demonstrated a loss of intimacy with the environment.[52] In the very first issue of the *Malay Nature Journal*,[53] Shebbeare describes a journey he made between 27 April and 21 May, 1940[54] to deliver a cow and calf elephant from Jalong in Kuala Kangsar District to the Taman Negara National Park,[55] a month-long journey, 60 miles as the crow flies, into the *ulu*, the deep jungle clinging to the main watershed between the states of Perak and Kelantan. No reason is given for the journey or justification provided for the decision to avoid the main roads, although it is possible to come to some reasonable conclusions about his motivation. Shebbeare set off with 'three Tharu Elephant-men' and 'Yeop Ahmad (our guide)'.[56] It takes a while for the reader to adjust to this new world Shebbeare presents in the article, where elephants are named as friends, where men are defined by the animals they share their working lives with ('elephant-men'). They become bewildered and lost and increasingly dependent on animal agency: 'we had to find our way as we went' Shebbeare tells us, 'using such paths and elephant tracks as existed.'[57] The terrain was so steep that the elephant spent 'almost as much of her time climbing on "nose and knees" or sliding downhill on her quarters'.[58] At the Luwak Jalak pass, at 3,700ft the highest point on the watershed before the drop down into Kelantan, Shebbeare noted that:

49. Royal Geographical Society Film Archive, *Everest – Shebbeare* 11 minutes, *https://player.bfi.org.uk/free/film/watch-everest-shebbeare-1933-online*.
50. Shebbeare Letters, Alpine Club Archive.
51. S Kellert and E Wilson (eds) *The Biophilia Hypothesis*, Island Press, 1995, p416.
52. B Weil, (2006), 'Conservation, Exploitation, and Cultural Change in the Indian Forest Service, 1875-1927', *Environmental History*, Vol 11, April 2006, pp319-43. K Sivaramakrishnan, 'Science, Environment and Empire History: Comparative Perspectives from Forests in Colonial India', *Environment and History*, Vol14, 2008, p56.
53. E O Shebbeare, 'An Elephant Trek', *Malayan Nature Journal*, Vol 1, 1940, pp9-14.
54. The first issue of the *Malayan Nature Journal* was published Vol 1, 1, August 1940. See Anon, 'Malayan Nature Society and Journal', *Nature*, No 3711, 14 December 1940, pp711-2.
55. *http://www.taman-negara.com/park_info.htm*
56. Shebbeare, 'An Elephant Trek', p9.
57. Shebbeare, 'An Elephant Trek', p9.
58. Shebbeare, 'An Elephant Trek', p10.

*'At first sight it looked awkward country for a loaded elephant but we were luckily on the three-day-old tracks of a small wild herd which led us by a traverse across the face to the rather steep head of a side ridge. The gradient of this eased off rapidly into an excellent elephant path.'[59]*

As well as a reliance on animal agency, Shebbeare is scrupulous in acknowledging the indigenous contribution to the co-production of knowledge that made the journey possible. He acknowledges:

*'Yeop Ahmad the Perak Museum Collector whose knowledge of the Temiar, their language and their country made the trip possible. The excellent "Reconnaissance Map of parts of the Ulu Kelantan and Ulu Perak," from which we set our course, was largely built up from his field sketches and observations during earlier treks with Mr. H. D. Noone.'[60]*

H D 'Pat' Noone, the Malayan government protector of aborigines, was already a legend for his anthropological studies of the Temiar and along with his brother Richard was part of Shebbeare's Frontier Patrol the following year in 1941. Noone's work emphasised the 'highly communal, violence-avoiding' character of Temiar society. Noone presented his theories in lectures in England in the late 1930s and in an extended radio talk broadcast from Singapore, he described the Temiar as 'communistic, or rather, co-operative'.[61] Guided by spirits, animal familiars and dreams, Temiar dream-songs and ceremonials mapped the jungle they lived in. According to Marina Roseman, their theories of existence and of the self indicated that they believed in 'a collegial permeability between entities that post-Cartesian Western cosmopolitan philosophy hierarchically differentiates as "human" and "nonhuman".'[62] Noone's work subsequently resulted in a great deal of anthropological controversy over Temiar and Senoi 'Dream Theory'.[63] Noone was also instrumental in the setting up of 'Temiar reserves in Perak state and for the enacting of protective legislation'[64] for aboriginal populations in 1939,[65] the very country through which Shebbeare's elephant trek took place. The *Malayan Nature Journal* that Shebbeare edited clearly saw its remit as wider than just natural history, incorporating an anthropological article in its first issue, and one suspects Noone's influence is behind Shebbeare's application to become a member of the Royal Anthropological Institute in 1940. Shebbeare published an article on 'The Senoi of Malaya'

59. Shebbeare, 'An Elephant Trek', p13.
60. Ibid, p14.
61. G Benjamin, *Temiar Religion, 1964-2012: Enchantment, Disenchantment and Re-enchantment in Malaysia's Uplands*, Singapore, NUS Press, 2014, pp25-7.
62. M Roseman, 'Singers of the Landscape Song: History, and Property Rights in the Malaysian Rain Forest', *American Anthropologist*, New Series, Vol 100, March 1998, p110.
63. G Domhoff, *Senoi Dream Theory: Myth, Scientific Method and the Dreamwork Movement*, Chapter Two 'What Do We Know About the Senoi?', 2003. D Holman, *Noone of the Ulu*, Singapore, Oxford University Press, 1984. R Noone & D Holman (1972) *Rape of the Dream People*, London, Hutchinson, 1972.
64. Benjamin, *Temiar Religion*, p25.
65. D Holman, 'The Frontier Patrol', *Noone of the Ulu*, Singapore, Oxford University Press, 1984, p66. M Burkitt, 'Herbert Deane Noone, 1907-1943', *Man*, Vol 49, May 1949, p55. T Harper, 'The Politics of the Forest in Colonial Malaya', *Modern Asian Studies*, Vol 31, 1, February 1997, pp1-29.

In 1947, following Indian independence, Shebbeare retired to Banbury, Oxford-shire. Raymond Greene, who knew him from Everest, continued to visit him: 'the most loveable, imperturbable and knowledgeable of men'.

in the anthropological journal *Man* in 1947 in which he stated that 'Mr. H. D. Noone' introduced him to the Temiar 'and accompanied me on some of my journeys among them; and when I crossed their country from west to east, his museum collector Yeop Ahmad, came with me as interpreter.'[66] Shebbeare clearly wanted an encounter with the Temiar (as described by Noone) and was frustrated on his 1940 trip in his goal of finding a 'simpler people' on his journey concluding rather glumly: 'If I wanted to meet simpler people I must look for them up side valleys.'[67]

66. E Shebbeare, 'The Senoi of Malaya', *Man*, Vol 47, 168, November 1947, p152.
67. Shebbeare, 'An Elephant Trek', p12.

Disappearing, getting lost, relying on indigenous knowledge, opening your-self up to animal agency, seeking out the primitive: techniques and encoun-ters Shebbeare actively sought out in his journeys into the ulu, techniques not wholly dissimilar from the shamanistic practices and animist belief systems of the aboriginal Temiar,[68] techniques that break down oppositions seemingly inherent in imperialism: between culture-nature, colonist and colonised, the human and the non-human. The anthropologist Michael Taussig, in his book *Mimesis and Alterity* (1993) theorized that colonialism entails at its core a 'dialectic of civilization and savagery',[69] facilitated by the human mimetic faculty which enables the traverse back and forth between these ways of being. This faculty is 'the nature that culture uses to create second nature, the faculty to copy, imitate, make models, explore difference, yield into and become Other.'[70]

In his openness to this process of 'othering' through wilderness encounter, Shebbeare seems to signal a new form of modernity, his biophilia entailing a loss of selfhood and a rejection of nature-culture binaries. Hard as some of us may find it to believe, our modern conservation sensibility has its roots in the work of late-colonial officials like Shebbeare, who moved beyond game-preservation policies designed to support hunting to a fully realised conservation ethic based on the value of all life.

As mountaineers, perhaps we know so little about Shebbeare because, in his encounters with the mountains, jungles and forests of Asia and the subcontinent he moved away from the unending struggle for the summit and learnt instead to 'think like a mountain'. The conservationist Aldo Leo-pold coined the phrase to 'think like a mountain' to express the sense of deep time and interconnectedness implicit in all ecosystems. To 'think like a mountain' is to understand the trophic catastrophes that cascade through an ecosystem when a key predator or prey species is lost. To 'think like a moun-tain' is to see far into the future and understand the unimaginable loss of a world of silent forests and dried up riverbeds. To 'think like a mountain' is to rediscover our affiliation with the community of life on earth. Anthropo-genic climate change finally nails the illusion that we are somehow outside of nature, that we are its conquerors. The historian Peter Hansen has made the case that the emergence of mountaineering in the late 18th century was symbolic of Enlightenment attitudes to nature, that 'the summit position' symbolised both self-mastery and the human mastery of nature.[71] The sum-mit position enabled us to believe that we were somehow outside of nature, looking in from above. The life of E O Shebbeare suggests a way back down from that particular summit.

68. M Roseman (2007) '"Blowing 'Cross the Crest of Mount Galeng": Winds of the Voice, Winds of the Spirits', *The Journal of the Royal Anthropological Institute*, Vol 13, Wind, Life, Health: Anthropological and Historical Perspectives, 2007, s55-s69.
69. M Taussig (1993) *Mimesis and Alterity: A Particular History of the Senses*, London, Routledge), xiv.
70. Taussig, *Mimesis and Alterity*, xiii.
71. P Hansen, *The Summits of Modern Man: Mountaineering After the Enlightenment*, Cambridge, Mass, Harvard University Press, 2013.

KOEN VAN LOOCKE

# All By Themselves

The Alpine Club and Guideless Climbing
in the Nineteenth Century

Edward Whymper's image of the Chamonix Guides.
*(All images: Alpine Club Photo Library)*

In the early days of mountaineering it was not done to climb without
guides. The superior knowledge and technical capacities of early mountain guides most often surpassed those of amateur mountaineers and hiring
guides was the obvious thing to do, as it is for many climbers today. Around
the middle of the 19th century this slowly began to change. Examples start
appearing of mountaineers setting out to climb without guides. In the 1850s
and 1860s this remained a relatively rare phenomenon but from the 1870s
onwards guideless climbing become increasingly widespread, first in the
eastern Alps, and then across the whole Alps and beyond.

While many mountaineers saw this development as the way forward, the
trend was not applauded everywhere. For a long time many influential members of the Alpine Club, together with several mountain guide associations,
remained potent adversaries of this new kind of mountaineering, even after
it was widely accepted elsewhere. It was a debate that raged within the Club,

as the addresses of successive presidents attest. Why was this? What were the differences between the Alpine Club and other associations[1] and the mountaineering community as a whole? From where did these differences come?

### The First Guideless Mountaineers

At the start of modern mountaineering guideless climbing did occur. British examples from these early days include the first guideless ascent of Mont Blanc in 1856 by Kennedy and Hudson, while Tyndall summited Dufourspitze in 1858 and Whymper tried, unsuccessfully, to climb the Matterhorn alone in 1862. The brothers Parker – Alfred, Charles and Sandbach – were the first to reach the summit of the Finsteraarhorn without the use of mountain guides in 1865. The Matterhorn would see a guideless ascent in 1872 from Cust, Cawood and Colgrove.

Yet even though it did occur, guideless climbing, especially amongst British mountaineers, remained rare. Many mountaineers, guides or local people were not happy with such 'heretics'. In 1876 Comyns Tucker, together with Douglas Freshfield, heard his critics ask 'what business had you to try a new peak without guides?'[2] Cust, Cawood and Colgrove left Zermatt for the Matterhorn 'without an encouraging word from anyone, on an enterprise apparently regarded by others of a rash or dubious nature.' The year before, in his book *The Playground of Europe*, Leslie Stephen spoke out against the practice: 'Meanwhile I will only delay my narrative to denounce one other heresy – that, namely, which asserts that guides are a nuisance.' This opposition was mainly based on the feeling that, as Stephen describes it, 'Amongst the greatest of Alpine pleasures is that of learning to appreciate the capacities and cultivate the goodwill of a singularly intelligent and worthy class of men.'

The capacities of local mountain guides were seen as superior to the potential climbing skills of amateur climbers. Up until the Golden Age (1854-65) this was probably true. However, during this period, more and more amateur climbers improved rapidly and started to outgrow many mountain guides. The reasons for this development were, among others, the improved organisation of mountain climbing (i.e. the alpine clubs) and the personal development of many mountaineers, but also the stagnation of the development of mountain guides in Chamonix and elsewhere.[3]

Before we can turn to the question why many mountaineers, guides, or associations were opposed to the practice of guideless climbing, we will take a brief look at why an increasing number of mountaineers actually started to climb without guides; why they felt 'climbing […] is in all cases very incomplete unless it is done without guides.'[4] The reasons given are not to be

1. For instance in France. A Lunn, *A Century of Mountaineering 1857-1957*, London, Allen & Unwin, 1957, p137. *'The guided climber hardly exists for the modernists of the French school, but they make an exception for Young.'*
2. C Tucker, 'The Cima Dela Vezzana', *Alpine Journal*, VII, 1876, p61.
3. K Van Loocke, 'The Shaping of Nineteenth Century Guiding, *Alpine Journal*, 2015, p273-83. The Alpine Club not only influenced the Chamonix mountain guides, they had a considerable influence on the outlook and organisation of Swiss, German, and Austrian mountain guiding. D Freshfield, 'Alpine Notes', *Alpine Journal*, VI, 1874, pp369-72.
4. J Stogdon, 'Random Memories of Some Early Guideless Climbs', *Alpine Journal*, XXX, 1916, p156.

seen as a complete list. On the contrary: every mountaineer has or had their own personal reasons. The reasons provided in this article are based on elements that frequently reoccur in Alpine literature, diaries, letters and so forth.

A first and often reoccurring motivation was, and still is, to attain a sense of freedom; to be able to ascribe the success as well as failure of ascents to one's own responsibility and qualities.[5] By hiring guides, according to A F Mummery, there is 'the absolute certainty with which the day's proceedings are carried out.' Surprises will not be met, and when it comes to memories, 'there is, similarly, infinite delight in recalling all the varying chances of a long and hard fought victory; but the memory of a weary certainty behind two untiring guides, is wholly colourless, and soon fades into the indistinguishable past.'[6] Imagination, creativity, responsibility and intelligence fade away 'under the unimaginative tyranny of any two chance peasants between whom they are advised to suspend the exercise of their own finer faculties and the direction of their very differently constituted frames.' According to G W Young, such mountaineers 'are in no sense mountaineers, and they may never become so, any more than those who cross the Channel in a steamboat are qualifying as sailors.'[7] Only without guides was a mountaineer truly in command of his own movement, was he solely responsible for the success or failure of his enterprise, and were his creativity, intelligence and imagination wholly challenged. This combined with a sense of *Ehrgeiz*[8] – ambition, the search for glory,[9] and especially the wish to attain difficult goals on their own, not aided by mountain guides – persuaded many mountaineers to let go of the aid of mountain guides. This same motivation, often in combination with a powerful need for individual freedom, urges mountaineers not only to climb without guides, but also alone.

There was a second, more pragmatic reason, which hindered the hiring of guides: cost. This socio-economic element was most notably present in the eastern Alps and so the region was responsible for an enormous growth in guideless climbing. German or Austrian working-class rock climbers – of which there were many – did not possess the same financial means to hire

5. Ibid. *'In any case the trade must be learnt under professionals, but the joy of performance, the pleasure of well-applied knowledge and the application of all the delicate arts of the game can never be really felt till a man depends entirely on himself.'* Also W Kirkpatrick, 'Ten Years Without Guides', *Alpine Journal*, XXII, 1905, p549. *'Moreover without guides you can go your own pace. You can halt as long as you like at, and after, yours meals and on top of your mountain. There is a delightful feeling of freedom and independence, and, above all, what you do you do yourself.'* And G Hastings, 'Over Mont Blanc, by the Brenva Route, without Guides', *Alpine Journal*, XVII, 1895, p537. *'One of the many merits of guideless climbing is that you are always free to discard old routes and attempt new ways.'*
6. A Mummery, *My Climbs in the Alps and Caucasus*, London, T Fisher Unwin, 1895, pp92-3.
7. G Young, Mountain Craft, London, Methuen, 1920, p101-2. *'The great public [...] cherishes one fixed idea on the subject of climbing – that the guide is a providence who knows and shows and goes the one sacred and impeccable 'path' which every genuine mountain possesses: to go without him is to tempt destruction deliberately; [...] The importance of the error is that its persistence permits it to dominate the minds of a large number of men who 'do mountains' every year from hotels. To them, mountaineering means only the traditional route up in the traditional way; and tradition demands the surrender of their intelligence and personal inclinations for a day to the unimaginative tyranny of any two chance peasants between whom they are advised to suspend the exercise of their own finer faculties and the direction of their very differently constituted frames. Their ambition is laudable, but they are in no sense mountaineers, and they may never become so, any more than those who cross the Channel in a steamboat are qualifying as sailors. But they form a considerable portion of those who go among the mountains, and include a large number of those who give the public their experiences. In so far their patronage contributes to confirm and perpetuate the long-lived error.'*
8. P Grupp, *Faszination Berg: Die Geschichte des Alpinismus*, Köln, Böhlau, 2008, p73.
9. This *Ehrgeiz* would influence the so-called 'heroic climbing style' practiced by mostly German and Austrian climbers during the 1930s under national socialism.

Celebrity guides, including Jacob Anderegg (1829-1878). Anderegg, from the Swiss village of Meiringen, is perhaps best known for the first ascent of the Brenva Spur in 1865, an achievement overlooked in the aftermath of the near-contemporaneous Matterhorn disaster. That summer he also made first ascents of the Piz Roseg, the Obergabelhorn and the Pigne d'Arolla.

Franz Andermatten (1823-1883). In his early days he climbed with Curé Imseng and also with Melchior Ulrich with whom, and others, he made the first recorded crossings of the Ried and Adler passes. Among his first ascents were the Strahlhorn, Lagginhorn and the Nadelhorn. In 1872, by then in his late 40s, he was one of the guides on the first ascent of the Zinalrothorn from Zermatt.

mountain guides every time they wanted to climb as their mostly middle-class British counterparts. Yet even the Alpine Club acknowledged the high cost of hiring mountain guides was 'a serious hindrance to mountaineering.'[10] For many mountaineers, hiring a guide was a luxury.[11]

The organisation of mountain guiding was also a factor. For some, guideless climbing was a way – often the only way – to oppose sclerotic rules or traditions hindering the development of mountaineering whether on an individual or wider level. For example, around Chamonix British mountaineers set out on guideless exploits motivated by 'love of adventure, by the hope of breaking through the exclusive Chamonix system.'[12] This Chamonix system blocked many mountaineering innovations during the 1860s

10.  F Grove 'Alpine Notes', *Alpine Journal*, VI, 1874, pp430-1.
11.  G Young, *On High Hills*, 1927, p39. *'But on many days during the first season in the Val d'Anniviers, I was alone. Because guides were luxuries, and, of still more consequence, it took long to overcome that shyness of mixing with men of a different language and class which weighs heavily upon a type of public-school-bred islander.'*
12.  W Longman, *Modern Mountaineering and the History of the Alpine Club*, London, Longman, 1878, p15. '… the wish to break down the oppressive and mischievous system on which the Chamonix guides were managed, and for this purpose they* [Hudson and Kennedy] *determined to go without guides.'*

Johann Joseph Bennen (1824-1864) was born in Steinhaus and based at Laax in the Conches valley. Not only did he make the first ascent of the Weisshorn with John Tyndall, he made attempts on the Italian ridge of the Matterhorn. Tyndall wrote in his Führerbuch that he bore 'the same relation to the common run of guides as Wellington to an ordinary subaltern.' He died in an avalanche on 28 February 1864 attempting a winter ascent in the Bernese Oberland.

Michel Croz (1828-1865) was born in Le Tour above Chamonix and began his guiding career when William Mathews hired him for an ascent of Mont Blanc. He quickly became one of the most sought-after guides of his era. Whymper wrote after their crossing of the Col de la Pilatte of the 'ability with which Croz led us through a dense mist'. Whymper continued: 'As an exhibition of strength and skill, it has seldom been surpassed in the Alps or elsewhere.'

and 1870s. Under pressure of mountaineers and alpine associations Chamonix would eventually modernise.[13]

Another reason to give up on mountain guides was insufficient expertise. Although mountain guiding improved throughout the 19th century, progress could be held up or even thwarted. Lack of clear rules, growing demand, the absence of training courses or professional organisations all had a serious impact on the qualities of guides. Many guides, especially before the 1870s and 1880s, but also later on,[14] had dubious mountaineering skills. In time, the professionalism of mountain guiding would dramatically improve but in this critical period the dubious skills of guides could persuade some mountaineers to set out on their own.

At the same time, many top alpinists simply outgrew their mountain

---

13. K Van Loocke, 'The Shaping of Nineteenth Century Guiding', *Alpine Journal*, 2015, p273-83.
14. The Alpine Journal of 1903 includes as causes of accidents that year *'an increase in the quantity and a decrease in the quality of the guides.'* This evolution or feeling may have encouraged some to start climbing without the use of guides, whether they were prepared for it or not. G Yeld (ed), 'Alpine Accidents in 1903', *Alpine Journal*, XXI, 1903, p552.

guides. Many Austrian and German climbers focussed almost exclusively on rock climbing, prompting rapid technical development in the late 19th century. This continuous improvement of rock climbing techniques and the urge to climb ever more difficult routes made climbing with guides more or less obsolete.[15] This reason corresponds to Mummery's explanation of why guideless climbing was more rewarding.[16]

A final reason can be found in the changing relationships between mountain guides and mountaineers. In the early days, mountaineers and guides often teamed up for long periods of time. Spells of several weeks were not exceptional.[17] As a result, the Golden Age is known for its profound relationships between guide and client. From the 1860s and 1870s onwards this changed. Each year, more tourists were coming to the Alps – a commodification of the Alps and mountaineering if you will – and often for shorter periods of time. The strong bond between client and guide that had once been common became increasingly rare. Among skilled mountaineers there was a sense that guides were no longer strong and independent but not much more than servants.

> *'The swarming of the tourist has brought with it the wretched distinctions of class, and the modern guide inhabits the guide's room and sees his Monsieur only when actually on an expedition. Cut off from the intercourse of the old days, the guide tends more and more to belong to the lackey tribe, and the ambitious tourist looks upon him much as his less aspiring brother regards his mule. The constant repetition of the same ascent has, moreover, tended to make the guide into a sort of contractor. For so many tens or hundreds of francs he will take you anywhere you like to name.'* [18]

Mountain guides, according to some, lost their sense of independence, creativity, and even strength. At the same time, many mountaineers must have felt as if 'the skill of the traveller counts for absolutely naught; the practised guide looks on him merely as luggage.' This was all the more reason to

15.  C Dent, 'Amateurs and Professional Guides of the Present Day', *Alpine Journal*, XII, 1886, p296. *'On rock mountains many seem to think that a guide's powers so conspicuously excel those of his amateur rival, that even an inferior professional is vastly superior to the best amateur. [...] That this is much less the case now than formerly, ascents of the Meije, or the still more notable instance of discovery by amateurs of the right route up the Monte della Disgrazia from the Val Malenco side, sufficiently prove. The latter, indeed, is perhaps the most conspicuous instance of amateurs succeeding where the best of guides had tried and failed.'* C Pilkington, 'Address to the Alpine Club', *Alpine Journal*, XIX, 1899, p297. *'But we are now* [at the end of the 19th century] *faced with the fact that only a few alpine peasants can acquire these qualities, and that the demand for good guides is larger than the supply.'*
16.  Even around the 1900s, guides in Chamonix were not always very well qualified, despite being urge to continually improve by the Alpine Club mountaineers and other alpine associations, particularly the Swiss Alpine Club, suggesting problems had not disappeared since the 1860s and 1870s. G Young, *On High Hills*, 1927, p163. *'On my first visit to the Aiguilles, four of us had spent some twenty wicked hours upon the insidious little peak. Misled as to the route by the misstatements of some worser Chamonix guides – from whose threats of maltreatment in the valley I had still, in those distant days, to protect my 'foreigner' Knubel – we had assaulted the great Requin buttress directly up from the Mer de Glace, and so made, unwittingly, a first ascent as difficult as that of the Dru.'* G Young, *On High Hills*, p258. *'It is a matter of experience that good guides are least enterprising in their own valley. The difficult and the unclimbed in their own region are familiar to them as such, traditionally; and the voice of an inferior herd of colleagues, clamorous against any challenge to the tradition, destroys their initiative. As the moment approached for defying the terrors of the east ridge, invested for him from childhood with the superstition of inaccessibility, Laurent, our own local providence, was evidently fighting a losing battle with the genius of valley pessimism.'*
17.  A Wills, *Wandering Among The High Alps*, London, Richard Bentley, 1856, p318.
18.  A Mummery, *My Climbs in the Alps and Caucasus*, p90-1.

climb without guides.[19]

The truth is that thanks to this growth in tourism mountain guiding actually improved rapidly across the Alps.[20] This period saw the establishment of mountain guiding associations, stricter regulations and training courses for guides. Even so, many skilled mountaineers during the latter half of the 19th and early 20th century were convinced that the increase in tourism had caused a negative effect on the overall qualities of mountain guiding and this perception also drove guideless climbing. But the fact remains that despite the increasing popularity of guideless climbing among the elite, mountain guides remained very important to the bulk of mountaineers. The growth in tourism allowed guides to make improvements and took guiding away from the pioneer scientists and mountaineers of the mid 19th century. At the same time, the rise in standards among elite mountaineers also drove a rise in technical standards among guides.[21]

Until the 1860s and early 1870s guides were seen as an absolute necessity among the vast majority of mountaineers. The Alps were scarcely explored and mountaineering techniques were mediocre at best. Mountaineers, with little or no local experience or knowledge had little choice but to entrust themselves to mountain guides[22] if they wanted to climb and explore hitherto untrodden places. Then, as knowledge and access to it improved, that dynamic changed.[23] In the eastern Alps this happened much faster than in the western Alps. In the western Alps, where most British mountaineers were active, the trend of guideless climbing developed at a slower rate. As the socio-economic element was of less importance, most mountaineers kept climbing with mountain guides. This socio-economic element also influenced the point of view of the Alpine Club with regard to guideless climbing.

While some welcomed the change, others did not. It's understandable that mountain guides and their associations were not best pleased, fearing their revenues might decrease and their status be diminished. As it happened, guided mountaineering experienced strong growth, a process that continues, and so guides didn't experience much, or even any, damage to their profession. Perhaps more surprising was the displeasure and even animosity of many British amateur mountaineers at the Alpine Club, where a majority remained opposed to guideless climbing until the late 19th century and even beyond. This opposition is illustrated in the numbers who continued to hire guides but also in the way that guideless climbers felt the need to defend themselves against attacks on the 'folly' of their enterprises.

These advocates were sometimes explicit in arguing that guideless

---

19. A Mummery, *My Climbs in the Alps and Caucasus*, p90-1.
20. A Hungerbühler, *Könige der Alpen*, 2013. K Van Loocke, 'Geld, Vriendschap en Sociale Tegenstellingen. Een onderzoek naar de paradoxale relaties tussen gidsen en alpinisten in de negentiende eeuw', master's dissertation, P François (supervisor), Ghent University, University of Hertfordshire, 2010, p201.
21. G Young, *On High Hills*, p98-103. *'I was making to train on a young and unspoiled guide.'* Also by associations representing mountaineers: K Van Loocke, 2015.
22. Although at this time mountain guides were mostly herdsmen and farmers who occasionally guided tourists on glaciers or mountain peaks.
23. For the vast majority of mountaineers, meaning tourists, guides remained almost indispensable. The story told here is applicable to elite mountaineers. These may be only a minority, but despite this, elite mountaineers did create and develop the framework wherein all mountaineers were active.

A pack of Knubels. Nicklaus Knubel (1841-1877) from his *carte de visite*. It was Niklaus who led Lucy Walker on the first female ascent of the Matterhorn and then Margaret Breevoort on the first female ascent from the Italian side. He died with his brothers Johann and Peter Joseph, along with their employers Lewis and Paterson, in the terrible Lyskamm tragedy of 1877, when a cornice collapsed underneath them.

Peter Knubel (1832-1919) was the first Swiss guide to climb beyond the Alps, having made the first ascent of Elbrus (5642m) with Frederick Gardiner, Florence Crauford Grove and Horace Walker. He was also on hand to assist in the terrible aftermath of the Lyskamm accident which killed his three brothers. He continued to guide into his 70s on the Matterhorn.

climbing was superior.[24] 'In 1892,' Mummery wrote, 'I once again started for the mountain. This time we were without guides, for we had learnt the great truth that those who wish to really enjoy the pleasures of mountaineering, must roam the upper snows trusting exclusively to their own skill and knowledge.'[25] Mummery had in his early career had a strong relationship with A Burgener but others who espoused the values of guideless climbing could also continue to climb with them, Geoffrey Winthrop Young being a good example. The paradox illustrates I think how guided climbing was part of the Alpine Club's cultural fabric.[26] While British alpinists towards the end of the 19th century did not have to defend themselves as strongly as before for their guideless undertakings,[27] this paradoxical stand remained present.

24. Especially in the second half of the 19th century when guideless climbing increased immensely. 'Alpine Notes', *Alpine Journal*, XXVI, 1912, pp215-6; G Yeld (ed)), 'The Alpine Club Library', *Alpine Journal*, XIII, 1907, p160; p487.
25. A Mummery, *My Climbs in the Alps and Caucasus*, p90.
26. Mountaineers did not always have much choice of climbing partner. Mountain guides offered a solution to this problem and were available for longer periods. Guide and amateur were to some extent bound to each other, seeing each other as partners and companions, rather than being in a straightforward client-guide relationship. Lunn considered Young's association with Knubel *'had far more in common with that which unites members of a guideless party.'* A Lunn, 'Geoffrey Winthrop Young', *Alpine Journal*, 1961, pp100-17.
27. Numerous entries in the *Alpine Journal* of guideless ascents confirm this.

Joseph Knubel (1881-1961) between H O Jones and Geoffrey Winthrop Young in 1911. The son of Peter Knubel, he qualified as a guide in 1904, continuing to work as a stonemason and lumberjack. Young spotted his abilities as a guide and they climbed together each year between 1906 and the outbreak of war, making some of the most impressive first ascents of the Edwardian area.

Geoffrey Winthrop Young and Joseph Knubel in Zermatt in 1948. Their accomplishments together were legendary: new routes on the Zinalrothorn, the Weisshorn, Lyskamm, the mountain that killed his uncles, and the Täschhorn. Arnold Lunn taught him how to ski and he went on to make groundbreaking ski tours. Young approved of guideless climbing in theory, but it practice enjoyed climbing too much with Knubel to give him up.

## The Alpine Club

The Alpine Club was founded by mountaineers accustomed to climbing with guides. Guideless climbing happened, but it was rare. The idea of amateurs tackling the same mountains on their own, let alone by more difficult routes, was unthinkable. Some members wanted the Alpine Club to speak out explicitly 'against mountaineering without guides, a practice I believe to be fraught with danger.'[28] Several of the first generation of British mountaineers feared that 'if ever it becomes fashionable for English travellers to attack the high Alps without guides and without due experience, the era of bad accidents will begin.'[29] This group was more or less convinced that amateurs could not attain the same mountaineering qualities as guides, not least because 'the guide has been practicing during his whole life, the amateur during a few vacations.'[30] Climbing without guides was, in their eyes, not completely impossible – for instance on smaller excursions, when

28. F Grove, 'The Comparative Skill of Travellers and Guides', *Alpine Journal*, V, 1872, p95.
29. L Stephen, 'Alpine Dangers', *Alpine Journal*, II, 1866, p280-1. Or: W Longman, *Modern Mountaineering and the History of the Alpine Club*, 1878, p37. '… *I think* [re: Tyndall] … *if climbing without guides were to become habitual, deplorable consequences would assuredly sooner or later ensue.*'
30. L Stephen, 'Alpine Dangers', *Alpine Journal*, II, 1866, p281.

guides were not available[31], or after years and years of training[32] – but for most it would be altogether risky and reckless.[33] Many of the early British guideless ascents often provoked 'an outburst of indignant criticism.'[34] Within the Alpine Club there was, however, from the beginning a discussion on this matter, even though many did not agree with the trend. A general agreement was found that 'the neglect to take [guides] when the party is not exclusively composed of practised mountaineers, is totally unjustifiable, and calculated to produce the most lamentable results.' Yet, the Alpine Club was convinced that 'it is impossible to give a formal code of rules upon the subject.'[35] Clear and distinct rules on when and when not to take guides on excursions never came into existence, yet warnings regarding the subject of guideless mountaineering appeared regularly in the *Alpine Journal*.

A negative stance on guideless climbing did not only arrive out of cautiousness. It was also caused by the fear of several mountaineers that their achievements might be devalued and they might appear to be second-class mountaineers: 'a standard was being set which was higher than that to which they could attain. [...] it was inevitable that those who could not lead a guideless party up a second-class peak would not welcome a development which threatened to divide mountaineers into the guideless élite and a guided proletariat.'[36] While the Alpine Club showed itself to be very progressive during the 1850s and 1860s when they were at the frontline in trying to urge the Compagnie des Guides de Chamonix to let go of their own conservatism and start opening up towards new trends and innovations, after a few decades it was the Alpine Club itself that became conservative and protective of the past.

Finally, this negative point of view was, perhaps often indirectly or subconsciously, based on a romanticised view of mountain guiding. One or more amateurs together with one or more guides were the 'ideal type', to use the terminology of Max Weber,[37] of a mountaineering partnership: *seilschaft* in German. In the 1860s this particular ideal type was its zenith. Travel stories and papers in the *Alpine Journal* often refer to the way amateurs looked up at mountain guides. It was a paradigm the first generation of mostly British amateurs helped construct and offered considerable resistance when people started to climb without guides. Opposition to this ideal

31. J Bryce, 'The Ascent of Ararat', *Alpine Journal*, VIII, 1878, p210. *'I am no disciple of that gospel of mountaineering without guides which Mr. Girdlestone has preached so zealously by example as well as precept. But if there is any justification for the practice, that justification exists when guides are not to be had.'*

32. D Freshfield (ed), 'Proceedings of the Alpine Club', *Alpine Journal*, VIII, 1878, p232: *'Expeditions without guides were, no doubt, highly enjoyable, but were only justifiable when the members of the party had first qualified themselves for the work by the training which all authorities agreed was necessary to make a good mountaineer.'* See also: C Mathews, 'New Experiences in the Old Playground', *Alpine Journal*, XVI, 1893, p22.

33. C Dent, 'Address to the Alpine Club', *Alpine Journal*, XV, 1891, p13: *'The truth is that the number of amateurs really competent to undertake serious expeditions without guides is considerably less than the number who think that they can do so.'*

34. C Mathews, 'The Growth of Mountaineering', *Alpine Journal*, X, 1882, p256.

35. F Grove, 'The Comparative Skill of Travellers and Guides', *Alpine Journal*, V, 1872, p96.

36. A Lunn, *A Century of Mountaineering 1857-1957*, 1957, p86.

37. M Weber, *Methodology of the Social Sciences*, New York, Free Press, 1949. L McFalls, *Max Weber's 'Objectivity' Reconsidered*, Toronto, University of Toronto Press, 2007.

type was perceived as harmful to the image of mountaineering, through a feared increase of accidents. This, of course, was to be prevented. British mountaineering had suffered very public disasters and been the subject of public disapproval. This had sensitised many in the Alpine Club to the prospect of further bad news. Innovation carried with it a threat.

This point of view, so common in the Alpine Club, could be called conservative. While other associations, French, German, Austrian and so on, embraced guideless climbing, the Alpine Club dragged its heels.[38] At the same time, this conservatism doesn't have to be seen as necessarily negative. By constantly informing mountaineers of the possible dangers, the responsibility and experience that is needed, and by being extremely cautious, accidents may well have been prevented. Seen over the long term, we can say that 'even if the Alpine Club tended in the past to overstress caution, this was a fault on the right side.'[39] While in the early days the Alpine Club was more or less opposed to the emergence of guideless climbing, in later years they accepted the new phenomenon, but at the same time maintained a prudent approach. This point of view can be summarized with the words of Frederick Pollock: 'As to climbing without guides, it is a thing neither to be lightly undertaken nor to be indiscriminately condemned.'[40]

This conservatism did not mean that guideless climbs were not acknowledged or guideless climbers were banned or even unwelcome in the Alpine Club.[41] Nevertheless, it was not encouraged and often contested. Until the 1880s, guideless climbers experienced difficulties in being acknowledged by the Alpine Club. They were 'told in a nice (I mean really nice) letter, […] that my conduct was utterly subversive of the highest mountaineering morality and might easily lead silly sheep astray.'[42]

38. A Lunn, *A Century of Mountaineering 1857-1957*, 1957, p137. *'The guided climber hardly exists for the modernists of the French school, but they make an exception for Young.'* While the Alpine Club might have been more reserved towards guideless climbing than other mountaineering associations, this does not mean those associations embraced guideless climbing without any debate. 'Reviews and Notices', *Jahrbuch des Schweizer Alpenclub*, vol XXIII, Bern, 1887-8, reproduced in *Alpine Journal*, XIV, p263. *'At the annual meeting at Bienne in August 1887, the question of mountaineering without guides was warmly discussed. It was finally agreed that any direction of the club* [SAC] *in the matter would lead to no good result, if it did not aggravate the evil.'*

39. A Lunn, *A Century of Mountaineering 1857-1957*, 1957, p239.

40. F Pollock, 'In Memoriam', *Alpine Journal*, X, 1882, p81. Even Leslie Stephen, a strong advocate of mountain guides, stated in the late 1880s that *'a man should, if possible, qualify himself to climb without guides. To take a guide is an obvious precaution, necessary for some people even in the simplest expeditions, unnecessary for others even in the most difficult. Every vigorous young man should try to place himself in the class which can dispense with guides. That is the way to restore the charm of novelty to peaks already climbed. […] And in this matter, I hold that the Alpine Club should do everything in its power to set a high standard, to condemn all rashness, and to point out that it is as dangerous to dispense with a guide as to dispense with a rope in crossing hidden crevasses, until you have skill and experience enough to be capable of acting as a guide to yourself.'* L Stephen, 'Alpine Notes', *Alpine Journal*, XIII, 1888, p469.

41. For instance: J Farrar, 'Passages in 1860' *Alpine Journal*, XXX, 1916, p25. *'The two brothers Alfred and Sandbach Parker were elected members of the Alpine Club, on guideless qualifications, in December 1860, and remained members for many years.'*. On the other hand, many, but not all, did oppose this new tendency to leave behind mountain guides. *'As regards guideless climbing, Mathews did not go so far as some older men, who protested against it altogether.'* F Morshead, 'In Memoriam', *Alpine Journal*, XXII, 1905, p597.

42. J Stogdon, 'Random Memories of Some Early Guideless Climbs', *Alpine Journal*, XXX, 1916, p147.

## A Change of Heart[43]

The Alpine Club's objection to guideless climbing was diminishing towards the end of the 19th century.[44] From the 1870s onwards guideless mountaineering had been properly discussed by the Alpine Club, but it was only then than it became widely accepted.[45] 'It may be said,' the president Charles Pilkington told the Alpine Club in 1899, 'that at no time in our history has climbing without guides been more popular than at present. In days of yore the words 'guideless climbing' have often been the prelude to a note of warning; but a glance over the names associated with recent guideless expeditions suggests that the time-honoured admonition may now be withheld.'[46]

The process of this acceptance can be seen in the way the *Alpine Journal* approached the subject. Before c1880 reports on guideless ascents were more or less absent. Over the course of the 1880s more and more first-hand reports of guideless expeditions were published.[47] These were accepted but the Alpine Club remained very prudent as they 'strongly felt that Messrs Gardiner and Pilkingtons' example was only to be followed with impunity by equally competent mountaineers; and that there is no reason for the club to alter its previously expressed opinion that 'mountaineering without guides' is for 'the general a highly dangerous form of amusement which it is its duty, as a body, to discourage.'[48]

The 'Alpine Obituary' in the 1884 edition of the *Alpine Journal*, written by the founding member C E Mathews, offers another excellent example of this Alpine Club point of view. Mathews warns his readers of the dangers of guideless climbing as well as solo climbing.[49] He does not condemn it but warns people about the possible dangers.[50] A few years later, guideless

43. Outside of the Alps, after early experiments in the Andes and Himalaya, the practice of using European guides quickly disappeared. Local men, often Sherpas, performed some of the functions of early guides, but were employed as high-altitude porters rather than climbing guides on the mountain. Only recently have they acquired the high technical skills of modern guides.

44. H Walker, 'Address to the Alpine Club' *Alpine Journal*, XVI, 1893, p288. *'Guideless climbing, which, under proper conditions, has received the approval of the authorities on mountaineering, has been increasingly practiced.'* D Freshfield, 'An Address to the Alpine Club', *Alpine Journal*, XVIII, 1897, p12. *'Then in some independent minds a bold counsel of perfection was broached – to climb without guides. The first Englishman to put it in practice succeeded only in proving that for some people, including himself, the experiment was too rash. The conservatives among us chuckled prematurely over the indiscretions Mr Girdlestone revealed to the world. For meantime another party, Mr Charles Pilkington, Mr Lawrence Pilkington, and Mr Gardiner, were steadily setting themselves to be as capable as guides. The experiment, in my opinion, was perfectly legitimate, it has proved successful, and it has led to a great advance in mountaineering. It may be granted that in the very front rank of mountaineers there will always be two guides to every amateur. [...] But I do not see my way to allow much more. I am conscious that this is indeed a change from the time – before 1885 – when to whisper that an amateur might become nearly as a good as a guide was held to be the mark of a vain boaster or an ignorant person. But, judging from recent experience, there are now members of the Club with whom I would rather go up a mountain that with any guide out of the first rank.'* C Pilkington, 'Address to the Alpine Club', *The Alpine Journal*, XIX, 1899, pp296-7. *'But whoever was the first offender, guideless climbing gradually came to be recognized as a necessary evil, and the older members of the Club slowly yielded their assent. But they only did so with many protests and much good advice, recognizing that in this matter we should move cautiously if we were to ensure safety.'*

45. D Freshfield, 'Proceedings of the Club', *Alpine Journal*, VI, 1874, p256. *'Mr. Macdonald observed that 'Mountaineering without Guides' had been recently fully considered the Club.'*

46. H Woolley, 'Address to the Alpine Club', *Alpine Journal*, XXV, 1911, p375.

47. F Gardiner, 'Mountaineering in Dauphiné Without Guides', *Alpine Journal*, IX, 1880, pp219-34. *'Mr. Gardiner and his companions (Messrs C and L Pilkington) were on all sides warmly congratulated on the remarkable success of their experiment.'*

48. D Freshfield (ed), 'Proceedings of the Alpine Club', *Alpine Journal*, IX, 1880, p240.

49. During the 19th century, and after, the Alpine Club seriously opposed the idea of solitary mountaineering. H Walker, 'Address to the Alpine Club', *Alpine Journal*, XVI, 1893, p288. *'There is one form of it, however, which has been unsparingly condemned from this chair, of which, I regret to say, sporadic cases still occur. I refer to solitary climbing.'*

50. C Mathews, 'The Alpine Obituary', *Alpine Journal*, XI, 1884, pp78-89.

The great A F Mummery and an unidentified climber on Cristallo in the Dolomites. It was Mummery more than anyone who articulated the philosophical foundations of guideless climbing.

climbing had become 'an interesting, and legitimate outgrowth of modern mountaineering,'[51] provided that the necessary caution was taken into account. Otherwise 'guideless climbing is likely to fall into disrepute, and a most admirable form of exercise would thus be condemned, owing to the carelessness of a few of the increasing number who find pleasure in such climbing.'[52]

But even though guideless climbing was no longer in theory problematic, the notion of guideless climbing by insufficiently trained, inexperienced or reckless climbers absolutely was. The long-serving *Alpine Journal* editor George Yeld wrote in 1907 of 'the dangerous increase in the numbers of unqualified, guideless parties attempting the great peaks. We have no quarrel with guideless climbing. An expert has every right to choose for himself, and there is far more of mountaineering and of holiday in crossing a small pass with tried friends for pleasure than in being treated as an item in the

51. C Mathews, 'The Growth of Mountaineering', *Alpine Journal*, X, 1882, p256.
52. W Coolidge (ed), 'Alpine Notes', *Alpine Journal*, XII, 1886, p423.

business of a big climb by an unsympathetic peasant.'[53] Snobbery aside, this is a point of view still held by most, if not all, mountaineering associations.

## The Impact of Disapproval

It is almost – if not entirely – impossible to measure the precise effects of the Alpine Club's position on guideless mountaineering towards its members. We can only speculate on the number of British mountaineers climbing with guides who would have taken on guideless climbing if the Alpine Club had been more indulgent. Notable guideless mountaineers G W Young and A F Mummery reflected thoroughly on their own stance towards guideless climbing.[54] They and others were strong proponents of guideless climbing in practice, but more so in their writings. Perhaps in the distinction between their practice and theoretical principles we can deduce some of the effects of the conservative approach of the Alpine Club.

Not only did Geoffrey Winthrop Young continue to climb with mountain guides, he formed strong partnerships, even comradeships with them, particularly Joseph Knubel. He identified, perhaps paradoxically, more than most with the romanticised ideal type observed above. Young struggled with his own views on guideless climbing. It was his theoretical ideal, but in practice he held on to 'his' mountain guide, just as many others did. Even though they were more often seen as chaperons than true mountain guides, this habit reveals the dominant vision within the British mountaineering community. Even on 'easier' excursions many mountaineers, even as late as the early 20th century, felt the need to hire one or more guides, even if it was only because they 'thought it discreet to engage a […] guide.'[55]

This culture of guided climbing was also reflected in how guided climbs were presented in the *Alpine Journal* and how there was an attempt to minimise the difference between guided and guideless ascents.[56] Top climbers tried to minimise the very real distinction between guideless and guided climbing: as for instance in the following passage from *Mountain Craft*, quoted in an essay on Young written by Arnold Lunn: '... he will not allow his decision to take a guide to be influenced by any fear that the credit of his party will be diminished in any competent mountaineer's eyes by the fact that a prejudiced or a thoughtless modern virtuosity might jeer at it as "guided".'[57] The influence of a more conservative tradition of mountaineering is set against a new and rapidly developing trend. Both had met in the seminal figure of Geoffrey Winthrop Young.

53. G Yeld (ed), 'Alpine Accidents in 1907', *Alpine Club*, XXIII, 1907, p638.
54. A Mummery, *My Climbs in the Alps and Caucasus*, 1895; G Young, *On High Hills & Mountain Craft*, 1927 & 1920.
55. G Young, *On High Hills*, 1927, p63. *'All the same, since the Finsteraarhorn was to be our training walk, we thought it discreet to engage a crabbed but respectable local guide as a chaperon, for our introduction at least.'*
56. If Young preferred guideless climbing, he mostly climbed with guides, particularly Knubel. *'I admit that I climb with a guide. The confession is painful but necessary, and I must hope that the weakness will be attributed not so much to a want of originality as to a preference for a sense of security. I find that, take him all round, the guide meets me in better training, lasts rather longer, and occasionally climbs even better than the majority of amateurs with a month's holiday ...'* Arnold Lunn considered Young's association with Knubel *'had far more in common with that which unites members of a guideless party.'* A Lunn, 'Geoffrey Winthrop Young', *Alpine Journal*, 1961, pp100-17.
57. A Lunn, 'Geoffrey Winthrop Young', *Alpine Journal*, 1961, pp114.

C A RUSSELL

# One Hundred Years Ago

The fine weather experienced in many parts of the Alps in January 1918 enabled Fritz Egger and Hans Lauper, both members of the Akademischer Alpen-Club Bern, to undertake a winter ascent of the Bietschhorn. After reaching the north summit by way of the west-south-west ridge and being too late to continue to the highest point they retraced their steps to the Bietschhorn hut by moonlight.

In February the Dent d'Hérens was ascended by Herbert Hafers de Magalhaes with the guides Adolf Schaller and Viktor Biner, using ski from the Schönbiel hut to the foot of the Tiefmattenjoch. In the following month two medical students, Hermann Rey and Ludwig Gelpke with Heinrich Supersaxo completed two successful expeditions to make the first winter ascents of three high peaks above the Saas valley. Starting from the Hotel Weissmies – later the Weissmies hut – they reached the summit of the Lagginhorn and three days later, climbing from the Mischabel hut, ascended the east-north-east ridge of the Lenzspitze, traversed to the Nadelhorn over the Nadeljoch and returned to the hut by way of the Windjoch. Other peaks ascended for the first time in winter included the Aiguille du Moine in the Mont Blanc range.

The weather during the mountaineering season was notable for long settled spells and it was unfortunate, as the First World War continued, that few climbers were able to take advantage of the favourable conditions. At Chamonix some guides were employed by American servicemen on leave who wished to ascend Mont Blanc whereas the Swiss climbing centres were often almost deserted.

One member of the Alpine Club who was able to spend a month at Zermatt was A C Morrison-Bell who, after being held in captivity in Germany for nearly three years, had been interned in neutral Switzerland under the terms of an Anglo-German agreement for the repatriation of prisoners of war. After completing a number of training walks Morrison-Bell engaged the guides Aloys and Heinrich Kronig with whom he climbed the Lyskamm and Dent Blanche. A few days later with the same guides he ascended the north-east, Hörnli ridge of the Matterhorn, taking the opportunity to inspect the Solvay hut: the first visit to the hut by a British climber to be recorded in the *Alpine Journal*.

For his final expedition, accompanied by Hermann Perren and Heinrich Kronig, Morrison-Bell climbed the Dom, traversed to the Täschhorn and descended the west-south-west ridge or Teufelsgrat to the Kinhorn, only the second time this long combination of routes had been completed in a single day.

In the Bernese Alps a notable expedition was the second ascent of the south-west, Rote Zähne ridge of the Gspaltenhorn first climbed by Geoffrey

Winthrop Young and his companions who had traversed round the third and highest tooth below the summit to complete the ascent. In August Jean Bernet and the guide Jakob Rumpf made the first ascent of this tooth, completing a direct line up the ridge.

As in previous years during the war some climbing was possible in other mountain regions not directly affected by the conflict. In South Africa members of the Mountain Club continued to make new ascents as they explored Table Mountain (1087m). During the year parties led by J W Fraser completed a number of notable climbs including *Postern Buttress Frontal* and *Footstool Crack*, both very severe routes for the period.

In New Zealand the weather in the Southern Alps was favourable for much of the season and several major peaks were ascended. The High Peak of Mount Cook (3724m) was reached by three parties led by Peter Graham, the chief guide at the Hermitage hotel. Another visitor at the Hermitage was Samuel Turner who had returned to continue his attempts to make a solo ascent of the High Peak. In January he climbed the Linda glacier and had reached the rocks below the summit before being forced to retreat. Turner then completed two further expeditions on his own, climbing the Footstool (2767m) above the Hooker valley and making the first ascent of Mount Nathan (2852m) in the Malte Brun range.

In the Canadian Rockies V A Fynn continued his exploration in the Lake Louise district. After climbing Pinnacle Mountain (3067m) above Sentinel Pass with his wife, the first lady to ascend the peak, and the guide Rudolph Aemmer, Fynn and Aemmer made the second ascent and first traverse of Glacier Peak (3283m). They then undertook two major expeditions, completing the second traverse of the long narrow ridge between the north and south peaks of Mount Victoria (3464m) and making the first ascent of the south-east cirque and east-south-east ridge of Mount Temple (3543m).

At home in Wales a notable climb was completed above the Idwal Slabs in Cwm Idwal. In May I A Richards, his future wife Dorothy Pilley and C F Holland opened the *Original Route* on Holly Tree Wall, the first line to be forced up this famous cliff.

In June an interesting paper by Alexander Kellas entitled 'The Possibility of Aerial Reconnaissance in the Himalaya' was published in the *Geographical Journal*. The paper evoked considerable discussion and it was suggested that 'by a rapid flight into the Himalaya in an aeroplane fitted with photographic apparatus, particularly in the direction of Nepal, one might really get valuable results, though only a rapid reconnaissance.'

A welcome event during the year was the publication of *The Playground of the Far East*, an account by the Rev Walter Weston of his extensive exploration in the Japanese Alps during his time as missionary and chaplain in Japan. The work was favourably reviewed in the *Alpine Journal* where it was described as 'altogether a somewhat tantalising account of what one would fain were not quite such a far country.'

In April the death occurred of Mary Isabella Charlet-Straton, one of the first ladies to undertake serious mountaineering, who married Jean Charlet

The south-east face of Mount Temple, Canadian Rockies.
*(Frank Smythe, Alpine Club Photo Library)*

her principal guide. During a successful climbing career she took part in several notable expeditions including the first ascent of the Aiguille du Moine and the first winter ascent of Mont Blanc.

At the annual general meeting of the Alpine Club in December the president, Captain Farrar, made a significant announcement, confirming that the Royal Geographical Society 'is about to submit to the Government of India proposals for preparing the exploration and ascent of Mt Everest as soon as circumstances permit. Mr Freshfield, who is never forgetful of his old Club, has been good enough to suggest that the Alpine Club should be joined in the proposed submission. I feel I may assure the RGS that we feel honoured in this and that we will do all in our power to further the project.'

# Area Notes

Capt G T Ewen (1879-1917), 3rd Manchester Regiment,
who joked his climbing experience allowed him to get out of his
trench quicker, died during the relief of Kut, Mesopotamia.

# LINDSAY GRIFFIN

# Alps & Dolomites 2017

The south pillar of the Pointe de Platé, one of the biggest limestone walls in France. The red line is *Le Royaume de Noir* (2017) and the yellow is the *Original Route* (1958). *(Emmanuel Ratouis)*

Although 2017 was a remarkable year for significant new ascents in the greater ranges, notably in the Himalaya, very little important pioneering appears to have taken place in the Alps, certainly in the 'upwards' direction. Much of the Alpine news these days centres on the burgeoning number of remarkable first ski descents of seemingly horrifying objectives throughout the range. In some cases these may have travelled over previously untouched ground, a good example being a series of ascents and ski descents opened recently by Vivian Bruchez and friends on the south-west face of the Aiguilles Rouges du Dolent in the Argentière basin. Summer in the Alps was particularly difficult for anything but objectively safe rock routes, with the peaks so dry that even seasoned visitors often found them unrecognisable.

Rick Allen on the lower east ridge of the Aiguille du Chardonnet during the first ascent. Behind is the Grande Fourche, on which the pair had recently completed a new route: on the face in profile to the right. *(Simon Richardson)*

Rick Allen on a pitch of thin ice (Scottish IV) under a chockstone on the lower east ridge of the Aiguille du Chardonnet. *(Simon Richardson)*

Let us begin with the new routes. Twenty years after establishing the famous *Voie Petit* on the Grand Capucin with Stéphanie Bodet, Arnaud Petit was back to create a new route called *L'Or du Temps* (470m, 12 pitches, 7c+). Put up over four days in August with Nina Caprez, the route starts up the first two pitches of the classic *Bonatti* before breaking out left and climbing independent ground until joining the *Ragni* near the top. The new route was not climbed ground up, but the French-Swiss pair only bolted where necessary: 27 protection bolts. Two weeks later, it was climbed ground-up, free, and in 13 hours, the first continuous free ascent, by Slovakians Martin Krasnansky, Pavel Kratochvil, who is 16 years old and led the crux, and Robert Luby. This team felt the fifth pitch crux to be 7c+ rather than the original grade of 8a. After their ascent the Slovaks discussed the grade with the authors, and both parties settled on 7c+.

Also in the Mont Blanc massif, but earlier in the season, Rick Allen and Simon Richardson climbed virgin ground when they made unusual ascents of the Grande Forche and Aiguille du Chardonnet from the Albert Premier hut. On 24 June the pair left the hut, crossed the Fenêtre de Saleina, and

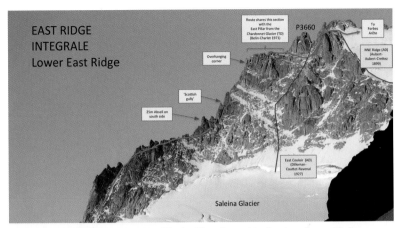

The lower east ridge of the Aiguille du Chardonnet to the junction with the north-north-east ridge. *(Simon Richardson)*

reached the south-east face of the Grande Fourche (3610m). This face is split by an east-facing couloir (AD) that rises to a point right of the summit. The *Adam-Crettex* (AD) slants from right to left up the spur to the right of this couloir, before crossing it and finishing up the central spur directly to the summit. The objective for Allen and Richardson was a complete ascent of the 500m central spur. This was achieved in 19 pitches, generally at 5a-5b but with several harder, including the first pitch crux (6a). The *Scottish Route* (TD) was harder and took longer than expected, forcing an unplanned bivouac with no gear near the summit. Fortunately, the night was warm: unfortunately, it rained. The two were relieved when morning arrived.

Poor weather then intervened, but when the forecast improved the pair returned to the Albert Premier for one of Richardson's characteristically well researched, long-term projects: a complete east to west traverse of the Aiguille du Chardonnet (3842m). Beginning from the Saleina glacier, the lower east ridge rises steeply to a crenelated arête leading to Pte 3660m, aka Pointe Alphonse Couttet, the south pillar of which was climbed in 2013 by Richardson and Tom Prentice. Above this point the ridge eventually meets the north-north-east ridge (*Aubert-Aubert-Crettez*, 1899), from where easy snow leads to the start of the Forbes Arête. In 1971 Belin and Char-let climbed a south-east-facing rock pillar from the Chardonnet glacier to reach the crenelated ridge, descending to the same glacier from below Pte 3660m. In 1929 Dilleman, Couttet and Ravenal had climbed the couloir on the north flank of the east ridge to the gap beyond 3,660m. However, there is no record of a complete ascent of the lower east ridge to the junction with the north-north-east ridge.

Allen and Richardson made their expedition from 4-6 July. They found a very old cairn low down on the easy introductory section of the ridge, which they feel was most likely constructed by crystal hunters. Higher, they passed an old rappel sling, after which the terrain became significantly

Looking back along the crenellated section of the east ridge of the Aiguille du Chardonnet, with the north face of the Aiguille d'Argentière behind. *(Simon Richardson)*

more difficult. The rock was rotten but fortunately the two were on the mountain just after a major storm, and a ribbon of thin ice through almost vertical gravel led under a chockstone (Scottish IV) to a steep corner (UIAA V+), and eventually the start of the crenelated ridge, where they bivouacked. At this point they had joined the *Belin-Charlet*. The following morning the pair climbed an overhanging corner (A1 and V) and continued over towers

A photo-diagram of the new route the *West Pillar Direct* (TD+, VII, 500m),
Aiguille du Jardin. *(Ben Tibbetts)*

on delicate and exposed terrain until below 3,660m. Belin and Charlet avoided these towers. Here, they traversed below Pte 3660m on the north flank to
reach a notch in the north-north-east ridge, where they made their second
bivouac. Day three along the Forbes Arête was fun, though time-consuming
due to lean conditions, and the descent to the west was particularly testing,
with black ice, rubble and two enormous bergschrunds cutting the glacier
below Col Adams Reilly. Needless to say, the Chardonnet had few ascents
during the 2017 summer.

The pair regained the Albert Premier at 8pm after three full days' climbing,
but Richardson had an airport transfer at 9am the following day, so after a
meal they walked down to the valley, arriving just after midnight. The *East
Ridge Integral* has a vertical height gain of 800m and an overall grade of TD.

On the Aiguille du Jardin, Will Sim and Ben Tibbetts have climbed a
direct route up the west pillar (TD+, 6b, 500m). This is the pillar immediately right of the couloir leading to the Col Armand Charlet. Their climb
is described in more detail in this edition of the *Alpine Journal*.

In cold stable weather over 15-16 March, Dani Arnold, Thomas Senf (Switzerland) and Alex Huber (Germany) added a new line to the north face of the Matterhorn by climbing directly through the long overhanging section of the Zmutt Nose to the left of the *Gogna* (Cerruti-Gogna, 1969). The three climbed approximately the first two-fifths of the *Gogna* to a small ledge below the start of enormous overhangs where the *Gogna* moves right. They bivouacked on the ledge after fixing a pitch above. The next day was 'Huber terrain', the German using sophisticated aid techniques to climb two pitches through a section as overhanging as the huge roofs on the Cima Ovest di Lavaredo. Bolts were placed at belays, and two bolts used to start the first pitch. After another steep pitch – 'there aren't many places in the Alps as steep and exposed as this' – the three continued up easier, mixed terrain for a further five hours to reach the summit. The route has been named *Schweizernase* (VII+, A4, 1000m).

On the north-west face of the Breitwangflue (2200m), north-east of Kandersteg at the western end of the Bernese Oberland, Dani Arnold made the first on-sight free solo ascent of *Beta Block Super*, (WI7, 300m), a steep ice route put up in 1998 by Daniela and Robert Jasper. Arnold took only one hour and three minutes to complete the ascent. It is the first time an ice route of this length and standard has been free soloed: there have been solo ascents of WI7 in the past, but far shorter routes. The ascent was well filmed and can be viewed on the planetmountain website.

On the famous Konigspitze (3851m) in the Ortler Group, Daniel Ladurner and Johannes Lemayer (Italy) climbed a new route on the north-east face. *Schattenspiel* (M6, WI5, 900m) follows the prominent line of thin ice gullies and smears 100m right of the classic *North-east Couloir*, a popular winter ascent and often skied, before joining the latter for its last straightforward 200m to the summit. The rock left much to be desired and the climbing was poorly protected. The route was climbed on 7 October and although an obvious line, it seems that it remained untouched in the past due to lack of ice build-up. Despite the 'good' conditions for the ascent, this is a serious route, which should only be attempted in autumn during very cold temperatures.

Over in the Dolomites, in just 9h 15m on 17 March, Simon Gietl and Michi Wohlleben made the first winter crossing of the 'Lavaredo Skyline', a west-to-east traverse of all the peaks in the Cime di Lavaredo group. This involved climbing the *Squirrels' Ridge* on the Cima Ovest then down-climbing the normal route, the *Dulfer* on the Cima Grande and descent of its normal route, the normal route up the Cima Piccolo and descent via the *Innerkofler*, a west-to-east traverse of Punta Frida, and finally the normal route on the Cima Piccolissima and descent of the *Preuss*.

There were two notable achievements in what could be termed pre-Alp terrain. Over five days during the autumn Christophe Bressard and Emmanuel Ratouis opened one of the longest routes on French limestone when they completed *Le Royaume de Noir*, 750m high, 19 long and equipped pitches, with difficulties of 7a+, 6b obl. The route is situated on the south pillar of the 2,554m Pointe de Platé in the Haut Giffre or Fiz Range north-west

A fine 5c pitch on *Le Royaume de Noir*, south pillar of the Pointe de Platé. *(Emmanuel Ratouis)*

of the Mont Blanc Range. It is basically a direct version of the classic, but little climbed, 1958 *Lenoir Wohlschlag* route (TD-, 5c, 5a obl). The new route took a lot of work, both cleaning and equipping, is sustained at 5c-6c, and has generally very good rock and some amazing pitches, particularly in the upper part. However, the limestone on the first two or three pitches, which include the crux, is a little friable, but can be avoided by an easier variant. This peak offers superb views of Mont Blanc and the approach, from the top of a ski station, is only one hour. Allow eight to 11 hours for the ascent, and two and a half for the scenic walk off the back.

Just west of the Mont Blanc range, a notable speed solo took place in the Massif des Aravis, when in September Paul Bonhomme took just 37h 20m to make a north-east to south-west crossing of this jagged limestone chain. This is a total of 76km, of which 35km are over relatively sharp, rocky (and grassy!) arêtes. The traverse involved a total vertical ascent of 7,230m. The main difficulties lie in the crossing of long sections of narrow, delicate and exposed ridge where the rock can be generously described as far from perfect. Maximum difficulties are 5+/6a on Pointe Percée's classic *Arête du Doigt*, though here the limestone is solid. Bonhomme, who travelled unsupported, stopped for the night on the Col des Aravis. This is the first solo traverse of the Aravis in this direction and the first completed in less than two days.

Patrick Bérhault and Christophe Frendo made the first known traverse in this direction over five days in winter. However, this pair understandably had logistical backup and descended each night to a hut. It should be noted that both the winter team, and Bonhomme, missed out a few sections of the ridge, but back in September 2013 Matthieu Gilbon had made the first (and only) integral crossing but from the other direction, from south-west to north-east. Gilbon, who took five days for the traverse, had made two attempts with partners the previous year and left certain sections equipped. His odyssey involved pioneering new ground on the ridge, both in ascent and descent. A successful unsupported integral traverse from north-east to south-west as well as complete winter traverses in both directions await ambitious future parties.

Looking south-east from high on the Arête des Bouquetins. The main chain of the Aravis is visible in middle distance, with the highest summit, Pointe Percée, on the left. Directly behind this peak is Mont Blanc. *(Lindsay Griffin)*

There were other worthy ascents of typically demanding and rarely climbed routes. On the Grandes Jorasses there were several notable successes on the harder coveted mixed lines. On 20-22 February Luka Lindič (Slovenia) and Ines Papert (Germany) climbed the Whymper Spur in quite dry conditions, using a combination of *No Siesta* and the middle section of the *Bonatti-Vaucher*. They made two bivouacs and estimate the difficulties at M7. This was the first time Papert had climbed a route on the north face, though Lindič had been there in 2014, completing the first free ascent of *Rolling Stones*.

A month later Leo Billon, Max Bonniot and Pierre Labbre made an almost free ascent of *Rolling Stones* (ED3, M8, 1200m). Beginning on 13 March, the trio made two bivouacs and climbed all pitches free, including the crux on pitch 23, apart from pitches 24 (M7+) and 25 (M7).

From 11-14 October Damian Granowski and Tomasz Klimczak (Poland) climbed the *Serge Gousseault* (aka *Desmaison*) on the north-east flank of the *Walker Spur* (ED3, M6+ WI4 A1, 1200m). Julien Desécures' 2012 topo guide recorded about 15 ascents of this route at the time of publication.

Another historic tour de force to receive attention was the *Guides Route* on the north face of the Petit Dru. Put up over eight days in February 1967 by the crack French team of Michel Feuillarde, Claude Jager, Jean-Paul Paris and Yannick Seigneur, this 850m route has rarely been repeated. It follows the left rim of the niche and required copious aid on the first ascent, though this was halved on the first British and third overall ascent in August 1975 by Bob Milward and Steve Parr. Jérome Para and Sébastien Ratel climbed the route in two days during March 2017, likely to be only the second ascent in winter. An outstanding challenge would be an all-free ascent of this route. Many ancient pegs remain in place and the French pair considered dry tooling to be the most logical way to climb this route without aid.

A month previously, in February, Max Bonniot, Sébastien Ratal and Pierre Sancier made the second free ascent of the 1992 *Rhem-Vimal* on the north face of the west summit of Les Droites, but were the first to complete the route free in one day. The climb had originally been rated 6b and A2 but when climbed free over two days in March 2009 by Eric Doiseau, who led the crux, Benjamin Guigonnet and Damien Tomasi, it was modified to M7/M8. Shortly after the ascent by Bonniot et al, the route was climbed again, free and in a day, by Mathieu Maynadier and Mathieu Détrie, who were full of praise for Doiseau's 2009 lead.

The young Italian Federica Mingolla continues to dominate female Alpine rock climbing. During August in the Dolomites she repeated three long, difficult free climbs. At the start of the month, with aspirant guide Francesco Rigon, Mingolla climbed the 600m *Chimera Verticale* (7c), established by Alessandro Bau and partners over the summers of 2007 and 2009. The route takes the big compact wall between the classic *Aste* and *Andrich* routes on the north-west face of the Civetta. Rigon led the lower pitches but then Mingolla took over and led through to the top, with no falls including the crux pitches. Four days later she was on the south face of Marmolada di Ombretta completing a successful ascent with Enrico Fedolfi of the 1988 Maurizio Giordani masterpiece *Specchio di Sara* (7c). This line offers vertical climbing on superb compact rock, sometimes run out, and with route-finding problems.

Next was the south face of Punta Rocca on the Marmolada and the *Via delle Cattedrale*, a 800m route originally climbed in 1983 by the great Italian activist, Graziano Maffei, and friends at VI+ and A4. Petro dal Pra managed to free climb it in 2004 at 8a+, and the route has since become a sought-after free test-piece, though few have climbed it as such. Partnered by Nicolo Geremia, Mingolla took a preliminary look at the first six pitches on day one, bailing when it started to hail. On day two she took the lead and led most of the pitches, on-sighting 7c, but not able to on-sight the crux. After a two-day ascent the pair rappelled the route and during the descent Mingolla led the crux pitch first go. It was probably the Marmolada that brought this Italian to prominence, when in 2016 she became the first woman to free climb *Fish*.

Another woman climbing hard free routes in the Dolomites is Austrian Lisi Steurer. With partner Hannes Pfeifhofer, and climbing ground-up over seven days, she put up *Hakuna Matata* (8a, 7b obl, 400m) on the right side of the south face of Tae in the Fanes region. Protection was a mixture of pegs, bolts and natural gear, and the rock was considered some of the best in the Dolomites. Both climbers returned at different times during the summer and climbed the route free in a day.

## SIMON RICHARDSON
# Scottish Winter 2017-18

Guy Robertson wrestling with the Great Cave during the first ascent of *The Holy Grail* (IX,10) on Buachaille Etive Mòr in Glen Coe. The route description comes with a serious health warning: 'the crux moves may cause nausea and dizziness.' *(Greg Boswell)*

The sad demise of *Climb* magazine signaled the end of regular reporting of Scottish winter climbing in the mountaineering press. The Internet, and social media in particular, has proved to be a more popular way of communicating domestic climbing information. This is particularly valuable for the transitory nature of the Scottish winter game where real-time conditions can be communicated to a high number of dedicated subscribers of climbing-related Facebook groups.

This wealth of data brings both advantages and disadvantages. For example, on-the-spot conditions reports and photographs has in recent winters boosted immensely the number of successful traverses of the Cuillin Ridge, once the holy grail of Scottish winter outings. The downside is that instant conditions info can focus several parties on a single route when in the past they would have been more spread out over the Highlands.

The immediacy of the Internet has also changed the definition of what makes news. Nowadays it is not cutting-edge new routes that set cyberspace buzzing but events verging on spectacle. In this regard three achievements stand out from the 2018 season. The first was a new record time for a winter traverse of the Cuillin Ridge by Uisdean Hawthorn in February. Uisdean casually mentioned his 4h 57m time on Facebook not intending to claim any record, but it was immediately noted as over an hour faster than Finlay Wild and Tim Gomersall's time from two seasons before. Record keeping for summer traverses has been in place for several decades but recording winter times is a recent phenomenon. It is interesting to speculate, but quasi-winter conditions of hard névé on the more straightforward sections on the ridge and dry rock on the steeper pitches may yield even faster times in the future.

The second major event was Helen Rennard's winter completion in 23h 30m of Tranter's Round: the 19 Munros of the Mamores, Grey Corries, Aonachs, Carn Mor Dearg and Ben Nevis. Not only was this the first completion by a woman, it was only the second time it had ever been done on foot in winter in under 24 hours. Although a significant part of the challenge is travelling 58km with 6,000m of ascent, the terrain is steep in places and the night navigation required in the depths of winter makes it a significant mountaineering challenge. Rennard was rather surprised by the attention her round achieved, and it was ironic that she was applauded for a non-technical achievement, whilst her Scottish winter climbing record, easily the most impressive achieved by any female to date, has been largely ignored. But similar to the Cuillin Ridge, Tranter's Round is something that many more people can relate and aspire to.

The third event was so mind boggling that it has to be classed as pure spectacle. In March, Dave Macleod completed his '24/8 Project' which involved climbing a Font 8a+ boulder problem, an E8 trad route, an 8a sports climb, a Grade VIII winter route and eight Munros within 24 hours. The rock climbing was quickly dispatched in Glen Nevis and followed by a long haul up to the top of Ben Nevis where Macleod and Iain Small climbed *Frosty's Vigil* (VIII,8) near the top of Observatory Gully. Then Macleod walked over Carn Mor Dearg and the Grey Corries to his home at Roy Bridge. MacLeod has lived in Lochaber for over 10 years and his success relied not just on his outstanding talent but his deep knowledge of the area. One wonders how many other British climbers currently have the skills to repeat such a feat.

From a winter climbing perspective the season had some of the best ice conditions in recent years. This resulted in dozens of ascents of much-prized routes such as *Gully of the Gods* (VI,6) on Beinn Bhan as well as time-honoured classics like *Crowberry Gully* (IV,4) on Buachaille Etive Mòr in Glen Coe. Paradoxically, very icy winters do not always produce the most innovative or technically demanding ascents. There are so many outstanding icy lines waiting for early repeats that even the most hardened mixed climbers are only too happy to ascend rarely formed ice routes if they are in condition.

There are exceptions to the rule however, and the irrepressible Andy Nisbet added a series of excellent climbs to the north-west face of Ben Hope in the far north. Ben Hope is Scotland's second biggest cliff, at around 500m high and 2.5km long, so it is rather surprising that it is only now being thoroughly explored. Six hundred metre-long routes such as *Blue River* (IV,4) climbed with Dave McGimpsey and *Turf Factor* (IV,4) with Steve Perry and Jonathan Preston will undoubtedly attract repeat ascents in the near future, especially when you factor in colder weather at the northern tip of the country and the short approach.

Other important ascents include two very difficult mixed climbs in Glen Coe by Greg Boswell and Guy Robertson. *The Holy Grail* (IX,11), which was hailed as 'one of the best grade IXs in Scotland', takes the very steep crack-line on the right side of Slime Wall on Buachaille Etive Mòr. Equally impressive was *The Lost Arrow* (X,10) on Church Door Buttress on Bidean, a direct ascent of the main front face of the crag that had previously been the preserve of high standard summer routes.

Iain Small and Murdoch Jamieson also had a productive time in Glen Coe with the first winter ascent of *En Garde* (IX,9) on Stob Coire nan Lochan and a winter version of the *Trapeze* on Aonach Dubh. This spectacular and as yet unnamed route, sits high up in the Grade VIII/IX category. The same pair also added a difficult Grade IX to the *Rogue's Rib* area in Coire na Ciste on Ben Nevis.

One of the most pleasing aspects of the season was a number of new faces pioneering new routes. Tim Miller had a good winter with first winter ascents of *Dingle* (VII,7) on the Buachaille with Callum Hicks and *Punter's Crack* (VIII,9) on The Cobbler with Martin McKenna, and visiting Polish climber Kacper Tekiele added the testing *Wolf Whistle* (VII,7) and *Jaws* (VII,7) on Lurcher's Crag in the Cairngorms in the company of Andy Nisbet and Sandy Allan.

Other younger climbers establishing themselves as the pioneers of the future include Michael Barnard, who ranged far and wide with new routes from the Northern Highlands to Glen Coe with Doug Bartholomew and

Steve Holmes leading *The Orphan* (VII,8) on Buachaille Etive Mòr in Glen Coe. Heavy snow conditions meant that accessing the route via Curved Ridge was a mini-expedition in itself. *(Duncan Curry)*

John MacLean. Steve Holmes added *Optimist's Arete* (VI,6) on Ben Nevis with Ken Applegate and made the first winter ascent of *The Orphan* (VII,8) on Crowberry Ridge on Buachaille Etive Mòr in difficult snowy conditions with Duncan Curry and Hannah Evans. With enthusiasm like this, the future of Scottish winter climbing is well assured.

TIMOTHY ELSON

# India 2017

Ben Silvestre on the headwall of the west pillar of Arjuna (6230m).
*(Uisdean Hawthorn)*

The major ascents in the Indian Himalaya in 2017 were in the Kishtwar-Zanskar region; this is an area that was very popular until the early 1990s when access became difficult due to the political situation. In the last few years, access has become less of an issue. Unusually for the Himalaya two of the major ascents of the year were on one mountain Arjuna (6230m), situated above the Kijai Nala. (A similar coincidence occurred on Hagshu in 2014). In June a Slovenian expedition made the first ascent of a difficult mixed route up the west face of the central summit while in the autumn a British team made the first ascent of the arête of the west pillar of the south summit of Arjuna South (6100m). In October a Swiss-German team climbed a difficult direttissima on the north-west face of Cerro Kishtwar (6173m). On the northern side of the range an American team made the first ascent of Barnaj I (6370m) via icy grooves in its north face and a separate US team made the first ascent of Rungofarka (6495m) by its north ridge. In the Garhwal an American team made an impressive first ascent of the south-west face of Nilkanth (6596m), overcoming difficult mixed and ice climbing.

The Indian Mountaineering Foundation have a new website and web portal for applying for permits, see: https://www.indmount.org/IMF/welcome. In access news the Himachal Pradesh government now aims to keep the Rotang pass open during the winter with the aim of keeping other high passes open as well. Travel to the south side of the Kishtwar is still via the Chenab road from Himachal Pradesh, as travel on the main roads in Kashmir is still not advised by the FCO.

### Arjuna

Arjuna is situated in the Kijai Nala, and was climbed by Polish teams in 1981 and 1983; in 1981 only the south summit was gained via the south-east ridge; in 1983 the south summit was gained again via a difficult route on the west face while at the same time the central pillar of the west summit was climbed. The 1983 ascents were highly technical climbs and were possibly a little overlooked at the time. A Slovenian super-team of Marko Prezelj, Urban Novak and Aleš Česen arrived at basecamp on 29 May and set about acclimatising, making the first ascent of Peak 6038m via the north ridge (D) on 4 June. On 16 June they set off up the west face couloir of the main summit, taking three days to climb the route experiencing considerable difficulties (ED+, WI5+, A0, M7+). They rappelled their line of ascent, and named their climb *All or Nothing*. During their trip they experienced only six days of good weather, managing to be in position to do both the climbs they completed when the weather was good. However, they note they could easily have left without having climbed anything.

In the autumn a British team consisting of Ben Silvestre, Pete Graham and Uisdean Hawthorn visited the Kijai Nala also with the goal of climbing Arjuna. Their goal was the west pillar of the south summit of Arjuna. After acclimatising the trio set off up the pillar on 2 October. Once on the pillar they spent 4 days climbing on perfect sounding granite covered in chicken heads; they named their route *Gandiva* (1400m E3/5.11 M5) after

The south and west aspects of Arjuna: the British route climbs the prominent pillar to the south summit, while the Slovenian route climbs a gully hidden in this shot. *(Uisdean Hawthorn)*

the bow Brahma give Arjuna in Hindu mythology. On the first day they simul-climbed the lower section and climbed six pitches to a comfortable bivy. The second day included a pitch described as similar to *The Strand* on Gogarth and improbably led to easier ground. Their second night out was chilly being exposed to wind. On the third day they climbed to the top of the pillar, and made a committing abseil to below the headwall, which they ascended with massive exposure to a small bivy ledge. The fourth day included traversing pitches and a tricky mixed chimney, where several further pitches led to the summit. They started descending on the fourth day and bivied half way down the descent gully. On the fifth day they arrived back at base camp.

The British team noted that the west face of Arjuna had excellent rock and was very much like the north face of the Grandes Jorasses with multiple spurs and couloirs that will keep teams busy for years to come. The Slovenians compared it to the Charakusa valley in Pakistan.

### Cerro Kishtwar

In October 2017 Cerro Kishtwar (6155m) got its fourth ascent via its imposing north-west face by a Swiss-German team made up of Stephan Siegrist, Julian Zanker and Thomas Huber. Siegrist had already climbed Cerro

Climbing the spectacular north-west face of Cerro Kishtwar (6155m). (Thomas Huber)

The Swiss-German route on the north-west face of Cerro Kishtwar. *(Thomas Huber)*

Kishtwar in 2011 via an ice gully on the right-hand side of the north-west face leading to the south ridge. In 2017 Siegrist was back to attempt a very similar line to that of Brendan Murphy (Ireland) and Andy Perkins' (UK) 1992 attempt, when they turned back 100m from the summit after 17 days on the mountain. Huber, Zanker and Siegrist arrived at their basecamp on 13 September and made an initial attempt on the face reaching about a third of the way up. Their second attempt started on 8 October and they reached the summit after seven days of climbing on 14 October. They had fixed some pitches on the lower third of the face and set up four portaledge camps on the face and reported difficulties of VII, A3+, 6b, M6, 80°, with the lower 400m being mostly ice and mixed climbing and the upper 600m consisting difficult rock climbing. They named their route *Har Har Mahadev*. Mick Fowler and Steve Sustad made the first ascent of Cerro Kishtwar in 1993 via a hidden gully on the left side of the north-west face to the north spur. The Swiss-German team reported cold temperatures, down to -20°C, and snowfall almost every afternoon. This contrasts with the British team who reported relatively warm temperatures on Arjuna, which was climbed at the same time and only a couple of valleys over. The different experiences reflect the different aspects of the faces they were climbing.

The north face of Barnaj I (6370m): the upper section of the route, which faces almost east, is hidden in a deep icy chimney. *(Seth Timpano)*

Looking into the ice chimney that defines the start of the upper east face of Barnaj I. Hennessey is standing on the bivy site where the pair spent two nights. *(Seth Timpano)*

### Barnaj I

From 1 to 4 October, Seth Timpano and Sam Hennessey made the first ascent of Barnaj I (6370m), via its north buttress. This aesthetically pleasing mountain is situated in Zanskar and is approached from Leh and the Hagshu Nala. Barnaj I had been attempted once before, by Timpano with Tim Dittmann and Jared Vilhauer in 2014. They were turned round by warm conditions and rock fall. After acclimatising on Castle Peak (5850m) at IV, 5.8 and attempting an unclimbed 6,200m peak, they were ready for their attempt on Barnaj. On 1 October they set off simul-climbing the lower slopes, following the same line as in 2014. The climbing soon turned more difficult with several long ice pitches and a few mixed steps to a bivy. On the second day they started late and climbed 250m to the 2014 highpoint; they bivied early here and set off at 1am to climb an ice gully in the cold temperatures of the night. They climbed to the summit that day and returned to their bivy that night, descending the rest of the face the next day. Timpano and Hennessey encountered difficulties up to M4 and WI5+, describing the route as every alpinist's dream: direct, sustained, and objectively safe climbing on an unclimbed peak.

### Rungofarka

The American duo of Tino Villanueva and Alan Rousseau made the first ascent of Rungofarka (6495m) via its north ridge between 30 September and 4 October. Their initial attempt was on the north face, which they retreated from, having not found a bivy site at the end of their first day. Changing plans for the north ridge, they ascended to the col at 5,700m on the first day.

On Nilkanth, Chantel Astorga leads out from the rock alcove onto mixed terrain and steep ice around the corner to the top of what the team dubbed 'the castle'. This section was the big question mark in the viability of their route and proved to be the crux of the south-west face. *(Jason Thompson)*

On the second they climbed 10 pitches of sustained climbing (M6) to a small bivy behind an ice pillar. The third day, they climbed 20 pitches of mostly M4 with some M6 and a final offwidth pitch with bad protection to a poor bivy and a sleepless night. The next morning they made a committing abseil from their bivy to the base of an ice runnel that proved to be the crux of the route, with thin mixed and ice climbing. They continued up the summit ridge and descended the west ridge via 20 abseils some 2,700m of vertical ground back to their base camp. They named the route *The T&A Show* (VI, M6, WI4+) consisting of around 50 pitches and 1,200m vertical technical terrain.

## Nilkanth

The US trio of Chantel Astorga, Anne Gilbert Chase, and Jason Thompson made the first ascent of the south-west face of Nilkanth (6596m) from 28 September to 2 October. Chase and Thompson had attempted the face in 2015, and climbed most of the west ridge. That proved useful as it formed their descent route in 2017. With a late monsoon, and ensuing heavy snowfall in September they managed to setup an advanced basecamp at 5,180m below the face but not advance any higher for acclimatisation. At the end of September and with a good weather forecast they set off up the route on 28 September from their advanced basecamp; the first day had several tricky mixed steps and a steep ice pitch to a bivi at 5,670m. The second day involved technical mixed ground and steep ice, and ended at an uncomfortable sitting bivouac at 5,944m. Their third day on the route proved to be the crux. Their intended route went up a feature dubbed the Castle however once close up it looked like big wall tactics would be required to overcome it; luckily they found a devious route around it that required difficult ice and mixed climbing. The day ended with a bivi on top of the Castle at 6,248m; on the fourth day they thought they would make the summit however the climbing was more difficult than anticipated, leading to a bivi at 6,523m.

Less than 60m from realising a three-year dream, Anne Gilbert Chase heading towards the summit of Nilkanth on the morning of the fifth day. Chase and Astorga are two of the world's leading female alpinists, making an ascent of the *Slovak Direct* on Denali this year: see page 63. *(Jason Thompson)*

On the fifth day they made it to the summit in a couple of hours and then descended the west ridge arriving back at advanced base camp at 2am. They named the route *Obscured Perception* (VI WI5, M6, A0, 70° snow, 1400m).

**East Karakoram**

In July and August, to celebrate the 90th anniversary of the Himalayan Club, an Indian team traversed a substantial portion of the East Karakoram. The team consisted of Divyesh Muni, Rahesh Gadgil, Vineeta Muni, Huzefa Electricwala, Ashish Prabhu and Sonali Bhatia. They set off from Rongdo on 5 July and ascended the Rongdo valley. They then crossed the Rongdo La (5800m) to the East Phunangma glacier and from a camp there made the first ascent of Nga Kangri (6165m), before traversing to the South Argan glacier via a huge icefall. The team crossed the Argan La (5950m) to gain the North Argan glacier and from there to the south Shukpa Kunchang glacier, which is dominated by Saser Kangri II (7520m) at its head. They spent two days ascending the glacier and crossed the Zamorian La (5860m) to cross to the Zamorian glacier and then down to the Sakang valley;

the team ascended up the Sakang valley before making the tricky descent back down the valley to civilisation.

In September and October a British team made up of Alpine Club members consisting of Derek Buckle, Drew Cook, Jamie Goodhart (who unfortunately left the expedition early due to a family bereavement), Rafal Malczyk and Howard Pollitt travelled to the Sumur valley in the East Karakoram. Malczyk, Cook, Pollitt and Buckle made the first ascent of Point 6088m via the south-west slopes (F) on 18 September. They named the top Deception Point as it turned out to be the convergence of three ridges with a good view rather than an independent summit. On 25 September they made the first ascent of Peak 6078m at the head of the glacier beyond the East Rassa col via the south-east face (PD). Finally, they made the first ascent of Peak 5991m on 29 September via its west north-west ridge (AD). The team reported unstable snow on all northerly faces limiting the options of where they could climb.

## Zanskar

The Zanskar range seemed to be the place for new routes in 2017 with many successful expeditions in addition to Barnaj I and Rungofarka. It lies on the north side of the Kishtwar range and is generally approached from Leh via the Kargil and Padum road, with numerous 5000m and 6000m peaks still unclimbed.

A Slovenian team consisting of Matjaž Dušič, Matija Jošt, and Tomaž Žerovnik visited the Hapal mountains during July and August 2017. Departing from the village of Tungri on the Leh-Kargil-Padum road they set up base camp on 20 July in the Rangtik Tokpo. They acclimatised by climbing a new route on Remalaye (6278m), also known as H5, at D+. They next made the first ascent of the spectacular looking Chakdor Ri (6193m), or H8, by the south-east ridge. The ridge was made of perfect granite and was climbed free (ED+, VII-) from 31 July to 2 August, calling it *Treasure of Zanskar*. On the summit they were caught in an electric storm. Following this success, they climbed Jamyang Ri (5800m), a rocky spire obvious from the road via its west face at ED, VII-, naming the route *Chunka*, which means chough in the Ladakhi dialect of Tibetan. The team note that there is massive potential for good rock climbing in the area, with the mountains seeming more Alpine than Himalayan, other than the altitude.

In August and September Savannah Cummins, Lindsay Fixmer and Anna Pfaff (USA) visited the Raru mountains. Travelling up the Tetleh glacier they set up base camp in the same location as previous expeditions. During their trip they encountered only five days of good weather, with 19 of poor weather: apparently the area experienced a late monsoon in 2017. On 9 September they attempted peak 5750m near the Kang La that leads to the Miyar valley; they climbed to just below the summit ridge but were forced back in back weather overcoming difficulties of WI4/M5. They returned to the same peak later in the trip but found unstable snow conditions. In between they made the first ascent of peak 5400m via 400m of 5.10 climbing.

The Austrian Alpine Club cadet team made up of Michael Groher, Thomas Holler, Lorin Etzel, Timo Moser and Barbara Vigl visited Zanskar in August 2017. Their original aim was to climb two virgin rock peaks beyond on the Poat La (5500m) but difficulties with employing enough porters meant they could not make that approach. They settled for climbing on peaks above Padum making four new routes and one repeat. On 10 August Holler and Vigl climbed Torre Fanni (5400m) via a 350m route they called *Inschallah* (M6, 5c, 60°), while Etzel, Groher and Moser climbed the south-east face of Peak 6060m (4, 55°). The full team then climbed the south-west face of Cerro Zanskar (5600m) in 15 pitches (6a, A1) over two days. Several days later, Etzel, Groher and Vigl climbed a 19-pitch route on a rock pillar (4500m) at 6a+ while Holler and Moser repeated a route on Shafat Fortress (5630m).

The Japanese pair of Yasushi Yamanoi and Takaaki Furuhata visited the Hagshu Nala and made the first ascent of Rucho (5970m), located off the true left bank of the glacier. They climbed the east face during the night and early morning of 1 August to meet the south ridge where they continued to the summit. They descended the south ridge and rated their route TD.

**Garhwal**

An Austrian-Italian team made up of Vittorio Messini and Simon Gietl climbed a new route on the north face of the iconic Shivling (6543m) in October 2017. Arriving in September they found very cold snowy conditions that led them to change plans from their original intension of repeating the *Shiva's Line* climbed by Thomas Huber and Iwan Wolf in 2000, the direct finish to the 1993 *North Pillar* climbed by Hans Kammerlander and Christoph Hainz. The 2017 line is to the left. Messini and Gietl spent the beginning of October acclimatising on the lower section of the route and fixing the steepest section. On 9 October they left base camp and set off on a summit push. Ascending the lower pillar, they joined the 1993 *North Pillar* before finishing up the 1980 *Japanese Route* to reach the summit on 11 October, descending their ascent route next day. The route was named *Shiva's Ice* (WI5, M6, 1500m) and was reported to be comparable to the *Colton-MacIntyre* on the Grandes Jorasses.

IAN WALL

# Nepal 2017

The Hillary Step, whose shape was altered in the 2015 earthquake to become more of a staircase, a fact only officially acknowledged in 2018.

Nepal seems ever more divided into two mountain seasons, spring for mountaineering expeditions and autumn for trekking although a little of each genre does filter through both. After the tragedy of the earthquake in 2015, all mountaineering activities came to a halt, and by the autumn not only was the country still reeling from aftershocks but India had imposed a blockade of Nepal and commodities were in short supply, again hampering tourism. However, 2016 proved to be a successful season and 2017 was eagerly awaited with high expectations by all in the Nepal mountain tourism sector. It did not disappoint.

Everest hogged the headlines as far as the rest of the world beyond climbing was concerned. The 2017 season illustrated how people are highly motivated to get information into the public arena as quickly as possible, even via communication systems taken on the route. Commercial expeditions are able to blow their own trumpets with expedition updates appearing in almost real time. The majority of information is, I believe, posted in good faith. Unfortunately the information is not always reliable or properly checked and some stories are hastily withdrawn or corrected.

One of the hot topics for 2017 was the Hillary Step. In 2016 there were no official reports of the status of this famous feature despite speculation it had been damaged in the earthquake. Before the 2017 season it was not mentioned in expedition briefings given by the tourism ministry and it appeared that there was a veil of silence pulled across the whole situation. It was not until the end of the 2018 season that it was acknowledged that the Hillary Step had fallen and is now a snow ramp: narrow, but not steep or technical.

**Right of Passage**
In recent years, fairly or unfairly, the 'Himalayan mountaineering world' has been split into two groups: those that sign up to commercial expeditions; and those that climb independently organising their own trips. There are obviously huge skill differentials within and between both sectors. However, by 2017 it was evident that a third group is developing, one that can be dubbed the 'following others' group. These people are not on 'commercial' expeditions but are in fact independent climbers or groups. Thirty years ago all the expedition members would pull together to get a route fixed. Some 'independent' expeditions rely on Sherpa route-fixers to get to the summit and make a safer and easier passage for others to follow. I have heard several of these 'independent' climbers who failed on their objective use the excuse that the Sherpas 'weren't strong enough to get the ropes in,' suggesting these 'mountaineers' didn't have the required skills or energy to make their own passage to the summit.

**2017 Expeditions**
There was significant activity on many of the 8,000ers across Nepal but all expeditions reported exceptionally high winds from late April onwards. Louis Rousseau, Adam Bielecki, Rick Allen and Felix Berg had plans for a new route on the northern side of **Cho Oyu** but these came to an abrupt end when they were prevented from entering Tibet because of Pakistani visas in their passports. The team switched to Annapurna but all agreed their adventure started badly with rushed planning, missed flights and finally lost baggage by the airline. Despite a good 'adventure' they failed to summit. Another **Cho Oyu** Expedition led by Di Gilbert also failed due to conditions on the route.

    **Kangchenjunga** also witnessed expeditions hit by high winds. Simone Moro and Tamara Lunger tried a new route following the 'Skyline Ridge', 5.5km and much of it above 8,300m, but their expedition came to a premature end. Matt Du Puy, Chris Burke, Chris Warner, Lakpa Sherpa and Tshering Sherpa were forced to abandon their climb because, according to the *Timaru Herald* 'the route to the summit had not been fully set and this was not known until the team were a few hundred metres from the summit, making it unsafe to continue.' The Nepali female climbers Maya Sherpa, Dawa Yangzum Sherpa and Pasang Lhamu Sherpa Akita also failed on their **Kangchenjunga** attempt due to rope-fixing issues.

    On **Annapurna** an Italian couple became the first couple to successfully

Dhaulagiri was busy in 2017, including an ascent from British climber Adele Pennington, but the Spaniard Carlos Soria Fontán missed out, his eighth failure on the peak. Now aged 79, he still has this peak and Shishapangma to complete his 14 8,000ers. *(Ian Wall)*

summit all 14 8,000ers. Romano Benet and Nives Meroi climbed without using the bottled oxygen. Meroi became the second woman to climb all the 8,000ers without supplementary oxygen after Gerlinde Kaltenbrunner succeeded in 2011. At least six Spanish climbers, including Alberto Zerain and Jonatan García were forced to abandon due to large avalanches and heavily crevassed areas on the Dutch route.

At least 255 foreign climbers from 35 countries had permits for Manaslu, the highest number of permits ever issued for the mountain in a season. There were 46 Chinese, 39 Russians, 18 Spanish and 13 German climbers among other nationalities. The Basque climber Juan Ramon Madariaga Abaitua was on **Manaslu** leading a six-member team but the weather put an end to their efforts. A Hungarian extreme skier and mountaineer Peter Wetzl tried to summit and ski **Manaslu**. He was not using supplementary oxygen but again conditions defeated the expedition with a lot of fresh snow and dangerous seracs.

Over on **Makalu**, Phil Crampton's expedition was short of the actual summit by about 10 or 15 vertical metres. All the Sherpas and the 25 climbers present that summit day deemed the corniced ridge a little too fragile to continue those last few metres.

**Dhaulagiri** also saw a lot of activity with over 60 people on expeditions during the season. The Indian Air Force successfully summited the mountain but tragically the guide Ang Nima Sherpa went missing from base camp. Guy Cotter and Dean Staples got their team to the summit on 22 May 2017. Adele Pennington also made a safe summit round-trip. Peter Hamor had a successful season on **Dhaulagiri**. Spanish climber Carlos Soria Fontán, then aged 78, tried twice in September to summit including once by 'going up the wrong couloir'. By the time they discovered their mistake it was too late with conditions worsening. They didn't get another chance as conditions continued to degrade thus ending his eighth attempt over nine years to summit.

The Nepal government issued 371 permits for **Everest**, of which 70 were permits carried over from 2014 and 2015. With at least one Sherpa or other high-altitude worker for every foreigner that meant approximately 742 heading for the summit. Some of these ascents would not have been recorded if they were completed by Nepali staff. The final count during the last week of May of 365 summits added to the 300 that had summited over the previous three weeks on both sides, making for a >600 summit season. The Icefall was prepared well in advance to lessen pressure but in fact fears of overcrowding weren't realised and the mountain was reasonably harmonious. Many teams acclimatised on nearby trekking peaks, especially Lobuche, to reduce the pressure and stress of multiple passages through the Icefall. However, high winds from late April caused delay in setting the route on the upper slopes. Route setting was stalled due to fatigue and the need to spend additional time checking for rope damage due to high winds. At this point a Gurkha expedition along with their Sherpa guides completed the task in good harmony with the rope-fixing team.

The **Everest** season saw an extreme effort put into the recovery of dead climbers from the mountain. Vladimir Štrba, a Slovak climber, was retrieved alive from above the Balcony, with one newspaper reporting he died before reaching the South Col, while Gautam Ghosh was retrieved from the South Col. The family of Indian climber Ravi Kumar had insisted that his body was retrieved and taken back to India. This involved a complicated high-altitude recovery as his body was near the Balcony at about around 8,412m. It is estimated the recovery cost over $60,000 but there was little consideration given for the safety of the eight to 12 Sherpas who had to spend a few days at extreme altitude to execute this task. Others who perished chasing their dreams were 54-year-old Australian Francesco Enrico Marchetti and the 50-year-old American physician Roland Yearwood. It was reported that four bodies were found in a tent near the South Col. According to tourism official Durga Dutta Dhakal no group of four had been reported missing. The facts surrounding these bodies are unclear.

On the north side the Chinese Mountaineering Association group tasked with rope-fixing withdrew their services at 8,300m due to conditions. An Indian expedition then stepped up to the mark and completed the task. The following day several Indian teenagers successfully reached the summit, as did Lhakpa Sherpa who made the summit for the eighth time and the first from the north, a female record.

The young Spaniard Kilian Jornet established what is known as a FKT (fastest known time) to the summit of **Everest** from base camp at 5,100m in 26 hours, without supplementary oxygen, fixed ropes or any form of human support. Illness slowed him and prevented him from setting a record for the round-trip. Within a week, on 27 May, he tried again, this time leaving ABC and

Ueli Steck, who died in a fall from Nuptse in the spring of 2017.

making the summit in 17 hours, just shy of Christian Stangl's record. The round-trip from ABC was completed in a stunning 29h 30m.

Mollie Hughes became the youngest Briton to summit from both sides and Andy Holzer became the second blind person to reach the summit. Kami Rita Sherpa summited for the 21st time in 2017, tying him with Apa and Phurba Tashi for most summits. (He would go on to break the record in 2018.) The main headline from this 2017 season was the tragic death of Ueli Steck the world famous alpinist and speed climber.

Steck was in the Western Cwm on Everest acclimatising for his expedition to climb the west ridge, descend the south-east ridge before completing the traverse across to climb Lhotse from which he would descend back to base camp. All this would be completed in his usual style, fast, solo and without protection. On the morning of 30 April 2017 he set off for what was thought to be an acclimatisation climb on **Nuptse**. A young Nepali mountaineer Vinayak Jay Malla had seen a climber at around 7,100m on Nuptse early that morning but a little later heard the sound of what he described as 'something falling'. With a colleague he went to investigate and discovered Ueli Steck's body at around 6,300m. It was reported that near to Steck's body was a large rock covered in blood. One of his crampons was missing and Steck appeared to have been climbing without a harness. Steck was estimated to have fallen 800m. His cremation took place during a three-hour ceremony at Tengboche monastery. Reinhold Messner suggested that Steck may have had his eye on the 'Everest Horseshoe', ascending the west ridge, descending the south-east ridge, traverse across to Lhotse summit before continuing along the ridge to Nuptse, an objective held in the minds of many a world-class mountaineer. The challenge is still there to be completed.

There was a pair of ice axes in Steck's tent along with a light rope and various other pieces of climbing equipment. Steck was well known for climbing 'axe-less', using adapted trekking poles instead if he thought he could manage the difficulties in that style. A journalist asked Vinayak Malla what piece of essential equipment he would  have taken to which

Malla dryly responded: 'a climbing partner.' There is no definitive conclusion as to what caused Steck to fall. Vinayak was quoted as saying: 'Perhaps we should think of Steck as a *bharal* (blue sheep), who although the master of their own terrain could fall for any number of unexpected reasons.'

In the last few days of 2017, the 36-year-old Spanish mountaineer Alex Txikon returned to Nepal with Pakistan's Muhammad Ali Sadpara to attempt **Everest** in winter without supplementary oxygen. This was Txikon's seventh winter expedition without supplementary oxygen. By 20 January it was reported that as part of the acclimatisation cycle the team had climbed Pumori (7161m), a first winter ascent of that mountain. However their attempt on the main objective failed due to extreme conditions. Sadly, his liaison officer Padam Jung Rai died as a result of altitude sickness near Lobuche on the walk in.

One hundred permits were issued for **Lhotse** in 2017. Well known South Korean climber Sung-Taek Hong, the 51-year-old National Geographic explorer, said he made a final summit attempt on 20 November but failed due to strong winds.

Controversy is never far away when it comes to **Everest**. South African filmmaker Ryan Sean Davy tried to climb the peak without paying the $11,000 permit fee, without going through appropriate channels and avoiding several other compulsory conditions. His excuse was he had no money, but on his own admission he had no real mountaineering experience either and added that he was motivated to help those climbers who got into difficulty and were not assisted by others. Tourism officials found him hiding near base camp in a cave. They may have saved his life. His passport was confiscated and he was ordered back to Kathmandu where he was fined, deported and banned from any form of mountaineering activity in Nepal for 10 years.

A second climber, 49-year-old Polish economist Janusz Adam Adamski, completed a traverse of **Everest** via the North Col in Tibet and then descended the South Col route into Nepal. This is said to be the 15th such traverse and the first to be completed by a Pole. Although he had a permit for the North Col route he did not have entry permission from Tibet into Nepal via Everest and he also failed to obtain a Nepali permit for Everest. Janusz said believed there are no borders in the mountains. He said he was well aware of immigration and climbing rules in Nepal and Tibet. 'As there is no provision for the issuing of traverse permits in either country, I had to traverse illegally for fulfilment of my lifetime dream,' Adamski claimed. He was also fined, deported and banned from mountaineering in Nepal for the next 10 years. His actions also resulted in China closing the 'big' mountains on its side of the border for the autumn 2017 season. In a statement China claimed: 'His actions have caused the industry related internal rules and regulations to be adjusted and improved.' The statement did not mention anything about the placing of the Tibetan flag as well as photos of the Tibetan spiritual leader the Dalai Lama on top of Everest's summit, images of which were widely circulated on social media during the spring climbing season.

Two very risky rescues were also carried out on **Everest**, although one was actually a recovery. In the first instance a 21-year-old and inexperienced Sherpa guide Dawa Sange Sherpa was leading his Pakistani client Col Abdul Jabbar Bhatti towards the summit of Everest when the weather started to deteriorate. The guide suggested they turn round, the client insisted they continue. Despite being told to descend without his client over the radio, Dawa Sange Sherpa stuck with his duty. (Abdul Jabbar Bhatti disputed Dawa Sange's version of events, claiming the Sherpa had not brought enough oxygen. He told the BBC: 'The porter asked me to stand down when we were still not very high up the mountain. I asked him why he wasted my time and money if he couldn't scale the mountain. When we reached closer to the summit, we ran out of oxygen and the weather was also becoming unfavourable. That's when

Dawa Sange Sherpa, who was rescued and eventually evacuated to Colorado to treat severe frostbite injuries he suffered after a forced bivouac at 8,500m on Everest while guiding a Pakistani client.

I told him we should go back down, but he insisted we should climb to the top.') The result was that after reaching the summit at 3pm, both collapsed in the snow on descent at around 8,500m. Ang Tshering Lama on his way to the summit came across the pair in the snow and realised they were still alive. Along with his two colleagues they roped the young guide and his client up and dragged them back down to a lower altitude where others were also able to assist before Ang was able to turn round to again ascend their route to the summit which they finally achieved a few days later. Dawa Sange was flown to Colorado for treatment on severely frostbitten hands. Abdul Jabbar Bhatti, the fourth Pakistani to reach the summit, arrived home after a week in hospital but to a muted reception.

The second instance concerned the death of Indian climber Ravi Kumar. Kumar was reported missing at about 8,400m, above the Balcony on **Everest**'s South Col route, his body was eventually located after a 36-hour search. Kumar had reached the summit with his guide. The Indian climber then collapsed during the descent at 8pm due to low energy and oxygen levels. The client had forced his guide to push for the summit even though it was late in the day and getting benighted was a high probability, according to the expedition organiser. The guide left his client, Kumar, on the Balcony making him comfortable and leaving oxygen. The guide then descended to

The upper portion of the first ascent route of Burke Khang (6942m).

Camp IV to send back a rescue team as he himself was also suffering from frostbite and snow blindness and could do little more to assist his client. It is generally accepted that the retrieval of an injured or dead mountaineer from extreme altitude is difficult and hazardous. Nevertheless, under instruction from the Indian external affairs minister Sushma Swaraj, the Nepali tourism ministry insisted on what would become the most complex retrieval ever carried out on Everest. The ministry insisted that the Indian government was providing all necessary support for the operation, apart, of course, from the all-important resource of people, adding that the bereaved family wanted the body back home 'at any cost'. Due to the risks involved in spending so much time at high altitude, many expeditions choose not to bring down the bodies of their members who die high on Everest. Ironically, one of the main arguments put forward for banning less able people on Everest is the fact that they are more likely to jeopardise the life of the Nepali support climbers. That argument apparently did not hold water in this case.

All Indian mountaineers, if in government service, receive enhanced employment benefits if they climb Everest, pushing people to lie, recorded recently, and also to take extraordinary risks to secure promotion. Obviously not every Indian mountaineer is driven by such motives; the majority enjoy 'the games climbers play.' But for a few there are large rewards also. It should also be noted that the 2017 season witnessed the highest number of thefts of oxygen bottles, full as well as empty, from locked tents on both the north and south sides of Everest. That pattern was repeated in 2018.

The first ascent of **Burke Khang** (6942m) in Khumbu was completed in Autumn 2017 when Noel Hanna of Northern Ireland, Naga Dorje

The south-east face of Larkya Lha (6425m), with the Georgian line and bivouacs marked, climbed big-wall style and comfortably the most technically difficult new route done in Nepal in 2017.

Sherpa of Nepal, Pemba Tshering Sherpa and Samden Bhote reached the summit on 5 October. The team was led by Bill Burke of the US and in appreciation of Burke's contributions to promoting mountain tourism in Nepal, the mountain was named after him by the government of Nepal in 2014. **Burke Khang** is a technical peak situated between **Everest** and **Cho Oyu**, on the border of Nepal and Tibet.

A German mountaineer successfully scaled the unclimbed **Nagpai Gosum II** (7296m) on 3 October. Setting out from Lukla the two-man team, Jost Kobusch and Raphael Schardt, established base camp on 14 August but the weather proved too unsettled to reach this technical summit on the first attempt. Kobusch then made a solo attempt setting off from camp two to reach the top.

Archil Badriashvili, Bakar Gelashvili, Giorgi Tepnadze from Georgia reached the top of **Larkya Lha Main Peak** (6425m) on 27 September via the south-east face, which involved 700m of big-wall climbing and four bivouacs. Paulo Grobel from France led a 12-man expedition to Dolpa and successfully climbed **Danphe Sail** (6103m). A team of Nepali guides succeeded in making the first winter ascent of **Langdung** (6357m) in December. The team consisted of Dawa Yangzum Sherpa, Dawa Gyalje Sherpa and Pasang Kidar Sherpa. Since then 27-year-old Dawa Yangzum, from the Rolwaling valley, has created history by becoming Nepal's first female international mountain guide.

On 19 October, Jürgen Schütz, André Günzel and Manuel Möller, together with Dawa Gyalje Sherpa and Pasang Gomba Sherpa, succeeded on the first ascent of the west ridge of **Chulu West** (6419m) The mountain is

The line of the first ascent of Nagpai Gosum II (7296m) climbed solo by Jost Kobusch.

located in Manang. Chulu West, first climbed in 1952 by a Japanese expedition, is a popular 'trekking' peak without major technical difficulties only if climbed by the normal north-east ridge route.

An Austrian climber, Markus Schett, died while attempting a winter ascent of **Lobuche East** (6119m) in December 2017. Markus along with his guide reached high camp on 19 December but then leaving his guide in camp Markus set out alone for the summit. Despite an air and ground search the body was not discovered until 29 December.

**Other Information**
The old system of the Nepal Mountaineering Association having an A and B list of peaks has now been abolished. All trekking peaks now come under one category and are subject to the appropriate fee as per the mountain's height as a royalty. Trekking, national park and conservation area permits remain unchanged. TIMS (Tourist Information Monitoring System) is required for all trekking areas but if trekking in restricted areas then TIMS is not required providing a restricted area permit has been purchased. There are two categories of TIMS: one for foreign independent trekkers (FITS) and for those trekkers who trek through a Nepali agency. If the trekker is also going to climb a trekking peak then a TIMS card is not required providing a peak permit has been purchased.

Since October 2017 foreign trekkers have been charged 2000NR or $18 by the Khumbu Pasang Lhamu Rural Municipality to enter Khumbu and

The west ridge of Chulu West (6419m), near Manang.

collected NR 44m in tourist entry fees between October and December. Despite local entrepreneurs' strong opposition to the entry fee, the policy has continued. The Trekkers' Information Management System (TIMS) card issued by the tourism ministry does not substitute for the entrance fee but both in Khumbu and Langtang the TIMS counters remain unstaffed and closed. The local municpality has said that funds collected will be used for tourism promotion of the region and to improve the trail between Lukla and Everest Base Camp along with increasing tourist infrastructure in the region. It must be noted that all Nepali mountain workers, including trekking staff are now subjected to insurance laws. The TIMS card provides automatic insurance cover and without a TIMS card the trekking staff may not be covered so alternative arrangements must be made.

The above represents the 'legal' permit requirements and costs as stipulated by the government, as of 1 February 2018, but other charges may or may not be levied on top of these by agents in Nepal. Nepal is now spending billions on trying to survey Everest to confirm the actually height, just to make sure it is still the tallest mountain on Earth.

## Nepal 2018
Sadly the beginning of 2018 started with news of the death of Miss Elizabeth Hawley. A full obituary appears elsewhere in this year's *Alpine Journal*, but suffice to say Liz was a well-respected and loved member of the mountaineering community and that was particularly the case in her adopted

home of Nepal. Not only was she a great friend but she was also a constant source of information for the *Journal*, slipping bits of news to Dick Isherwood and then to me when I took over from Dick. The Himalayan Database will continue with its recording of Himalayan ascents but now under the guidance of Billi Bierling and team.

In February the government finally clarified the situation regarding summit certificates for Nepali climbing staff. Over 500 high-altitude climbing guides who made it to the summit of different mountains in recent years can now receive their summit certificates according to officials at the tourism ministry.

News that the government was banning disabled climbers from Everest was met with outrage in some quarters. One of the victims of this decision was Hari Bahadur Budha Magar, a former British Gorkha war veteran who lost both his legs while serving with British forces in Afghanistan in 2010. Hari Bahadur had hoped to attempt the summit in 2018 and become the first double amputee 'above the knee' to climb Everest. Although Nepal's supreme court overturned the decision, it came too late for the 2018 season, so the ex-Gurkha will try again in 2019.

There was also a breakthrough in the vexed question of insurance fraud. The tourism ministry announced an investigation into corruption among trekking, expedition and helicopter companies that has cost insurance companies millions of dollars. In 2017, an operations manager representing insurance companies was sent to Kathmandu to assess levels of care provided at hospitals and to ascertain why the 2017 spring climbing season had been the most expensive on record for medical claims, particularly for helicopter rescues and evacuations. After further investigation, it was found that 30% of helicopter evacuations billed to the insurance companies concerned were completely unnecessary and in six cases completely fictitious. Since then, Traveller Assist has launched an operations centre in Kathmandu and its head has met with justice ministry officials to share information and establish a line of communications between the government and trusted providers to tackle the corruption, stop unnecessary helicopter lifts from happening and improve the situation in Nepal. As yet there have been no official comments regarding future insurance provision from the industry as a whole.

TIMOTHY ELSON

# Pakistan 2017

Approaching the north-west face of Shispare. *(Kazuya Hiraide)*

The 2017 summer season in Pakistan saw 35 registered expeditions. (Expeditions to peaks under 6,500m do not need a climbing permit.) Of these, 16 were to 8,000ers and a further five were to Spantik. On the whole, these were commercial expeditions. There were two stand-out climbs: the first ascent of the north-east face of Shispare (7611m) by the Japanese climbers Kazuya Hiraide and Kenro Nakajima; and a difficult new route of the south-west face of Gasherbrum I (8080m), also known as Hidden Peak, by Czech climbers Marek Holeček and Zdeněk Hák. The two climbs share some similarities as they were both climbed in impeccable alpine style and required multiple attempts over several years to achieve success.

In addition there was a very impressive ascent of Badal Peak and traverse to K7 West (6615m), and there was a strong attempt of Latok I's (7145m) north ridge that got the highest on this much-tried objective, with the first attempt dating back to 1978. In general, August was very wet and did not have much stable weather, with July being more stable. A continuing welcome trend in the Pakistani Karakoram is for increased tourism from Pakistanis rather than from hitherto predominant foreigners. Unlike some recent years there does not seem to have been any major issues with permits. The FCO continues to recommend not using the Karakoram highway between Islamabad and Gilgit; there are regular flights from Islamabad to Gilgit and Skardu that overcome this difficulty, though delays are still a common occurrence.

The north-west face of Shispare. The Japanese climbed the left hand spur topping out to the left of the summit pyramid. The American team's aim was the central spur. *(Steve Su)*

**Shispare**

Kazuya Hiraide had attempted Shispare three times previously: the north-east face in 2007, and the south-west face in 2012 and 2013. In 2017 Hiraide and Kenro Nakajima arrived at base camp on 26 July and then acclimatised on the initial section of the first ascent route of Shispare and then on nearby Passu Peak (7478m), where they reached 6,750m before being forced back in bad weather. After eight days of more of this, they made their first attempt on the north-east face, however continuing bad weather turned them back low down.

On 18 August they set off with a slightly improved forecast: the whole of August saw high precipitation with more frequent than usual landslides. Their second day on the climb proved most trying, dodging avalanches on the lower exposed slopes and then climbing until late to a poor bivy on a snow arête.

The third day provided the crux climbing (M6, WI5), then they spent the fourth tent-bound at 6,850m in bad weather before finally reaching the summit on 22 August. They spent the next two days descending the long and complex original route arriving in base camp on 24 August. Hiraide is no stranger to this type of climb, having won the Piolet d'Or in 2009 for his ascent of the south-east face of Kamet. Shispare has been climbed twice: its first ascent in 1974 by a Polish-German team and its second in 1994 by a Japanese team. Both teams climbed the very long and complicated *Borchers Ridge* in siege-style, named for Heinz Borchers who died on the first ascent.

# Gasherbrum I

Marek Holeček and Zdeněk Hák climbed a new direct route up the southwest face of Gasherbrum I in an eight-day tour de force, with three days spent climbing the headwall between 7,400m and 7,700m with reported difficulties of M7 and WI5+. The south-west face had been partially climbed by two separate routes first by Jerzy Kukuczka and Voytek Kurtyka in 1983 where the headwall was avoided and more recently by Viktor Afanasiev and Valery Babanov who climbed the left side of the face and then joined the upper south-west ridge. Holeček first attempted the face in 2009 with Zdeněk Hrubý where they reached 7,500m at the headwall; the pair returned in 2013 but Hrubý fell to his death with all the technical climbing gear and ropes leaving Holeček facing an epic retreat. Holeček returned in 2015 with Tomáš Petreček and reached 7,400m before furious weather forced retreat; Holeček came back again in 2016 with Ondřej Mandula and reached 7,700m where the pair were trapped for several days in a terrible storm before making their way back to base camp after 13 days out. Holeček suffered frostbitten feet as a consequence of this.

In 2017 Holeček returned and after acclimatising set off with Hák on 25 July. They climbed the lower section of the *Afanasiev-Babanov* route to meet the *Kukuczka-Kurtyka* route before heading directly up the headwall. They reached the summit on 30 July and arrived back at base camp on 1 August after descending an avalanche-prone normal route. This seems to have been the only ascent of the mountain in 2017. They named their route *Satisfaction* in memory of Zdeněk Hrubý.

# K7 West

In August a Japanese team of Katsutaka Yokoyama and Takaaki Nagato made the first traverse from Badal Peak to K7 West (6615m). The pair, along with Ryo Masumoto, had climbed Badal Peak in 2014 via the massive south-east ridge (VI, 5.11c, C1, M5, 1600m) but considered it incomplete as they had not traversed to the summit of K7 West. Badal Peak is the shoulder south-west of the summit of K7 West and was first climb by a Spanish team in 2007. In August 2017 Yokoyama and Nagato were back and after fixing some of the initial pitches on 2 August, set off in a single push. They climbed 2,300m of technical ground over five days, from 5 to 10 August, ascending the south face of Badal Peak then traversing to K7 West. In the upper part of their route they joined the 2012 *Slovenian* route on the north-west face. They abseiled down the north-west face to arrive at base camp on the 11 August. They called the route *Sun Patch Spur* (ED+ 5.11cR, A2, M5, 90°). This impressive alpine-style ascent of a highly technical route was considered one of the 'last great problems' of the Charakusa valley.

# Latok I

The north ridge of Latok I (7145m) is one of the great outstanding problems in the Karakoram. It has repulsed around 20 strong teams that have included some of the best climbers in the world. The closest attempt to date was by Jeff Lowe, George Lowe, Michael Kennedy and Jim Donini in 1978, when they reached approximately 150m from the summit before being forced to retreat. The 2017 Russian team consisted of three climbers: Alexander Gukov, Anton Kashevnik and Valery Shamalo. They climbed in pure alpine style. On the approach Shamalo fell in a river and was submerged, which resulted in him getting a lung infection.

After acclimatising, the trio set off on 17 August, climbing a gully left of the ridge initially then onto the ridge itself. They took ten days' food with them and climbed through never perfect and sometime terrible weather for 12 days. On the 12th day they reached around 6,700m and felt they were almost at the end of the difficulties. However, they were also at the end of their tether and with no improvement in the weather, plus Shamalo's deteriorating condition, they thought it would still take three days to reach the summit, so decided to descend. On 29 August, while abseiling, a mistake led to one of their packs being dropped, unfortunately the one that contained the tent and sleeping bags. That day they did 14 abseils and spent a terrible night huddling under a hammock. The consequence was the team suffered bad frostbite: Shamalo lost all of his toes and parts of several fingers and Kashevnik several toes. After 14 days out, at 5am on 31 August they reached the glacier and took a further eight hours to wade to their base camp after a heavy accumulation of snow. By this time Shamalo had developed full pneumonia. This is an incredibly impressive attempt that clearly pushed them to their limits.

### Pakistan's 8,000ers

The five Karakoram 8,000ers saw the main volume of high-altitude expeditions in the summer of 2017. The majority were of a commercial type with almost every team attempting the 'normal' routes in a siege-style with oxygen. K2 (8611m) saw its first ascent in three years with Vanessa O'Brien and Mingma Gyalje Sherpa's team of 12 reaching the top on 29 July, despite deep snow that turned back all other expeditions. Mingma Gyalje Sherpa had a remarkable year, climbing five 8,000m peaks: Dhaulagiri (8167m) and Makalu (8485m) in Nepal in the spring and K2, Broad Peak (8051m) and Nanga Parbat (8126m) later in the year. He had got very close to the summit of Nanga Parbat in June, in fact claiming an ascent until doubts were raised. On 2 October he undisputedly made the summit and was very late in the year to make such an ascent.

On Nanga Parbat in June the very experienced Argentinian-Spanish team of Mariano Galván and Alberto Zerain attempted an alpine-style ascent of the massive Mazeno Ridge, first climbed to the summit in 2012 by Sandy Allan and Rick Allen. However, they disappeared and, after an aerial search was made, are presumed to have been caught in an avalanche. Also of note was an experienced Spanish team attempt on the Gasherbrum I-II traverse, which they abandoned. The Pakistani government requires foreign expeditions to employ Pakistani high-altitude porters in an attempt to discourage expeditions from bringing Nepali Sherpas to do this work, although many expeditions have Nepali Sherpas in addition. This is only really relevant for siege and commercial expeditions.

## Winter

The 2017-18 winter season in the Karakoram was dramatic: a large Polish expedition attempted the first winter ascent of K2 while a French-Polish pair attempted the second winter ascent of Nanga Parbat. The 13-strong Polish team, led by Krzysztof Wielicki who made the first winter ascent of Everest in 1980, arrived in Pakistan at the end of December, set up base camp and started climbing the *Česen* ridge. Meanwhile on Nanga Parbat, Elisabeth Revol (France) and Tomek Mackiewicz (Poland) were climbing the *Messner-Eisendle-Tomaseth* route in alpine style without oxygen. They had attempted the route twice together in winter, getting to 7,800m in 2015. Mackiewicz had attempted the mountain a further four times. They summited on 25 January but Mackiewicz was soon suffering from frostbite, snow blindness and altitude sickness. They spent the night in a crevasse at 7,400m and managed to reach their camp four at 7,200m the next day.

At the same time a rescue effort had begun, with a crowd-funding campaign started and co-operation from the K2 winter expedition. Revol made Mackiewicz as comfortable as possible and continued her descent and late in the afternoon of 27 January Adam Bielecki, Denis Urubko, Jaroslaw Botor and Piotr Tomala were helicoptered from K2 base camp to Nanga Parbat base camp at 4,900m. Urubko and Bielicki immediately set off up the *Kinshofer* route and climbed through the night up more than 1,000m of ground to find Revol at 2am on the morning of 28 January at 6,100m. Revol had severe frostbite by this point and Urubko and Bielicki provided first aid before making the heart-breaking decision not to continue up to Mackiewicz who was unable to move unaided according to Revol. On 29 January Urubko and Bielicki lowered Revol down to camp one where she was airlifted to hospital in Islamabad. This was a truly dramatic and daring rescue on the part of the climbers and Pakistani military pilots, though sadly it did not manage to save Mackiewicz.

Following the drama of the Nanga Parbat rescue, the Polish K2 team continued, establishing three camps. However, with a dry winter rock fall was a constant danger. After Adam Bielicki was hit in the face, breaking his nose, and Rafal Fronia sustained a broken arm they decided to switched routes to the classic *Abruzzi* ridge. By 23 February, Bielicki and Urubko were at camp three and Urubko proposed to Bielicki to make a summit attempt. An argument ensued and on 24 February Urubko set off on a summit push alone against the wishes of the team. By 26 February Urubko had abandoned his attempt and descended to base camp, where he left the expedition. Urubko's attempt was in part due to a disagreement over what 'counts' as a winter ascent. Officially the winter season ends on 28 February while the astronomical end of winter is 20 March. The rest of the team continued but failed to make much headway due to heavy snow that did not let up. The expedition was abandoned in the middle of March.

**Baltoro**

In the Baltoro region, the most notable news was the first ascent of Praqpa Ri South (7026m) via the east-south-east ridge (TD+, M3, 90°, 1500m) from the Khalkhal pass (5705m) by the Chilean team of Andres Bosch and Alejandro Mora. They approached via the Khalkhal valley and acclimatised first via a new route on Khalkhal West (6250m) via its south-west ridge (D, 1000m). Their ascent still leaves the main summit of Praqpa Ri (7156m) unclimbed. Also in the Baltoro region, Bruce Normand, Billy Pierson and Marcos Costa made an attempt on the unclimbed east face of Gasherbrum IV (7925m). They reached 7,300m but were defeated by a band of unprotectable marble, only about five metres high. They felt that in a deeper snow year the wall would have been possible. See page 79 for an account.

**Biafo**

In addition to the strong attempt on Latok I there were attempts on Ogre I (7285m), also known as Baintha Brakk, and on Ogre III (6950m). A strong Swiss-German-Austrian team comprising Alexander Huber, Dani Arnold, Mario Walder and Christian Zenz attempted the east pillar. They experienced very high temperatures, only being able to move on their route between midnight and 5am, describing the snow at 6,100m as slush; this forced them to abandon their climb as they felt the risks were too high. Huber, who has been on numerous expeditions to the Biafo over a 25-year period, felt this was a consequence of climate change and that teams attempting technical routes on lower altitude peaks in the Karakoram are better aiming for the end of August and start of September rather than the traditional Karakoram climbing season of July into August.

At the end of August a young German team consisting of Xari Mayr, Rainer Treppte and Fritz Miller attempted the south pillar of Ogre III. They fixed ropes on the lower part of the climb through a complex icefall and established two camps, before retreating back to base camp. They then made two attempts on the summit: on the first their highest camp had been destroyed; on the second attempt the forecast good weather did not materialise and they retreated. Sadly, in January 2018, Mayr died in an avalanche in the Dolomites. He was only 22.

**Hispar**

The Hispar region was fairly quiet in 2017. There was an interesting attempt on an unclimbed peak called Machu (6630m) from a British team consisting of Peter Thompson and Aiden Laffey. They tried the south-west ridge to west ridge and reached 5,650m where they reached an impasse they could not overcome. In June Symon Welfringer (France) climbed a new route on the south face of Emily Peak (c5850m), which he called *La Vengeance de Robîne* (AI4, M4, 1000m).

**Batura**

In the Batura area, in addition to the Japanese success on Shispare, there was a Pakistani expedition to attempt Passu (7478m), which was turned back by bad conditions in the icefall approaching their intended route. The American pair of Steve Su and Rusty Wills aimed to climb a new route on Shispare but after a reconnaissance Wills learned his mother was in hospital and returned to the US. Steve Su stayed on and climbed a new route on Maidon Sar (6085m), climbing through the night on 5 August up the south face and east ridge with difficulties up to M4.

### Shimshal

In August 2017, a British-Pakistani team consisting of George Cave, Ross Davidson, Steve Carratt, Clay Conlon and Karim Hayat visited the Gunj-e Dur glacier system off the Shimshal valley. Davidson and Hayat made the first ascent of Yad Sar (6,015m) via a 900m long Scottish II-III gully on the south-east face. They did not reach the highest point but rather the most prominent one on the multi-summited ridge. At the same time Conlon and Carratt were making the first ascent of a 5,855m peak from the Second East Gunj-e Dur glacier via the loose west ridge (PD). Also in the Shimshal valley were Tim Sheers, James Lawson and Will Smith (UK), whose original aim was to attempt the unclimbed Khurdopin Sar (6,310m) from the Virjerab glacier. However, on arrival they found that the Khurdopin glacier had advanced by a kilometre over the winter blocking access to the Virjerab glacier so they changed plans to attempt peaks above the Boesam pass (c5000m). They set up base camp south-west of the pass and then made four first ascents and attempted three other peaks over three weeks. They climbed a 5,700m peak via its north-west face (PD) from the pass, a 5,503m peak immediately south-east of the pass at AD, followed by ascents of Imtiaz Sar (5930m) and Arman Sar (5970m).

### Charakusa and Kondus Valley

A strong US team of Chris Wright, Steve Swenson and Graham Zimmerman based themselves on the Kaberi glacier in the far east of the Pakistani Karakoram to attempt the east face of Link Sar (7041m). They were unsuccessful, turned back by a combination of bad weather, hard climbing and complex route finding. However, they marvelled at the potential of the opposite site of the valley and the views up the Kondus valley where the Actual Ground Position Line between India and Pakistan lies. They approached up the Kondus valley, which has been closed to foreigners for the last 16 years, although the authorities seem to be  allowing expeditions into the area again. Also active on Link Sar at the same time were Tom Ballard (UK) and Daniele Nardi (Italy), who attempted the north-east face. They reached 5,700m and retreated in bad weather; they noted that Link Sar seemed to attract the bad weather. Link Sar is unclimbed. Andy Houseman and Jon Griffith climbed the lower west summit (6938m) in 2015. An Italian team made up of Federica Mingolla, Simone Pedeferri and Luca Schiera visited the Kondus valley in July inspired by photos from the 2000 American expedition there. They set up base camp an hour's walk below the start of

Beautiful rock peaks near the snout of the Kaberi glacier. The striking tower on the right is Tahir Tower, climbed by Brady Robinson, Jimmy Chin, Steph Davis and Dave Anderson in 2000. *(Graham Zimmerman)*

Looking down the Kaberi from the lower flanks of Link Sar's east face. *(Graham Zimmerman)*

the Sherpi glacier and attempted some rock climbs but found the rock to be sandy and vegetated. They moved base to the Kiris valley and climbed a big-wall-style route (7b, A2) on a 4,900m peak they named Peak Nic.

### Hindu Raj

In June and July, an Italian team of Francesco Rota Nodari, Tarcisio Bellò and Mara Babolin visited the Hindu Raj, situated north of the main Karakoram on the border with China, a region infrequently visited. Between 30 June and 1 July the team made the first ascent of the last unclimbed 6,000er in the Chiantar glacier area, which they named Jinnah Peak (6177m) after the first president of Pakistan. They climbed the south-east face via an ice and mixed route they named *Ghotolti Dreams* (TD, IV, 70°, 1500m), climbed in a single 27h 30m push.

# HUGH THOMAS

# Central Asia 2017

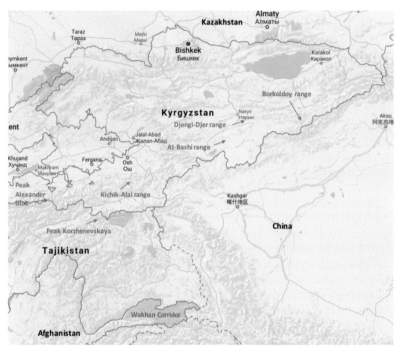

Areas mentioned in the text are highlighted in red.

Compared to 2016, there was relatively limited new routing activity in Central Asia. The reason for this is slightly unclear. Visas, flights and permits remain relatively straightforward and cheap for most countries in the region: Kyrgyzstan, Tajikistan and Kazakhstan. In addition, straightforward access to many areas, particularly in Kyrgyzstan, and generally lower altitudes than the Himalaya, allow for quicker acclimatisation for anyone without time for long expeditions.

Kyrgyzstan saw most activity in 2017, with notable new ascents on Pik Aleksandr Blok (5239m) by Slovak and German teams; a new route by Denis Urubko and team on Pik Chapaev (6372m); and two exploratory British expeditions to the Djengi-Djer and Borkoldoy ranges. A team led by the Czech climber Michal Kleslo explored the Kichik-Alai range, and a large team from the International School of Mountaineering explored the At-Bashi range.

281

On pitch 15 (6c) of *Alexandra Supernova*, with wild rock formations above. *(Benno Wagner)*

There is unfortunately very little information on expeditions to Tajikistan and Kazakhstan in 2017. A Russian and Kyrgyz team made the first winter ascent of Pik Korzhenevskaya (7105m) via the south face in Tajikistan, but there is limited detail on other first ascents.

Afghanistan remains the exception in terms of access in Central Asia as there are increasing security concerns in the north of the country. In particular, although some reports say the Wakhan corridor itself is fairly safe once you are there, the approach through Ishkashim is not considered safe, and in May 2018 the FCO was advising against travel to the Wakhan corridor, a warning that may present difficulties in obtaining travel insurance.

Weather reports from the expeditions that took place are variable. Generally, the further east in Kyrgyzstan, the better the weather. The Slovak team on Pik Aleksandr Blok in the western Ak-Su region of Kyrgyzstan reported one day of good weather in three weeks during August, whereas both British expeditions towards the east reported generally stable conditions in August which grew significantly colder and snowier through September.

### Kyrgyzstan

The ease of access and well established local tour operators, who can arrange overland transportation and helicopter access, combined with a wide variety of both rock and alpine objectives and first ascent potential has made Kyrgyzstan the top choice in the region for many mountaineers.

In addition, Vladimir Komissarov's guidebook to Kyrgyzstan's mountains was updated in 2017 and contains comprehensive information on all areas of Kyrgyzstan as well as suggestions on unexplored and unclimbed areas. There remains significant potential for further new routes and first ascents. Komissarov is president of the Kyrgyz Alpine Club.

Pik Aleksandr Blok in the western Ak-su region of Kyrgyzstan, plagued with poor weather in the summer of 2017. *(Paul Sass)*

Djengi-Djer Peak (4519m), Kyrgyzstan. *(Sally Hudson)*

The line of ascent of the new Slovak route *Summer Bouquet* on Pik Alexandr Blok. *(MANOfactory, Martin Grajciar)*

In August 2017 Denis Urubko and Maria Cardell visited Pik Chapaev (6372m), just west of Khan Tengri in the far east of Kyrgyzstan and succeeded in putting up a new route on the 2,000m south face, reaching the summit on 27 August. They named their route *Saber* (Russian 5A, IV/4, M4, 900m). On 1 September Denis made the first ascent of Pik Irbis (5350m) with Vera Rogovaya and Vladimir Ryazantsev via a 22-pitch route on the north face fuelled merely by a cup of coffee and some chocolate over an unexpected 29-hour push.

Pik Aleksandr Blok (5239m) is in south-west Kyrgyzstan in the Aksu valley (not to be confused with the other Aksu area in the east of Kyrgyzstan). This area offers much potential for rock routes and has been compared to Patagonia. Over three weeks in August 2017 a Slovak team of

Jozef Krištoffy on the hardest pitch (UIAA 9+) of *Summer Bouquet*.
*(MANOfactory, Martin Grajciar)*

climbers consisting of Martin Grajciar, Ondrej Húserka, Jozef Krištoffy and Vladimír Linek climbed an impressive new line up the west face of Aleksandr Blok using some aid and summited on 24 August. They subsequently freed each pitch and called their route *Summer Bouquet* (UIAA 9+, 70°, 22 pitches, 900 m), probably one of the hardest free climbs in the area.

Also in August, Toni Lamprecht, Benno Wagner, Paul Sass from Germany and Henry Francis from the UK succeeded in putting up *Alexandra Supernova*, an 800m route (18 pitches up to French 7b) on a summit (4800m) of the west ridge of Pik Aleksandr Blok. They highlighted excellent Joshua Tree-type granite but suffered from similar changeable weather conditions as the Slovak team: warm conditions at the start of the expedition led to significant rock fall, which was followed by much colder conditions a few days later.

Two British expeditions explored the Borkolodoy and Djengi-Djer regions. Both were extremely successful in terms of number of new peaks climbed. Full expedition reports are available from the MEF and BMC. The seven-member Borkoldoy expedition was supported by the Mount Everest Foundation and the BMC and climbed 14 new summits including one over 5,000m during August 2017. They reported generally stable weather and good snow and ice conditions, and noted there is still potential for first ascents and new routes. However, rock quality was poor.

The Djengi-Djer was explored by a team of six, also with support from the MEF, BMC and the John Muir Trust. They climbed 12 new peaks, a mixture of rock and alpine routes up to 4,716m, during the first three weeks of September. Weather conditions were generally good in the first half of the month, but they experienced significant snowfall at the end of their expedition, and low overnight temperatures at base camp (down to -15°C). They noted limited future potential on high peaks in the area, but did comment on the rock climbing potential on a kilometre-long band of solid limestone offering four or five-pitch routes.

Michel Kleslo and David Brezovjak led a nine-member expedition to the little visited Kichil-Alai region in south-eastern Kyrgyzstan. They made the first ascent of Korly-too (4913m) via the north ridge at a grade of Russian 3A. They also climbed the standard route up Gezart (4935m) and highlighted the potential of the area for first ascents on virgin 4,000m peaks, also noting that the area is easily accessible from Osh, which is a bus ride or flight from Bishkek.

The largest expedition in 2017 was probably the 15-member team from the International School of Mountaineering, which went to the At-Bashi range in the centre of Kyrgyzstan near the Chinese border, accessing the area from the Kashkaratash valley. This trip was led by Adrian Nelhams and included Vladimir Komissarov, the author of the guidebook to mountaineering in Kyrgyzstan. Not surprisingly, it was very successful and summited 10 virgin peaks up to 4,801m in the last week of August. According to Vladimir Komissarov's guidebook, this leaves approximately 50 more unclimbed mountains for future expeditions to the area.

### Tajikistan

A four-man team of Russian and Kyrgyz climbers led by Sergey Seliverstov made the first winter ascent of Pik Korzhenevskaya (7105m) via a new route on the south face in January 2018. They experienced bitterly cold temperatures down to -40°C with high winds and ice pitches up to 60°.

# ANTONIO 'SEVI' GÓMEZ BOHÓRQUEZ
# Peru 2017

The Gocta waterfalls, variously described as the
third and fifth-highest in the world. *(Jorge Yamamoto)*

## AMAZONIA

### Catarata de Gocta (Gocta Falls)

The brothers Iker and Eneko Pou spent a month in Peru with climbing
companions Pedro Galán and Manu Ponce, joined by Luis Rizo and
Lina Schütze as camera operators. From the town of San Pablo de Varela
they walked two or three hours to the Gocta Falls. (There are two waterfalls,

The line taken by Simón, Crave and Baró on the south face of Pucarashta Central, Cordillera Blanca. *(Simón, Crave, Baró)*

the smaller 540m high, the taller 771m, although these figures have been disputed they are generally regarded as the world's fifth-highest. They are near the villages of Cocachimba and San Pablo, in the district of Valera 700km north-east of Lima. The airport at Chachapoyas (2235m) is inactive. Tarapoto airport is about 334km from Cocachimba by paved road, then 6km of unpaved road to the falls). They had planned to start with a route near the lower waterfall, but the rock was broken and so they opted to climb just to the left side of the upper waterfall, a total of six rope lengths up sandstone cracks of variable quality. On 3 July 2017 they completed *Yaku Mama*, which means 'mother water' in Quechua (7a+, 185m). For future ascents they recommend a machete, two sets of cams and two ropes for rappelling down the line of the route. They later went to the Rúrec canyon of the Cordillera Blanca; please see Quebrada Rúrec later. (Source: Desnivel.es, 8 September 2017; *AAJ* 2018.)

## CORDILLERA BLANCA

### Pucarashta Central
The Eqipo Femenino de Alpinismo (EFA) of the Spanish climbing federation (FEDME) to the Cordillera Blanca comprised Rith Craven, Vicky Vega, Diana Calabuig, Ester Simón and Fátima Gil, led by Marc Subirana and accompanied by the guide Oriol Baró and the doctor August Cavaro, lasted from 5 June to 12 July 2017. After acclimatising in the Quebrada Santa Cruz, Simón, Craven and Baró climbed the south face of Pucarashta's central summit (c5450m), a snowy peak situated to the north-east of Alpamayo and to the south-west of Pucahirca Oeste, for a mixed climb *Para*

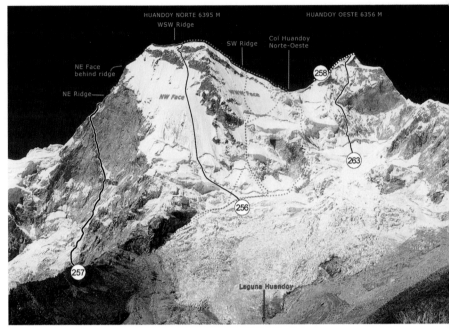

Nevado Huandoy North and West from the base camp of Cerro Parón. 257: *Slovenian* route of 1987; 256: *North American 1971* route; 258: *North American 1954* route; 263: *North American-British 1985* route. The blue dotted lines indicate the likely options for the *Swiss 1959* route. The line of red dots indicates the line taken by Nathan Heald in 2017. It's approximate because this photo is from the 1988 book *Cordillera Blanca*.

*Casa de Zarela* (MD+, 600m) that coincideded for half of the face with the route first climbed by Phil Moores, Mick Davie and Steve Di Ponio with a bivouac on 16 June 1991. The line of this route publised in 1995 in the David Sharman guide is not so accurate, meaning that it was difficult to determine exactly which sections were shared with the 2017 route. The author names the peak Pucarashta Central to distinguish it from the two adjacent peaks east and west and gives the altitude 5,650m. Four days later Moores fell rappelling down the south face (*AAJ* 1992) of Pucarashta Este (c5500) and he died the next day while he was being evacuated. (Sources: personal communication Oriol Baró; www.fedme.es; *AAJ* 1992, p152; D Sharman, *Climbs of the Cordillera Blanca de Peru*, Scotland, Whizzo Climbs, 1995.

**Huandoy**

The North American Nathan Heald, a guide resident in Peru, and the Peruvian Yjegual Camasa travelled on 17 October from Huaraz to the Parón gorge, approaching via the north-west to Lake Huandoy (c4750m) and cached some gear, then descended to Lake Parón (c4150m) for the night. Next day they again climbed with their remaining gear picking up their

Top left: The *Berg-Roberts* route on the east of Chacraraju Este. *(Quentin Roberts)*
Above left: Roberts leading the crux pitch on the main rock wall of their new line on Chacraraju Este. *(Roberts, Berg)*

Above right: Berg in the exit ice gully. *(Roberts, Berg)*

cache and continuing to the north-west up lateral moraine to the left of the lake. They arrived at the moraine field (c5200m) close to the base of the rocky buttress on the left side of the north-west face. Camasa would wait here. On the same day, at 10.15pm, Heald crossed the glacier to the right below the buttress and the seracs at the base of the north-west face to reach the foot of the rocky rib that separates the north-western and west face. Once under the west-north-west face he crossed the bergschrund, climbed an ice slope (60°-70°) to cross the left side of the barrier of seracs located between Huandoy North and West. Overcome this barrier, Heald climbed slightly diagonally to the right. The last 300m were climbed on hard ice to reach the south-west edge, which reached about 6,100m. He climbed this ridge (*Schatz-Reiss*, 1959) at an angle of about 50° to the foresummit. He continued to the north-east (*Hein-Schneider*, 1932) reaching the summit (6395m) at 8.30am on 19 October under a clear, calm sky, with low temperatures. Heald calculated he climbed 1,200 m, with an overall difficulty of TD. On the descent, by the same route, he used 22 abalakovs and abandoned three snow pickets. He carried a 60m 7.5mm rope and three ice-screws. It took nine hours to regain the moraine field, arriving at 5pm. (Sources: Nathan Heald; *AJ* 1933-4; *AAJ* 1941 et al; *Annales*, Groupe de

Haute Montagne, 1959; A Gómez Bohórquez, Cordillera Blanca, Escalada, Parte Norte. Murcia, Andes Info, 2004. J Ricker *Yurac Janka: A Guide to the Peruvian Andes, Part I Cordilleras,* Blanca and Rosko, Banff, Canadian Alpine Club, New York, American Alpine Club, 1977; R Schatz, 'Anden-Expedition 1959 des Schweizer Alpen-Clubs', *Berge der Welt,* Zürich, Schweizerische Stiftung für alpine Forschungen, vol 13 1960-1.)

### Chacraraju Este

The Canadian climbers Alik Berg and Quentin Lindfield Roberts approached via the Yanapaccha gorge to Lake 69, then crossed the east col between Chacraraju and Yanapaccha, camped under the east face of Chacraraju Este (6001m), which they watched the following day while they rested. Next day, the two Canadians opened a route they called *The Devil's Reach Around* (M6 5.10, 90°), the first without aid on the east face of the peak. They waited out the warmer hours of the day to climb a rocky section, then waited until the ice and snow areas had shade. The face seemed to fall apart when the sun was hot, but they found shelter where they waited a few hours for the cold to bite. Roberts published the following text on alpineinsight.com: 'We went for it and we charged. We climbed to the base of the headwall overnight in 12 hours. I lead the first block negotiating the first cliff band in the dark, and Alik lead the next, finding a long Rockies style traverse to negotiate the central cliff band at sunrise. This traverse soon became dubbed the 'reach around traverse' and was the key that we needed to unlock access to the headwall. Both blocks proved easier than anticipated, and we were handling the thin air well. We motored and felt good. But then the sun came out and baked us to the face. Like lazy flies we sat there as the face started to fall apart. Ice was delaminating and falling from the summit mushrooms above. The falling ice and rock would clear the steep headwall and explode on our tracks below. We couldn't climb in this. Eventually we chopped a platform for the tent in a fin of snow. We planned to fix the first headwall pitch once the face cooled off, and fire the rest of the route the next day.' They descended with 20 abseils down the south face. For more details please see: *https://www.alpineinsight.com/single-post/2017/07/19/To-burro-ornot-to-burro-Chacraraju-Este.* (Sources: *www.alpineinsight.com*; Alik Berg.)

### Nevado Hualcán

On 28 and 29 July 2017, the Basque-Peruvian guide Aritza Monasterio and the Canadian Alik Berg, who had never climbed together, opened possibly the first route on the north face of Nevado Hualcán (6125m), one of the last virgin walls of the Cordillera Blanca in the Andes of Peru. They named their route *Nadie Sabe Nada* (ED1, M6, 85°, VI, 1000m). In descending the south face, they completed a 'an integrale traverse in the best Andean style', which, according to Monasterio, means 'no support personnel, muleteers, donkeys, porters, camp security or communications equipment such as satellite phones or simple cellphones for external contact, etc. It was a lightweight effort for two people for six days, with everything on their back from

The new *Monasterio-Berg* route on the north side of Nevado Hualcán (6125m east), at the head of the Cancaracá Grande river. The blue circles mark each bivouac. *(Aritza Monasterio)*

Aritza Monasterio on the mixed climbing of the upper wall of the north face of Nevado Hualcán, on the second day of climbing. *(Alik Berg)*

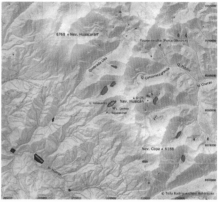

The red line shows the approach of Monasterio and Berg from Carhuaz. The Cancaracá Grande creek is shown below the east summit (6125m) of Nevado Hualcán. *(Toño Rodríguez, Sevi Bohórquez, IGN)*

beginning to end. The day before leaving they bought public bus tickets and organised equipment and food in the backyard of Monasterio's home. On day one, 25 July 2017, they travelled from Huaraz by bus, through Carhuaz to the Ulta pass and then got off at the bend where the Cancaracá canyon begins. That same day they climbed through this gorge to camp at 4,200m on one side of the lateral north moraine. The second day they camped on the glacier at about 5,000m, at some distance from the wall to avoid being hit by avalanches and rockfalls. They spent the third day watching the north face to choose the definitive line, oriented slightly north-northwest. On the fourth day they climbed to camp on the wall (c5900m) at the foot

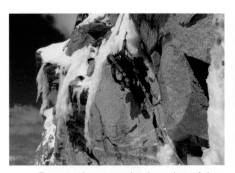

Berg on the crux mixed section of the upper wall, during day two. *(Aritza Monasterio)*

Monasterio climbs towards the east summit (6125m) of Nevado Hualcán at dusk on the second day of climbing. *(Alik Berg)*

of the rocky, mixed upper face. The fifth day they exited the wall, reached the summit and descended to bivouac (c6075m). On the sixth and final day they completed the traverse of the mountain, descending the southern slope to Lake 513, reaching the city of Hualcán from where they returned to Huaraz. (Source: Aritza Monasterio.)

**Huantsán**

Between 4 and 8 June, from the Alhuina gorge, Oriol Baró and Marc Torralles climbed the north-east arête of Huantsán (6395m) via the international route of 1974. It is the fifth ascent to the summit via the ridge and the first in alpine style. The two Catalan guides climbed mostly snow and ice, with sections of rock; the route was ED+, 1,700m. Baró explained on Desnivel. com: 'The weather was typical and for the last bivouac we had to endure heavy snow, but we were inside a cave and it was quite good. Every day we were able to pitch the tent, even digging a platform on the crest of the ridge. All the different types of terrain were difficult: vertical ice, poor rock and a lot of bad snow that was almost vertical. We had to overcome sections of A0 with snow stakes, something that is very scary. There were long stretches without protection. We only had four stakes, which we abandoned on the rappels, in addition to about 18 abalakovs and some rock rappels.'

On a brief historical note, the first ascent of the complete north-east ridge to the summit of Huantsán needed the collaboration of two expeditions: one of 13 French (nine men and four women) and another of three French, two Americans an Australian and a Peruvian porter. The first of them to reach the summit were the French Batard, Parmentier, Maire and Missilier on 18 August 1974. The second were Normand, Neff (both from USA) and Johns (Australia) on 19 August. The third were Fournier, Minisini and Penin (France) on 20 August. The last were Muisant, from Naurois (France) and Seibel (USA) on 20 August. A month earlier, a team expedition of North Americans Rick Ridgeway and Chris Chandler, who had prospected the ridge a year earlier, Bill Lahr, Craig McKibben, Malcolm Moore and Patrick Padden had climbed almost the entirety of the same ridge in semi-alpine style. From camp three, Lahr and Ridgeway continued to the rocky band at about 6,250m. They only needed to climb 145m in altitude to reach the top and were in good physical condition, but the lack of equipment to secure the rock, ice and deep snow forced them to give up. A French expedition the previous year fixed ropes to 6,000m but abandoned in bad weather. (Sources: Desnivel.com; *Annales*, Groupe de Haute Montagne, 1975; *AAJ*, 1972-5; *La Montagne*, 111, 1978; Rick Ridgeway.

### Huantsán Oeste
On 17 June 2017, Nathan Heald published the following on his Facebook page, but this information needs elaboration and confirmation: 'We made it to the west summit of Nevado Huantsán at 6,250m after two ice cave bivouacs. There was a 60m rappel to the col [north-west with the south-west ridge of the main summit] and then the final 150m [of the east ridge] and a wicked summit block, which we realized the team did not have the energy or margin of error to finish. Nonetheless, it was only the sixth time in history the west summit of Huantsan has been reached. I am very proud of my partner Duncan McDaniel, and our bro Devin Corboy for enduring the sufferfest. It was Devin's first 6,000m peak and a great intro to extreme alpinism.' A French expedition in 1989 reached the west summit, descended to the north-west, continued towards the main peak and had to retreat only 50m short of it on ice of 60° to 70° because of unstable seracs.

### Itsogwanka (Itsochuanca)
An expedition led by Italian climber Pietro Rago went to Quebrada Rúrec with two disabled professional athletes, Silvia Parenti, who is blind, and Kevin Ferrari, whose right leg was amputated above the knee, and expert climbers Roberto Conti, Enrico Piccinelli and Gabriele Tonoli, as well as Peruvian mountain guides. They equipped a pair of routes with bolts for sport climbing in the low walls of the ravine and tried to open a route that reached the middle of the west face of Itsochuanca. Its Quechua name comes from itsog 'left') and wanka ('large, long or tall stone'), meaning 'the tall stone on the left'. It is on the north side of Chaupihuanca or Chaupiwanka. See *AJ* 2003 pp287-8 and 2006 pp321-2. (Source: *www.arrampicande.it.*)

### Chaupiwanka (Chaupihuanca)
The brothers Pou, Galán, Ponce, Rizo and Schütze travelled 24 hours by bus from Gocta (see above Gocta Falls, Amazonia) to Huaraz, then by car beyond the town of Olleros to walk to a base camp (c3850m) on the pampa under the towers of the Rúrec gorge. Attempting Chaupihuanca (c4750m), 'the tall stone in the middle', in Quechua, the Spanish spent 11 and 12 June on the wall trying to repeat the Italian route *Qui Io Vado Ancora* free (see *AJ* 2008, pp329-30; *AAJ* 2007 pp216-7). This route of 585m had an original grade of 7c with two pitches of A1: these went free at 7c+/8a. When it began to snow, they abandoned the climb. Then they went down to Huaraz, rested for two days and returned to Rúrec. Here they stayed five days, in-

From left to right the western faces of Itsochuanca (Itsogwanka), Chaupihuanca (Chaupiwanka) and Allachuanca (Allaucawanka) from the Rúrec valley.

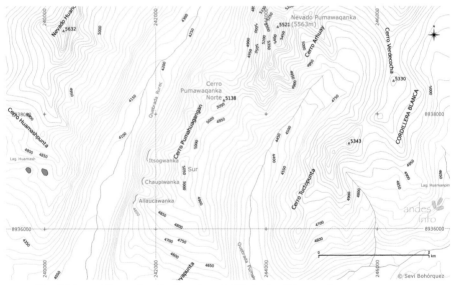

The IGN map illustrating the location of cliffs in the Rúrec valley.

cluding three nights on the wall of Allachuanca or Allaqwanka (see below), located to the right of south-west side of Chaupihuanca. *Qui Io Vado Ancora* terminates at about 4,600m according to the Italians, joining the Spanish route *García-Sandoval* (VI, 5.11, A4, 850m) completed on 23 August 2003 with fixed ropes, sometimes with capsule style, after 16 nights on the wall. (*AJ* 2003 p287-8 and 2006 p122, *AAJ* 2006 p241 and 2007 p216.) The peak was termed Pt c4800m in *AJ* 2003 and as Punta Numa (NPUGI: name proposed, unacceptable to a geographical institution) in *Desnivel* 134

(November 1997) and in other publications later. (Sources: *AAJ* 2018; www.hermanospou.com.)

### Allaucawanka (Allachuanca)

The Pou brothers' team climbed a route they called *Zerain* (7a+, A1, 860m), dedicated to the Himalayan climber Alberto Zerain, who was buried by an avalanche next to the Argentinian Mariano Galván on the Mazeno Ridge of Nanga Parbat. From 17 to 22 July 2017, spending three nights on the wall, the Pou team did not have time to free three pitches, (from nine to 11) of the 20 climbed in total. Many media have reported that this climb is one of the most significant of the Pous' career, due to its height, the size of the wall, its quality and difficulty: estimated at 8a when freed. The team suggested that pitch nine could 7c+, pitch 10, in a crack in a dirty corner, could be 8a, and pitch 11 that continues up the corner was roughly 7b.

The highest point of this rocky wall, whose name means 'the long stone on the right', ends at about 4750m or 4800m on the western slope of Puma-huagangán South (Cerro Pumahuacanca Chico, c4950m) of sheet 20-i Recuay published by the Peruvian National Geographic Institute (IGN). This hill should not be confused with the snow peak of the same name: see photo in *AJ* 2013 p306. The first route on this wall, the north-west face of Allaucawanka, was put after almost two and a half months of siege, by Spaniards José L García and José Pardo in 2004, with Antonio Noguera in charge of support, logistics and communication with the media. This expedition reported it had climbed 'Chopiwanka', an incorrect transliteration of Chaupiwanka. Both words refer to the same thing, 'the great long stone of the centre', although about different wankas. (Sources: Desnivel.com; *AAJ* 2018; www.hermanospou.com.)

## CORDILLERA HUAYHUASH

### Jirishanca

With 12 days until their return flight to Spain, guides Roger Cararach, Marc Toralles and Iker Madoz travelled eight hours by taxi on 17 July from Huaraz to Queropalca. With their equipment on donkeys they walked about a day to the foot of the east face of Jirishanca (6094m). The next day, with two rucksacks and a haul-bag, they walked three hours to its base. Their goal was the route put up on the north-east spur in 2003 by French alpinists Didier Jourdain and Aymeric Clouet called *Tambo, Churros y Amigos* (ED+, VI, 7a, A2, 95°, 1200m). Iker Madoz described the attempt:

'This isn't the simplest way to climb the rocky east face of Jirishanca, since on its right-hand margin is the Italian route, full of bolts and therefore less dangerous and with lower grades [...] Our main goal was to try to repeat the French route, achieved without the use of bolts, only natural gear; this added great integrity for those who did the first ascent, as to their commitment, since they had only that protection that already existed on the wall. The first two days were the trickiest, and we only managed to climb

The east face and north-east spur of Jirishanca (6126m) with the route climbed in September 2003 by Aymeric Clouet and Didier Jourdain, *Tambo, Churros y Amigos* (ED3/4, 7a, A2, 95°, M4, 1100m) marked in September 2003. This was repeated to the north-east ridge by Iker Madoz, Roger Cararach and Marc Toralles blue line. *(Koky Castañeda)*

Iker Madoz on pitch 15 *Tambo, Churros y Amigos. (See page 329) (Marc Toralles)*

the first three pitches. The cracks were full of earth, mud and plants, preventing us from climbing free, so we had to clean them on aid. Because of that, we decided to return to base camp for more food. After a day of rest in camp, we got up early [on 22 July] and at first light had reached our high point. Our progress accelerated and we were able to climb free. So, to cut a long story short, we reached a bivouac at the end of the ninth pitch.' They reported this pitch as being the best on the route: 60m and 7a.

'The second day on the wall we climbed nine pitches, the most intense section of the route. All three of us climbed all the pitches, without using jumars. From 6.20am to 12pm we climbed in the sun, which then disappeared behind the ridge and in the afternoon we climbed in temperatures close to 0°C.' This middle day had the highest concentration of hard climbing, again with rock up to the seventh grade and aid of A2, as well as snow and ice. They bivouacked at 5,650m.

'The third day on the wall we managed to finish the French route and reach the north-east ridge, the route of the first ascent. After passing the first ice roof we found a snow ramp on which to bivouac. Roger was left to chop out a good ledge while Marc and I climbed the next ice roof to leave it fixed so we could climb light next day to the top. In the morning we woke to cloud and strong winds. Thanks to our satellite phone we contacted Huaraz, and discovered a few unstable days of windy weather had arrived. We didn't think it prudent to be on a ridge at 5,900m so we made the decision to collect our gear and retreat. After many rappels down the face we reached the foot of the route and a few hours later, still with light, our base camp. No top, but happy to have reached that point and have repeated a route done in the best style.' (Sources: Iker Madoz; www.andesinfo.blogspot.com.)

From left to right, Nevados Siulá (6344m), Jurau B (5727m), Jurau A (5617m) and Yerupaja (6634m). The red line on the right is the first attempt of the Italian-Swiss rope on the east side of Jurau B and the line on the left is the attempt on the east pillar of Siulá. *(Koky Castañeda)*

## Jurau B and Siulá Grande

The Italians Matteo della Bordella and Matteo Bernasconi and the Swiss climber Titio Arosio arrived in Peru in July planning to spend a month at base camp to climb the middle of the east face of Siulá Grande (6344m). This rocky limestone wall is to the right and above the Espolón Este – the eastern spur – the beginning of the route taken by the French Bonniot and Jourdain in 2016. With their cook, Pio Pollo, the two Italians and Swiss travelled by minibus to Queropalca (3831m). A day later, with their gear carried by mules, they walked six hours to base camp (c4300m) next to Lake Siulá. They spent the following days transporting material to the base of the wall and equipping what they called 'the plinth' of Siulá. This 'plinth' is in fact the east face of Jurau B (5740m, DAV 1936, or 5727m, ÖAV 2008), which climbs up to where the rock is covered by the southern glacier. They overcame the seracs on the front of this glacier and ascended diagonally to the left (to the north-west) to a point at c5400 m where it meets the south-east ridge that falls from the top of Jurau B. Because of glacial conditions they decided to descend; from this point it was too dangerous to reach the rocky east wall of Siulá. Days later they tried to reach the base of the wall on the south side of the east pillar of Siulá Grande (6356m or 6344m), starting to the left of the 2016 Bonniot-Jourdain route. The trio climbed diagonally right, crossing the east pillar to its northern side, reaching an altitude of 5,200m, where the weather forced them to abandon. Sources:

Pariacacca Sur (5758m) left and Norte (5699m) with the line of Jurado, Huamán and Mendoza marked. *(Marco A Jurado)*

On the south summit of Pariacacca. *(Marco A Jurado)*

On the south-east ridge heading for the south peak. *(Marco A Jurado)*

www.ragnilecco.com; *AAJ* 2017-8; Cordillera Huayhas (Perú) Alpenvereins-karte 0/3c, DAV 1936 and ÖAV 2008.

## CORDILLERA HUAROCHIRÍ

### Nevado Pariacacca Sur

In the Cordillera Huarochirí or Pariacacca, the central Andes of Peru, the Peruvian guide Marco Jurado, Frank Huamán, and Misael Mendoza travelled from Huancallo to the Nor Yauyos Cochas nature reserve. They camped (c5070m) next to a lake, either Trajíncocha, west of Cerro Trajín or Tullujutucocha, the lake below the north-east face of Nevado Pariacaca Sur (5758m): exact details are awaited. The three started their ascent on 8 August at 6.30am. The crossed the glacier up to the rocky spur of the north-east ridge. Then they traversed snow and across rock to the south side, which continued to a shoulder where Mendoza waited while his two companions climbed the final 100m of the arête, which twists towards the north, with a serac and a short rocky section, up to the summit. They named the route *Waka Ñan* (AD+, UIAA, V+, M3, 650m), descended on the east side, and arrived at base camp around 6pm. Waka Ñan means in Quechua 'way of men'. The upper part of this route seems to coincide with that of several previous ascents.

Pariacaca (Pariacacca, Pariakaka, Paryaqaqa, Tulluqutu or Tuyucoto) is a snowy mountain with two well differentiated peaks: the north (5699m,

W F Jenks) and the south with 5758m (5752m, Jenks) in the official carto-graphy. This does not attribute the name to this mountain located south-east of Nevado Collquepucro. Tullujuto means in Quechua 'lots of bones'. T A Dodge reached both summits, the north with his carrier D Dionisio in 1936 and the south in 1938 when Dionisio waited for him. Sources: Marco Antonio Jurado; *AAJ* 1948, p174; *AJ* 2001, pp83-8.

## Nevado Tunsho Suroeste

The Peruvian guide Víctor Rimac Trejo, with Greg Meyering and Susie Young (USA), travelled to the nature reserve Nor Yauyos Cochas, to the east of Lima, walked from the town of Pachacayo to Azulcocha (lake c4400m) and camped for five days to acclimate. The three of them then went to the base of the south-west peak of Nevado Tunshu (5420m) and camped (c4600m) for two days. On 17 July, at 5am, they climbed 200m on the south-east side via a snow ramp (40°-50°) diagonally to the left, followed by mixed terrain (70°) to a shoulder (c5300m) on the south ridge about 300m from the top. The route, about 400m in length, was graded D+, 70°. They abeiled the west-south-west face.

Sheet 24-l La Oroya of the National Geographic Institute (Peru) marks the main Tunshu peak as 5,730m but does not indicate specific height or name to the central summit located to the west-south-west. The topograph-ical sketch Cordillera Central Yarumario-Gruppe (1:60,000) published in 1969 by the Munich Academic Section of the DAV indicates the north-east-ern peak as 5,650m, the central at 5,560m and the south-western 5,420m. See AJ 2013, p304. See also First Climbs in Tunshu at http://andesinfo. blogspot.com, 27 January 2012, where it says 'Cordillera Central', it should in fact read 'Cordillera Huarochirí or Pariacacca'. (Sources: *AAJ* 2018; www.facebook.com/VictorRimacPeru.)

## Nevado Paca

*Marcelo Scanu adds this information:* Argentines Nehuen Conterno and Pablo Maximiliano Laumann spent three weeks in the Cordillera Blanca and then visited the Cordillera Central [Editor's note: see above for nomenclature] near Lima. The pair had many objectives in mind in this poorly explored region. They firstly ascended Tatajayco (5342m) to see the south face of Nevado Paca (5500m). On 5 August they began their ascent of Paca, climb-ing a line below the summits seracs. They did 250m unroped before the difficulties began. They found only one belay because of bad snow con-ditions using a snow stake. only a stake as a kind of security. After seven and a half hours of tricky snow they switched to the ridge 20m below the summit. Only Nehuen, carrying 15kg less than Pablo, went to the summit. Descent was via the north face and some little creeks reaching their base camp at Lake Rinconada after 16 hours. They called the route *Una Realidad Diferente* (MD, M5, 800m). Because of conditions they didn't attempt other mountains in the region.

Line of the route climbed by Heald, Urquizo, Gálvez and Putallaz on Nevado Terijuay (5380m), with the central and east peaks to the right, in the Urubamba range. *(Nathan Heald)*

## CORDILLERA URUBAMBA

### Nevado Terijuay

In mid August 2017 Nathan Heald, Jorge (Coqui) Gálvez Aramburu, Andrés Putallaz and Manuel Urquizo Cereceda met in Calca, sacred valley of the Incas, and traveled 98km in a truck to Lares, a town north-east of the Urubamba mountains. An SUV took them 18km to Cachín, where the locals, surprised and distrustful because few tourists come to this village, asked them what they were doing, while also asking them to write it up in their community newspaper. The three backpacked west through the Quecha de Cochayoc. After a couple of hours they crossed the Yanacocha pass (4268m), descended towards the Yuraccocha lake and rested. From here they climbed up a slope almost directly towards a ridge behind which was Terijuay (5330m) but they camped before reaching it because night began to fall and with it drizzle. Heald writes: 'We heard then the strange song of a girl who was taking care of her alpacas below; she sang with all the strength of her lungs to ward off the evil spirits that she believed we were. Next morning we reached the ridge and went to the small Tambillo lakes, located at the base of the south side of Terijuay. A few dozen or so villagers, a couple with machetes, were waiting a few hundred metres away. They had climbed a path from Quelcanca (Quelccanca) and wanted us to go down to this village, located a couple of hours away, where they would decide if

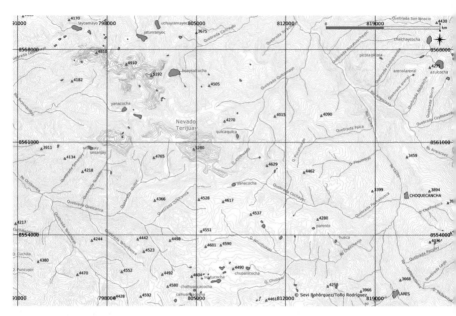

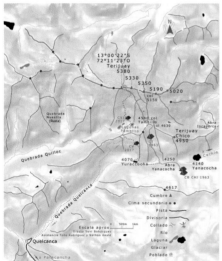

Above: Portions of IGN sheets 26-r Quebrada Honda and 27-r Urubamba showing Nevada Terijuay. *(Toño Rodríguez / Sevi Bohórquez)*

Left: The Urubamba range. The position of the secondary tops, marked in blue, is approximate. The Italian expedition of 1963 reached the peaks marked with red. The line of green points indicates the route of Heald, Urquizo, Gálvez and Putallaz to the summit of Nevado Terijuay, the orange dotted line is their descent to Quelcanca. Where it says 'Quebrada Nuestta', read 'Quebrada Ñusta'.

they would allow us to ascend. After an intense discussion they allowed us to follow our path. We reached a moraine crossing between the lakes and camped in a safe location at the foot of the southern glacial basin, formed by the three highest peaks of the Terijuay massif. We left the camp late at 5.30am on 17 August in unusual weather: it had snowed and the fog slowed our progress between serac barriers. We reached about 150m below the two western peaks without being able to distinguish which one was higher. We chose the west peak, covered in ice, which we reached just before noon.

Our ascent was 400m, with difficulty AD and we estimate that the peak we climbed was about 5,330m. This same summit was reached from the east and called Terijuay Grande (5380m) by the Italian expedition of 1963 [see *AAJ* 1964] thinking that it was the summit of the snow-capped mountains. However, from its other two peaks to the east, we could see the central rocky peak was higher. As we descended the clouds thickened and we arrived at our camp with only an hour of light. It snowed all night. It continued to snow in the morning, so before getting caught we started our difficult descent between precipices and clouds towards Quelcanca.'

Anyone planning plans to visit the Terijuay massif should know that it covers two cartographic sheets, the 26-r Quebrada Honda and the 27-r Urubamba, from the National Geographic Institute (IGN) of Peru, with scale 1:100,000 that limits the graphic representation of the terrain. In addition, as noted on other occasions, some heights on official Peruvian maps barely coincide with those of other cartographers and many place names bear little correlation to those in common usage or with those contributed by some expeditions, especially Spanish and Italian. The Terijuay massif (T'iriqway) has three prominent peaks, which could be named Terijuay Oeste, Terijuay Central and Terijuay Este or, as in similar cases, Terijuay I, II and III. The Italian expedition that reached these summits, in August of 1963, kept the name Nevado Terijuay that is marked as the main summit next to elevation 5,330m on sheet 27-r Urubamba, but the expedition leader calculated it was 50m higher. To the central summit, which lacked name or elevation on the map, the same expedition gave the name of the nearby town, Nevado Quelccanca (5330m), thus baptising with Italian names that were acceptable to the Peruvian geographic authorities the rest of the 'conquered' eastern peaks. (Sources: Nathan Heald, Servei General d'Informació de Muntanya (SGIM) de Sabadell; *AJ* 1969, pp262-70; *AAJ* 1964, pp217-8; 1971, pp408-9; F Ratto, 'La spedizione 'Città di Biella' 1963 alle Ande del Sud Perù', *Estratto dalla Rivista Mensile del Club Alpino Italiano*, No 9, September 1964. pp413-32.)

## CORDILLERA VILCABAMBA

### Humantay South?

At the end of October, Nathan Heald (USA-Peru), Jack Barker and Emil Tjonneland, both 18 years old and from Maryland, left Soraypampa to trek the Salcantay-Machu Picchu route, with their loads on a couple of horses, heading for Nevado Humantay South (5459m), a peak marked on the 27-q sheet Machupicchu of the Peruvian IGN. These three, now carrying loads, climbed steeper terrain to camp on a rock tower at about 4,900m below the south face. They left this camp at 2am on 31 October and climbed the south face, crossed the top of the south-east ridge, continued to the east side and reached the summit at 9.30am having followed a new route (AD, 500m). The altimeter on Tjonneland's watch measured 5,455m. They descended on the opposite side, the north-east, 'making the final rappel with one core-

Nevado Humantay in 2008. *(Consuelo Amorós)*

The line of Heald, Barker and Tjonneland on Humantay (Sur?). *(Sevi Bohórquez)*

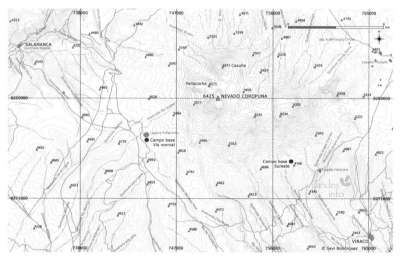

The IGN map of the Coropuna region. The normal route of ascent is from the south-west and base camp is marked.

shot rope just after dark.' Having camped in moraine they spent two says descending the Rayancancha gorge to the Ahobamba valley. The precise details of the summit the three reached aren't confirmed.

The peaks of the Humantay mountain – North-east (5217m), North (5473m) and South (5459m) – are on the ridge that extends from the western slope of Salcantay Nevado (6264m IGN and 6279m Heald) and branches to the north and northwest. Heald led a group that may have achieved, unless proven otherwise, the first ascent of the Humantay North in July 2014: see *AJ* 2016 pp309-10. (Sources: *AJ* 2015 p205; *AAJ* 2018; Nathan Heald.)

Entrance to the north-east glacier. *(Julieta Ferrari)*

Coropuna Casulla and Nevado Palla-cocha. *(Julieta Ferrari)*

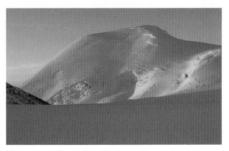

Coropuna Casulla. *(Julieta Ferrari)*

## CORDILLERA OCCIDENTAL

*Marcelo Scanu adds the following:* The **Nevado Coropuna** (6425m) is the highest volcano in Peru, located in Arequipa. For years it was regarded as the highest mountain in the American continent. Hiram Bingham explored it before the discovery of Machu Picchu and disproved that theory. It has three principal summits: the main summit (6425m), Coropuna Casulla (6377m) and Coropuna Este (6305m); and four secondary summits: Coropuna Este II (6234m), Pallacocha (6171m), Coropuna Central I (6150m) and Coropuna Central II (6161m). Argentine Julieta Ferreri and Brazilian Marcelo Motta Delvaux were active here during June and July climbing new routes. From 13 to 19 June the pair climbed Coropuna Oeste and Coropuna Norte. They started up the north-east glacier placing camp one at 5,057m, camp two at 5,357 masl, camp three at 5,823m and camp four

Nearing the top of the south face of Pallacocha. *(Julieta Ferrari)*

at 6,020m. This was new ground until 6,020m where they switched to established routes: Coropuna Oeste by its south face and Coropuna Norte by its south ridge and east ridge.

Between 2 and 8 July the same pair ascended Coropuna Este via its north-east glacier with camps at 4,875m, 4,951m, 5,055m and camp four at 5,537ma. On 6 July they finished this new approach reaching the summit by its north-west face. The standard route is from the south, from the village of Viraco. Coropuna has the largest tropical ice cap in the world.

MARCELO SCANU & ROLO GARIBOTTI

# Argentina & Patagonia 2017

Base camp for El Muerto at 5,455m. *(Lis Sablé)*

There has been a new right-wing government in Argentina since December 2015 that has liberalised the economy. Transportation has improved making it easier to reach the mountains as low-cost airlines start to operate. Depreciation of the peso has made the country more attractive to climbers from abroad with hard currency. The weather in the Argentine Andes has not been stable because of the El Niño-La Niña phenomenon. The north-west, a high desert plateau, had a terrible amount snow and rain. As I write this, in the first days of April, the weather is stable once again. Aconcagua remains the principal attraction and one of the few mountains in Argentina that requires a permit. Acclimatisation can be done in nearby mountains or in Vallecitos, with huts and mountains that reach almost 6,000m. The country is still on the ever-diminishing list of countries where real exploration is possible.

*Rolo Garibotti writes:* Patagonia is as popular as ever, but the season was also marked by very unstable weather. This prevented any ground-breaking ascents but a good time was had by most and there were virtually no accidents. It had been some years since the Patagonia season was so accident free. If bad weather is what it takes to accomplish that, then let's hope it continues. We can all agree there has been far too much death in our community of late. On a related topic, there are now to private helicopters stationed in El Calafate in the Chaltén massif. Although they won't be able to perform technically difficult rescues, using long lines for example, they can retrieve injured climbers from most valley bottoms or glaciers, saving precious time and effort.

There is no funding available to pay for rescue flights so climbers should make sure they have rescue insurance coverage in excess of $10,000. Consider joining the British section of the Austrian Alpine Club to take advantage of their comprehensive rescue and repatriation coverage. Note that rescue insurance is mandatory in the Torres del Paine national park. Although online fund-raising appeals are moving spectacles, not having adequate rescue insurance is irresponsible.

The other big news in the Chaltén massif was the change of ownership of the south side of the Río Eléctrico valley, around 8,000 acres, which gives access to the northern flank of the massif, via Piedra Negra, one of the most popular advanced camps. The land was purchased with funds provided by the Wyss Foundation, from Swiss-American philanthropist Hansjörg Wyss, with hopes to donate it to the national park. The NGO Banco de Bosques is in charge of the land for now and unfortunately has decided to keep charging the access fee the previous owners had in place. However, during the second half of the season, the concessionaire, a third party, decided to stop charging climbers.

To become part of the national park, the land first has to be transferred from provincial to federal control. The law proposal that was presented to the provincial legislature includes several other national park expansions, totalling over one million acres. Such a vast land transfer has resulted in strong opposition from farming and mining groups. The proposed law was brought up twice for a vote, and both times it was blocked and sent back to committee. An agreement seems improbable.

Another concern with the land purchased by the Wyss Foundation is that Banco de Bosques, with funding from American Richard Butler, has taken a rather unexpected turn in the Perito Moreno national park, neighbouring Cerro San Lorenzo. They have installed five new huts in what was an otherwise pristine area, which until now received only 800 to 1,200 visitors per year. The fear is that Banco de Bosques might intend to install similar levels of infrastructure along the Río Eléctrico valley. In Argentina there has been an 80-year debate regarding the management of wilderness areas, between the non-interventionist model copied from North America, and the much heavier handed vision of the outdoors that European immigrants brought. The installation of huts under the guise of 'conservation' sets a particularly bad precedent. There is also a proposal to place a hut below Cerro Colorado, aka Cerro Apidame, a beautifully pristine climbing destination outside of Chile Chico, in the Aysen region.

A view of the south glacier on Vola-ceán El Muerto. *(Lis Sablé)*

Negro Jerez belayed by Carlitos Torino on the fourth pitch of *Providencia*, graded 7a. *(Nachele Karle)*

## Jujuy Province

*Marcelo Scanu writes:* Chañi (5986m) is the highest peak in Jujuy and also sacred, first climbed by the Incas, who sacrificed a little boy at its summit. This boy was found in 1905 and his remains deposited in a museum in Buenos Aires. During two weeks in November of 2016, an Argentine-Chilean party was active in the area, Argentines Negro Jerez, Nachele Karlen and Carlitos Torino and Chileans Nicolás and Nicole Valderrama and Papeliyo. They walked the old Inca route to access the military hut and from the refugee continued 40 minutes farther to a series of walls called **Grupo Arista**, located north of the Chañi massif. The Chileans climbed in the Torrecillas sector and made an ascent of *Rocasfoncas* (6a, 60m) while the Argentine group made the first ascent of the **Aguja Janajman** (5151m) via *Wash'n'go* (6b, 250m). To the left of Aguja Janajman, the Chileans made the first ascent (6a+, 100m) of **Aguja Chilena** (5050m). The next day Argentines made the first ascent of **Aguja Iñaki Coussirat** opening *San Percutori* (6b+, 230m) with an off-width as the crux of the climb. They then had to wait out many stormy days so the group cleaned and improved the military shelter.

The ascent of **Pico Nordenskiold** was done, climbing three needle-like features to the summit. The first needle, **Aguja Julio Altamirano** (5150m) had a crux chimney and an overhang they rated 7a. After climbing five pitches, they reached a col and continued by climbing **Aguja Flor de Pupusa** (5270m), encountering nice plated rock with 6b cracks for three rope-lengths. From the top of Aguja Flor de Pupusa, they crossed the col to **Aguja Intihuasi** (5430m) and climbed three pitches up and into the clouds. From there, they took the easiest route in a storm, avoiding difficult zones and climbed with difficulties of 5+ and 6a. Towards the summit, the rock quality decreased and it began to snow, causing them to retreat 50m short of the top. The storm became violent so they quickly descended via a scree gully between Pico Nordenskiold and Morro Von Rosen. They freed nearly all the 1,000m of the route, which they called *Providencia* (7a, 11 pitches).

On the 10th day, in unstable weather, they left the shelter and after a two-hour trek, the Chileans reached the base of **Morro Von Rosen** (5450m) and the Argentines the base of the 1,000m wall of Pico Nordenskiold (5470m).

Carlitos Torino on pitch eight (6b, 50m) of the first ascent of *Providencia*, on Aguja Flor de Pupusa, the second of three needles on Pico Nordenskiold. *(Nachele Karlen)*

The Chilean party ascended a variant of *Qhapac Ñan* located south east of Von Rosen called *Variante Antofaya* (6b, 400m). On their 13th day, thanks to locals and their pack animals, the group were able to descend. The Chañi area still has a lot of potential for new routes on virgin walls of good granite.

**Catamarca Province**
**Incahuasi** (6638m)is a volcano on the border with Chile. It means 'Inca house' in Quechua and has the world's second-highest ruins near the summit, an open-air Inca temple. Incahuasi has many routes established but Argentine Diego Cavassa opened a new one in the first days of January 2018. He acclimatised with his fiancée Cari Weber, ascending **Cerro Pastos Largos** (4125m) on 31 December. They arrived at Incahuasi base camp at 4,400m on 1 January. Camp one was established at 4,911m and camp two at 5,350. The pair ascended a line left of the archaeological route. Diego summited alone, Weber reaching 6,350m.

**Volcán El Muerto** has its name because of an ancient legend that says its profile resembles a dead man. The official high of this Argentine-Chilean peak near Incahuasi is 6,488m but many climbers think it is a few metres above 6,500m. It has a nice big glacier with an 800m slope and there's a record of this route being climbed in March 2005, courtesy of Swede Janne Corax and Nadine Saulnier, a native of Québec, as stated by Andean authority Guillermo Almaraz. During 2012 there was another ascent, this one from Vasques Arkaitz Ibarra, living in Argentina, and Jabi Txikon, as part of an extensive 6,000m traverse. On 19 January it was climbed once more. An Argentine team comprising Griselda Moreno, Liz Sablé and Lauro Gutiérrez found a route through some crevasses and Lauro ascended the last part on rock. Moreno and Gutiérrez summited, Sablé was very short of doing so and stopped near a secondary summit.

During December an Argentine team consisting of Andrés Fabeiro, Luis

Pontoriero and Marcelo Scanu were active in the Chaschuil zone. They found an archaeological site, explored the region and found interesting wildlife including a venomous snake living at 3,350m. They camped at a spring known as Guanaco Yacu, from the Quechua meaning guanaco spring, on the slopes of **Cerro de los Caranchos** (4225), one of the highest unclimbed mountains in the are. On 9 December Fabeiro and Scanu reached the summit by its north-east ridge while some condors flew a few metres above their heads. In Witold Paryski's 1956 map the peak is known as Guanaco Yaco.

## La Rioja Province
During July 2016 an Argentine team comprising Lucas Alzamora, Roberto Rivas Jordan and Juan Guerra climbed a new route on the south-east face of **Negro Overo** (5780m), a mountain first ascended by the Incas. The snowy route has an average of 45° with a final section of 55°. During September 2017 Lucas teamed up with Argentine Diego Nakamura and climbed the highest virgin summit of the massif, which is unnamed and has a height of 5,849m. They summited in a second attempt via its east-south-east face. They also had a snowy slope that ranged between 45° and 55°. The only recorded previous attempt on the mountain was via its east ridge and ended 100m short of the top.

## Mendoza Province
Glauco Muratti has been exploring Mendoza for years. He joined another Argentine, Lisandro Arelovich, and headed to the remote Quebrada Chorrillos, a creek with many obstacles and great rock cliffs that have kept it in a virgin state. On 7 February 2018 they left Punta de Vacas (2400m) taking the Tupungato river and then the Chorrillos creek ascending the Paso de los Guanacos (4200m) with some difficult sections and the Paso Modesto (also 4200m), descending to the south branch of the Chorrillos creek, certainly unvisited. On the fifth day the pair summited a virgin 5,150m peak by its north ridge with tricky terrain, some delicate steps and rotten rock. They named it **Cerro 34 Leguas** because of the long journey to reach it. They took a different route back, from Paso Modesto traversing directly to Paso de los Guanacos, ascending **Cerro Horqueta** (4565m). On Muratti's previous ascent, the first in 2016, he had climbed from the west. Now they climbed the south face, up rotten rock of about III and descending to the Valle de las Huellitas (3600m). After a long journey the pair reached Quebrada Potrero Escondido, finishing in Punta de Vacas.

## Chaltén Massif
*Rolo Garibotti writes:* The following is a list of new routes climbed, listed in geographical order, from south to north along the west side, and back south along the east side. Two lines were climbed on the south-west and west faces of **Cerro Solo**: *French Connection* (WI4, M6, A0, 600m) by the British climber James Monypenny and American Austin Siadak, and *Los Gringos No Comen Llajua* (90°, 5.8, 600m) by Monypenny and Bolivia's Rodrigo Lobo

In its first third, and just four hours from the river mouth, the Quebrada Chorrillos valley presents this step of c300m that prevented exploration of the upper part of this valley. It was only climbed in 2013. *(Glauco Muratti)*

Villarroel. On **Cerro Adela Sur**, the Romanians Vlad Capusan and Török Zsolt climbed a variation in the middle section of the *East Ridge* route (Aikes, Monaco, Pellegrini, 1967), up a steep wall involving six pitches with difficulties to M5+ and WI4. On the north face of **Punta Filip**, Tad McCrea and Jonathan Griffin, both from the US, climbed *Espera que te Pegue* (5.10+, C1, 10 pitches), to join *Amigos Perdidos*, retreating without continuing to the summit. On the north-west face of **Cerro Pollone**, Matteo della Bordella and Luca Schiera from Italy climbed *Maracaibo* (5.11+, C1, 250m), descending east without continuing to the summit.

Earlier in the year, in early September, Austrian Markus Pucher did the first solo winter ascent of **Aguja Guillaumet** via the *Amy-Vidailhet* couloir. A short five-pitch pillar immediately left of that route was climbed by Aurélien Bessot of France and Brazilian Marcelo Machado: *Pilar del Quinto Sol* (5.10, C2, 190m). The *Comesaña-Fonrouge* also on Aguja Guillaumet got climbed in 11 hours car-to-car, and American Cristopher Alcocer and Canada's Sam Lambert climbed a five-pitch variation to the south summit: *Plata o Plomo* (5.11+). Unreported last season the Belgian climbers Seán Villanueva and Siebe Vanhee did the first free ascent of *Disfrute la Vida* (Pitelka-VonBirckhahn, 2009) on the west face of Aguja Guillaumet, now 5.11.

On the east face of **Aguja Mermoz**, the French team of Johanna Marcoz, Jeremy Stagnetto and Jerome Sullivan climbed a direct start to *Jardines*

After the step Cerro Tito Magnani (4905m) towers above, first climbed by Muratti and Arelovich in January 2016. The mountains here are the product of glacier erosion, the rocks being sedimentary. *(Glauco Muratti)*

*Japoneses* (Haley, Holsten, Schaefer, 2010), up a striking ice filled corner (AI5, 150m). On the east face of **Aguja Val Blois**, the German trio of Lutz Zybell, Felix Getzlaff and Tom Ehrig climbed *La Torcida* (7a M4, 450m) to the junction with the first ascent route from where they retreated in the face of strong winds. The route follows a left-leaning system of cracks 80m left of *Couloir Este*. Ehrig, who led all the pitches, desribed the route as a high-quality rock climb that offers a more amenable challenge while waiting for bigger adventures.

On **Cerro Chaltén** Americans Colin Haley and Austin Siadak repeated the classic French *North-west Ridge* route (aka *Afanassieff*) in 10h 37m, taking 23h 57m from Piedra Negra to Piedra Negra descending via the Francesa. On **Aguja Poincenot**, Seán Villanueva and Siebe Vanhee freed all the crux sections of the un-repeated *Whisky Time* (Eggler-Pitelka, 1994), originally A4, now 5.11+. The second crux was climbed via a variation, traversing left into the off-width crack right from the belay. Unfortunately around pitch 10 and with only three more 5.9/10a pitches left, high winds forced them to retreat. On **Aguja Rafael Juárez**, Argentines Matías Korten and Agustín Mailing climbed five new pitches to join the west ridge (*Los Millenials*, 5.10).

Very little got done in the Torres del Paine massif. **Aleta de Tiburón** was the most visited feature, with more than 30 parties attempting it this season, out of a total of 45 climbing permits issued for the entire range, and for good reason. The *French* route from 1981 on the south-west face offers 10 pitches at 5.8 on good quality rock and in one of the most stunning settings one can possibly phantom.

Climbing out of the Bader valley and on the east face of **Aguja Descon-ocida**, north summit of **La Máscara**, a feature originally called The Thumb,

The German team approaching the Fitzroy group and their advance base: a snow cave at Paso Superior. In the background from the left to right, Fitzroy and the Pilar Goretta, Aguja Val Blois, Aguja Mermoz and Aguja Guillaumet. *(Tom Ehrig)*

The crux pitch of the new German route *La Torcida* on Aguja Val Blois: hard from the start, with strenuous moves up the thin finger crack. At the back looms the Pilar Goretta of Fitzroy. *(Tom Ehrig)*

The Fitzroy skyline with Aguja Val Blois and the line of *La Torcida* marked. *(Tom Ehrig)*

Seán Villanueva and Siebe Vanhee climbed *El Matédor* (5.11c, 500m), a new line just to the left of *Chi Dorme non Piglia Pesci* (Amore-Angelini-Polacci-Vietina, 2002), with which it shares a couple of pitches in the upper section. A Catalan team made a valiant attempt to repeat the *South African* route (5.12d, 1200m) on the east face of Torre Central, but were forced to retreat one or two pitches shy of the summit ridge. Later in the season Villanueva and Vanhee attempted a one-push ascent of the same route but encountering very bad conditions retreated a couple of pitches above the Boeing ledge.

TOM HOYLE

# New Zealand 2017

On the Maximilian Ridge of Elie de Beaumont
during the first winter ascent. *(Ben Ellis)*

An exceptionally warm and dry spring in the Southern Alps made for a short season last year. The rapid removal of snow coverage during this warm spell made glacier travel increasingly arduous and good freezes scarce as early as October. As climate change seems here to stay, this is likely becoming the norm and serves to discourage all but the most committed – see the Maximilian Ridge climb below – from accessing the more demanding routes with longer approaches in the Aoraki Mt Cook region. It also means that ice and snow conditions on lower peaks are harder to come by outside of winter. These conditions, combined with an increasingly time-poor population, have pushed trends towards shorter and more accessible objectives, with ski touring and alpine rock climbing trending in popularity over more traditional mountaineering.

The glacial retreat has also lead to geological instability in a few key sites on moraine walls and terraces, further increasing the difficulty of access. Murchison hut, at the head of Murchison glacier, has been closed due to slope instability and the opening of a large fissure nearby. The traditional route over the Main Divide from Hooker glacier, via the cable route up to Copland Pass, is now unsafe, and the removal of Copland shelter is imminent.

Despite these challenges, the alpine community continues to seek adventure in these regions. New winter ice routes are added each season, helped by the focus of the Darrans Winter Climbing Meet based out of Homer hut, and the Remarkables Ice and Mixed Climbing Festival. The boom in ski touring has contributed to activity in searching for first ski descents of peaks and the completion of the 'Ski Rhapsody' addition to the classic Symphony on Skis traverse of the Southern Alps. This eastern link by Richard O'Neill-Dean and David Hamilton completes the traverse by skis from the headwaters of the Rangitata river in the east, all the way to the west coast through the heart of Aoraki Mount Cook national park.

The Maximilian Ridge of Elie de Beaumont (3109m) was first climbed in January 1951 by Ed Cotter, Ed Hillary, George Lowe and Earle Riddiford but had never been climbed in winter. In August, three Cantabrians, Jack Grinstead, Josh Mitchell and Ben Ellis headed to the Whataroa valley for a second try at the Maximilian. Their first, a summer effort the previous Christmas, was thwarted by cloud. The climbers concluded they would have better luck during the winter season. Over six days, the trio made the long approach via the remote Whataroa valley, on the west coast of South Island, then completed the climb and descended the Tasman glacier, on the opposite side of the range, to Mt Cook Village. Ellis offered a grade of 4+ on the Mount Cook scale, with a crux of about seven pitches leading to the summit ice, with powder snow on the south side of the ridge and mixed climbing on the north. On the third day, a huge cornice collapse persuaded the trio to take a diversion: descent to the Burton glacier and then re-joining the ridge via the first ascent route to the north of Roderick Peak.

On 27 October Ben Briggs and Tom Grant (UK), and the Italian Enrico Mosetti made the first ski descent of the Caroline Face of Aoraki Mount Cook (3724m). The Caroline is the most dangerous and difficult face on Aoraki and consequently the last to have been ascended, on 6 and 7 November 1970 by John Glasgow and Peter Gough. Almost 2km in height, the face had featured in Devon O'Neil's notorious list of un-skied challenges and had already cost the lives of Magnus Kastengren and Andreas Fransson, like the successful party based in Chamonix. Tom Grant had skied big faces in New Zealand on a previous trip in 2015 but fickle conditions kept him off Mount Cook. This time they found the line had changed, and for the better, and immediately flew to the Plateau hut to take advantage of the first available weather window, despite not having skied since the previous May. An inspection from the air convinced them that their proposed line was feasible. The team found deep snow on the east face and the east ridge, reaching the summit at 9am. They made two abseils on abalakovs to reach the face and found cold powder: ideal conditions. Grant reported that while they had skied steeper faces in the Alps, the critical aspect was staying on route. Mosetti said: 'The biggest thing I've ever skied, the biggest line I could imagine to ski, and in great powder conditions!' The three still had time to ski the central *Zig-Zag Route* on Malte Brun while working up a number of future projects.

The route of the ski descent of Mount Cook's Caroline face. *(Tom Grant)*

# Mount Everest Foundation Expedition Reports

## SUMMARISED BY GLYN HUGHES

The Mount Everest Foundation (*www.mef.org.uk*) was established as a registered charity following the successful ascent of Everest in 1953. It was initially financed using the surplus funds and subsequent royalties from that expedition. It provides financial support for expeditions of an exploratory nature in mountain areas, and is administered by trustees appointed by the Alpine Club and the Royal Geographical Society.

The exploration is usually mainly of a geographical nature, but may also cover disciplines such as geology, botany, zoology, glaciology and medical research. In return for the funding the MEF requires only a comprehensive report, and copies of these reports are lodged with the AC and the RGS. The reports can be consulted at these establishments, or alternatively on line.

The MEF has made total grants of well over £1m to more than 1,600 expeditions with members from the UK and New Zealand, and donations to allow us to continue with this work are always welcome. We particularly encourage donations from former beneficiaries of MEF grants.

In 2017 we supported 25 expeditions with grants totalling over £97,000, and the following notes summarise the reports from these expeditions.

### ANTARCTICA

**Spectre Trans-Antarctic Expedition** – Leo Houlding, Jean Burgun and Mark Sedon (November 2017/January 2018).
The primary objective of this ambitious expedition was to carry out technical Alpine-style first ascents in the Organ Pipe Peaks in the Queen Maud Mountains of Antarctica, the most southerly rock spires on the planet. On the outward journey a flight from Union glacier camp to the optimum start location was followed by travel with power-kite to the mountains. The intended target of the S spur of Spectre (2020m) was deemed to unsafe in the conditions encountered, but a new route was completed on the N face and NW ridge of Spectre, involving about 750m of climbing. They also made a route on the N face of the unnamed first spire of the Organ Pipe Peaks which they named Alpha Tower. The return journey to Union glacier was completed by power-kite. The total distance travelled under kite power was 1,650km, with only 60km of man-hauling.           MEF ref 17-01

## ARCTIC

**British Stauning Alps Expedition** – Molly Thompson, Jesse Dufton, Alistair Everett, Oliver Mentz and Jennifer Roberts (April-May 2017).
This expedition had both mountaineering and scientific objectives. They flew in to Constable Point in East Greenland, and from there travelled by skidoo to the base of the Roslin glacier. They skied up the Roslin taking scientific measurements on the way, then down the Bjornbo glacier attempting climbs on the way, and finally back to Constable Point by skidoo. The scientific work involved the installation of ablation stakes at locations in the Roslin glacier to repeat measurements collected in the 1970s, and to provide new data on melt rate as a function of elevation. In addition snow temperature and density measurements were taken at the stake sites. The climbing included first ascents made by the full party of two peaks: Pt2237m (PD) and Pt2191m (AD), but an attempt on a third peak of 1,777m was abandoned because of high avalanche danger.        MEF ref 17-03

**Svartisen** – Paul Weber and Lauren Knight (July/August 2017).
A scientific expedition with an exploratory element, to find the best route through the Vesterdalen valley in Arctic Norway, which separates the western and eastern Svartisen icefields, and collect scientific data relating to the behaviour of the two icefields since the Little Ice Age. Full details of the research will be included in the final report.        MEF ref 17-36

## NORTH AMERICA

**Kichatna Spires, Alaska** – Twid Turner and Miles Bright (April-May 2017).
Twid's original partner for this trip was Paul Ramsden but at the last minute Paul found he was unable to get a visa because of business trips made to Libya. Miles Bright was a short notice substitute. They were flown in to the Tatina glacier for the Kichatna Spires. These are in the extreme west end of the Alaska Range, renowned for bad weather, and they lived up to their reputation. The team were unable to move from their camp for five days. When conditions improved they found that this had been dry season, with very little ice formation on faces or in gullies. They climbed to the col between the Tatina and Monolith glaciers in avalanche conditions and saw there had been no ice formation on Triple Peak, one of the possible objectives. The weather turned bad again, giving appalling snow conditions. They did manage some rock climbing in Anchorage while waiting for their flight home.        MEF ref 17-31

## SOUTH AMERICA

**South Face of the South Tower of Paine** – Calum Muskett, Tony Stone and Tom Livingstone (December 2016-January 2017).
The primary objective was the first ascent of a new route on the S face of the

South Tower of Paine. They reached the base of the face, but did not climb a single pitch due to bad weather, heavy and frequent snowfall and strong winds. The S face is very impressive but weather windows seem to be short and infrequent. They moved to El Chaltén and experienced bad weather until the end of Calum's trip. The others stayed on at Chaltén for another three and a half weeks, and managed to climb *Supercanaleta* on Fitzroy just before their return flight. They walked into the mountains six times for attempts on routes, and succeeded on one major alpine route during seven weeks in Patagonia.                                    MEF ref 17-05

**Graham Hawthorn Patagonia Expedition** – Peter Graham and Uisdean Hawthorn (January/February 2017).
Objectives were various first ascents on peaks in the Fitzroy massif, Patagonia. The team was based in Chaltén for two months but due to the particularly bad weather they were not able to attempt any of their major objectives. One day after their arrival in Chaltén the weather looked good for 24 hours, so they climbed Aguja Guillaumet via the N ridge, *Brenner-Moschioni* route in 18 hours road to road. After a fruitless trip to the Torre glacier, they took advantage of another short lull to climb *Chiara de Luna*, a rock route on Aguja St Exupery. During their descent the wind again rose and it snowed. Another attempt on Cerro Torre, this time on the *Ragni* route, resulted in another retreat.                                           MEF ref 19-09

**APEX 5** – Christopher Graham, Ellie Lee, Becky Dru and 27 student volunteers from the University of Edinburgh (June 2017).
This was the latest in a series of scientific expeditions carrying out research into aspects of the human response to hypoxia. Blood samples were taken from a large team of student volunteers before and after exposure to altitude at Huayana Potosi, in the Cordillera Real, Bolivia. Of specific interest were changes to gene expression in human leukocytes following prolonged exposure to low oxygen levels.                                    MEF ref 17-20

**Huagurunchu South Face** – James Monypenny and Harry McGhie (August /September 2017).
The intended aim of the expedition was to climb the central spur of the SW face of Huaguruncho in Peru, a mountain first climbed by a team including George Band and Mike Westmacott in 1956. After acclimatising on the original route on Esfinge (5320m) in the Cordillera Blanca they headed for Huaguruncho but Monypenny was taken ill with a chest infection and they descended to sea level for medical treatment. There was then a poor forecast with no weather window for the next month, so they decided to head south to Cuzco and Bolivia seeking drier conditions with the intention of returning to Huaguruncho if the weather improved, although it never did. After an unsuccessful attempt on the S face of Humantay, they made a new route on Pk 24, and a route on Pk Maria, on the east side of Illampu in the Cordillera Real. Monypenny then soloed the *French* route on Huayana

Potosi (6200m) as well as a new route on the S face of Illimani (6400m). He then made the first ascent of the SW ridge of Piruhata (5700m).

MEF ref 17-37

## PAKISTAN

**Boesam Pir Expedition** – Tim Seers, Will Smith and James Lawson (June/July 2017).
The original objective was Yashkuk Sar II in the Chapursan valley, but the permit for this was not issued in time. An alternative in the Virjerab glacier was chosen but on arrival in Shimshal they discovered that access was impossible because of movement of the Khurdopin glacier. They discussed options with local guides, who suggested that they head north to Boesam Pir, and a high concentration of unclimbed peaks. They attempted a total of seven routes, and believe they made five first ascents, with heights in the range 5,500m-6,000m and grades PD to AD. The weather was good for all ascents but snow conditions less favourable.

MEF ref 17-11

**Kondus Valley Expedition** – Graham Zimmerman, Chris Wright and Steve Swenson (July/August 2017).
The original objective was to be Link Sar but they were advised it was unlikely a permit would be granted. They subsequently changed their target to Muchu Chhish in the Bartura Group of the Pakistan Karakoram, believed to be the second highest unclimbed peak in the world. Unfortunately the permit for this was not issued in time but unexpectedly the permit for Link Sar was issued. The approach was made by air from Islamabad to Skardu, and then by jeep to base camp. They combined acclimatisation with investigation of the proposed route, making forays up to 5,300m. Two attempts on the face of Link Sar, to 6,000m and 5,500m, were terminated by bad weather, which unfortunately continued, meaning no further attempt could be made.

MEF ref 17-13

**Gasherbrum IV** – Bruce Normand, Billy Pierson and Marcos Costa (May-July 2017).
An attempt of a new route on the E face of Gasherbrum IV (7925m). From base camp twelve days were spent setting up a series of three camps on the route. The climb from camp two to camp three involved snow to 50°. From camp three repeated climbs were made to 7,300m. The line thereafter was of snowfields interspersed with previously invisible compact white marble slabs, which were completely unprotectable. In the absence of worthwhile belays the route was considered too dangerous to attempt and three days were spent in the descent cleaning the route. It was considered that in a year with more snow it might be possible to climb over some of the marble bands but on unprotectable snow. A bid on the Bonatti route was cancelled due to bad weather and although 'Gasherbrum 4.5' was climbed to 6,700m, further progress was prevented by dangerous snow conditions.

MEF ref 17-15

**British Shimshal** – George Cave, Ross Davidson, Clay Conlon, Steve Carratt and Karim Hayat (August/September 2017).
The main objective was the first ascent of a 6,150m peak in the Gunj-e Dur glacier system, with other secondary objectives nearby. After a three-day walk in from Shimshal they established a base camp in the valley, and then an ABC from which the attempts were made. Cave and Davidson set off for an attempt on Pk 6150 accompanied by their local guide, Karim Hayet. Unfortunately Cave suffered altitude sickness and retreated. Davidson and Hayat continued up the SE face to the summit ridge. The highest point of the ridge was deemed unclimbable in the snow conditions so they climbed a nearby peak of 6,015m at Scottish II/III, and with a 900m gain in altitude, and named this Yad Sar. Meanwhile Carratt and Conlon climbed an unnamed peak of 5,855m, also in a single day from ABC. Both are believed to be first ascents.                                    MEF ref 17-24

**Hispar Expedition** – Peter Thompson and Aiden Laffey (June/July 2017).
The attempted first ascent of Machu, (6630m) in the Hunza valley of the Pakistan Karakoram, by either the SW or W ridges from the Machu valley, or by the SE ridge from the Chaghuta valley. From a viewpoint above Hispar village the Chaghuta approach looked difficult, so they set up a base camp at 4,442m in the Machu valley near some huts and one day from Hispar. They established ABC at 4,760m, and from there climbed a 700m couloir to get onto the SW ridge at 5,530m. Unfortunately heavy snowfall forced a retreat from here. They returned and climbed to 5,550m in very poor snow conditions, but found their route blocked. They then looked at snow couloirs further up the Machu glacier, which appeared to lead close to the col, and W ridge leading to the summit, but snow conditions were too difficult, so the attempt was abandoned.                          MEF ref 17-42

### INDIA

**Glacier Melt and the Ganges River** – Alexandra Winter-Billington, Michele Koppes, Surendra Badwal, Gajendra Badwal, Ramanchandra Shankar and Argha Banerjee (May/June 2017).
The objective was to carry out scientific research on the Satopanth Bamak glacier. Experiments included ground penetrating radar survey of the rock debris that blankets the glacier, measurement of the change in surface elevation since the last visit to determine melt rate, collection of data from instruments installed during a previous expedition, movement of temperature sensors from one location to another to increase the spatial resolution of the dataset, and moving four of their twelve rain gauges from the Himalayan foothills onto the glacier to measure on-glacier precipitation. The most time consuming activity was using GPR to measure the thickness of debris, which involved moving the equipment by hand along a total of twelve transects at two metre intervals across the glacier.    MEF ref 17-06

**Sumur Valley Expedition** – Derek Buckle, Drew Cook, Jamie Goodhart, Rafal Malczyk and Howard Pollitt (August/October 2017).
The plan was to ascend the Sumur valley in Ladakh with the objective of exploring the complex glacier system at its head, and to climb one or more virgin peaks, before crossing to the Upper Rassa glacier where only one peak had been climbed previously. From a base camp at 5160m by the Sumur Lakes they explored the extensive Sumur glacier system, and first ascents were made of Pt 6068 (Deception Point), Pk 6078 (Tsagtuk Kangri aka Twin Peak), and Pk 5991 (Sumur Kangri). The peaks were graded F, PD and AD respectively. All peaks were climbed in excellent clear weather, but options were limited by unstable snow lying on northerly faces. There was evidence of recent avalanches, and this prevented them from venturing onto the Rassa glacier.                                            MEF ref 17-14

**British Arjuna Expedition** – Ben Silvestre, Pete Graham and Uisdean Hawthorn (September/October 2017).
The objective was Arjuna South (6100m) via the arête of its W pillar. From the road head at Gulabgarh they walked in via Kijai Nala to base camp. They acclimatised on an unnamed peak directly above the base camp, reaching 5,200m. They established a gear cache at the base of Arjuna South, from which they made the ascent. The first day involved loose rock, snow ramps, and then good steep rock to a large bivy site. The second day was continuous steep rock climbing following the arête to an exposed cold bivouac. The following day they reached the top of the pillar and continued to a final bivouac at 6,000m, and the next morning reached the summit. The descent, largely by abseil, occupied the rest of the day, and the following morning. They described the route as continuously steep and sustained at E1/E2, and occasionally E3.          MEF ref 17-16

## NEPAL

**British Gokyo Expedition** – Simon Yates and Paul Schweizer (October /November 2016).
An attempt on the N face of the unclimbed Kangchung (6103m) in Gokyo, Solu Khumbu. They set up their base camp in an ablation valley at Gyubanare, and from here they scoped the approach and route, deciding on the NW ridge as the best option. They bivouacked on the Gyubanare glacier and on the first day followed a gully line to a bivouac on the Kang La at 5,700m. There was no sign of any bivouac sites on the ridge above so they decided on a single-day push to the summit without bivouac gear. Still 200m below the summit they had to turn back after running out of time and having no bivouac gear. They experienced good clear postmonsoon weather.                                               MEF ref 17-02

**British Gorakh Himal Expedition** – Julian Freeman-Attwood, Jim Fother-ingham, Nick Colton, and Luke Hughes (April/May 2017).
An expedition to visit a remote part of the Gorakh Himal on the border between Nepal and Tibet, and to make the first ascent of an unclimbed 6,000m peak in the Gorakh or Kangla Himal. After an approach of 12 days on foot they reached Kang La on the border. From here they made three attempts on Kangla Kang (6150m), a peak to the immediate east of Kang La. In the worst pre-monsoon weather in Nepal for several years they experienced snow, thunder and lightning during part of each of the 14 days spent above base camp. There was also consistently poor visibility and severe wind-slab avalanche danger. In spite of this they managed to reach a high point of 5650m. This was the first expedition to this part of the Gorakh Himal.                                           MEF ref 17-04

**Far West Nepal Expedition** – Rebecca Coles and Simon Verspeak (October /November 2017).
The primary objective was an ascent of an unclimbed 6,246m peak in the Humla region of the far west of Nepal. Base camp was reached in a four-day trek from Simikot. Reconnaissance to the edge of the glacier from the north reached two tent platforms, and rubbish including polypropylene rope, presumably for fixed lines. They established a high camp to attempt the N ridge, but discovered steep loose rock. They then made another attempt, this time on the E ridge, which they climbed in a three-day round-trip. The route was estimated as 1,300m in length, and graded AD+. They found a section of fixed rope low down on the glacier but none higher up, which led them to believe that this was a first ascent. They subsequently found that the local name for the peak was Lasarmu La.            MEF ref 17-08

**Khumbu Valley Meteorology** – Emily Potter (April/May 2017).
Emily Potter's aim was to carry out high-altitude meteorological analysis in Khumbu valley and on the Khumbu glacier. She worked alone on this project, although other researchers were carrying out separate studies in the same region. She set up a series of nine temperature sensors in the Khumbu Valley to measure air temperature lapse rates, and a further ten temperature sensors on the Khumbu glacier over an the altitude range 4,920m-5,260m to compare temperature variation with levels in the valley. She also set up a fully automatic weather station and anemometers on the glacier. Measure-ments were carried out over a period of eighteen days, and some monitors were left over the monsoon season to be recovered in October. Two weeks were spent carrying out measurements. Details of results will be given in a fuller report at a later date.                              MEF ref 17-27

**Annapurna South Glacier** – Rachel Carr, Arminel Lovell, James Linighan, and Jack Oxtoby (October/November 2017).
A scientific expedition with objectives to quantify changes in the ice surface elevation, thickness, and velocity, and assess their relationship with debris

characteristics; to evaluate how ice surface debris thickness and characteristics vary over space and time, and their influence on glacier melt rates;
to investigate the impact of supraglacial melt ponds on ice loss, and their
linkages to the hydrology of the glacier; analyse ice cliff formation processes
and their impact on glacier melt rates. Techniques employed included use
of an Unmanned Aerial Vehicle (UAV) with ground penetrating radar,
which yielded several kilometres of radar data, as well as melt stakes and
temperature sensors. Analysis of data will be covered in the final report.

MEF ref 17-33

**Ardang** – Emily Ward and Mark Bielby (October/December 2017).
The original target was Ardang (6034m) in the Humla region of West
Nepal. Unfortunately they were told they could only get a permit for this
peak if they agreed to take a guide, and so they chose to explore the nearby
and lower Phupharka Himal. They attempted an unnamed 5600m peak,
which appeared to be the highest peak in this range, but turned back at
about 5300m in bitterly cold conditions. At their second attempt Bielby
summited, Ward retiring about 100m below the summit suffering from altitude. The climb involved a height gain of 700m, with 400m of climbing and
scrambling up a rocky ridge, and the most difficult section being Scottish
Winter II. They then moved up the Talum Khola and climbed an unnamed
peak of 5,401m via a snow gully up to 50° incline ending with a short scramble to the summit. Two further peaks were attempted but they were turned
back by weather or rock conditions. On the walk out they climbed a peak of
4,900m which included a frozen waterfall section with four 50m pitches
of WI4, and easy angled ice for a few hundred metres above and below.

MEF ref 17-38

## CENTRAL ASIA

**Djengi-Djer Expediiton** – Sally Hudson, Will Rowland, Connor Holdsworth, Mark Chambers, James Cooper and Simon Tietjen (September
2017).
The objective was first ascents of unclimbed peaks over 4,000m in the
Djengi-Djer mountains of Kyrgyzstan. The only previous expedition to the
range in 2016 approached the range from the east, and travelled along its full
length. Time spent travelling limited that available for climbing. This team
approached from the west via Naryn, selected one valley in which to set up
a base camp, and thoroughly explore the area over a two and a half week
period. This plan worked well, and they completed ten first ascents in the
range 4,000m to 4,700m.                                    MEF ref 17-18

**Breaking in Borkoldoy** – Neil Cox, Stuart Gillian, Tom Harding, Scott
Martin, Matthew Lewis, Hannah Meinertzhagen and David Lyons Ewing
(August 2017).
The principal objectives were attempts on two unclimbed peaks of about

5000m, and various smaller peaks in the range of 4,000-4,700m, in the Borkoldoy range of southeast Kyrgyzstan. The team gained access to the eastern part of the range after negotiation with local hunters, who had obstructed previous parties. None of the team had previous experience of major mountaineering expeditions. However, from a base camp by Kainar Lake they climbed 14 unrecorded peaks in the height range 4,400 to 5,000m, and with alpine grades of F to D-. They also documented local distribution of key species of flora and fauna.                MEF ref 17-23

## EAST ASIA

**Mulu Caves, Malaysia** – Andy Eavis and a team of 28 cavers (March/April 2017).
This was the 24 Anglo-Sarawak Expedition to Gunung Mulu national park. Objectives included further exploration and surveying of cave systems discovered in previous expeditions, search for connections between known systems, and scientific study of paleomagnetic sediments. A total of 21km of new cave passage was surveyed using modern digital techniques, plus resurvey of known cave systems. They came away with new leads and questions to be answered, and without any reportable incidents or accidents.
                MEF ref 17-28

# Reviews

2nd Lt N S Done (1881-1917), Royal Fusiliers,
killed at the Somme, one of 70,000 men with no known burial place
whose names are recorded at the Thiepval Memorial.

# Reviews

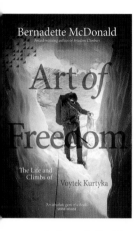

**Art of Freedom**
The Life and Climbs of Voytek Kurtyka
Bernadette McDonald
*Vertebrate Publishing, 2017, pp247, £14.95*

The Polish mountaineer Voytek Kurtyka never breached the wall of wide public acclaim that many mountaineers have enjoyed, even though few, if any, have equalled his phenomenal record. He resisted celebrity and his letters to the committee seeking to award him the Piolet d'Or, recognition for his life's work of bold and innovative climbs, became increasingly but politely terse. He argued that media pressure to create a number one star meant the degradation of climbing. Would they publicly award a hermit for years of spiritual practice? According to his declared view of the world, climbing is art, advertising poison and self-advertising the oldest disease of the human soul.

So spoke the man who treated the stupendous west face of Gasherbrum IV to its first ascent in exemplary style, made a complete and sensational traverse of Broad Peak as well as so-called 'night naked' speed climbs up Cho Oyu and Shishapangma, each of them staggering achievements. Kurtyka's life and philosophy are now brilliantly and sensitively described in *Art of Freedom*, a biography by Bernadette McDonald tracing Kurtyka's development from a young, slightly built but ferociously strong rock addict known as 'the animal', to an Alpine and Himalayan climber of the highest distinction.

Born in 1947, the first son of a well-known author, he studied electronics at university but quickly forgot most of what he had learned as he concentrated on climbing. Poland had survived the Nazi regime and endured the onslaught of communism; mountains were an escape. Kurtyka was among the first climbers to develop fast ascents. It was essential to climb quickly because their 'gulag' quality clothing and poor equipment allowed no time to linger. Only speed ensured survival. Even so Polish climbers earned a formidable international reputation when Kurtyka and four others spent 13 days on the first winter ascent of Europe's tallest cliff, the 1,100m Trollveggen Wall in Norway, made even more daunting by rock so overhanging the climbers spent long periods in mid air jumaring or rappelling in the dark on poor-quality Polish ropes put under heavy stress.

Kurtyka and his regular partners reached the highest levels of mountaineering long before the Polish mountaineering establishment grudgingly acknowledged their success and officially accredited them as mountaineers.

'What fun!' was Kurtyka's reaction to their reluctance. He was born to question and to rebel against life in a totalitarian regime that expected him to report his fellow mountaineers should they criticise the system. Experience taught him how to bend and manipulate rules. Rules, regulation and the approved way of doing things were anathema to him, as was his father's strong Christian belief. Freedom, he demonstrated, was indeed an art although he was benevolent towards those who felt it necessary to use aids such as bottled oxygen at altitude. 'Thou shalt not blame thy neighbour for using spectacles, condoms or oxygen,' he declared.

Bernadette McDonald's examination of Kurtyka's attitudes and relationships with his fellow mountaineers and her descriptions of the bold lines they forced up the highest summits are thorough and totally absorbing. Between 1970 and 2003 Kurtyka organised or took part in a total of 49 expeditions, mostly with Polish climbers. Although he realised that his ethos of lightweight style on difficult new routes meant failure was always a distinct possibility, he much preferred this approach as an alternative to siege tactics carrying heavy loads and fixing ropes up the mountain. Regardless of success or failure he declared that returning from each climbing adventure brought a new perspective on everyday life.

'The mountain worked like some giant broom that swept away all the junk, all the trivialities, all the burdens I took with me from my neurotic everyday life. I came back from the mountains an immaculate and clean person.' It was an almost mystical or spiritual experience for Kurtyka; it was his record of illegal ascents, his self-styled 'collection', which gave him greatest pleasure. 'Being illegal is part of a creative life. Restrictions are mostly applied by the brutes of this world and they turn our lives into slavery.'

In 1977, in the grip of cold war tensions, an international climbing exchange between Britain and Poland introduced Alex MacIntyre and John Porter to the east European climbing scene. Kurtyka helped them keep a low profile by introducing them as Porterwich and MacIntyreski. With Kurtyka they climbed a new route alpine style on the north-east face of Koh-i Bandaka (6812m), after cunningly substituting the name on the original permission for a more demanding option. The following year they forged another new route, again alpine style, on Changabang (6864m) in the Garhwal.

Kurtyka was still climbing hard well into his sixties, soloing some of the hardest rock routes Poland could offer. He can look back on an impeccable safety record. Apart from a few bruised knuckles and skinned fingers he emerged without injury. Despite a penchant for extremely difficult and dangerous climbs, he avoided accidents or tragedy; not only for himself but also for his partners. In his seventies he at last relented by acknowledging official recognition of an exceptional climbing career. In 2016 he agreed to accept the Piolet d'Or marking his lifetime of mountaineering achievement – but only on condition that all his close mountaineering friends joined him on the platform, which they did.

*Ronald Faux*

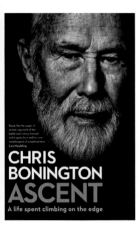

**Ascent**
A Life Spent Climbing on the Edge
Chris Bonington
*Simon & Schuster, 2017, pp432, £20/£9.99*

The front cover of the hardback edition of Chris Bonington's autobiography, *Ascent*, features a striking black and white headshot of the author. Commissioned by Simon & Schuster and taken by photographer Robert Wilson, it certainly belies Chris' 84 years. But what else might be hiding behind this enigmatic mask? Eyes slightly narrowed and close set, a family trait, lips lightly together, skin finely weathered, beard neatly trimmed and rendered a distinguished silvery grey rather white against the dark backdrop; I found myself looking back at this portrait after almost every absorbing chapter – and wondering.

Death haunts climb after climb during Chris' storm years: John Harlin, Eiger Direct, Ian Clough, Annapurna south face, Tony Tighe, Everest southwest face 1972, Mick Burke, ditto 1975, Nick Estcourt, K2, Pete Boardman and Joe Tasker, Everest north-east ridge. All of course were enthusiastic participants in a high-stakes game. Nonetheless one finds oneself looking hard at the photo; does it betray guilt or regret, or perhaps just stoic acceptance?

We know from Chris' own words here of the strain his frequent and lengthy absences imposed on Wendy, whose loving forbearance verges on saintly. It was she who consoled the widows of her husband's adventures and was so often the single parent to two boys who resented their dad's disappearances, suffered at school from famous father syndrome and became wayward.

*Ascent* is, to an extent, confessional. But for all the admissions of obsession and selfishness, there is no suggestion from Chris that with hindsight he would have done anything differently, stayed at home more or lowered the risk threshold on expeditions. As for how he has survived when so many climbing friends have died: 'the answer must be plain luck.' For those of us – and surely we are the majority – already familiar with the Bonington oeuvre, the fascination of an autobiography is any insight it gives into the personality behind those blockbuster expedition narratives. It does not disappoint.

To say Chris was brought up in Hampstead, went to public school and later to the Royal Military Academy, Sandhurst, smacks of privilege, and in it you imagine the makings of a bold adventurer, a leader of expeditions with columns of porters and pack animals. Yet this is a caricature. *Ascent* reveals a timid child, frightened of bullies and cricket balls, brought up in a dysfunctional, sometimes cash-strapped family, an absent father overly fond of booze (a sometime journalist, I note), Mum sectioned and hospitalised for 18 months. Chris cried on failing his English A-level, and cried again on failing as a pilot at RAF College, Cranwell.

Transferring to the army, Chris loved Sandhurst and 'unconsciously' tried to fit in with fellow cadets from top public schools, his own school having been comparatively minor, by adding a posh veneer to his north London accent. But he remained socially awkward; serving in the Royal Tank Regiment in Germany he was 'too conscious of the pips on [his] shoulders', too proud to take his veteran sergeant's advice, yet also too shy to emulate his fellow subalterns in pursuing German girlfriends.

So thank goodness for climbing. Chris's bubbling enthusiasm for rock seems to have remained undimmed from his love-at-first-sight taste of it as a teenager on the sandstone of Harrison's Rocks near Tunbridge Wells. 'I had discovered the passion that was to guide my life,' he writes. More than sixty years later he was still 'getting out,' marking his entry to a ninth decade with one more ascent of the Old Man of Hoy, this time with a touch of tight rope from Leo Houlding.

Leo had suggested the climb shortly after the death of Wendy Bonington in July 2014. Chris had nursed her through two years of cruel decline with motor neurone disease. His grief was intense but climbing offered the possibility of relief, just as it had done in 1966 when Tom Patey invited him to make the first ascent of the Old Man following tragic death by drowning of Chris' first son, Conrad, aged three. 'I think [Tom's] aim had been similar to Leo's, to help me through my bewildering sense of loss.'

*Ascent* is dedicated to three women: Chris' mother Helen – only recently, he confesses, has he come to appreciate how great was her love for him – Wendy, the epitome of 'selfless love', and his second wife, Loreto Herman, widow of his old friend Ian McNaught-Davis. Frequently the book reads like a tribute to Wendy, an expiation of the guilt he must have felt at so many goodbyes.

After the epic crawl down the Ogre in 1977, Chris with three broken ribs, pneumonia and a broken wrist, Doug Scott with both legs broken, he arrives home to Badger Hill in Cumbria 10 kilos lighter and barely able to walk more than a few hundred metres without a rest. He goes on: 'For a while just being reunited with Wendy and the boys was enough but time was passing and I had an expedition to plan.' And so to K2. Such single-mindedness. The drive of the man is formidable.

Chris's last 'real' expedition was to Arganglas in 2001, but hot-rock trips continued well into his late seventies, notably annual sojourns with old friends new routing in the Anti-Atlas of Morocco. By then, of course, he was a knight of the realm, the public face of British mountaineering and also of a clutch of charities whose aims he believed in. He was president of Lepra, combating leprosy, for almost 30 years, a very active president of the Council for National Parks, and until recently chancellor of Lancaster University. Even now, as he jets around the world, any kind of carpet slipper retirement remains unlikely.

With more than 80 years of an incredibly active and varied life to pack into four hundred pages, *Ascent* of necessity has pace. Chris describes the effort of writing the book as 'a challenging exercise of introspection', which,

It's a dog's life. Chris Bonington and friend, featured in *The Climbers*, a collection of climbers' portraits from Jim Herrington, who brings a rock'n'roll eye to the world of rock and ice. *(Jim Herrington / Mountaineers Books)*

by his own earlier admission, is a condition that does not ordinarily detain him for long. The past has never much concerned him, he says. He has never kept scrapbooks of his career. 'Curiosity and enthusiasm are what drive me: the joy and pleasure of new paths.'

One of those new paths has been falling headlong in love with Loreto and getting married again. Thanks are due to her for helping ensure *Ascent* reached its publisher, supporting Chris through days of 'literary struggle' and applying the occasional kick up the backside whenever her mountain man had a tantrum with writer's block. Loreto's foot has hit its target to splendid effect. That cover photo, however, remains inscrutable.

*Stephen Goodwin*

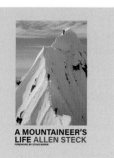

### A Mountaineer's Life
Allen Steck
*Patagonia, 2017, pp256, £21.99*

The old Silver Fox is a good sport, despite his naming me Fat Badger. On the day after the International Festival of Mountaineering Literature we would always take visitors out onto the gritstone, whatever the weather. When Steck questioned whether we always went out when there was actually snow on

Allen Steck, front left, in Pakistan. In 1976, Steck led a first ascent of Payu Peak above the Baltoro glacier but decided he wouldn't go to the summit as a gift to his Pakistani team. *(Mountaineers Books)*

the ground, Curran replied that it was a necessary Sheffield religious observance to climb every Sunday. We delighted in getting photos of this Californian climber brushing snow off the holds at Froggatt Edge. However, I also remember Jerry Lovatt bringing Steck to Stanage to fulfil his ambition to climb *Right Unconquerable* following a London AC lecture. The local welcoming party was gathered in the rain under the trees in the Plantation. We observed an umbrella slowly approaching uphill through the wet bracken. Upon close inspection we noticed that Steck had on his formerly polished, now quite sodden, city shoes. He'd no intention of being sandbagged this time. So he could only be impressed when Dick Turnbull, being characteristically so fired up to lead it, went ahead and led it in the rain to prove a point.

This is not an autobiography in the conventional sense. The book opens with a series of accounts of Allen Steck's most famous climbs in chronological order, after a summer in the Alps in 1949 in the company of a similarly young, inexperienced but equally ambitious Austrian, Karl Lugmayer, in which near catastrophes matched bicycling idylls between big climbs. Then follows the *Steck-Salathé* route on Yosemite's Sentinel Rock in 1950, an account concluded by the story of the 'astonishing hubris' of attempting the climb on the 50th anniversary of its first ascent when Steck's 75-year-old body lost all energy at the Narrows Chimney and he was benighted. Perhaps the most remarkable story is that of the first, and still unrepeated, ascent of the Hummingbird Ridge of Mount Logan by a party of six over 37 days in 1965. Steck still produces for astonished guests the steel shovel that he perforated to take on this climb, the key to the famous Shovel Traverse of the narrowest part of the three and a half mile long corniced ridge.

The laconic, easy-going humour that makes this book such a delight is exemplified by the opening of the story of the third ascent of the Salathé Wall, when, gathered at the bottom of the climb, 'to our surprise, Long brought with him a Super 8 movie camera he had just bought. Now it seemed we were to make a film of the climb. We dutifully read the instructions for this machine by headlamp, eventually drifting off to sleep.' This amazing film languished for decades until Steck and Steve Roper made a voiceover commentary in Steck's kitchen, complete with popping cork for their second bottle of wine towards the end. It was first seen in the UK at the 2015 Kendal Mountain Festival. This would be the only opportunity for a UK audience to get a sense of the hilarious double act that Steck and Roper perform daily together over lunch in that kitchen.

The book shifts gear into a section titled 'Childhood, Family and Business'. The briefest of biographical facts are often the most telling, especially when set against family photographs, and in this way Steck gets himself to the editing, with Roper, of the Sierra Club's mountaineering journal *Ascent* which set the bar for innovative climbing writing for a whole generation. Inevitably for a lifelong resident of the Bay Area, the Sierra Club played a crucial role in Steck's story, introducing him to climbing and then accepting Steck and Roper's proposal for an elegant, large-format, photo-essay-enhanced publication that the club supported for 25 years and 13 issues, helping launch the careers of writers like David Roberts and photographers like Glen Denny. Of course, those *Ascent* lunches eventually had their own wine label, chosen from a phrase in an Ed Drummond *Ascent* article. Thus was created Incubus Hills California Barefoot Burgundy.

In 1976, Steck led a first ascent of Payu Peak above the Baltoro glacier for the Alpine Club of Pakistan and decided that he would not go to the summit as a gift to his Pakistani team. (With amusing candour he admits that he changed his mind as he sat on a ledge below the summit and called for a rope, but it would not reach. 'Just as well.') His respect for different cultures and love of mountain travel led to Steck setting up a trekking company called Mountain Travel (USA), allowed to use this title by Col Jimmy Roberts who had pioneered trekking in Nepal under this name. Even after the ten years that he led this company, Steck continued to lead treks for them, especially to the Greek islands. One suspects that there are many stories untold about these journeys, but the book gathers pace in order to celebrate climbs at Joshua Tree and Jebel Rum, a lucky escape from being buried in an avalanche for 20 minutes and an epic walk through the Grand Canyon with his brother George who was writing guide books to his amazing journeys in the Canyon. Imagine planning a through-hike along the remote north side that would take 80 days and seven caches of food and water. Such was George's enthusiasm, canyon experience and tenacity that they not only made it but remained the best of friends until the older brother's death. This capacity for easy-going friendship is one of the understated themes of the book, represented at the end by an affectionate portrait of John Salathé, a loner who was obviously not easy to get to know well. But Steck hangs in with him, finding the 82-year-old recluse in his camper van wintering out near the Mexico border, then ten years later visiting with Roper a nearby nursing home where the Swiss blacksmith recalls making his revolutionary hard steel pitons from Ford axles.

Amongst our literature's books of epics and suffering, agonies and anger, falls and fallings-out, Allen Steck's *A Mountaineer's Life* stands out for the warmth of its friendships, its sustained quiet humour, the joys and the beauties of a life not only fully lived, but clearly fully loved. Steck says that he and Roper were pleased that the first issue of *Ascent* 'demonstrated our desire for innovation and whimsy'. In today's hard edged, hard hitting literary climate these are undervalued qualities that are to be found beneath the veil of self-deprecation that the old Silver Fox weaves through *A Mountaineer's Life*.

*Terry Gifford*

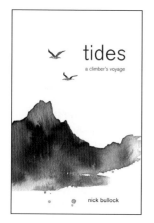

**Tides**
A Climber's Voyage
Nick Bullock
*Vertebrate Publishing, 2018, pp256, £24*

It's 2015 and a newly released film, 'All Roads Lead to Scotland', is doing the rounds online. Nick Bullock and Tim Neill are featured, despatching *Feeding Frenzy* and *Han Solo* on Ben Nevis to the beat of a pounding guitar. 'That's a run-out, i'n't it?' Nick says at one point. 'Nutter,' I think, closing my laptop. 'Absolute nutter.' Satisfied that I had Nick correctly pegged as unhinged I swiftly put him from my mind. A year later and I encounter him again in front of a packed audience at the 2016 Kendal Mountain Festival. Laughing, joking, scratching his head and generally looking manic he is compering an event on Scottish winter climbing with a winning combination of morbid humour and enthusiasm. The lecture hall pulses. Having survived a bear attack in Canada alongside Greg Boswell the year before, his conscious self-deprecation in the face of eye-watering danger reinforces my impression of a one-dimensional eccentric. Useful for selling jackets and entertaining audiences, I reason, but leaving the auditorium I again put Nick to one side.

How wrong could I be? My no-fixed-abode caricature of a certified maniac who thinks little and laughs a lot imploded reading *Tides*: so much so that I swiftly acquired *Echoes*, Nick's 2012 book, soon afterwards. Moving from UK rock and winter climbing, to the Alps, South America and the

Himalaya, *Tides* is a deeply meditative book in which climbs take on significance not simply for their difficulty, but for the questions they raise when Bullock is back in the valley. The writing is restless, constantly interrogating the validity of his motivation, his place in society, and his relationships with friends, family and partners.

Early on, the writing moves impressively between climbs, people, emotions and memories with a pace that leaves the reader immersed in Nick's disorientation. Some might argue that bolder editing could have make the collection clearer, yet I personally consider such ambiguity a welcome challenge to much of our modern climbing discourse. Here is not a glossily packaged sponsored athlete, but an intelligent and refreshingly uncertain human portrayal of what it is like to give one's life to climbing.

The strain on Bullock and the pressure he places on himself and those around him are all too real. Insecurities about his ability and comparisons to the likes of Matt Helliker and Jules Cartwright are not shied away from, and translate to a very real internal anxiety and desire to push ever further. This journey, mirrored against that of his parents selling up and retiring to a touring nomad lifestyle on board a canal boat, gives a poignant honesty to the book's ruminations on death, commercialism and what it might mean to be fulfilled in modern society.

Written in a poetic style that to me had echoes of Ed Drummond's essay 'Mirror Mirror', Nick's opening climbs often lack a moment of conclusion or resolution. The *Supercouloir* and Chacraraju's east face are two examples, but even success on the likes of *Omega*, the ED3 on the Petites Jorasses and a notable British first, consciously cuts short so the moment of euphoria is left hanging incomplete in the mind. Summits hold little importance to Nick, and make this a challenging book to read, not just because of deaths of Jules Cartwright and Nick's own mother, but because no matter what the success, the only thing it appears to lead to is further personal uncertainty.

These are not, however, the disingenuous musings of a self-absorbed mountaineer looking for Instagram followers, but questions posed with absolute sincerity that reach to the heart of what it means to be human in modern society. Painfully personal memories from his childhood are set against the difficulties faced by his own aging parents and this makes for a wide-ranging book. Teenage angst, wilful youth, mid-life uncertainty, and old age come under scrutiny; one perhaps wonders whether Nick's mental restlessness is because he can never retreat from this intensely critical perspective.

In this context, scenes of running over Tryfan and the Glyder plateau in 2008 mark a notable switch in tone; we begin to see a more relaxed individual. A near epic with Nico Favresse on Dinas Cromlech's *Nightmayer* during the BMC International Meet is told with Bullock's familiar morbid humour but his perspective is broader and more light-hearted, a poignant contrast to the book's earlier mood. On a successful third attempt of *Surgical Lust*, a bold E7 on Scimitar Ridge in the Llanberis Pass, Nick sits at the top feeling that he almost understands this new life. Almost. Because if this collection makes one thing apparent, it's that Nick is never truly fulfilled.

I wonder how I failed to appreciate this complexity in Nick before I read *Tides*. Perhaps I had been guilty of judging him by his vividly exuberant cover. Or perhaps it is because today's climbing media is defined by increasingly reductive narratives that it is difficult for us to appreciate that our relationship with climbing is rarely simple, often contradictory and likely to be fraught. Either way there is a boldness to *Tides* that deliberately attempts to break from this reductive trend and challenge such conformity. It is still be the fast-paced account of the man I saw on stage in Kendal, where drama plays out on blank rock faces and at extreme altitudes, yet *Tides* is also the questioning and discursive memoir of a thoughtful and candid mountaineer. I happily stand corrected.

*Jonny Dry*

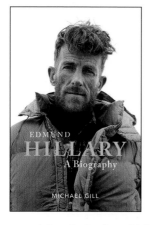

**Edmund Hillary**
A Biography
Michael Gill
*Vertebrate Publishing, 2019, pp532, £24*

Michael Gill modestly subtitles his book 'A biography' rather than '*The* biography', but make no mistake: this is a heavyweight tome, which aims to give a comprehensive account of Hillary's life, before and after Everest. It's a fascinating piece of work, both for readers who know Hillary well and for those who are new to his story. Currently there only seem to be imported hardbacks available but its New Zealand publishers, Potton and Burton, have done a beautiful job, printing it on high quality paper and filling the book with both black and white and colour photographs. It might look like an archetypal 'doorstop' but in fact it's a surprisingly fast read, written with pace, honesty and humour.

When it comes to telling Hillary's story there are already several other books in print. Ed wrote two full-length autobiographies, *Nothing Venture* and *View from the Summit*, as well as several other books detailing his adventures on Everest and elsewhere. Over the years there have been several unauthorised biographies and most recently, the New Zealand biographer Alexa Johnson published a lavishly illustrated coffee table biography. Where Michael Gill scores however is in his access to Hillary's letters and personal documents as well as his long friendship with New Zealand's most famous son.

Gill first got to know Hillary in the early 1960s when he was a young student 'working towards an unrecognised degree in mountaineering.' Hillary invited him to take part in the Silver Hut expedition in 1960-1, a scientific and sporting expedition to Khumbu, which aimed to combine a rigorous study of high-altitude physiology with a wild yeti chase and forays onto nearby mountains, including the first ascent of Ama Dablam. After that the two men stayed friends, with Gill becoming one of the founding members of the

Himalayan Trust. His biography breaks down into roughly four sections: Hillary before Everest, the Everest story, life as a global adventurer, and Hillary's last two decades when he re-married and became an elder statesman.

One highlight of the first section is a chapter on his father Percy's First World War experiences, based on recently discovered diaries. Percy was a crucial figure in Hillary's life, a role model with whom he fought a running battle for much of his early years. Percy didn't talk about his wartime experiences, but the horrors of the Gallipoli campaign, turned him into a lifelong pacifist. Ed's work ethic and sense of social commitment can all be traced back to his father, as he readily acknowledged.

Gill's re-telling of the Everest story includes a three-chapter diversion into the history of pre-war Everest expeditions but becomes more pointed when he takes a swipe at what he calls Harriet Tuckey's 'revisionist' version of the 1953 Everest story, as recently told in her biography of her father Griffith Pugh. Gill queries Pugh's elevation into 'the man who made it possible', and declares that if anyone deserved that epithet, it was John Hunt, the expedition leader, a much maligned figure in Tuckey's book.

It's the chapters that deal with life after Everest that are the most interesting. The problem Ed Hillary faced was shared by all the great heroes of 20th century exploration: what do you do after the headlines stop? It wasn't always easy for him but Hillary's answer was a life of almost constant movement. As Gill emphasises he became the consummate professional adventurer, who as a writer, filmmaker and public speaker was very adept at telling and retelling his story.

What set him apart, however, weren't his adventures in Antarctica or his epic river trips, but the long-term commitment he made to improve the lives of the people of Nepal. One of the most touching notes in Mike Gill's book is a simple letter from the village of Thame asking him to build them a school. 'Though our children have eyes,' they wrote, 'but still they are blind.'

Long before the concept of 'giving something back' became a cliché, Hillary and the volunteers he recruited built schools, hospitals and airstrips all over the Sherpa region and raised tens of thousands of dollars to further the cause. It was a chapter in Hillary's life that Gill dubs 'the best decade of Ed's life' and is all the more poignant when it ends in tragedy, with the death of his wife and daughter Belinda in an air crash in Kathmandu. The letters written by Ed and his family afterwards as they try to come to terms with the deaths are painful and raw; the fact they continued their work in Nepal in spite of what happened, a testament to their exceptional grit and dedication.

In his final years, Hillary got the diplomatic job that had been predicted for him since the 1950s, and settled into the role of an occasionally grumpy elder statesman.

Like all heroes, he had his flaws and weaknesses. Gill does not shy away from the difficult periods in Hillary's life but you cannot get to the end of this warm-hearted book without thinking: 'Boy, what a life.' What more could anyone want from a biographer?

*Mick Conefrey*

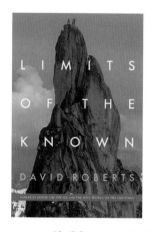

**Limits of the Known**
David Roberts
*W W Norton, 2018, pp306, £18.99*

David Roberts is seriously ill with throat cancer and so this is very much a valedictory book. When he started it he was so weak that he hired a researcher to visit libraries and conduct interviews for the 'texts and testimonies' that have always given authority to his writing. But for his 75th birthday in May 2018 he was sufficiently improved by radiation treatment to be able to hike in Cedar Mesa and share 'Anasazi wonders' with friends. His Facebook page reveals that he has even been teaching Alex Honnold to play golf. Of course, his book with Honnold, *Alone on the Wall*, was his most recent and Roberts' fascination with Anasazi culture has been a major part of his later work. Some of us, of a certain generation, have been following his prolific writing career almost since the beginning with the Alaska narratives that established his reputation for gripping but elegant story-telling that was also well-researched and emotionally explorative. Superficially, *Limits of the Known* appears to revisit the themes and sometimes the subjects of his writing career, but Roberts' intelligence and spirit of enquiry drives the book to do more than that and to circle back to his current challenges.

So this book is driven by a reassessment of the life of a freelance adventure writer. The initial question 'Why have I spent my life trying to find the lost and unknown places of this world?' is now followed by a more penetrating reflective inquiry: 'What has my passion cost me in missed opportunities to connect with those who do not share my desire?' This is really only addressed in the book's self-examining last chapter where Roberts has become dependent upon his wife of 50 years, whose hand he desires to be holding in his final moments, 'unwilling to let go.' 'It isn't a journey,' he snaps at one friend at his lowest point. 'It's an assault.' Then immediately and typically, he half-justifies, half-regrets his correction. 'In my pedantry, I was cruelly fending off my dear friend's love.' The implication is that journeys only unfold as stories in retrospect. At the time you are in it, it is something else that is more immediate, somewhere on a scale from urgent survival to ecstatic epiphany. It is only in the retrospective telling that meaning can be made of it. So Roberts searches for meanings in the adventurous stories of this book as a way of circling back into his own adventures, chosen and unchosen: 'What have the passions of explorers across human history delivered to our understanding of life?'

In a chapter on Nansen's *Farthest North* Roberts reveals that his father was an astronomer operating a telescope at the highest town in the United States. A combination of snow and an awareness of the expanding universe led the child to an interest in polar discovery and Himalayan expeditions. A chapter on Shipton concludes with Roberts meeting him in Alaska in 1966, the gracious elder and the gawping young admirer. Then, in his early forties, Roberts 'gradually drifted into a fascination with the Anasazi' in south-eastern Utah: their canyon caves, petroglyphs and archaeology. Without realising it, this new passion came to replace climbing new routes. In a brilliant analysis Roberts reflects upon the difference between the two obsessions, pointing out that the discovery of new cultural sites led to wider questions about their mysteries. Drawn into writing assignments on first river descents, Roberts then tells the story of Leahy and Dwyer's first contact with unknown civilisations in a traverse of Papua New Guinea. Again, Roberts questions his interest in the long gone Anasazi as 'dilettantism' and admits that his mountaineer's need for control would preclude any immersion in another culture to really experience its beliefs and practices. Indeed, it is the exercise of control, in its purest form of complete isolation, which Roberts regrets as having been lost from modern forms of easy communication in adventure travel. It is caving, he points out, that has been least 'adulterated by the machinery of communication', and it is as a caver rather than a climber, he admits, that he would launch his career if he were starting now. Talking to the American cave diver and explorer Bill Stone, 'basking in the full force of the man's intense volition', Roberts realises that, 'This is the kind of brilliant zealot that Columbus must have seemed to his shipmates, or Shackleton to his comrades – a man to be feared but followed.'

And this is the kind of insight, combining immediacy with historical depth, experience of human spirit with reflective distance that a valedictory book from a vastly experienced, questing and questioning writer can offer. In the final chapter David Roberts tries hard to turn the hardest questions upon himself, identifying his vocation as that of an adventurer above all. He is sceptical about this delivering self-knowledge, broadening the mind, or the value of personal joy, which 'for its own sake is a selfish thing.' He pulls back from psychic adventure, although psychotherapy has been 'an endeavour that led me to a better understanding of myself', more than exploration.

'But back to adventure,' he rather clumsily interjects at this point. His swerve is understandable, although it does perhaps avoid reflection upon one aspect of Roberts' career that should preoccupy his biographer. I remember Bob Bates telling me when I visited him just before his death that Roberts had probed him for possible lines of fracture in his partnership with Charlie Houston and left, finding none. Friends of Jeff Lowe in Utah still bristle at Roberts' prurient writing about Lowe's marriage and his relationship with Catherine Destivelle during Lowe's new route on the Eiger. It can be argued that searching out the truth has benefitted history, whatever the consequences for relationships, in work such as *True Summit: What Really Happened on the Legendary Ascent of Annapurna*. That there are still questions to be explored is perhaps something that an adventure writer would want to leave behind.

This absorbing and unsentimental final book, if that is what it becomes, will take fans of Roberts' writing beyond what has gone before in ways that will tell them more about its writer and his quest than any previous book.

'As much as anything, I started climbing because I was bored,' Roberts admits, seeking adventure as a boy away from comfortable security. This book is an intellectual, historical and personal journey into what followed, told by the freelance adventure writer who set the standard for a generation.

*Terry Gifford*

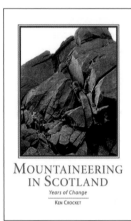

**Mountaineering in Scotland**
Years of Change
Ken Crocket
*Scottish Mountaineering Trust, 2017, pp371,£25*

Ken Crocket is a past president of the Scottish Mountaineering Club, was editor of the SMC journal for over a decade and has written an authoritative history of Ben Nevis. In 2015 he published a history of the early period of Scottish mountaineering from the late 19th century up to the First World War. The present volume covers the period from 1914 until the early 1970s, when winter ice climbing changed dramatically with the introduction of curved picks.

Crocket has done a phenomenal amount of research and covers the history in considerable, if not exhausting, detail. Readers unfamiliar with Scottish climbs may find themselves overwhelmed; almost every significant new climb done in a 60-year period is mentioned, with the full names and birth and death dates of the pioneers. The text is enlivened by extracts, often dramatic and well written, from the accounts of first ascensionists and there is a fine selection of historic black and white and colour photographs. In addition, Crocket sets the history in context with asides on progress in technical equipment, the development of mountain rescue, access and conservation issues, significant disasters such as the 1971 Cairngorms tragedy and the broader socioeconomic background, for example the effects of the depression in the 1930s. He is assiduous in giving modern grades for most of the climbs described, as well as original grades, with reference, of course, to the amount of aid used and the clothing, footwear and weather associated with the first ascent.

So far as climbing in the Cairngorms is concerned, Crocket acknowledges having borrowed freely from Greg Strange's masterly history, published in 2010. The latter is more comprehensive and has more historic photographs. The large overlap would, I suppose, be justified by the fact that Crocket embeds Cairngorm climbing history and the activities of its great protagonists like Brooker and Patey in the wider context of climbing all over Scotland.

There are brief portraits of all the famous names in Scottish climbing history: Bell, Nimlin, Macphee, Murray, Kellett, Cunningham, MacInnes, Marshall, Smith and many, many others. Evocative accounts of the first ascents of classics such as *Observatory Ridge*, *Mitre Ridge*, *Fluted Buttress* and *Minus One Buttress* add greatly to the reader's enjoyment.

Crocket has been at pains to follow up every trail he can, explaining for example the etymology of route names such as *The Bullroar* on Ben Nevis' Carn Dearg. His work is replete with amusing details: we learn that John Bernard Meldrum, who made an early ascent of the *West Buttress* in Coire Mhic Fhearchair on Beinn Eighe was a bachelor until the age of 90, then married and lived on to the age of 107. He recycles the story that Norrie Muir persuaded his GP to prescribe a pair of big boots for self-medication allowing him to continue climbing, while conceding that this may be an urban myth.

Despite many attractive features the book has not been well edited. There is a significant amount of repetition and the writing does not flow well, with the author too often allowing himself to lose the thread with his side-tracks; changes of topic are not signposted. As an illustration here is an extract from page 77.

> *Elsewhere new venues were being explored. Coire an Lochain, one of the three northern corries of Cairn Gorm, is the most popular modern climbing area in the Cairngorms, largely due to the ski road which greatly eases access. Central Crack Route (120m Moderate) was the first climb recorded here, by Alexander (Sandy) Harrison and Louis St Clair Bartholomew. The latter was a JMCS climber from Edinburgh and one of the Bartholomew family firm of cartographers which is credited with the introduction of hypsometric tints, or layer colouring on maps. This indicated low ground in shades of green, and higher ground in shades of brown, leading to still higher ground in purple then white. Leonardo da Vinci was probably the first to produce a map using a basic colour scheme to indicate high ground, with his map of central Italy in the early 16th century.*
>
> *Louis St Clair Bartholomew appears not to have paid [sic] a very active role in the family firm, however, perhaps saving his energy for mountaineering.*

There are some surprising errors, for example the photo of Hamish MacInnes opposite page 249 is said to be on Rannoch Wall. One hesitates to disagree with Crocket, a past author of a Glen Coe climbing guide, but the author of the latest guide in preparation pointed out to me that it looks far more like the east face of Gearr Aonach. The photo of Dougal Haston is wrongly dated as July 1977, six months after Haston's death. I was pleased to see a print of a cartoon of Dougie Dinwoodie by Norman Keir, a talented Aberdeen climber who produced some excellent magazines in the 1970s; but there is no reference to this illustration within the text, and as it dates from the late 1970s, it does not really belong in the time period to which the book is ostensibly devoted, indeed it is strangely placed next to a set of photos of wartime ascents in Arran.

There is no list or index of illustrations. There are two somewhat un-attractive maps in an appendix, one of which was far better presented as a full colour endpaper in Strange's Cairngorms history. Some aspects of the book design are unappealing, particularly the ugly tables, which appear to have been copied straight from a Word document. The page headers for

Chapter 14 have Corriemulzie misspelt, and for Chapter Seven 'The War Years' are given as 1910-1944.

Negative comments notwithstanding I feel that Crocket deserves our gratitude and praise for his long labours. Like most 'official' histories it is perhaps best consumed in small portions rather than all devoured at once. As a source book it is unlikely to be outdone. Anyone who loves Scottish climbing will derive great pleasure and learn much fascinating information from dipping into it.

*Geoff Cohen*

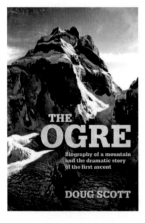

### The Ogre
The Biography of a Mountain and the Dramatic Story of the First Ascent
Doug Scott
*Vertebrate Publishing, 2017, 178pp, £20*

When I was young expedition books were all the rage. There were still a few gaps on those maps of the Greater Ranges that were then available, and every expedition seemed obliged to produce a book upon its return. Most differed only in the names of the members and the name of the objective: most narratives were all but interchangeable. Irrespective of whether or not a summit was reached – and give or take the odd accident – armchair readers could enjoy a whiff of an exotic adventure that was quite beyond their own reach.

In due course expeditions became two-a-penny. So-called mountain adventure, even a billet on an 8,000m peak, is available for purchase to every Tom, Dick or Harriet. The question is, can they write? It takes an epic happening, a talented writer or an unusual treatment to make an expedition book of more than passing interest to those of us who actually climb mountains ourselves.

On the face of it this book is what it says on the tin: yet another expedition book. However, it's not a run of the mill story and its author is a real, highly respected mountaineer with a worthwhile tale to tell. It's historical, in as much as the expedition it recounts took place over 40 years ago, yet three of the four dramatis personae are still around, aged but active. And although at the time the bare facts of the expedition were reported in the *Alpine Journal* and distorted and dramatized in the tabloid press, the full gripping story has never before been recounted in depth, move by move.

The treatment too is unusual for the book is divided into two distinct parts: the context and the adventure. Part One opens with a discourse on Karakoram geology and geography followed by what can, in the space available, be only a précis of the history and exploration of the region, spanning from Darius the Persian and Alexander to Moorcroft, Godwin-Austen, the Great Game, Conway, Tilman and Shipton. Apparently it was Conway who during his 1892 expedition, first remarked on 'Point 23,914' (now Pt 7285m) and dubbed it the Ogre, despite some confusion as to which mountain was what. For the armchair reader Part One should prove a useful, scene-setting backdrop to the adventure described in Part Two, which Doug Scott recounts in the first person, aided by access to the diaries of his colleagues.

It is not for me to retell his story here; suffice to say that Scott and Bonington, who happened to be professional climbers, reached the summit of the Ogre successfully but were both badly injured on the descent, indeed Scott completely crippled. They were subsequently stormbound, still very high on their complicated descent route, together with their two very experienced but nevertheless amateur companions, Mo Anthoine and Clive Rowland. To whom they undoubtedly owe their survival.

Writing in retrospect after all these years, Scott is not averse to sharing his feelings, doubtless still imprinted vividly on his mind. While obviously in great pain he is able to admire the view; he explains how while crawling on hands and knees each obstacle must be overcome one at a time. Never once does he appear sorry for himself, his concern is with the worsening frostbite of his mates. Unlikely though it seems to the reader, he never questions the prospects of survival.

I might well have skipped the initial two chapters, a standard 'expedition book' lead-in covering the approach march to Advanced Base Camp, and who did what, when and where. However, I was able to understand how the expedition had come together and appreciate why all was not necessarily sweetness and light among the original six expedition members. Although united in their desire to climb the Ogre, their climbing ethos ranged from single-minded to ambitious-but-laid-back, that is until the chips were down when the ethos became 'one for all and all for one'. Even then, marooned in their snow hole after five days of storm, one climber suddenly announced, 'We're going to make a fortune out of this'. Had Scott been a lesser man, both physically and mentally, it's unlikely that he'd have survived. While the same probably applied to his companions, it was Anthoine and Rowland who averted a tragedy and are surely the heroes of the tale.

Still in a very bad way, Scott was treated at Askole by a couple of doctors from a passing American expedition who told me months later how impressed they had been, not only by his cheerful fortitude despite thirteen days of continuous pain, but especially by his selfless concern for the porters who so had carried him so gently 35 rugged miles down the Biafo glacier on a makeshift stretcher. Without local porters, expeditions in the Karakoram would be impossible, and after his Ogre experience and several subsequent expeditions, Scott was determined to honour the special debt he felt to the Balti folk of Askole. Learning that the village's 50% infant mortality had been traced to polluted water, he set about raising $10,000 to lay a mile of deeply buried pipeline into the village from a fresh water spring, which alleviated the problem. This was the germ of the idea that has since become Community Action Nepal, the charity for mountain people of which Scott is the prime mover. All power to his elbow!

This book is an excellent read, although as the author admits, much of it was hurriedly dictated to a typist, so the flow can be a little bumpy. The book is nicely produced and well designed, despite Galen Rowell's aerial photograph being bisected at the crucial place by the spine. The protagonists' own colour photographs are well reproduced and usefully placed on the appropriate pages. Four annotated photographs of the Ogre enable the reader to follow most of the route, but by definition such photographs are foreshortened and can be initially confusing; diagrammatic artwork from a hypothetical viewpoint with height lines added would have been useful. But these are minor quibbles. *The Ogre* is a worthy addition to the mountaineering genre. For Mo Anthoine's own perspective on the incident, *Feeding the Rat* by Al Alvarez (Bloomsbury, 1988) is also recommended.

*John Cleare*

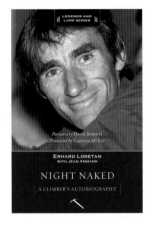

**Night Naked**
A Climber's Autobiography
Erhard Loretan, with Jean Ammann
*Mountaineers Books, 2016, pp256, £16.95*

On 28 April 2011 the Swiss guide and Alpine Club honorary member Erhard Loretan fell to his death from a ridge on the Gross Grünhorn (4043m) in the Bernese Alps. The accident was prosaic: a crampon slip by his client and girlfriend Xenia Minder on an easy route and perhaps the most audacious high altitude climber of the 1980s and 1990s was dead on his 52nd birthday. As Jean Ammann, Loretan's collaborator on *Night Naked*, observes, it was an ordinary death for a mountain guide. 'Dying in the course of one's duties. The Grünhorn succeeded where 14 8,000ers had failed.' Ms Minder suffered a broken arm and scratches.

Six month's earlier I'd had supper with Erhard in London following his participation in 'First on Everest', a fund-raiser at the Royal Geographical Society in aid of Community Action Nepal. Few were better qualified to speak at such an event. When Erhard and his fellow Swiss Jean Troillet reached their advance base camp at 5,850m on the Rongbuk glacier late on 30 August 1986 they had set a new record in extreme alpinism: to the summit of Everest (8848m) and back in only 43 hours, no sherpas, no rope, no bottled oxygen, for the last 1,000m they did not even take a rucksack.

The above I already knew of Erhard Loretan. This and the heart-wrenching fact that in 2003 he had received a four-month suspended prison sentence after pleading guilty to the negligent manslaughter, in December 2001, of his seven-month-old son Ewan. Erhard admitted to the police that he had shaken Ewan 'for a couple of seconds' to stop him crying. The case led to research showing many parents were unaware that infants, because of weak neck muscles, could die from being shaken for only a few seconds.

Erhard had never been one to seek the limelight and after the tragedy he became, for several years, a virtual recluse. It is unlikely we would have this memoir before us now had not the original French language version, *Les 8000 Rugissants*, been published way back in 1996 when Loretan's star was riding high with the Swiss public.

This first English language edition takes as its title *Night Naked*, the graphic term coined by Voytek Kurtyka for the audacious, super-light, pushing on through the night style of alpinism employed by Loretan and his companions. Jean Ammann, a journalist for *La Liberté*, has brought the story up to date with a moving final chapter, 'Erhard *Humanum Est*', and David Roberts has supplied an insightful foreword.

To summarise *Night Naked* simply as Loretan's campaign to climb the 8,000ers would be to invite a yawn. But while, yes, we are taken sequentially through Erhard's extraordinary career, starting with the west ridge of the Dent de Broc near his home in Bulle (okay, not *so* extraordinary, until you learn that Erhard was only 11 years old at the time) to solo ventures in Antarctica, healing wounds, *Night Naked*, for the most part, bowls along with all the pace appropriate to the man along with candid opinions.

Reflecting on the death of Benoît Chamoux below the summit of Kangchenjunga in 1995, when both Loretan and the Frenchman were set on their last 8000er, Loretan suggests that if millions of radio listeners had not been following Chamoux's final stumbles maybe he would 'have listened to his body instead of his pride.' By now Loretan had become disillusioned, believing that the heroic era was over and mountaineering was entering the 'sad category of mass sports'.

In late 1994 he *Desnivel*: 'Urban hell, including all its problems, has migrated to the mountains. Mountaineering has lost its sense of ethics, and thereby its spiritual dimension.' Loretan and Jean Troillet had recently returned from Lhotse and witnessed the Everest base camp circus. '[We] laughed at these pseudo-mountaineers who have money but no skills. At the same time, this appalling spectacle made us feel tremendously sad.'

Loretan's gloomy tone here in the 1990s stands in contrast to the first two-thirds of *Night Naked* where he treats a storm of first ascents in the Andes and Himalaya, plus *enchaînements* in the Alps, more as some kind of cosmic joke. 'I never asked myself why I climbed, because I never asked myself why I lived.'

In 1983, along with Marcel Rüedi and Jean-Claude Sonnenwyl, Loretan became the first person to climb three 8,000ers on the same expedition (Gasherbrum II, Hidden Peak or Gasherbrum I, and Broad Peak) in only 15 days. Loretan was hooked. Eight-thousanders, he quips, are like salted peanuts: 'it's better never to start.' Yet there is a duality to Loretan. Just a few pages earlier comes a less jokey observation that perhaps better encapsulates Loretan's character: 'I was [alone] on top of Hidden Peak. To live happily, let us live hidden!'

David Roberts first read the book in the French original and thought it one of the finest memoirs ever written by a mountaineer, a high-wire performance with Loretan's vision of life springing from a sense of the absurd invigorated all the same by a driving quest for joy and transcendence. Yet even before the awful event of December 2001 it seems there was a more insecure personality beneath the free-spirited exterior. Roberts was dumbfounded when a biography by the French climbing journalist Charlie Buffet, *Erhard Loretan: Une vie suspendue* (Éditions Guérin, 2013), revealed Erhard to be not the 'blithe absurdist' Roberts supposed, but someone who went to the mountains fretful and anxious. Troillet also described his friend as by instinct a private and retiring man.

Reading this memoir with the benefit of Roberts' foreword, Buffet's analysis and most particularly Jean Ammann's thoughtful commentaries between each chapter along with his 2013 postscript, the paradox is perhaps not so hard to grasp. Those words ('To live happily, let us live hidden!') become more than a throwaway line. Exuberant, visionary climber, yes, but Loretan was no less a complex human being. *Night Naked* is a fascinating story.

*Stephen Goodwin*

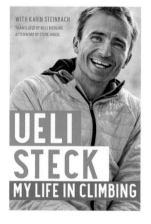

### My Life in Climbing
Ueli Steck
Translated by Billi Bierling
*Mountaineers Books, 2018, pp224, £16.95*

Most books do not have the Sword of Damocles hanging over every page, but that is how I felt reading Ueli Steck's *My Life in Climbing*. Ueli's fate is known from the first page to the last, a fate he predicts at times in sad reflections that uncover layers of self-doubt and self-rebuke: concern that he is being driven by selfish vanity and the commercial image of himself as the indestructible 'Swiss Machine'. And then, elsewhere and in equal measure, he reassures himself with the self-confident view that he holds the key to a long life, as he strives for ever-increasing levels of fitness through extreme training on trails, bikes and mountains, trusting that in speed he will find safety. A couple of decades ago, no one would have predicted that the north face of the Eiger would be used as a running track, but that is what it was for Ueli Steck.

The last time I saw Ueli was during the 2014 Kendal Mountain Festival. He was just arriving to register, looking smaller than I remembered and somewhat nervous, not at home with all the crowds. He was surprised when I addressed him out of the blue: 'Hello Ueli. Well done on Annapurna. You probably don't realise that Alex MacIntyre predicted your single-day ascent of the south face over 30 years ago? He shuffled slightly, and then gave me a smile of recognition as I explained what Alex had written back in 1982 for the Karrimor Technical Journal, predicting the coming of a future where individuals would be so fit and technically adept that new routes in a day on 8,000m peaks would be the norm for the very best.

My encounter with Ueli came a few months after he was awarded the Piolet d'Or, but also at a time when there was growing controversy over his claimed solo ascent. Could he really have done such a thing? Where was the evidence? The Sword of Damocles that hangs over this book is double-edged. It is not only that of his eventual fate, but one that could also destroy his legacy.

But why would he lie? His account in the chapter that deals with the Annapurna experience is vivid and plausible, yet there are some unexpected clues as to his mental state:

> At this moment, I realized how much risk I was prepared to take, and how high I had already climbed up the face. It did not really matter now whether I carried on or turned back. I had accepted the risk. It occurred to me that I might not come back from the face. Suddenly there was no longer an afterward... no matter what happened I had accepted the situation.

Later in the same chapter, he answers the challenge regarding lack of evidence, the absence of photos, his GPS turned off, despite wearing it as part of his watch, the staggering rate of progress at high altitude, by saying he concentrated on the climbing with no thoughts of providing evidence afterward. Many other ascents have been believed with no evidence. Yet the writing also reveals an ill-tempered annoyance with mistakes made by both his partners and Ueli himself. He did not like or accept failure. There is little doubt that he was fit enough and technically able to make the solo ascent of Annapurna, but it is possible that he got into a mental paradox in which what was possible for him to achieve became for him what he wanted the world to believe was true.

The Annapurna experience cast a huge shadow over Ueli's last years. He was a half-broken man as the Swiss journalist Mario Casella reported:

> Steck was doubly hit by this personal experience: he felt offended by the insinuations, but what really made him waver was the realisation that he had overcome the limits of his own mind. This point was revealed by Steck himself in a documentary on the post-Annapurna days. In a highly emotional sequence, the Swiss mountaineer explains with a choked voice: 'I think I found myself in the same condition of the first men who came back from the moon. Everyone commented on those missions in space. Common people, however, do not understand, they cannot understand. Astronauts were the only ones who could understand what they had experienced up there. They were the only ones to have lived that experience! And they became depressed afterwards... It's normal! No?'

Whether he did or did not climb Annapurna, this book stands as a testament to everything that Steck did achieve. It is a remarkable diary of his climbs. I say diary rather than autobiography because there is little else in the book: about his childhood, loves and home. His life appears from this, as the title suggests, to exist almost entirely 'in climbing'.

To balance the dark moments experienced on Everest in the infamous encounter with a violent group of Sherpas, and the deaths of friends on Shishapangma in an ill-judged summit push, there are moments of joyful ebullience, especially during his solo crossing of all the 82 alpine 4,000ers when every climb, every meeting with friends, every cup of coffee is expressed vividly and joyfully, and puts the reader firmly in those moments.

The translation is not perfect, usually in technical areas, which sees Ueli placing or clipping bolts when we know pitons are meant. Sometimes the editing isn't clear. I had to read the detail of his Eiger speed ascents several times before I understood that he hadn't contradicted himself on the tactics he used to take back the record in 2015.

The Eiger chapter is the last in the book. Steck concludes: 'The most important thing was to stay aware of the risk at any given moment and control it. If I managed to do this, I would certainly be able to experience more exciting and beautiful moments in the mountains without killing myself.' Sad to say Ueli could not live by that maxim on Nuptse. Extreme solo climbing is no doubt the purest of all alpinism no matter what some may think about the risks. Steve House is absolutely right when he says in his afterword: 'Ueli Steck shaped the sport of climbing for the better by seeing what was humanly possible and then achieving it.'

*John Porter*

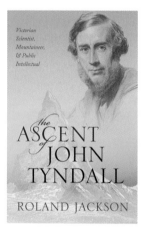

**The Ascent of John Tyndall**
Victorian Scientist, Mountaineer, and Public Intellectual
Roland Jackson
*Oxford University Press, 2018, pp576, £25*

John Tyndall (1820-93) was born in Ireland to a family of modest means but rose to be a revered scientist and thinker. He was involved in politics, the oil and gas safety board, the design of the organ at the Royal Albert Hall, lighthouse safety, and became a key figure at the Royal Institution, as well as being, eventually, married into the aristocracy: all this during the early days of the Alpine Club and some landmark ascents in the Alps. Science historian Roland Jackson has boldly taken on the monumental task of sorting through the many volumes of Tyndall's writings: to give an idea of the scale, the Tyndall Correspondence Project has so far catalogued 7,500 letters, Tyndall himself authored 180 scientific papers, and the project is expecting to fill 18 volumes.

Tyndall began his career as a surveyor for the railroads in England and was hired in 1847 to teach at Queenwood College, where he was able to attend lectures on chemistry and botany and learned about discovery-based and child-centered learning. It was at Queenwood that he became aware of Ralph Waldo Emerson's writings, which, along with those of Thomas Carlyle, influenced his work. Eventually, Tyndall began to teach physics at a time when laboratory science was largely absent from the British school system, something that Tyndall helped to remedy later. He debated his options of going to Germany to gain a doctorate or staying in England but ultimately pursued studies in Germany, where he developed his belief in the importance of molecular structure and his craft of experimental design and execution.

As Jackson writes: 'he must have found personal resonances in German ideas: aspects of idealism; ideas of consciousness and will; the importance of the individual; moral duty.' His thinking on science and theology was nuanced; he noted that society should be wary of 'making it the foundation of moral or religious convictions' and advocated for a fairer system for workers who are exploited but have little share of profit. Unfortunately, his suggested solution was to wait for 'noble-hearted men' in the upper classes to fix this. And so Tyndall largely pursued his own agenda, working constantly, summering in the Alps and not marrying until his fifties.

It was Tyndall's work that led to the discovery that Earth's atmosphere retained heat. He also established heat conduction in glaciers, worked on the structure of matter, promoted a scientific curriculum for schools and performed classic demonstrations of science: all of this ensured he was famous in his own time. He also disproved the theories of other scientists; it was for his dispute with James Forbes that I knew him. This controversy features throughout a great deal of this book and shows Tyndall's true character to be somewhat like Whymper in my imagination: a bit of a bore with great stamina for feuds. People began noting Tyndall's showmanship in some of his work. Thomas Archer Hirst, a friend of Tyndall, reprimanded him for a disagreement in print and Jackson points out that Hirst was 'concerned that success was going to Tyndall's head.' The dispute with Forbes, centring on who exactly should be credited for the various aspects involved in understanding the science of glaciers, proved so long-lived it outlasted Forbes by a considerable number of years.

Tyndall thought the blue of the sky was due to a scattering of very fine particles (our modern understanding is that it is a scattering of molecules in the atmosphere) and he argued this with George Airy who was forced to admit he didn't have a satisfactory explanation. As well as intriguing the scientific community, Tyndall could also thrill his audiences. He generated coloured clouds by the 'cooling effect of a sudden expansion of the vapour in a tube' and 'artificial blue skies that he created in his laboratory and the lecture room'. These 'were sensational.' Tyndall associated with literary worlds as well, as Jackson notes 'not only because of his advocacy of the need for creative imagination in science as in poetry but also because of the ethos he supported at the Royal Institution and those who spoke there.' If he was cast as a bore in later life, he was one that couldn't be ignored.

This book lacks the dynamic narrative that seems to have been his life. Perhaps it would have had a stronger heartbeat with more context. Tyndall saw a great deal change. It was the time of railways, the Ordnance Survey, the rise of tourism. It's the time of John Muir, activism, war in Europe and America, workers' rights, the beginnings of feminism, and the rise of the British Empire, but we don't see too much of this amidst the minutiae of Tyndall's life. It's as if Tyndall is too interesting a character, involved in too much, writing too many letters and papers, to allow an engaging read. Just as Tyndall advocated for more imagination in science, I wanted more imagination from his biography. As Jackson says: he was a 'remarkable man, complex, often infuriating, and reflecting all the prejudices, tensions, and opportunities of his age.' But the book for a large part is lists: lists of friends he writes to or visits and the lectures he gives. In between there's lots of physics, which required some scientific background to understand. The combination felt heavy, even burdensome.

We do get glimpses of major events. On 23 June 1848, Tyndall left Paris only just missing the start of the June Days uprising, when the city revolted against the conservative turn of the Second Republic. Outside of Paris he hears 'rumours of 20,000 killed' and finds himself 'weeping with anxiety over the safety of Frankland, who was still in Paris.' But if Tyndall seems to be at every party and friend to all the major figures of the day, we hear too little of it. A surfeit of diary and letter extracts impedes the narrative's flow. We miss the impact of his discoveries: it would benefit the reader of how Tyndall's discoveries filter into the present, especially as one of his key discoveries is the greenhouse effect.

Jackson tackles Tyndall's racism and misogyny at various stages in the book. Tyndall wanted to overhaul the inadequate education system of the time but criticises women for their inferior intellect, which makes him not quite the force for good that he imagines himself to be, even if science education still carries traces of Tyndall's work. On receiving a request for a subscription from the editor of *Woman* magazine in 1872, he declined, judging 'the present movement as leading to mischievous results.' Tyndall doesn't stop there. He suggests 'the men of the day have become to some extent women' meaning a 'few of the women aspire to be men.'

Tyndall, unlike contemporaries such as John Stuart Mill, was no advocate of women's emancipation. He was perplexed to find that women could indeed conduct scientific experiments, and even write books. He was a product of his society, not the force for change he thought he was. He used science to claim it was right and true to think this way. He held objectionable views on race: 'we do not hold an Englishman and a Jamaican negro to be convertible terms, nor do we think the cause of human liberty will be promoted by any attempt to make them so.' When the governor of Jamaica declared martial law to quell a rebellion and ordered the execution of innocent men, Tyndall joined Carlyle in the governor's defence. Thomas Huxley shared Tyndall's attitudes on gender and race, but took the side of the liberal John Stuart Mill, the only significant issue apart from the American Civil War on which Huxley and Tyndall ever differed. (Tyndall had Confederate sympathies).

Tyndall belonged to the great gentlemen's clubs of the day, which all restricted women of course. His friend Emily Peel joked after an abortive attempt on Mont Blanc 'when worthy of the distinction you must enroll me amongst your Alpine Clubbists, if such an honour is ever accorded to one of the weaker sex!' Jackson points out that the Alpine Club didn't allow women members until 1974 but then adds incorrectly: 'Unless one includes Tschingel, William Coolidge's canine companion, who was made an Honorary Member in 1869.' I doubt the Alpine Club Committee had that good a sense of humour. The enlightened did exist: the American Alpine Club (1902) and the Appalachian Mountain Club (1876) never restricted membership. But while there were some in the Alpine Club sympathetic to women alpinists, Tyndall certainly wasn't one of them.

Tyndall did some very significant climbs, such as the first solo of Monte Rosa, which Jackson tells us occurred in a rather unplanned way, with Tyndall 'waking before 6am [... thinking] the view from the summit [of Monte Rosa] must be unspeakably fine [... so] he set off [...] to make the first solo ascent.' It's this side of Tyndall that I admire the most, just doing something to see if he can. It's the experimenting side of him. Tyndall was ahead of his time in some respects. If he saw future disaster in guideless climbing becoming commonplace, he complained to Mary Egerton '[of the] small amount of originality developed by English climbers, Girdlestone is the only man who has shown anything of the kind [...] infinitely more creditable to him than hanging on to the skirts of a guide to whom you delegate the skill of scenting out the proper way, and the labour of leading, your own inventive powers being for the time perfectly torpid.'

This is a lengthy book about a remarkable man, unremarkable in its narrative. I need a biography to connect dots. I want a spider's web of the world with the subject at its centre, to make sense of their world. Tyndall was a well connected and remarkable man interested in just about everything, but Jackson's biography is simply a chronological plod through meetings, letters, dinners and discoveries, a lengthy, difficult book albeit a triumph of research and a testament to archives and the efforts to preserve them.

*Nigel Buckley*

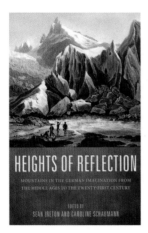

**Heights of Reflection**
Mountains in the German Imagination from the
Middle Ages to the Twenty-first Century
Edited by Sean Ireton and Caroline Schaumann
*Camden House, 2017, pp406, £15.99*

**The Flying Mountain**
Christoph Ransmayr
Translated by Simon Pare
*Seagull Books, 2018, pp336, £18.99*

*Heights of Reflection* is a collection of essays from European and North American academics on mountains in the German imagination from the Middle Ages to the 21st century. First published in 2012, it has stood the test of time and is now usefully available again for a sensible price. It starts, musically enough, with what is termed a 'Prelude', and a pleasing quotation from H W Tilman's 1946 book *When Men and Mountains Meet*. 'Like the desire for drink or drugs,' he wrote, 'the craving for mountains is not easily overcome, but a mountaineering debauch, such as six months in the Himalaya, is followed by no remorse.' Tilman's third book covered his disastrous pre-war expedition to Assam and other adventures, but much of its subject was his brave and exciting military service, including his time fighting behind enemy lines with Albanian partisans. Tilman had taken a dim view of Germany's mountaineering ethos on Nanga Parbat in the 1930s but his judgement, you feel, could equally stand for his view of their military ethos too: 'They spent a lot of time and money and lost a lot of climbers and porters, through bad luck and more often through bad judgement.'

I don't wish to endorse Tilman's opinion *in toto*. The fact large numbers of climbers died on Nanga Parbat was not because they were German, more because they were German in the 1930s. The upwelling of nationalism as Germany emerged from the humiliation of Versailles only to run into the Great Depression readily explains the inane levels of risk-taking. British climbers were more risk-averse, but saw admirable qualities of virility and self-sacrifice in its campaigns on Everest. I used to laugh at the idea of Everest as a 'British' mountain and Nanga Parbat as a 'German' mountain, but in terms of critical theory, these terms seem rather apposite in the context of this book. The attempts to climb them reveal much about two cultures that once ran in parallel but then, as the nineteenth century wore on, diverged.

So how does the British mountain experience differ culturally to that of the Germans? Tilman's laconic explanation for his addiction is one answer.

Dan Hooley, the author of this excellent 'Prelude', a climber himself and professor of classics at the University of Missouri, offers the term *jouissance*, coined by the psychoanalyst Jacques Lacan. The term was a kind of retort to Freud's pleasure principle: that suffering has its place in self-fulfilment. One can take an educated guess at Tilman's reaction to that sort of psychological speculation: 'Any fool can be uncomfortable.' But Hooley strikes me as a man who can take an acerbic joke.

He also says, very shrewdly, that the book's subject, mountains in the German imagination, often a Romantic one, 'inform the mountaineer's pleasure but do not, as they are often said to do, explain it.' It reveals the deep cultural continuity that links Goethe to von Humboldt, the poet Ludwig Tieck, Richard Strauss and Thomas Mann, all of whom are the subject of essays included in the book. English Romanticism feels like a distant historical artefact compared to this. Notions of the sublime have collapsed into the sort of fuzzy sentimental glow that characterises much landscape photography, the type loved by tourist boards. Within mountaineering, the laconic irony of Tilman, doubtful of anything too philosophical, is what's endured: Mick Fowler is a good example of a modern exponent. In mainstream culture, humanity's encounter with the extremes of nature has been reduced to a pastiche of imperial explorers, a knowing wink that accompanies predictable stories fashioned to satisfy consumers and certainly not challenge their thinking: adventure as product.

These things are true in Germany too, but the blaze of German Romanticism lives on, judging by representations of mountains and mountaineering in contemporary German culture. Two recent German feature films, *Nordwand*, directed by Philipp Stölzl, and *Nanga Parbat*, directed by Joseph Vilsmaier, are ambitious attempts to explore the motivation and character of mountaineers, respectively Toni Kurz and the Messner brothers. (Angela Merkl was at the premiere of the latter, pictured alongside Reinhold Messner, which speaks volumes.) They both reject the supposed ideology of the post-First World War *Bergfilm* but draw on its aesthetic tropes. *Nordwand* is the more successful film, but the ambition of both directors is for serious, enquiring work, a contrast with the frothy mountain entertainments Hollywood puts out. It's hard to imagine an English equivalent to Werner Herzog, who has made ambitious mountaineering films: *Gasherbrum: Der leuchtende Berge* (1985) and *Cerro Torre: Schrei aus Stein* (1991). Herzog's work frequently draws on nature as a context in which to explore who we are precisely because he springs from the intellectual universe outlined in this book. In English, only Kevin Macdonald's 2003 *Touching the Void* has come close to engaging in the same way, and his antipathy to his subject gives that film a kind of alienating disinterest.

The English passion for the work of W G Sebald, a German writer working in East Anglia who would most probably have won the Nobel prize for literature had he lived, shows how galvanising this German tradition can be. (It pleases me immensely that the documentary filmmaker Grant Gee has made films about W G Sebald, the band Joy Division and Jim Perrin.)

Sebald is adored here partly I think because of his use of irony: so very English. Scott Denham's essay on Sebald in this collection touches on this and how Sebald drew on the work of Thomas Mann, who walks a similar line in *Der Zauberberg*, or *The Magic Mountain*. It's the sublime as a favourite ageing relative, loved, necessary even, but gently mocked. 'If Mann,' Denham argues, 'ironically questions the potential of mountain experiences to expand human understanding, then Sebald affirms that potential, but questions the potential of humans to live with the understanding of themselves that they have gained from the experience at the top of the mountain.' Perhaps the best we can hope for is a sequence of intense experiences to string as beads on a rosary, and then count them off, as the shadows lengthen.

There is irony too in Christoph Ransmayr's critically acclaimed novel *Der fliegende Berg* (2006), now capably and sympathetically translated into English by Simon Pare as *The Flying Mountain* and long-listed for 2018's International Booker. It's a genre-defying work, sufficiently allegorical and oblique that you can read into it more or less whatever you like. Having read the essay by Olaf Berwald dedicated to it in *Heights of Reflection*, I wondered if we'd read the same book. It is the story of two brothers, Liam and Pádraic, with radically different philosophical responses to their shared upbringing by a loving mother who escapes their father, an Irish Republican dreaming of old grievances. After a long career at sea, Pádraic, the narrator, has come to live on a remote island with Liam, who has settled there after making money in digital geo-information. The island is a perch from which Liam is attempting to wrestle the complexities of the world into some semblance of order. Late on in the book, Pádraic remembers the gift they made their father for the first Christmas after their mother runs off to – horror! – Belfast: a papier-mâché topographical model of the valley where Michael Collins was ambushed and murdered. It's a metaphor for the whole book: lost men trying to orientate themselves in the world they think they inhabit.

The book opens with the brothers separated and Pádraic expiring high on the Tibetan peak of Phu-Ri, the eponymous flying mountain. Or at least, he believes himself to be dead, because soon his brother is bullying him awake, having found him unconscious in the snow. One thinks of Beck Weathers returning from the dead on Everest in 1996. (Olaf Berwald argues that Pádraic is in fact dead. Perhaps I'm being too literal-minded.) Then, as they continue their descent, Liam is swept away to his death in an avalanche and the rest of the book is an exploration of what it was that put them there. Thrown into the mix is Pádraic's passionate affair with a Tibetan nomad widow, whose presence deflects him from sharing his brother's determination. Her presence also allows Ransmayr to invoke Tibetan mythology, in which notions like flying mountains are readily accepted, on the basis that we shouldn't become too attached to the ground beneath our feet: it's not as solid as we might imagine. Nyema's love for Pádraic is arguably the truest thing in the book, but it still doesn't keep him on the ground.

The text appears as blank verse, although Ransmayr himself has spoken of 'flying lines' to go with his flying mountain. Some readers will find this too unconventional, but it does add to the dream-like quality of the novel. Towards the end, after Liam's death, Pádraic says: 'I sometimes have the feeling / that I must wake from another / and then another dream / to arrive at last where I really am.' Perhaps it's not surprising that most alpinists don't leap into such philosophical rabbit holes. Most of us don't intellectualise what we do in this way. Except that we love mountains because, as Dan Hooley suggests, they 'persistently escape human efforts to chart or control them.' Of course, that isn't really true: you can dam a river or place a bolt and the spell is broken. But that's what we're looking for. The climbing scenes in *The Flying Mountain* may not convince the expert eye but the extreme psychological ground it covers will feel familiar to others who have been there and are prepared to think, and think deeply, about what it is they learned.

*Ed Douglas*

**Unknown Pleasures**
Collected Writing on Life, Death, Climbing and
Everything in Between
Andy Kirkpatrick
*Vertebrate Publishing, 2018, pp232, £24*

For Andy Kirkpatrick writing is 'the urge to make a reality.' He explores many realities in this roller-coaster of a book, with their common denominator his unswerving fascination with himself. This has nothing of the congratulatory, of self-aggrandise-ment or hubris: instead it speaks of a constantly observing inner eye which pays attention to the smallest detail of his experiences and preoccupations in order to 'see the vital importance of the seemingly unimportant.'

He discovered his love of and skill at drawing from an early age and this helped him make the stories that his severe dyslexia prevented him from writing. He took the trouble to study the intricacies of his subjects, the nu-ances of their shapes and angles and he kept looking: artist and fledgling writer together. Climbs of extreme and extended difficulty became 'frozen puzzles' to unlock, drawn on the rock for those who take the time to see and have the skill to interpret. That Kirkpatrick has those skills is beyond doubt.

The long-delayed decision to test for dyslexia was finally made when he was sixteen and his papers produced a near-perfect score on the spatial test, eliciting a comment from the examiner that the best choice of career would be one that involved three-dimensional problem solving and crea-tivity. Little wonder then, that where others might find fear or self-doubt on seemingly impossible rock or ice, he sees pattern and possibility. His accounts of Scottish winter climbing, Yosemite ascents, struggles on the Dru and extended travails on the Troll Wall all bear this out.

He is adept at vivid descriptions, which place the hapless reader in these hostile environments: the Troll Wall is 'a brutalism set in stone.' His descriptive skills illuminate the book as a whole; he has learned to view writing, too, as a pattern which can be deconstructed and manipulated, beginning with the recounting of his social security days living on £24 a week amongst 'people who were spread as thin as they can be on their small slice of life.' He injects humour to leaven the grim realities of this life on the wrong side of government benevolence, especially when he offers a snapshot of his brief career as a Happy Shopper Cheddar thief.

The surreal has its place, too, as he takes a female celebrity presenter who has never climbed before up Moonlight Buttress in Zion National Park. Whilst the climbing element of the undertaking was difficult enough for his newly recruited partner, it was the lack of an indoor toilet on the wall that generated most anxiety for her. Kirkpatrick's account of teaching her the techniques of relieving oneself on a high, vertical wall are both cinematic and unflinching.

*Unknown Pleasures* encompasses far more than climbing experiences: Kirkpatrick's focus is wide-ranging and keen and his honesty is unswerving. This is particularly apparent when he writes about personal relationships. There is a confessional feel to his prose. His thoughts, 'a little raw, a bit edgy, car-crash uncomfortable', mine their way into his subject, think on their feet and the overspill of feeling carries the reader along. There's pride in his family, too; when his 13-year-old daughter climbs El Cap with him his joy in her achievement is matched by his admiration at her modesty.

His later essays step confidently into wider arenas, including political controversy: his piece on the SS massacre of the inhabitants of the village of Oradour-sur-Glane in WW2 is fuelled by a quiet anger and the grim satisfaction that the only child to survive the atrocity was a boy who disobeyed the soldiers' orders because he knew that Germans were bad and would hurt them all. This narrowing of focus, a spotlight on the exceptional, resonates throughout Kirkpatrick's work. The essay 'Everest Sucking on the Barrel' punches fast and hard, a short diatribe the pounds furiously along the well-worn path of climbing deaths on the mountain. Kirkpatrick wonders why there are not more when 'you consider the ratio between fuck-off scary mountain and clueless out-of-their-depth tourist.'

This is a beautifully bound edition on good-quality paper enlivened by Kirkpatrick's monochrome line drawings. All credit to Vertebrate Publishing for having it produced in the UK. This sort of quality is, of course, reflected in the price but it's a book well worth having on every level.

*Val Johnson*

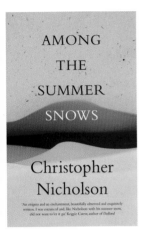

AMONG THE SUMMER SNOWS

Christopher Nicholson

'An enigma and an enchantment, beautifully observed and exquisitely written. I was entranced and, like Nicholson with his summer snow, did not want to let it go.' Reggie Carew, author of *Dadland*

## Among the Summer Snows
Christopher Nicholson
*September Publishing, 2017, pp170, £14.99*

A good writer should be able to make anything interesting, even lingering summer snow patches in the Highlands. But for the length of a whole book? Well, if it is then short-listed for the Boardman Tasker Award perhaps this is confirmation that it not only holds the reader but also offers a special sparkle in the prose. Holding the reader is achieved by structuring this book as a kind of detective's journey (from Kent!) for clues that lead to further clues around the Highlands's highest corries in August. But this is also a journey of 'a complication of thoughts and feelings': 'Within this complication, among much else – curiosity, admiration, melancholy, elation – is uncertainty … It's the lateness of the snow, the rareness of the snow, the improbability of the snow, that draw me up to the Highlands.' And already here's the sparkle of the prose, those emotional modulations that qualify uncertainty, and the rhythm of repetition that coveys obsession in that last sentence.

Partly because the author is regularly questioning the absurdity of his obsession and partly because of the sheer physical demands involved as he increasingly comes to feel his age, the reader is drawn into the roller coaster ride of Christopher Nicholson's in-the-moment emotions and lone walker's wandering mind: 'I even had a snow-related thought: that ice was water pretending to be a rock. No, ice was water trying to be a rock. Trying and failing, but trying. As humans yearn to escape gravity and fly like birds, do rocks ever yearn for the fluidity of water?' Then a Burns love poem comes to mind with the line 'Till … the rocks melt wi' the sun'. Literary memories like this are so lightly handled that they are accepted naturally as part of the rich cargo carried and informing Nicholson's quest that is really a journey into himself, alone since his wife died we are told, almost incidentally, at the beginning of the book. It is telling that the photographs, a surprisingly effective part of the book, are not captioned. This is far from a scientific survey. It's a personal quest to express the last unmelting, improbable, resilient and ridiculous reasons why we love being in mountains.

*Terry Gifford*

## The Magician's Glass
Ed Douglas
*Vertebrate Publishing, 2017, pp192, £14.95*

In these eight essays on climbing and the mountain life, Douglas goes on a quest to track down and reveal individual climbers behind their more public or popular persona. Not only does he examine and tease out their deeper motivations through detailed research, he explores their enduring impact on others, both during their lives and for many, after their deaths. The temptation when reading a collection such as this is to search for common threads, to understand the author's choice in assembling these particular eight essays. In this book the reader is presented with a conundrum. Certainly words such as ego, pride, freedom, spirituality, risk, commitment, love, loss and death appear frequently, but to paint all personalities with the same brush is both reductive and inaccurate. Maybe one common thread is that all these men had a need for the mountains more than a need for people? But that too is reductive and misses the point. What is clear is that their lives were (or are) not all that they might first appear and Douglas casts a shaft of light onto figures that, even with his revelations, remain intriguing.

The anthology starts with the story of Nick Colton and Tim Leach on Annapurna III; it is one of impressive commitment and bravery, and ultimately failure. It serves to justify the title of the book, reflecting on how these two individuals differently recall their shared experience. Not only were their lives affected, their views on climbing and its inherent risks were forever altered. With this essay, Douglas introduces the notion of climbing as an art form. He ends the book with an essay on Andy Parkin who has literally made climbing into an art form with his paintings and sculptures. Parkin himself makes reference to the likes of Joe Brown, Johnny Dawes and Ben Moon who have the ability to see and climb the rock in a way similar to that in which a sculptor creates his work of art. The stories in between allude to climbing as something much more than a sport or even a compulsion, often a deeper spiritual pilgrimage, as subject to interpretation and criticism as art itself.

Stories of Tomaz Humar, Patrick Edlinger and Ueli Steck, and even the more happy-go-lucky Kurt Albert, are of men passionate and driven in their climbing and in achieving success. They are compelling to their associates, godlike to admiring climbers, yet vulnerable to the demands of notoriety and the more pedestrian needs that infiltrate all our lives. The essay 'Stealing Toni Egger' is an attempt to reclaim the achievements of a young man whose life and death, purportedly on Cerro Torre, has been overshadowed by the stories surrounding his climbing partner, Cesare Maestri. A particularly sensitive interview with Egger's sister both elevates the memory of Toni and remembers him as a beloved and sorely missed brother.

All five died young: three in the mountains, one in a fall from a via ferrata, and one at home, each leaving a legacy of mystery alongside their impressive climbs. How, I wonder, would a verse in McGough's poem 'Let Me Die a Youngman's Death' read for mountaineers? 'Let me die a young-man's death / not a free from sin tiptoe in / candle wax and waning death / not a curtains drawn by angels borne / 'what a nice way to go' death.'

*The Magician's Glass* was shortlisted for the Boardman Tasker Award in 2017. There is no doubt that Douglas has a way with words, and his ability to delve rigorously and insightfully into the inner lives of climbers and the mountaineering world sets his writing at the pinnacle of mountain literature.

*Adele Long*

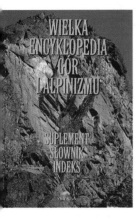

### Wielka Encyklopedia Gór i Alpinizmu
Compiled and edited by Jan and
Małgorzata Kiełkowski
*Stapis, 2003-2017, 620zł / £127, seven volumes, pp5402*

In the last three or four decades, several studious mountaineers have endeavoured to produce encyclopaedic works that cover both the entire mountain world and its connection to world mountaineering. Usually, this vast scale of information has been compressed into a single, rich volume. Outstanding in this respect, to mention one, was Edward Pyatt's *Guinness Book of Mountains and Mountaineering* (1980). But the vast scope of this subject clearly needed to be treated in several volumes. In 1975, the Italian publishing house De Agostini launched its eight-volume *Grande Enciclopedia Illustrata della Montagna*. In 2003, updating and greatly enlarging the Italian work, a Polish couple, Jan and Małgorzata Kiełkowski, began to publish in Polish their *Wielka Encyklopedia Gór i Alpinizmu* (Great Encyclopaedia of Mountains and Mountaineering). With its seventh and final volume now on the market, this Polish collection, the most ambitious accumulation of information about the topic ever known, reached its completion.

I hasten to confess that I know no Polish, but I believe any mountaineer more or less well versed with mountains everywhere and the development of mountaineering at home and abroad will be able to follow the Polish text of most entries. For many readers it could be a rewarding effort, since no other printed source will offer what this collection contains: accuracy, quantity and quality. Quantity, in this case, must be emphasized. The seven volumes total 5,402 pages. The text of most entries ends with a bibliography from international sources. Illustrations, in black and white, appear on almost every page of the entire set. Each volume also carries two sections of colour prints. Art illustrations, particularly European, often appear. The first volume, *Wprowadzenie*, works as a general dictionary of mountaineering in every aspect. Volumes II to V could be said to be the core of this ambitious encyclopaedia, since they treat mountain ranges, individual peaks and even small rock pinnacles on every continent. Charts and sketch-maps, simple and functional, appear in every one of these four volumes. Volume VI is purely biographical. It seems to me that no person could possibly dare to count the number of mountaineers included, but I risk to say this volume must contain at least eight thousand of them, with several thousand graced with a small portrait. The seventh and last volume, *Suplement / Slownik / Indeks*, carries some 1,600 additional biographical entries and portraits, a dictionary of international mountaineering terminology (from 108 different languages), an addenda and corrigenda section and closes with a massive index of 789 pages.

Such are the raw statistics. Some time the editors Jan and Małgorzata Kiełkowski will have to explain to their readers how they were able to accumulate so much information and such a large and varied number of illustrations. No doubt, the computer age with its 'memory' loaned a helping hand. And besides, a number of mountaineers from Europe and South America contributed information and photographs. But we must also keep in mind that the editors were experienced travellers, climbers and even explorers, having made first ascents in the Andes of central Peru. But still, this collection must represent on the part of the editors at least 15 years of hard work, patience, knowledge, correspondence and then even more hard work.

The practical usefulness and merits of this collection are evident. The wealth of its content will make it a reference work for constant consultation. Being so completely international it will also compel readers everywhere to become more knowledgeable about the mountain peaks of our whole planet and more aware of the accomplishments of those unknown explorers climbing mountains in their own distant lands. One can only hope that the entire set will be translated into other languages. Its illustrations alone will make readers realize that there are expeditions yet to be undertaken, new peaks still to be won, new routes yet to be braved, mythology still to be made and history yet to be learned.

*Evelio Echevarría*

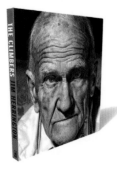

### The Climbers
Jim Herrington
Essay by Greg Child
Foreword by Alex Honnold
*Mountaineers Books, 2017, pp191, $60.00*

This is a sumptuous coffee-table book, taking in the realms of mountaineering, photography and fine art. Described in its blurb as a 'one-of-a-kind' collectors' volume', it is certainly a niche product and priced to match. It's also the outcome of the personal project and journey (in more ways than one) of Jim Herrington, known for his magazine photography of famous

Gwen Moffatt, among the very few women to feature in Jim Herrington's *The Climbers. (Jim Herrington / Mountaineers Books)*

American rock musicians but also a climber. For the past 18 years, he has turned his lens to capturing images of key figures from what he judges to be 'the golden age of mountaineering'.

The images, all black and white, are beautifully captured and reproduced and cover familiar and some unfamiliar names. They all qualify on grounds of serious contributions to climbing, from the micro (John Gill) to the macro (Reinhold Messner). Many were photographed in their last years or even their last days. Herrington certainly captures late life well: mixing vulnerability with obvious strength of character. For those climbers I knew more about, the portraits – by dint of clothes, location or expressions – were often hugely insightful of their histories and personalities. Maybe this isn't surprising given Herrington's day job (his photos have graced the covers of high-end fashion and lifestyle magazines) and a climber's appreciation of his subject's achievements and reputations. Capturing their humanity, often through the quotidian, is a useful levelling device and counterpoint to our imbued memory of their god-like years. Occasionally, symbolic props are a little too obvious (Joe Brown in an old cotton anorak?) or overly ironic (John Gill with an ice axe?). Some photos are just weird (Robert Gabriel in his underpants and long socks). But most of the images are simply stunning.

The choice of climbers is obviously personal and spans back to some early US pioneers, including Jules Eichorn, Glenn Exum, Glen Dawson and David Brower. European names are well represented: Cassin, Maestri, Paragot and so on. There are many less well-known climbers whose achievements deserve greater recognition. An accompanying essay by Greg Child – richly informative but necessarily selective – reveals and contextualises some of their achievements. I had no idea David Brower, of Sierra Club and Friends of the Earth fame, was a pioneer of desert rock climbing. But sometimes it feels Child is trying too hard to shoehorn all of this 'golden age' into a neat narrative, with some rather too obvious 'cap-doffing', including an all-too-short section on female climbers. But it's a personable account that doesn't shy away from questioning Herrington's 'bucket list' ethos. Here Child quotes from Voytek Kurtyka's frank but friendly 'thanks, but no thanks' letter: '... it's too difficult to take part in this spectacle which is, whatever the noble intention [...] behind it, a display of "the death of heroes" or with a bit of imagination "the march of death". Forgive me. I'm not ready yet.'

Despite its quirks, Herrington's project has done climbing history a service although its necessarily selective approach will raise hackles for some.

*Andy Tickle*

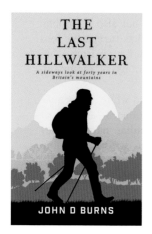

**The Last Hillwalker**
A Sideways Look at Forty Years
in Britain's Mountains
John D Burns
*John Burns, 2017, pp314, £9.99*

John Burns begins his book with a winter ascent of Green Gully on Ben Nevis. The ice is fragile, his protection is poor, he is struggling for footholds and night is falling. He heaves himself past an overhang, then teeters up a final stretch of ice-glazed rock to reach the security of the summit plateau. He brings up his partner and the two savour the dusk.

Inexperienced climber out of his depth on a dangerous route is a familiar trope, and there are more to come. A young man ventures into the hills and on to the rocks for the first time, poorly equipped, making mistakes, somehow surviving. He takes us to the Lakes and Highlands, summer and winter, walking and climbing with inadequate or second-hand equipment, teaching himself to navigate as he goes along. There are encounters with tyrannical Youth Hostel wardens (now, happily an extinct breed); epic drinking bouts; and the inevitable car-crash, while heading for the Highlands through the night in a Morris Marina, from which he crawls out almost unscathed.

At first Burns' self-deprecating rites of passage seems all too familiar. But he lures you on with his precise and witty writing, his eye for evocative detail and his ear for dialogue, together with a sense of both time and place. Gradually the innocent abroad matures into a climber who tests himself in the Alps and Yosemite, and then joins the Cairngorm Mountain Rescue team, at which point we discern that this *faux naif* is more accomplished and capable than he wanted to let on.

An intriguing personal story is laced through the narrative. Burns grew up in Bebington, Merseyside, studied sociology at Leicester in the 1970s and became a social worker in Yorkshire, followed by a posting in Inverness. For a time he believed he had achieved his nirvana, a salaried job in the Highlands. But then he made two abrupt decisions: he gave up both climbing and his salary in order to try his luck as a stand-up comedian. After achieving some success, he wrote a one-man play based on the life of Alesteir Crowley, followed by another about George Mallory. Both have the wit and rhythm of his writing, and I found the Mallory piece, which I saw at Kendal in 2016, poignant and affecting, notwithstanding some poetic exaggerations, which a Mallory biographer is likely to spot.

Following another epiphany, Burns returned to the hills, with the initial aim of rediscovering the joy of bothies. He now tells us how, walking to Ryvoan in the Cairngorms, he finds he is out of condition, overtaken by older walkers, feeling an imposter again. But the old sensations are rekindled, and he relates the pleasures of seeking out remote bothies, navigating through storms with map and compass, crossing swollen rivers, nights spent with chance companions or alone, experiences which lead him to evaluate the forty years of his life that the book has traversed.

The early explorations and transgressions assume a new context, so that his story is likely to appeal to mountaineers and beyond: about how we forge connections to the wild, how we can enjoy our own company, how we come through adversity and how we assess our lives. Not only is our tottering Green Gully leader a far better mountaineer than he initially implies, he is a gifted and elegiac writer, escorting us on a journey that we all must make.

*Peter Gillman*

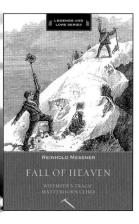

### Fall of Heaven: Whymper's Tragic Matterhorn Climb
Reinhold Messner
Translated by Billi Bierling
*Mountaineers Books, 2017, pp204, £15*

Much has been published on the first ascent of the Matterhorn but Whymper's letter to *The Times*, which appeared 25 days after the ascent, has remained the standard account. Whymper re-used this account in his book, *Scrambles amongst the Alps*, which was mostly written three years later during 1868, and this became his own accepted version of the climb over the last 40 years of his life.

The events of June and July 1865 make a wonderful tale of mountaineering success, chance meetings and national rivalry, in the middle of which were Whymper's astonishing six days of the Grandes Jorasses, the crossing of the Col Dolent and the Aiguille Verte. The drama of the summer culminated in two rival teams climbing on opposite sides of the mountain at the same time in a race to the unclimbed summit. The cast of characters – among them Whymper, Carrell, Hudson, Croz, McClintock, Francis Douglas, and (largely unknown to Whymper), Quintino Sella, Giordano and the aspirations of the Italian Alpine Club – only adds to the story.

Hence, to find that the legendary mountaineer Reinhold Messner had attempted to tell the story from the point of view of his compatriot Carrell, who played such a significant part in Whymper's life, was intriguing. Unfortunately, the book is disappointing. Credit is given to Alan Lyall's excellent bibliographic work on the Matterhorn ascent, but otherwise no use is made of the available resources on Whymper; anecdotes and, often incorrect, hearsay from different periods of Whymper's life are muddled together to give a simplistic view of a complex figure. As someone who worked for his living, Whymper was aware of the value of money, but he was not 'parsimonious' and could not be described as a 'dandy'. Conversations are created with no attributions; Whymper's book is randomly quoted as a record of events, but on other occasions is questioned. To say, as Messner does,

Gustav Doré's famous and famously imaginative lithograph of the first ascent of the Matterhorn: 'Arrival at the Summit'. He and Whymper met and both agreed that the £300 raised for the family of Michel Croz was 'not much for the life of a man'. For more on Doré's interpretation of the Matterhorn disaster, see A Lyall, 'The Matterhorn Lithographs of 1865', *Alpine Journal* 1995, pp215-21.

that Whymper was hoping to find an Inuit in Greenland to take him to the North Pole shows a surprising lack of historical knowledge, as well as an ignorance of Whymper's well documented trips to Greenland.

Messner is muddled about the events of 1865. That Whymper and Carrell climbed the Grand Tournalin in 1863, not 1865 as Messner says, is only one of many small errors. He wants to show that Carrell's foremost care was for the safety of his party, and that Whymper was a cavalier English *monsieur*, but he does not try to understand Whymper. He says that 'Old Taugwalder was responsible for Douglas, and he would never have put his client's life at risk,' while ignoring the near catastrophe on the Obergabelhorn, where Douglas and Taugwalder fell through the summit cornice but were, by good fortune, held by their companion Viannin. Such a selective choice of which events to describe characterises Messner's book. It is disappointing that Messner does not use his undoubted knowledge of climbing to understand what it was actually like to be on the ridges of the Matterhorn in the 1860s. He questions why Croz was first on the rope descending, but this was exactly what Hudson and Croz had done one week earlier on the Aiguille Verte.

Messner does quote Whymper's words to imply that Whymper spent the rest of his life avoiding responsibility, and blaming the Taugwalders, but the real problem was that no one had responsibility, as Whymper well knew. Whymper was not directly involved in the accident, was not involved in arranging either the descent or roping up (although with hindsight he knew he should have been). The euphoria of finally succeeding, seeing the Italians still below them, the summit untrodden, and the lack of agreement about who was actually in charge – Hudson, Croz or Whymper – led to carelessness on the descent.

Whymper in public was always considerate of the deceased but in private knew that Hadow should not have been there, and that Hudson was at fault in not belaying his young friend correctly. Whymper also knew that he should have been more involved, that someone should have been in charge, and this haunted him for the rest of his life. Whymper did criticise the behaviour of the Taugwalders on the descent, but he always paid credit to Old Peter's feat of holding his position and his prompt belay, and ruefully recognised that if the rope had not broken, he would not have survived.

Whymper made no further entry in his journal after 2 July, so our knowledge of the events leading up to the ascent and the accident itself is dependent on what Whymper made public, but no one who spent any of this time with Whymper, for example Girdlestone and Lucy Walker, contradicted his account. It is therefore disappointing that Messner misses the opportunity to give an informed view from the Italian side, and merely relies on preconceived dislike of Whymper.

*Ian Smith*

**Classics Routes in the Écrins**
A Mountaineering Guide
Sébastien Constant
*Éditions Constant, pp192, 2018, £27.95*

Seb Constant is a well-known and experienced mountain guide based in L'Argentière-La-Besse in the east of the Écrins and is an expert in those parts of the southern Alps – the Écrins itself, Cerces, Queyras – which are wilder and less travelled than the main centres like Chamonix and consequently more appealing to those who like their mountains a bit more *sauvage*. This useful little guidebook offers a rich selection of the best low and middle-grade routes in the broader Écrins from snow and ice, to mixed and pure rock climbs. 'So many of the routes presented here,' Constant writes, 'were pioneered by W A B Coolidge in the 1870s that this book could have been entitled In Coolidge's Footsteps. In fact, I have long drawn inspiration, in both my writings and my climbing, by his approach to mountaineering.' For those familiar with Coolidge's taste for controversy, this might seem surprising, but Constant is clear in his admiration, quoting from the preface of the 1905 guidebook to *The Central Alps of the Dauphiny*, co-authored with Henri Duhamel and Félix Perrin: 'It is only by the joint labours of many that our book can be made, as we earnestly desire it to be, the standard work for climbers who propose to explore the highest mountain group lying entirely within French territory.' This book sets itself up as that pioneering work's successor. Alongside more famous climbs, Constant has included a number of lesser-known objectives culled from his decades of experience and finishes with ten multi-day alpine tours, including, as an example, a six-day tour of the Ailefroide, starting at the Sélé hut, an east to west traverse of the Col du Sélé to the Pilatte hut, an ascent of Les Boeufs Rouges, the traverse of Mont Gioberney via the Says glacier to the Temple Écrins hut, an ascent of the Col des Avalanches and a return to Ailefroide via the Col de la Temple. As Constant regularly mentions, you need to be fit, especially in a region largely free of cable cars. Beautifully illustrated, clear and concise, the paucity of modern guidebooks to the Écrins makes this a more than welcome addition.

**Farewell to Yak and Yeti?**
The Sherpas of Rolwaling Facing
a Globalised World
Ruedi Baumgartner
Foreword by Ngawang Tenzing Lama
*Vajra Books, pp315, 2015, £32.50*

As it should be, Sherpas are increasingly reflecting for themselves on their meteoric journey: from
remote pastoralists and farmers, via mountaineering,
to an international diaspora that spans the world.
This book, for example, has a blurb from the Sherpa
sociologist Pasang Sherpa, who has written his own
book on the subject. How to explain and comprehend such a rapid and
disorienting journey? The Sherpa community in Brooklyn is these days
bigger than that of Khumbu. Eighty percent of Rolwaling Sherpas had
settled in Kathmandu at the time of the last census in 2011. What is it,
if anything, that holds these remarkable people together? 'To know where
to go, we need to know where we came from,' Pasang writes, and so this
long perspective is vitally useful. Ruedi Baumgartner first visited the Rolwaling, Khumbu's near neighbour, in the 1970s to conduct his PhD research
and has worked in development aid ever since. This is his account of the
change in Rolwaling Sherpa society over the past 40 years, covering three
generations that have seen as much change as any other since the migration
of Tibetan communities across the great divide got underway.

Mountaineering has been one of the catalysts in this transformation.
(One Sherpani quoted in this book recounts how when her husband was
working on expeditions, he earned more than she did running their restaurant. When he was trekking, it was the other way round. That's what
climbing can mean in Nepal.) Longstanding relationships with western
climbers gave Sherpas opportunities denied other marginalised groups in
Nepal. That economic leverage led on to improved education so that the
children of climbing Sherpas didn't need to take their lives in their hands
to offer a better future to their children. (It's interesting that local monks
were suspicious of the Hillary school built in Rowaling. Secular education
might persuade young Sherpas to join the police or the army, where they
might be required to kill. There is a hint here as well of the suspicion of
the Nepali state, which had marginalised ethnic minorities for centuries.)
You can track this process to increasingly remote corners of the Sherpa
world. Rolwaling Sherpas, off the beaten track in comparison to Khumbu,
were consequently later to the game and had to struggle for their place in the
sun but have taken a similar road since. Everest guides will tell you that it is
increasingly difficult to find good Sherpa workers on the mountain even as it
transforms their economic stars. Given the risks and exploitation they have
experienced, the worst of it from local operators, even Sherpa operators,
it's hardly surprising that Sherpas are moving on from climbing. Equally,

the culturally rich and physically demanding world that existed before tourism – yak herding and potato cultivation – is also under threat.

Although he is an academic, Baumgartner is a lively writer, mixing personal stories, history and a firm grasp on the literature to produce a valuable and important book, one which many climbers with an interest in Himalayan culture would do well to acquire. Something like a quarter of Nepali mountain guides thus far qualified are from Rolwaling, including the first and only woman, Dawa Yangzum; it's a district with a central place in the mountaineering scene in Nepal. Beautifully illustrated, the highlight for me among the many excellent photographs was Tom Weir's portrait from 1952 of the six-year-old Lama Thupten Zopa Rinpoche, one of the founders of the Kopan monastery in Kathmandu. A curiosity to Weir, this small, self-possessed boy would go on to carry the resurgence of Buddhism in Nepal to the capital, propelled there in part by a transformation in Nepali society that had mountaineering as its catalyst. We should tread carefully, because we so often know not what we do.

*Ed Douglas*

# Obituaries

Capt C J Reid (?1875-1915), Royal Warwickshire Regiment,
killed in a Turkish counterattack at Gallipoli.

# In Memoriam

As usual, the editor will be pleased to receive obituaries for any of those above not included in the following pages.

## John Ashburner
## 1944 - 2017

John Edward Ashburner, who died on 5 May 2017 at the age of 73 after a five-year battle with cancer, was born in Hest Bank, Lancashire and raised in Chellaston, Derby. John had the good fortune to attend Derby School when it was run by Leslie Bradley, a disciple of Kurt Hahn. The school maintained a strong emphasis on both academic and outdoor pursuits, and John's vintage entry year of 1955 included two other boys, Rod Gallagher and Brian Chase (*AJ* 1988-9, pp322-3), who with John were destined to become excellent mountaineers at a young age.

John Ashburner in the Hindu Kush in 1966.

Their early forays occurred under the auspices of the Duke of Edinburgh's (DoE) Award scheme and the Combined Cadet Force, but it was a young master at the school, Bob Pettigrew, who would prove transformational. Bob became their mentor, instilling in the boys self-reliance and the unspoken rule to leave no one behind. Trips to the mountains followed and excursions included classics such as Striding Edge, Crib Goch and Scafell. They began rock climbing on Tryfan's Milestone Buttress and on gritstone outcrops closer to home, such as Black Rocks at Cromford. By the summer of 1960, aged 16, John was leading Very Severe rock climbs, and the group had climbed in winter on snow and ice in Scotland as well as Wales and the Lakes. They climbed with Doug Scott who was a couple of years older and who had also been a pupil of Bob Pettigrew. Meanwhile they all completed the DoE gold award, receiving their awards from Prince Philip himself at St James' Palace.

Thus, when they entered the sixth form they were already thinking beyond the UK for their next adventures. Bob Pettigrew packed them off to Saas Fee for a first Alpine season in 1961, unaccompanied, guideless and all aged just 17. Their preparations included walking the fourteen 3,000ers in Snowdonia in about 18 hours. Also, that summer half term, John led *Longland's* on Clogwyn Du'r Arddu on sight, without any of the modern aids and few of the old ones. His run-out took almost all their available rope and he wore ordinary climbing boots.

The choice of Saas Fee could not have been better. They enjoyed perfect weather and moved from hut to hut taking in more than a dozen peaks.

John, Rod and Brian's second alpine season the following year was divided between Zermatt, Zinal and Arolla before a move to Chamonix in deteriorating weather. They realised the key to the Hörnli ridge of the Matterhorn was simply to go up ahead of the crowd and after that they went on to climb Dom, Zinalrothorn and the Obergabelhorn traverse, Täschhorn, Weisshorn, Breithorn and Dent d'Hérens, Mont Collon, Besso, Aiguille de la Tsa and Mont Blanc de Cheilon.

Thus John Ashburner and Brian Chase, two very different characters, were already both fine rock climbers and experienced young mountaineers when they went up to Cambridge, King's and Christ's Colleges, to read engineering and natural sciences respectively. On arrival, both were accepted into the inner circle of the CUMC, and in due course John became secretary the year Brian was president (1965–6). During his first long vacation in 1964, he climbed in the Dauphiné and in Chamonix with D L Bevan climbing the Mer de Glace face of the Aiguille du Grépon.

Early in our second year John told me that he needed somewhere wilder, more uncertain and more distant than the Alps, though preferably with better weather, and to that end jumped at my proposed expedition to climb in the Ala Dağ range in southern Turkey in the summer of 1965. I already knew John as the friendliest and most modest of the CUMC rock stars and was thrilled to have him on board as the lead climber. Our party of six drove out to Turkey in an overloaded Bedford minibus, but we didn't pick John up until we reached the Dolomites. There we found him being discharged from hospital in Cortina following an epic ascent with Bob Keates of the north face of the Cima Ovest di Lavaredo, which he described in *Cambridge Mountaineering* (1966) in an article entitled '*Un Bruta Aventura*' ('Quite a little adventure … '). A combination of severe weather with serious route-finding difficulties had led to multiple bivouacs, and their route ultimately combined pieces of both the *Swiss–Italian* and *Cassin* routes.

Moving on towards Istanbul, the team paid a visit to Sidney Nowill, AC member and Turkish mountaineering expert, at his home there for last-minute advice. Then it was across the Bosporus, most of us for the first time. We left our minibus in Çamardı at the foot of the Ala Dağ and used donkeys to set up base camp in the Kara Yalak gorge. During a month and a half of settled weather, we clocked up more than 20 peaks, including several first British ascents and traverses, one on the highest peak, Demirkazık (3756 m). While many of our routes were relatively easy, John led several hard lines, including a new route on the north wall of Direktaş (Yedi Göl area). John's climbing report in the form of a 'Brief Guide' (*Cambridge Mountaineering*, 1966) became a key source for future climbers.

During the next long vacation, John teamed up with Henry Edmundson who had been climbing in Kishtwar with Charlie Clarke's expedition the previous summer. I was delighted to be invited, and we settled on the Afghan Hindu Kush, driving there in a second-hand Land Rover. Research led us to the Darrah-e-Abi ('Blue Valley') leading up from the village of Iskasr, just above the confluence of the Anjuman and Munjan rivers. The approach march up the Panjshir valley and over the Anjuman pass took two weeks with horses and then donkeys. We made first ascents of six peaks including Rast Darrah (5959m), the highest in the Darrah-e-Abi, according to an old aeroplane altimeter. Leaving, we crossed a difficult pass into Nuristan before returning to the road after almost seven weeks on the march. The expedition ticked almost every box (*AJ* 1967, pp65-75).

After Cambridge, John obtained a VSO posting in Allahabad, India, a springboard for little-visited parts of the Himalaya. In 1967 he joined an expedition led by Bob Pettigrew to attempt the first ascent of Papsura (6451m) in Kullu. Disaster struck when Bob and two other expedition members slid 2,000ft down a 70° slope in a couloir avalanche. Bob sustained a dislocated hip whilst the others were badly shaken but uninjured. John rushed to the scene and immediately improvised a stretcher from an air mattress, skis and aluminium pickets, lashed together with a climbing rope. With the Sherpa Pasang Lhakpa he then made a series of double marches, over heavily crevassed glaciers and steep rock spurs, to reach the Kullu valley and raise the alarm. Without resting, he recruited a rescue team of hill men and returned at once to supervise Bob's evacuation to hospital in Manali. During their absence, teammates Geoffrey Hill and Colin Pritchard climbed the mountain (*AJ* 1968, pp158-66). Hill tragically died on Mukar Beh (6070m), also in Kullu, later that year. Word of that accident reached Pettigrew who was still bed-bound with his dislocated hip. He cabled Ashburner in Allahabad, who travelled back to Kullu to organise a search party in Manali and succeeded in recovering the bodies of Hill and his three companions. John's most notable Himalayan climb was on that same peak, Mukar Beh, the following year (*AJ* 1969, pp58–66). With Sonam Wangyal, a Ladakhi high-altitude porter, John made a long and intricate first ascent traversing several subsidiary peaks en route. By now he had been elected to AC membership, serving on the AC Committee in 1972.

At the Allahabad Agricultural Institute John worked on agricultural machinery development, an area he continued to pursue on returning to the UK. In 1968, he took an appointment as lecturer at the National College of Agricultural Engineering (later Silsoe College) in Bedfordshire, while completing a PhD on tractor safety. There was time in 1969 to join a University of London Graduate Mountaineering Club expedition to the Kristians glacier area of East Greenland (*AJ* 1970, pp240-2). Thereafter a long and distinguished career as an agricultural engineer specialising in rural development overseas began in earnest, initially on British aid projects in Chile and Ecuador, and then, from 1981, in Algeria and Niger for the UN's Food and Agriculture Organisation (FAO).

From 1989 he became an independent consultant working worldwide, based in Ecuador where he met his wife Patty (née San Martín), where they built their family home at 3,000m on the slopes of the Rucu Pichincha volcano overlooking Quito. The family moved to the UK in 1997, and in 2000 John returned to the FAO as senior agricultural engineer in its regional office for Africa, based in Accra, Ghana. John worked for the

FAO until his retirement in 2006 and promptly resumed his consultancy. From his early days as an expert on the engineering of animal traction through to his return to the Panjshir valley decades after the Hindu Kush expedition to assess the mineral resources offered by derelict Russian tanks and other military hardware, to his final years as a prominent advocate of 'conservation agriculture' as a means to promote enhanced food security, John made his mark. His CV included eight books and more than 100 other publications and reports in English, French and Spanish.

John's youthful mountaineering publications appear in the *AJ* and elsewhere. Recently, after celebrating the life of fellow climber Dick Isherwood at a memorial weekend in Cumbria in 2013, it was John who undertook to compile an anthology of Dick's writings and published *Dick Isherwood: Mountaineer* in 2014.

John's last five years were hard, cancer of the larynx robbing him of his voice. But he remained courageous and good-humoured to the last – and Patty and their daughters Wendy and Jenny never ceased to be cheerful and effective interpreters. John lived to see the 50th anniversaries of his Cambridge expeditions and to celebrate in fine style. Torn from us slowly and painfully, all of us who had the privilege of sharing his life will remember the man with immense gratitude and affection.

John's own writing gives a flavour of what mountains meant to him. Here he is, writing about a first trip to Snowdon: 'Although agony at the time, I still remember the beautiful sight in the valley once day had broken. The colours, the surrounding cliffs and the general magic of the surroundings ... Progress was slow and tiring ... It seemed strange that anyone could think of taking pleasure from such an excursion. The summit was reached, but I felt none of the sense of achievement one reads about. The air was bitterly cold, and I was exhausted. We proceeded down the Crib Goch ridge. It narrowed, and momentarily the mist parted to reveal sheer drops on either side. Something stirred within me, and it was not fear. It was perhaps my first experience of the indescribable sensation which affects climbers at odd times and in odd places, and draws us back to the hills time and again.'

*Paul Newby et al*

## Fred Beckey
### 1923 - 2017

There are so many superlatives in modern climbing that it's often difficult to sort the wheat from the chaff. But when the name Fred Beckey comes up, there's no question of his place in mountaineering history: he was simply the greatest American climber of the 20th century. Physically, his climbs stretched from Alaska to Mexico and were crafted on all manner of mountain terrain, from the loosest desert sandstone to iron-like Bugaboo granite; mentally, his climbs clobbered the imagination, a perfect realisation of those oft-sought aesthetics of line, location and movement.

Fred Beckey with his friend Megan Bond, author of a forthcoming biography of America's most prolific climber. *(Cameron Burns)*

Fred Beckey's passion for exploration kept him climbing for eight decades. *(Cameron Burns)*

Wolfgang Paul Gottfried Beckey was born on 14 January 1923 in Zulpich, near Düsseldorf, during the years after the First World War when the country was reeling economically from the Treaty of Versailles. Young Fred moved with his family, father Klaus, a physician, mother Marta Maria, an opera singer, and newly born brother Helmut or 'Helmy', to Seattle in 1925.

Fred's parents liked car-camping trips and growing up Fred and Helmy were exposed to the rivers, lakes, and valleys of north Washington's majestic mountains. It didn't take Fred long before the mountains themselves became the goal. On an early trip to Olympic Hot Springs, 13-year-old Fred saw and decided to climb Boulder Peak, a 5,672ft mountain in the Olympics – alone.

'The story of these early years is one of self-doubt and self-reliance, the excitement and ecstasy of every moment of fresh adventure and chance for bravery,' Fred wrote in *Challenge of the North Cascades*. His concerned parents enrolled him in the scouts – Fred was assigned to 'Comet Patrol' – and under the tutelage of Leon Allers, Fred and his newfound friends hiked extensively in the mountains. In 1937, Fred joined a scout trip that covered 75 miles in the Olympics, climbing The Brothers and other peaks between the Hamma Hamma and Dosewallips rivers. Additional scout trips followed, including multiday cross-country ski trips, which culminated in a 1938 ascent of Mount Olympus.

'Scouting had its alpine limitations, of course, and through the suggestion of scout leaders … I joined the Mountaineers in the fall of 1938 as a junior member,' Fred wrote. 'In spring 1939, I took the climbing course.' With like-minded climbers Bob Craig, Jim Crooks, Ed Kennedy, Bob Lee, Wayne Swift, Lloyd Anderson, founder of REI, and others, Fred reached 35 summits during the summer of 1939, including the first ascent of Mount Despair, a 7,296ft peak in the North Cascades. That number astonished the local hard men, for whom a summer that included 20 successful summits was a banner season. He and brother Helmy also got as far as the Tetons and climbed 'all of the main peaks,' including the Grand.

By 1940, Fred was immersed in Cascades exploration and experiment-ing with aid climbing. During the summers of 1940 and 1941, the number of summits Fred & Co reached was, at 50, smaller, but the quality of the climbing had risen to a level Cascade climbers had never seen. Of those 50 ascents, half were firsts, and included peaks like Forbidden, Gunsight, Fisher, Inspiration, Crooked Thumb, Phantom, Twin Spires and Cloudcap. By then, 17-year-old Fred Beckey was considered the leading explorer of the continent's most significant alpine range south of the 49th parallel.

The following year, 1942, was the most important of Beckey's early climbing life. Aged 19, and with his younger brother Helmy, he made the second ascent of Mount Waddington (4019m) in British Columbia. Waddington's first ascent had come after 16 attempts spread across two decades. Fritz Wiessner, who nearly made the first ascent of K2 in 1939, and partner Bill House conquered the 'mystery peak' in 1936. So the sec-ond ascent was a huge prize for the Beckey brothers. Waddington was also the early culmination of a dual-pronged philosophy the Beckeys adopted during their extensive 1939–41 Cascades period: first, *really* exploring, seeing mountains and walls other people wouldn't really know about until decades later; second, and perhaps explaining why Beckey would remain such a force in the climbing world, is that the brothers were delving into the limits of physical endurance, traveling huge distances through impossi-ble scrub and across maddening mountain terrain to apply their advanced climbing skills on outlandish-looking peaks no one had ever heard of.

By the mid-1940s, Helmy had 'retired' from mountaineering, but Fred was just starting: the next stage of his career involved much bigger trips, striking out for climbing objectives that were often hundreds, even thou-sands of miles away. In 1946, he made his second expedition to Alaska and climbed Kates Needle and the Devils Thumb, both firsts. The late 1940s and 1950s saw Beckey continue on a heavy diet of alpine goals, mostly in Alaska and Canada, where he made first ascents of peaks like Hunter and Deborah, and climbed the huge *North-west Buttress* of Denali, the third route on the peak.

In the mid-1950s, Beckey tried his hand at the expedition game when he was invited to join an international team attempting Lhotse. High on the mountain, a storm turned Beckey and his Swiss climbing partner, Bruno Spirig, around. Beckey reportedly left Spirig, who was sick and suffering hallucinations, and descended. Stories circulated, including unfounded rumours, and Beckey was less than enamoured by the expedition exper-ience. It was one reason Beckey's climbing never again strayed far from the metrics he'd established in adolescence: a small team, reliable people, hard objective, fight like hell. It was also the reason a climber of his calibre was overlooked for the American 1963 Everest expedition.

Those metrics also matched Beckey's development as a climber. By the early 1960s, his sheer technical ability on both rock and ice put him in a realm that included only a handful of American climbers and arguably fewer European climbers, most of whom were either vastly experienced rock technicians, like Yosemite's hard men, or talented alpinists, such as the Teton climbers of the day, but not both. Few other contemporaries were as well rounded as Beckey.

Then there were the road trips. Early in his career, Beckey began to think little of the vast distances that separated him and the climbs he wanted to do. He would regularly drive a thousand miles to attempt something. If thwarted by unmanageable personalities, the weather, or just a bug up his ass, he might then turn around and drive a thousand miles to another objective. He was always on the move, always reaching for the next great climb, always searching for the next horizon.

As he moved beyond the Cascades, and Alaska, and Canada, all of which he returned to sporadically anyway, his first ascents began to include towers in the deserts of the South-west, walls in the Wind Rivers, clean white Sierra Nevada faces, and facets of just about every other mountain range in the Lower 48. His name can be found hundreds of times in guidebooks of all persuasion, mostly attached to now-classic climbs.

Early on, Beckey's keen intelligence prompted a literary career that, like his climbing, would span generations. His publishing activities started nearly 70 years ago when he wrote a *Climber's Guide to the Cascades and Olympics of Washington* for the American Alpine Club (1949). His iconic, three-volume *Cascade Alpine Guide* has been in print for decades, and his other books, ranging from coffee-table fantasies like *The Mountains of North America* and *Mount McKinley: Icy Crown of North America* to the dizzyingly researched 527-page *Range of Glaciers* about the history of the North Cascades, are masterworks. Starting in 1942, Beckey wrote 22 feature articles and hundreds of reports for the *American Alpine Journal*. As *AAJ* editor Dougald MacDonald noted in 2014: 'No climber in the 88-year history of the *AAJ* has written more reports or had more climbs cited in these pages than Fred Beckey.'

He never sought recognition for his climbs. In a 1994 interview, Don Liska, Beckey's late, legendary climbing partner, told me he'd written a letter to Jimmy Carter in an attempt to get Beckey a medal or some sort of presidential decree. When I told Beckey about it, his reaction was: 'But who cares about that stuff?'

In his later decades, he struggled to keep up with his own desire for more rock, new places and vivid experiences, and although the 1970s and 1980s were reasonable in terms of his new-route output and travel, by the 1990s he was starting to slow down. Climbing with Beckey, as I did between 1991 and 2000, you could see the frustration on his face. Still, it was also obvious that he enjoyed living out of his car, not washing for days or weeks, and stealing Fed-Ex envelopes to use as a makeshift filing cabinet along with condiments from fast-food restaurants. As he always had, he still loved living without rules.

In the 2000s, he continued making trips across the globe, notably several to China, but his aging body couldn't do what his brain was anticipating, and most of the time he came away empty-handed. Beckey also enjoyed shocking his climbing partners with bursts of profanity, and comments with the sort of prejudice that these days can prompt a social media storm. Yet, although he presented himself at times as something of a base and foul character, he had a keen intellect. In 1997, during a 10-day stay at my home, he grunted out a command that: 'I need to send an email to Lindsay Griffin.' I set him up with my computer, and after an hour and a half, came back into my office to read some of the most commanding and absorbing language ever written about mountains and geology. It was, literally, unbelievable. 'Send it, will ya?' he grunted. 'I'm hungry.'

In a decade of occasional adventures, I never felt like I was Fred's friend. He never asked for anything, except perhaps the rack, as he'd sized up whatever we were doing long before we got there and knew the plot, page by page. He was, in short, a climbing machine. A lot of climbers seem to feel the same way; I hear them calling themselves 'former Beckey partners' and such, but no one, as far as I can tell, was ever Fred's friend. I don't think anyone was ever really close to Fred, except perhaps Megan Bond, who became Fred's best friend in the mid-1990s, and eventually his biographer in the mid-2000s. Her biography is due out in 2020.

Perhaps it will reveal more about the astonishing drive that kept Beckey going for so long. Climbing partners and friends have often wondered about this perfect storm of motivation: his drive, his upbringing, his route tally, his gear, his next goal, his 'secret sauce,' and even if the bonks he suffered on his head over the years affected his judgment. But one outcome is undeniable: Fred Beckey's mountaineering career has never and will never be surpassed by any American mountaineer.

*Cameron M Burns*

*John Porter writes:* Back in the 1960s, when I was a student at the University of Oregon and not too far away from Washington, we all idolised Fred. But our paths didn't cross until I had the pleasure of editing his interview for *Mountain* magazine in 1975. The last time I saw him was at the Old Crown in Hesket Newmarket where he gave a talk to the Hesket Spiders in 2013. As AC vice president, I had the pleasure of introducing Fred and announcing to everyone that he had just been made an honorary member of the Alpine Club. With a wide grin, he stood up and shook my hand: 'Well that's really swell. I'll put that straight on my CV.' It was quite the CV. Fred was undoubtedly North America's most prolific alpinist with too many routes to remember. His was a life lived in and for the mountains.

*Stephen Venables writes:* In November 1996 I was speaking at the annual gathering of the American Alpine Club in New York. At midday I escaped the conference room to find some food, and found myself in a Manhattan sandwich bar chatting with another speaker at the conference: a grizzled, wiry, septuagenarian with a stubbly face as deeply furrowed as the canyons of the wild west. Dreaming aloud in a gravely croak, he reeled off names of all the Himalayan mountains and valleys he still hoped to visit. Then, pulling out a wad of grubby greenbacks, he paid for my lunch and beer. It was only afterwards that it dawned on me just how privileged I had been. This was the man who never had any money: the original climbing bum, the mountain tramp who had spent 70 years on the road, scrounging and making do, living out of the back of cars, stashing odds and ends at friends' houses all over the USA. This was also the man who had made more first ascents than anyone else in America. In fact he had probably made more first ascents, than anyone, anywhere in the world. And he had bought me lunch.

## Adrian Clifford
## 1955 - 2017

Adrian Clifford, a well-known and respected GP in Keswick, died suddenly and unexpectedly at home on 8 September 2017. He became a GP in Keswick in 2001, was a member of the Keswick Mountain Rescue Team, and although retired as a GP in 2013, he qualified as a holder of the UK UIAA/ICAR/ISMM diploma of mountain medicine just six months before his death.

He was born in 1955, and studied medicine at the University of Edinburgh where he was an active member of the mountaineering club. It was as a junior hospital doctor, on a EUMC meet, that he introduced Joe Simpson to snow and ice climbing in the winter of 1980. Memories differ, Simpson recalls in his *Game of Ghosts* that the climb was *Red Gully*, Clifford remembers it as *Spiral Gully*,

Adrian Clifford on *Thomsons Route* (IV), Ben Nevis, in March 2009.

in Coire an t-Sneachda. The climb was nearly finished when the pair witnessed the abrupt, spectacular and uncontrolled descent of Nick Rossiter from the adjacent *Rundle*, fortunately without consequent injury.

When Adrian applied for full membership of the Club in 2005, he had amassed considerable experience on classic mixed routes in the Alps, and many snow and ice routes, which he preferred to rock, and made a number of first ascents in the Lake District, including several on Black Crag in Ennerdale. He was the doctor and support climber for two expeditions to the Himalaya led by Mal Duff. In 1981 to Nuptse and in 1984 to the Muztagh Tower, described in Andrew Greig's lively account, *Summit Fever*: 'Medicine is the first thing in his life and he takes his role as expedition doctor very seriously. He doesn't like or approve of risk, yet courts it.'

His professional career as an RAF doctor took him to Germany and the Falkland Islands. Later he was a GP in Lincolnshire, before he returned to the mountains he loved around Keswick. He had many climbing friends in the Fylde Mountaineering Club of which he was a long-term member. He is remembered with great affection in the spring 2018 edition of the *Fylde Mountaineering Club Magazine*.

His interest in the great outdoors was wide ranging, extending from climbing to running, swimming, scuba diving, skiing, sky diving and flying micro-lights. He was fortunate to be able to continue to enjoy all these activities until his end.

*Roderick Smith*

*Sandy Allan writes:* I first met Adrian when he came to Muztagh Tower in Pakistan for our 1984 expedition when he was invited by Mal Duff to be the doctor for our expedition. He was an incredibly nice man and excellent doctor. He was rather shy about his climbing abilities but turned out to be a very competent mountaineer. I last saw Adrian climbing on Ben Nevis the winter season before his surprising untimely death and he was overflowing with enthusiasm for climbing and always keen to share tales. He was indeed a very active climber and is sorely missed.

*Andrew Greig writes:* I got to know Adrian on our Muztagh Tower expedition in 1984. I loved his sense of mischief and enthusiasm that sat alongside serious dedication to his role of team medic as well as support climber. Both came into play when in Askole. He was asked to treat a sick yak that had been badly scarred by a snow leopard. He estimated its bodyweight and injected it with a large part of the expedition's antibiotics. On his way back from the hill, the yak had recovered, and he was fêted as a star in Askole. Adrian was an orderly person who rather enjoyed disorder, and as such was an excellent friend and apt member of our team. We miss and mourn him.

## Nicholas Scarth Dixon
## 1930 - 2017

Nicholas Scarth Dixon, my maternal uncle, was born on 13 January 1930, in Rugby, third and youngest child of Mr and Mrs William Scarth Dixon, his father being an AC member and headmaster of a prep school, Hillbrow, which Nick attended. Hillbrow was evacuated to Featherstone Castle in Northumberland in 1940 when its building in Rugby, Overslade, was damaged by bombs. All the windows were blown out on the night of the biggest German bombing raid on Coventry. From the age of 10 therefore Nick was brought up in the wilds of Northumberland in accommodation not dissimilar to a mountain hut, the 13th century castle affording rather basic facilities.

His father's enthusiasm for mountaineering meant Nick was surrounded with pictures of mountains on the school walls and the proximity of the Lake District provided the opportunity to venture out on the fells. It was not only a love of the mountains that Nick inherited from his father but also strong links to Switzerland, his father, together with J A B Bruce, having helped form the Association of British Members of the Swiss Alpine Club (ABMSAC) and funded the Britannia hut at whose opening in 1912 he and Bruce were present.

Nicholas Dixon

After leaving Hillbrow, Nick continued his education at Oundle School and from 1951 Gonville and Caius College, Cambridge, where he studied history and theology and won his oars in the college first boat. After a year at Westcott House Anglican Theological College in Cambridge he was ordained deacon in 1956 at Carlisle Cathedral. His ministry thereafter was largely in Cumbria, near his beloved Lake District with spells away in Aden, where he was chaplain to the forces in 1959-62, and Norfolk, as rector at Blofield in the Diocese of Norwich 1970-77. He enjoyed getting out into the mountains in Aden, although an occasion when he was nearly shot at discouraged further explorations; in Norfolk he found the country a bit flat, although it was a comfort that he was less likely to be shot at, unless, of course, it was for a disagreement with an 'over-zealous evangelical'.

He did his national service in Gibraltar and Wales before going up to Caius. History doesn't relate whether he climbed on the rock of Gibraltar. However, back home a story is told that he took a group of boys to Snowdonia and is remembered for leaving them to tackle the tricky mountain ridges on their own and then meeting them with an elaborate tea after their exploits. At this time, he climbed numerous routes in the Lakes and in Scotland, Skye being a favourite haunt.

At Cambridge he joined the University Mountaineering Club and with them in 1953 went to the Pennine Alps where, blessed with good weather, he completed nine major routes including a traverse of the Matterhorn via the Hörnli and Italian ridges. Nick was known for his absentmindedness, his mind being 'on a higher plane', his family said, and so it was not entirely out of character that on arrival at the Italian border post Nick found he had left his passport at the Hörnli hut and had to return via the Theodul pass to collect it.

Nick had further Alpine seasons in 1956, 1958 and 1960, mainly in the

Zermatt area, before being accepted for membership of the Alpine Club in 1961, proposed by Christopher Simpson and supported by his father and Johnny Walker, another schoolmaster. The 1958 season was an exception, Nick taking a youth group from his parish in Walney Island to the Austrian Alps. All his Alpine climbing was guideless, save for the Austrian visit when two guides were hired and undertaken with Cambridge or family climbing partners. Looking at his AC application I note with interest the familiarity of the peaks climbed, the same ones I have climbed, not knowing I was following in family footsteps, some of which his father had also climbed before him: Dom, Matterhorn, Allalinhorn, Weissmies, Portjengrat, Nadelhorn, Mont Blanc de Cheilon, Pigne d'Arolla and many others. I note also a familiar lack of concern about climbing the same routes more than once.

After becoming a member of the Alpine Club, Nick climbed in the Dolomites, where he did the Third Sella Tower, and in the Bernina Alps, but Saas Grund was his favourite, taking his young family there on holiday: he was married in 1968. Although having a family slowed his climbing down a little, for Nick his mountaineering was no passing interest, no hobby. As his son, John, memorably said, in Nick's mind going to the mountains 'was somehow IMPORTANT.' Whether it was an outing with the mountain rescue team or a family picnic perched atop a rocky knoll in pouring rain, he was never happier than when in the mountains. Until his health no longer permitted it he climbed Scafell Pike in the Lakes every year.

Nick inherited a good sense of humour from his father, about whom it was said 'his wit was often too subtle for the solemn,' but in Nick's case the humour was quirky. He chuckled at human foibles and had a keen eye for life's absurdities. I remember him telling stories to myself and my brothers when we were young, stories told with great inventiveness and innocent mischief. He was, apparently, a believer in the existence of antlered aquatic creatures in the waters of the Lake District. He had his likes and dislikes, however, about which he was capable of making his feelings known unambiguously. Nick died on 26 February 2017 and is survived by his widow, Gillian, two sons and four grandchildren: all potential Alpine Club members. He left his collection of mountaineering books to the Alpine Club Library.

*Danny Clark-Lowes*

# Richard F Gilbert
## 1937 - 2018

Richard was born on 17 November 1937 in Lancaster. He was educated at St George's School in Harpenden and at Worcester College, Oxford, where he read chemistry. In between school and university, Richard did national service, commissioned into the Royal Electrical and Mechanical Engineers. De-mobbed in 1958, he celebrated by hitchhiking to Skye with his brother Oliver to climb in the Cuillin. In later life he gleefully remembered that

Ken Wilson and, right, Richard Gilbert, a formidable partnership on several important hill walking books. *(Ken Wilson Archive)*

their lift from Glen Garry to Sligachan was with Dame Flora MacLeod of MacLeod, 28th chief of Clan MacLeod, in a chauffeur-driven Rolls Royce.

He married Trisha Roberts on 1 September 1962, raising a family of four children: Tim, Emily, Lucy and William. They lived in the village of Crayke in North Yorkshire. Richard's professional career was as a chemistry teacher at the Benedictine Ampleforth College in North Yorkshire over some three decades, despite being an atheist and a member of the York branch of the British Humanist Association. By all accounts he was a popular and excellent teacher, with pupils in his classes frequently attaining examination grades far above expectation.

His other great claim to fame as a schoolmaster was his love of climbing and mountaineering and in taking charge of the Ampleforth College Moun-taineering Club, among the first to embark on overseas expeditions. He taught the boys to rock climb on local crags, one of the early participants being Joe Simpson of *Touching the Void* fame, and led groups on frequent trips to Scotland, enjoying back-packing and camping adventures in the Cairngorms and up challenging peaks, often in winter conditions in March and April. These Scottish adventures prepared him and the boys for five overseas trips: to the Mýrdalsjökull ice cap in south-east Iceland in 1968; the High Atlas of Morocco in 1970; the Tröllaskagi of northern Iceland in 1972; the Lyngen peninsula of Arctic Norway in 1974; and, finally, Kolahoi in the Indian Himalaya in 1977, for which Richard was awarded a Winston Churchill Travelling Fellowship. The story of these expeditions have been preserved for posterity in his book *Young Explorers* (1979) and the Kolohoi expedition, reputedly the first climbing expedition by a group of British schoolboys to the Himalaya, which concluded in the successful ascent of the 5,456m peak, is recounted in an article by Richard in the *Alpine Journal* (*AJ* 1978, pp174-7).

While Richard was fairly bitter about the fact that the Young Explorers' Trust (YET) in those days did not support his school expeditions financially, on the grounds that they lacked scientific fieldwork, his plans did gain the coveted 'approval', and in later life his vast experience as a mountaineer and as a schoolmaster engaged in outdoor activities made him an extremely valuable member of the YET expedition vetting panel for many a year, when he cheerfully 'got his own back' by strongly supporting purely activity-based plans. He understood the need that school governors and headmasters (even headmistresses) had for reassurance that the plans of their enthusiastic members of staff were sensible and within the capacity of the young students involved but he remained excited at all times by those plans that broke away from the norm and went a little 'out on a limb', as had his own ground-breaking Kolohoi expedition.

As soon as he left school he and two friends attempted the Three Peaks Challenge, Ben Nevis, Scafell Pike and Snowdon in 24 hours, with a Renault 4 Chevaux support vehicle, but they ascended the Ben too quickly (2h 35m from Glen Nevis) and burnt out in the Lakes.

At Oxford he had joined the OUMC, of which he was eventually president. Most term weekends were spent rock climbing in north Wales or Derbyshire with vacations in the Lake District and Skye and winter climbing in Scotland. He remembers that his hardest climbs were probably *Diagonal* and *Central Buttress* on Scafell and a full winter ascent of the *North-East Buttress* on Ben Nevis, and one of his most memorable was the whole Cuillin Ridge on Skye in a summer's day. Summer vacations were spent climbing in the Alps with OUMC friends such as Nigel Rogers, Colin Taylor, Alan Wedgewood, and his own brother Christopher.

Richard was quick thinking. On a ridge on the Allalinhorn with Alan and Janet Wedgewood, Richard was roped to a less experienced person who slipped and fell. So he leapt off the other side to arrest the fall. Other memorable Alpine days while a student included the ascents of the Matterhorn and the Dent d'Hérens. He pretty much gave up pushing hard on technical rock climbs after a fall off *Agrippa* on Craig yr Ysfa in the 1960s. While he was leading, a hold came free in his hand and he took a massive fall, stopped by a single runner and left hanging upside-down, his head an inch from the ground. This took away his enthusiasm for hard rock.

Even so, Richard was elected a member of the Alpine Club and was also a member of the Oxford University Alpine Club, perhaps for their excellent reunion dinners. His love of the Scottish hills, especially in winter or spring conditions, helped divert his interests away from rock climbing and onto hill walking, concentrating on the Munros and non-technical Alpine ascents, as well as mountaineering in Norway, Iceland, Atlas, the Rockies and similar. In 1971 he completed all the Munros, ascending Bidean nam

Bian on 12 June, becoming the 101st Munroist, recounted in his book *Memorable Munros* (1976).

Richard and Trisha had frequent family holidays in the Austrian Tyrol, hut-to-hutting and ascending peaks, often with their children. These family climbs began in 1982 as soon as the children were deemed old enough, when Tim was 16 and Lucy was 11 years old; too small to wear crampons, they ascended, amongst others, the Zuckerhütl (3505m), highest peak in the Stubai. Most other family holidays were based on hill walking and camping on islands and remote areas of north-west Scotland where Richard bought a plot of land on the Braes above Ullapool and had a small house built in 1970, looking over Loch Broom.

Often with Trisha, he undertook several long-distance walks, such as the Welsh three-thousanders, the Lakeland three-thousanders, the Lyke Wake Walk, Marsden to Edale, the Yorkshire Three Peaks, and several mountain marathon events. There were trips to the Wind Rivers in Wyoming, climbing the highest peak in the range, and a traverse of the Karakoram, up the Biafo glacier to Snow Lake and down the Hispar glacier to Hunza. In 1990 they joined a Karakoram Experience expedition to climb Mount Elbruz (5642m), highest peak in Europe. Due to the cold war, this was the first formal expedition from the UK to visit the range since John Hunt's expedition in 1958 (*AJ* 1992-3, pp137-43).

Richard was a prolific writer. As well as articles for the *AJ*, he wrote a column for *High* magazine, 'Richard Gilbert's Walking World', where he defended the UK's wild spaces from assault. He wrote several mountaineering and hillwalking books, particularly for Ken Wilson's bestselling coffee-table series: *The Big Walks* (1980), *Classic Walks* (1982), and *Wild Walks* (1988). A 1980s Channel 4 TV series 'Great Walks' was based on these books, two of which featured Richard (Malham, with his brother Oliver, and Cape Wrath to Sandwood Bay with Trisha and younger children, Lucy and William). His other great success was *Exploring the Far North-West of Scotland* (1994).

Richard was an active campaigner for outdoor access, for the natural environment and particularly Scotland's wild spaces and was a long-term member and supporter of the John Muir Trust and the Scottish Wild Land Group. What he termed 'vandalism' of wild places, such as hydroelectric schemes and pylons marching across wilderness, angered him immensely and he was at the forefront of many campaigns to preserve wild spaces. Fittingly, he had a deep love of music, Mozart and Haydn particularly, and was a friend of the Ryedale Festival and a frequent attender at its concerts. As a nature lover he simply could not stand cruelty to animals, especially hunting with dogs, and could not understand the passion for shooting. He was a great cricket and rugby fan, playing cricket at school and university, and enjoyed accompanying friends to Test matches in Lancashire, Yorkshire and even as far north as Durham.

As known to many but not all his friends, Richard suffered from polycystic kidneys, a hereditary disease where kidney function progressively worsens.

He had to start dialysis in 1998 and nine years later received a kidney transplant. Before that, however, he needed open-heart surgery for a mitral valve replacement to make him fit enough for the transplant operation. He suffered a major stroke in 2014 that partially paralysed his left arm and left leg, but he maintained his positive attitude and outward spirit by acquiring an automatic car with steering wheel gadgetry that enabled him to drive to the Lakes, the Dales and even, in 2017, to Ullapool and Scotland's north-west.

Richard's was a full life of eight decades, even latterly when he defeated his illness on many occasions, built around his professional career, where his teaching went so far beyond the classroom, his family, in whose many successes he rejoiced, and the hills, where he went to repair his spirit. He leaves behind his wife and children, of course, but also his books and so very many friends and colleagues around the outdoor world, all mourning his passing but celebrating his friendship.

*Brian Needham*

## Livia Gollancz
## 1920 - 2018

Livia Gollancz, who died on 29 March 2018, was born into a well-to-do London Jewish family on 25 May 1920. She was the eldest of the five daughters of Ruth and Victor Gollancz, who at that time was just beginning his career in publishing. The success of Victor Gollancz Ltd allowed her parents to buy a large country house in Brimpton, Berkshire, where Ruth instilled a love of gardening and the outdoors in all her daughters. However, when Livia visited Austria with her parents in 1934 it was to attend the Salzburg Festival, not to climb in the Alps.

Music was Livia's passion from an early age. She went to the opera alone as a schoolgirl, sitting high up in the gods at the Royal Opera House. Her principal instrument was the violin, but she bought herself a French horn too with her pocket money, and after studying at the Royal College of Music it was this instrument she played professionally. The Second World War created opportunities for women musicians, and her professional career took her to Glasgow and Manchester, with the Hallé, back to London and then again to Glasgow, where she went with friends to the Highlands for the first time, and discovered her other passion in life.

She soon went further afield, visiting the Alps both in summer and winter. Though she tried skiing she did not persist with it, but returned to climb and walk the Alps again and again. Her career as a professional musician was cut short by problems with her teeth, and she started working at her father's publishing house. Through the 1950s and 1960s she spent much of her spare time walking and climbing. She completed her circuit of the Munros, and at weekends might be climbing in north Wales, or walking the North Downs. She joined many climbing clubs: the Ladies' Scottish Climbing Club, the Pinnacle Club, the Ladies' Alpine Club and the Fell

Livia Gollancz in the Dolomites c1960.　Livia in conversation with the feminist rock climber Jill Lawrence, left, in the 1990s. *(Ed Douglas)*

and Rock. Her finest achievement was to ascend the Matterhorn in 1964.

By then she was the second-in-command at Victor Gollancz, her father still firmly in control. She started editing and publishing mountaineering books at this time, a list which was to grow much further following Victor's death in 1967, when she took over as head of the company. Chris Bonington, Joe Brown, Dennis Gray and Tom Patey were amongst the mountaineers whose books she published.

She had always maintained a life in music, through singing with a variety of choral and opera societies – combining both music and mountains memorably according to the Pinnacle Club history by keeping a railway compartment from Bozen uncrowded for her climbing companions by a judicious selection of operatic arias.

With increased age, she ceased to climb, but carried on walking for as long as possible. After Christmas with family in London, she would head north to spend Hogmanay in a Scottish bothy. It was not until 1988, at the age of 68, when she accompanied Hamish Brown on a two-week coast-to-coast walk, that she realised her body might not be up such exertions, although that might have been as much due to Hamish's relentless pace as age.

Livia retired in 1990, and though no longer carrying a full pack, joined commercial treks around the world, including trips to Bhutan and Nepal to see the rhododendrons and azaleas in flower. As well as her garden at her home in Highgate, she cultivated an allotment into her 90s. She had been a vegetarian since the war, qualifying for the extra cheese ration by first saving sufficient meat ration tokens to prove her credentials, and grew much of her own food.

Although no longer going for long walks, her social activity was still hectic. Her singing voice having aged, she returned to the violin, and played string quartets multiple evenings every week. She was also an active member of the Highgate Literary and Scientific Institution and other local societies. Never happy to accept the infirmities of age, she still enjoyed hearing about the mountain experiences of her friends and relatives up until the end.

*Benjamin Jeffryes*

*Hamish Brown writes:* A look at any bookshop in the 1970s showed Victor Gollancz as the publisher of mountaineering accounts and biographies (Joe Brown, Tom Patey et al) so I contacted them about publishing my book on doing the Munros in a single walk. In the event I dropped off the manuscript in London while driving out to Morocco and on reaching Marrakech found a postcard from Livia accepting the book. Typical, efficient Livia.

She saw all the mountain-y titles through from start to finish, was always accessible, stern and friendly, a joy to work with. When she read and edited my book (a chapter a night after supper) I received it next day and had to return it pronto. Miss a day and Livia would be on the phone. 'Where's my manuscript?'

She lived across the road from Ernst Sondheimer, one-time editor of the *Alpine Journal*, who had climbed with me in Skye, Alps, Corsica and Atlas so on my infrequent visits to London there were pilgrimages to Highgate. Ernst was a keen alpine gardener, Livia tended her allotment to a ripe old age and made music to the end, both were cultivated, full of life characters who would come to know some of the cruelties of being old. Livia would rather have been a professional musician but, as the only remaining Gollancz, gave her loyalty to the family firm.

In 1988 I persuaded Livia and another friend to join me on that year's Ultimate Challenge (now TGO Challenge) to walk across Scotland from Loch Duich to Arbroath. Livia had not had such a physical demand in years and found it hard graft. Most of the Mamores were bagged then the following day we started off from Mamore Lodge (Kinlochleven), passed the Blackwater dam, took in Beinn a' Chrulaiste and, finally, crossed Rannoch Moor to Rannoch Station. I'd gone on ahead to ensure supper was available and was sitting with a bowl of venison broth when *forfochan* Livia (a vegetarian) arrived, grabbed my bowl and drank it off. 'I needed that.' Working visits to Victor Gollancz in Henrietta Street inevitably took in lively lunches in London's best veggie curry houses. I've an image of Livia, near the end of that Ultimate Challenge crossing, *crawling* up the stairs to bed in Kirkmichael: 'I can't limp on both feet simultaneously!' The crossing however would spur Livia on for several years of trekking in mountain regions worldwide, including Bhutan.

Livia, the last Gollancz, eventually had to retire. Gollancz was sold with a proviso that mountaineering publications would continue but that went when it was sold on again into the conglomerate mess of publishing we see today. Mountaineering lost a very good friend.

## Norman Hardie
## 1924 - 2017

I first met Norman Hardie in May 1983 in his hometown of Christchurch outside my favourite old bookshop in New Regent Street. At the time I was field operations officer for the New Zealand Antarctic Research Programme

Above: Norman Hardie with Susan
Band, who died in 2018. Right:
Norman Hardie

so I introduced myself and asked Norman if he fancied a 5-month stint
as leader of Scott Base. I knew that Norman had been to Antarctica before
as a survival instructor in the early 1960s and, in 1967, as a surveyor with
Sir Edmund Hillary's New Zealand expedition that went on to make the
first ascent of the elegant Mt Herschel in North Victoria Land.

I felt sure that Norman's prestige as an internationally recognised mountaineer and his reputation as a skilled, no-nonsense civil engineer would
be the perfect skillset to take charge of not only the Scott Base staff but to
solve the complex logistic puzzle that is New Zealand's summer science
programme. Sure enough, a few weeks later, Norman sat beside me to start
his indoctrination into how some 300 people would meld together into a
cohesive team. A friendship started here at my desk and carried on during
that summer at Scott Base endured and deepened over the years.

Norman David Hardie was born in Timaru on 28 December 1924, one
of three sons and five daughters of George and Mabel Hardie. He was educated at Timaru Boys' High School then at the University of Otago and the
University of Canterbury, graduating in civil engineering. His first job, in
1948, was with the ministry of works at Lake Pukaki. In 1950 he moved to
the Wellington Hydro office. By 1951 Norman was in London and for the
next four years worked for a consulting engineering company on structural
and water scheme designs. While there, in 1951, Norman married University of Canterbury friend Enid Hurst, daughter of Colonel H C Hurst.

After his first expedition to Nepal in 1954 Norman returned to Christchurch to work for E G S Powell as a consulting engineer. From 1958 to
1963 Norman was a partner in Stock & Hardie consulting engineers, then
Hardie & Anderson, structural engineering consultants (1963-83). Norman
was a site engineer for Baigent's timber mill (1984-85) before retiring to

work as a private consultant working from homes in Halswell and Cashmere. He was chair of the Canterbury branch of the Institution of Engineers (1969-71) and a director of Farrier Waimak Ltd. Norman was also made a distinguished fellow of the Institution of Professional Engineers.

His mountain life started during the late 1930s as a government deer culler mainly in the Canterbury high country, work he continued during his years at university. On one hunting venture, after cycling from Timaru to Bealey, he shot four deer in the Waimakariri river basin. Tired out, he broke into Cora Lyn farmhouse to sleep the night, leaving a note about his actions upon leaving in the morning. Twenty-four years later, he and Enid bought that house, owning it for 22 happy years.

During his final university years Norman's interest in hunting led him to join the Canterbury University Tramping Club and this soon fostered a desire to take up mountaineering. Climbs at the head of the Rakaia followed in 1946, as did ventures into the Landsborough river catchment, a region that held a lifelong fascination. Here he completed numerous new routes on peaks such as Decken, Strauchon, Fettes and Elliot. During Norman's time at university he fostered enduring friendships with climbers Jim McFarlane, Bill Beaven, Bill Packard and Earle Riddiford who all went on to join the New Zealand Alpine Club. As fresh graduates bound for employment at the end of the 1947 summer, Bill, Earle, Jim and Norman completed the first ascent of the still rarely climbed south ridge of Sefton, approaching it from Fyfe Pass, the Landsborough and Harper's Rock.

Based at Pukaki in 1948 as an engineer Norman was awakened one night by Bill Beaven to tell him he was needed to help rescue Ruth Adams who lay badly injured close to the summit of La Perouse. Adams had fallen during a climb with Ed Hillary and guides Mick Sullivan and Harry Ayres. Ruth's subsequent lower down the West Ridge of La Perouse and epic stretcher-carry down the Cook river to Fox has entered New Zealand mountain folklore, with Norman's role being written up in his autobiography *On My Own Two Feet* (2006). Norman told me in recent years that he felt the rescue became a pivotal point in New Zealand mountaineering whereby amateur climbers like Ed Hillary who had always climbed with a guide saw what other amateur climbers were capable of. In turn, the amateurs learned much from the professionals. The bushmen who cut the track up the Cook river taught much also. Norman and his mates realised that the time was right for them to tackle bigger objectives, with luck overseas. As one, their dreams turned to climbing in the Himalaya.

Engineering work and marriage in London followed, interspersed with climbs in the European Alps. While in England he befriended famous English climbers Eric Shipton, Bill Tilman, Charles Evans and John Hunt. Lacking Himalayan expedition experience, his application to join John Hunt's 1953 Everest team was turned down. However, as a mountaineer based in London, he was asked by John Hunt to volunteer his time and expertise to co-facilitate the groundwork for the 1953 Everest expedition.

Norman finally got his break to climb in the Nepal Himalaya by sailing out to Bombay to join the 1954 New Zealand Alpine Club Barun valley expedition led by Ed Hillary. Some 20 new climbs were completed in what is now the Makalu-Barun National Park, including the 7000 metre plum Baruntse. I always envied Norman's first ascent of Pethangtse, an elegant outlier of Lhotse that straddles the Nepal-Tibet border. He used the summit as a survey station as part of his expedition-mapping programme. Charles Evans was invited on this highly mobile Kiwi trip, in part as repayment for New Zealanders being invited on British expeditions starting with Dan Bryant in 1935.

Norman's friendship with Charles Evans deepened and this led to him being asked to be deputy leader of the 1955 British expedition to Kangchenjunga, the world's third-highest mountain. Norman helped to refine the oxygen equipment for this venture that was ostensibly a reconnaissance though it quickly turned into a full-blown assault on the summit. Joe Brown and George Band reached the summit first with Norman and Tony Streather following the next day; all four climbers avoided treading on the actual summit in deference to local beliefs. I always liked Norman's tale from base camp of Evans asking him to take two of the climbers who eventually summited aside to teach them how to use crampons.

After the Kangchenjunga climb Norman and some Sherpas set out to walk all the way to Khumbu where he met Enid. This journey forms the basis of Norman's first book *In Highest Nepal* (1957) that was later translated into German and Japanese. Following Norman's participation in Ed Hillary's 1960-61 Himalayan Scientific and Mountaineering Expedition that wintered under Ama Dablam, the Khumbu became central to Norman's life for several decades. In 1963 he developed and constructed an improved water supply from a spring above Khumjung village. He played a key role in the functioning of the Himalayan Trust, remaining on its board from 1966-88. During this period Norman and Enid made 14 visits to Nepal for school building, national park work and re-afforestation programmes. In 1986, sponsored by the New Zealand government, Norman went to Khumbu to report on the state of their forests and to make recommendations for their future care, which led to the establishment of the Sagarmatha National Park.

Norman served for 21 years on various New Zealand Alpine Club committees and was president from 1973-75. He also served on the Arthur's Pass National Park Board from 1967-79 and on the Craigieburn Forest Park Committee 1980-87, being chairman for two years. He was a member of the Christchurch Civic Trust Board 1988-92 and The College House Board 1971-97. In 1992, Norman was awarded the Queen's Service Order for services to mountaineering and conservation. He was an honorary member of the Alpine Club, the Himalayan Club, the New Zealand Antarctic Society and the New Zealand Alpine Club.

Norman retained a deep interest in engineering and mountaineering throughout his life, attending and giving lectures and offering advice to younger climbers who found their way to his door. He helped innumerable authors get Nepali facts straight as well as offering editorial advice to draft manuscripts and journal articles. Many of New Zealand's top climbers owe a debt of gratitude to Norman's mentoring and instruction during their formative years.

While living in a semi-rural property in Halswell, Norman and his 'Last of the Summer Wine' enthusiasts bottled their own vintage. It's time to raise a glass to Norman Hardie, one of New Zealand's outstanding mountaineers.

Norman died 30 October 2017 and is survived by his wife Enid and daughters Sarah Jane Hardie and Ruth Wells and grandchildren Henry, Tamar and Roslyn Wells and David Turton.

Colin Monteath

## Elizabeth Hawley
## 1923 - 2018

Liz Hawley. *(Ed Douglas)*

Born on 9 November 1923 in Chicago, Elizabeth Ann Hawley became famous in the mountaineering world as 'the keeper of the mountains', the title of Alison Otto's documentary film as well as Bernadette McDonald's biography about the American journalist who settled in Nepal in 1960 and never left. 'I guess inertia has kept me here,' was her rhetorical answer to those wondering why she never went back to her native America, although inertia is not a term I would have associated with Miss Hawley. For five decades she hunted down mountaineers all over Kathmandu in her 1964 baby-blue VW Beetle, often ringing them in their hotel just as they put down their bags to summon them for interrogation about what they were up to, tireless in her quest to find every single mountaineer intending to climb an expedition peak in Nepal and grill them about it, something I witnessed for myself as her assistant for 14 years.

This astonishing era ended in spring 2016, when Miss Hawley was 92 and suddenly decided to give up her career as an archivist. It happened after she had interviewed a North American team who were attempting an unclimbed peak in the Everest region. 'When in the middle of the interview my mind went blank, I knew it was time to stop.' And so she did, and never once looked back. There were no hard feelings, no regrets: complete pragmatism was simply Miss Hawley's style. 'Why would I be upset about it? I started it, I finished it and now it's your job to continue,' she said when I asked her whether it was hard to stop doing something she was so passionate about. The question about passion actually came as a surprise to her. 'Passionate about my archives?' she responded. 'How can you possibly be passionate about a database? I have never been passionate about anything,' was her retort.

Maybe passion is not the right word to describe Miss Hawley's tenacity and devotion for the things she cared for such as her favourite writer, the English crime author and poet Dorothy L Sayers. Whenever I entered her dimly lit flat in the Kathmandu district of Dilli Bazaar over the past two years for my daily visits, Miss Hawley would sit at her sturdy oak table hunched over one of Sayers' books which she had already read countless times. 'The people in these books are my friends,' she would reply to my question why she was ignoring all the other books sitting on her table. 'Why would I read a book with people I don't know and I don't like,' she would say, often giving me instructions to re-adjust the big pile of paperbacks that were given to her by friends and acquaintances, but would never be read.

Reading had always been high on Miss Hawley's list of things to do. In previous years, when she was still interviewing expeditions, she would start her day avidly scouring the *New York Times* followed by a Nepali paper, and once a week *Time* magazine. Having read it daily since she was 12 years old, the *New York Times* was certainly her first choice and she often talked about the day when one of her stories made it to the front page. On 21 July 1982, she had found herself on the same flight from Bangkok to Kathmandu as the ailing prime minister B P Koirala, the great Nepali politician of the post-war generation, who was returning home after medical treatment in Thailand. 'They had taken out the seats in the front row and laid him down there. It was immediately clear to me that he was being flown home to die,' she recalled of this last encounter with a man she deeply respected. 'I spent the entire flight writing the story and kept checking with B P to make sure I got all my facts right.' Later that evening, just as she was sending her story to Reuters via telex, she received a phone call informing her that the prime minister had died. 'It was a sad moment as he was one of the few remarkable men we had in Nepal and a political leader who stuck to his beliefs.' She did not spend long pondering it, quickly changing the ending of the story and landing a scoop. 'I felt very proud,' she told me.

Miss Hawley's father was an accountant, her mother a labour relations professional for the League of Women Voters. She majored in history at the University of Michigan and then moved to New York where she landed a job as researcher for *Fortune* magazine. In 1946, when she started work, being a writer was an exclusively male preserve. She had taken a keen interest in world politics at university and afterwards began to travel, often alone, first in post-war Europe and then much further afield. She summarised these journeys as her favourite verandahs: Karen Blixen's in the Ngong hills outside Nairobi, the St George Hotel's verandah in Beirut, where she met Kim Philby, and one in Khartoum, where she drank whisky with a cultured administrator called Mamoun El Amin, whom she met on a Nile riverboat.

She arrived in Kathmandu in February 1959, having quit her job at *Fortune* in 1957 to travel. The refusal to promote women had turned her career into a dead-end. It was only a short visit, but Hawley fell in love with the city, which wasn't anything like the sprawling and polluted chaos it is today, and she returned for good in September 1960. She worked part-time as a journalist, first as an accredited correspondent for *Time*, then Reuters, but in 1985 her factually correct report of a bomb exploding by the royal palace gates cost her official recognition for three years. In 1990, she was appointed as a paid honorary consul for New Zealand, perhaps surprising for an American, but Miss Hawley was a longstanding friend of Ed Hillary and served as executive officer for the Himalayan Trust, managing the finances and using her local contacts to smooth the way for new schools and health posts. It was Miss Hawley who flew to where Ed Hillary was working in the field to break the news that his wife and daughter Belinda had been killed in an air-crash taking off from Kathmandu's airport. Until her last days, rumours persisted that they had had an affair, rumours she patiently denied. 'Ed was one of the finest people I ever met, but I never had an affair with him,' she told me in what I considered to be complete honesty. 'I have actually never had an affair in my life,' she said, looking sheepish.

Where Miss Hawlay made her greatest mark was with her impressive archive of interviews with mountaineering expeditions in the Nepal Himalaya, an archive that later became known as the Himalayan Database, released into the world in 2004 with the help of American climber and data analyst Richard Salisbury. Her modest and austere apartment, where she lived from 1963 until her very last days, was lined with bookshelves and filing cabinets containing handwritten accounts of thousands of expeditions. The mothballed papers were all neatly arranged and put together with high-quality paperclips. 'I don't like Nepali paperclips, they get rusty,' she said when she asked me to bring some from Europe. 'But don't dare buy the cheap plastic ones either.' Over the years, I must have taken about a thousand high-quality German paperclips to Kathmandu.

For more than half a century, Miss Elizabeth Hawley collected forms, notes, newspaper clippings and scrap papers, which were all held together by sturdy German paper clips, from her interviews with expedition leaders. She would grill mountaineers about their expedition details, their own personal data as well as the exact origins and personal data of their Sherpas, which was extremely important to her. 'Some people don't even know the names of their Sherpas,' she would angrily comment. 'And if they do, they often don't know how to spell their names properly.' Spelling was something Elizabeth Hawley was incredibly fastidious about. She would immediately spot a spelling mistake by just glancing at one of the handwritten forms I used to hand to her. I later found out why. 'I see my vowels in different colours and I immediately notice when a particular shade is missing.' In this case, there was a lack of yellow. I had obviously spelt the name wrongly.

Elizabeth Hawley met many well-known mountaineers and became close to a few of them, apart from Ed Hillary. One mountaineer she thought very highly of was the Italian Reinhold Messner. She met him in the 1970s when he came to Nepal for the first time. 'He was young and inexperienced and it was interesting to see him develop over the years.' The respect was mutual and in a recorded voice message for her 90th birthday, Reinhold Messner returned the compliment: 'I met many climbers over the last 40 years, but nobody is as strong in my memory as you, Liz. You understand the climbers and know how they tackle the big mountains. You are the Himalayan spirit.'

Miss Hawley's spirit will certainly live on in Nepal's climbing community. She was well respected and even though feared by some, she became a true icon of the Himalayan mountaineering scene, known for making some big mountaineers look small in the interviews. During the last two years of her life, she spent most of her time in her first-floor flat: moving up and down the stairs had simply become too difficult for her. She did not mind. She actually enjoyed finally having the time to sit and read all day long and whenever she was asked out for lunch, she would decline. 'I am happy where I am, I don't want to go out,' she would say.

She was hardly ever alone though. Her two nurses Dawa Sherpa and Rista Rai lived with her full time for the last five years of her life, and her long-time cook Man Bahadur served her lunch at 10.30am and dinner at 4pm. She adopted these early eating times when her 88-year-old mother came to live with her. Then there were the many visitors eager to meet the *grande dame* of the Himalaya and have their photo taken with her. She was always happy to receive strangers in her home and have chats with them, although sometimes not without a cheeky comment after they had left: 'They were on a sightseeing tour of Kathmandu, and I think I was one of the sights.'

*Billi Bierling*

# Iain McMorrin
# 1938-2017

It was a Tuesday evening in 1960 at South Audley Street and an interesting lecture was scheduled. In those days, however, young unknown alpinists not yet members were largely ignored by the City-suited AC regulars, thus Tony Smythe and I soon found ourselves in conversation with another young unknown with an unusual accent. Iain McMorrin, newly arrived from Southern Rhodesia, and a climber of course, happened to be looking for digs and Smythe and I had a spare floor. Iain proved a congenial flat-mate and in the Avon Gorge the following weekend proved no slouch on rock. Within the month we were pioneering new routes together at Swanage.

Forward 38 years. By the time he retired as director of Oxford's Woodlands Outdoor Centre, he'd become a leading specialist in the field of outdoor education. Among many appropriate advisory and committee appointments, he'd chaired the BMC Access and Conservation Committee and the Mountain Leader Training Board, sat on the Duke of Edinburgh Expedition Panel and the Health and Safety Executive, and campaigned

Left: Iain McMorrin
Above: Iain McMorrin and Cadi
exploring the Pembrokeshire coast.

vigorously on rights of way and access in Wales. He'd even seen his name given to an Antarctic glacier.

Hailing from Salisbury, now Harare, where his parents were in business, Iain enjoyed an outdoor childhood and learnt to climb with the Rhodesian Schools Exploration Society, and by the time he left school he was making first ascents on the big crags of the Chimanimani and Inyanga mountains near the Mozambique border, earning the sobriquet 'Steaming Jim'. He trained as a cartographer with the Rio Tinto Corporation and on an expedition to Kenya, among other climbs, reached the summit of Batian via the south-east face of Nelion. But dispirited by the looming political situation, Iain eventually booked a passage to Britain. On the day of departure from Cape Town, he set off to Table Mountain with Rusty Baillie to do a final climb, which they were still struggling to complete when the Union Castle liner in the docks below started blowing its siren to signal final embarkation for Southampton. Then one of them took a short fall. Two pegs came out and both climbers found themselves swinging on a single bent piton high over Table Bay. Needless to say, Iain caught the boat, but only just.

After sitting various exams in London Iain applied to join the British Antarctic Survey – or the Falkland Islands Dependencies Survey (FIDS) as it then was – and in 1961 he was posted to the Stonington Island base on the west coast of mountainous Graham Land as a surveyor-mountaineer. Here he befriended Johnny Cunningham, another Stonington resident. Over the course of three seasons Iain learnt to ski and became enamored with the ethos and techniques of dog sledding. Besides making frequent multi-day journeys and climbing several virgin peaks, he completed a notable and particularly gruelling expedition mapping the coast of the Larsen Ice Shelf on the eastern side of the peninsula, travelling 900 miles over 115 days by dog sled. Subsequently the Directorate of Overseas Surveys named the McMorrin glacier on the northern arm of Marguerite Bay. Not surprisingly his sojourn down south had a profound effect on his life thereafter.

Back in Britain Iain took a teaching qualification at St Luke's College in Exeter, where with Peter Biven he made first ascents on the limestone at Chudleigh and Torbay, before moving on to teach at Lindesfarne College near Llangollen. Earlier, at the AC, he had met Wilf Noyce, who was then starting work with publishers Thomas Nelson on what was to become the *World Atlas of Mountaineering*. Wilf consulted Iain on his embryo African chapters. He'd expected that once he'd returned to Britain, Iain would contribute the Antarctic material for the book, but in 1962 Wilf had been killed in the Pamirs and Nelson commissioned Iain to complete the book. The task occupied his spare time for several years but when finally published in 1969 the book was well received and was the only authoritative reference volume of its kind. He then went back to Rhodesia for nine months working with the Rhodesian Broadcasting News Division and he got involved in subversive activities against the rightwing forces of Ian Smith's government, passing documents on to the Central Africa Party.

An incident occurred in the Alps on which Iain dined out for many years. It was 1967 and Iain, Peter Biven and I happened to be descending, at speed, what was essentially steep névé on the Envers du Plan glacier. Out in front Iain was actually running. Suddenly a rogue crevasse appeared. Attempting to stop he snagged a crampon right on the lip. He leapt into the air, described a perfect somersault and landed safely on his feet on the far side. He continued running, much to the incredulity of a guided French party who were standing debating exactly how best to cross the crevasse. Later, he and I enjoyed the north face of the Chardonnet before going off with Bev Clark, Mick Burke and Mike Kosterlitz to shoot a movie on the Aiguille Brenva. Proposed by Fred Dangar, deputy editor of the *Alpine Journal*, Iain was elected to the AC in 1968.

While spending several months in 1970 plotting the results of his Antarctic work at the DOS, Iain became a prime mover in planning an Anglo-American expedition to the Sentinel Range, where at the time only the highest peaks had been climbed. When this fell through he started organising an expedition to untrodden Smith Island in the South Orkneys – Tilman's objective when he disappeared in 1977 – where FIDS was keen to plant a navigation beacon. Surrounded by imposing ice cliffs, this tiny island rises to Mount Foster (2105m), a worthy prize. But after overspending its 'exploration' budget on a failed northern polar junket, the BBC withdrew its backing, while navigational developments made the beacon redundant. Iain was bitterly disappointed and Mount Foster was left to a Bulgarian expedition 30 years later.

That same year he married Gaynor, a talented young artist, at Gresford, not far from Llangollen, and I was best man. Iain was anxious to bid a fitting farewell to bachelordom, so on the morning of the wedding he insisted we should repeat one of his own routes on a steep limestone crag in the Dee valley. High on the wall, spread-eagled at the crux with minimal gear, he discovered that the vital aid peg he'd left on the first ascent had since been chopped. He unroped, I climbed down and finding my way to the cliff-top dropped him a rope. We eventually arrived at the ceremony, flustered, sweaty and rather late. He remained happily married for 47 years.

When Iain took an advanced teaching diploma at Oxford, his tutor and soon to be close friend was the educationalist Robin Hodgkin, the well-known AC member who had been on Masherbrum in 1938. Impressed with Iain's ideas on the value of outdoor education and adventure in the shaping of young minds along with his strong sense of fair play, Robin pressured him to apply for the directorship of Woodlands, the Oxfordshire Outdoor Education Centre at Glasbury-On-Wye, where Colin Mortlock was about to retire. Iain was appointed and ran the centre for the next 28 years, teaching youngsters to live together and appreciate the environment through the gaining of outdoor skills – climbing, canoeing, caving, gorge walking and other adventurous activities – while supervising a busy staff. Unflappable, dependable and yet always up for a personal challenge, he and Gaynor bought a Macwester 27 sailing boat in Aberystwyth, sailed it to Fishguard and then crossed to Ireland and back without serious incident despite never having sailed.

When at last he and Gaynor, she still a working artist, retired to their cottage in north Pembrokeshire, Iain maintained his links with outdoor education by setting up a charity, the Oxford Outdoor Learning Trust. Involvement with committee work and consultancies continued but he still found time to enjoy steep rock, while taking a special pleasure in exploring the wild Pembrokeshire coast in his sea kayak, often with his Jack Russell terrier, Cadi, complete with little life jacket, riding pillion. A highly cultured man and an excellent photographer, he travelled widely with Gaynor investigating the art of India, Ladakh, Japan and Mexico. As his health deteriorated in later years he enjoyed his writing, his music, his poetry and his books while delighting in living so close to the sea. He was naturally proud of his two daughters, one a successful marine consultant, the other MP for Cardiff North, elected during the last months of his life. Iain died, peacefully, in Withybush hospital, Haverfordwest on 22 October 2017.

*John Cleare*

## John Sylvester Monks
## 1940-2017

I first met John in September 1962 when he was just 21. He had been offered his first job in Oldham but unsurprisingly turned it down when he was offered the modern languages post at Monte Rosa College in Montreux, Switzerland. We both started teaching at this co-ed boarding school offering O and A-levels with skiing for four half days a week. The teachers were nearly all under 30 and we slotted in very easily.

My earliest memories of John were of him holding forth in one of the local smoke-filled cafés, a cigarette in one hand and a pint in the other. We did not seem to have much in common as he was an Anglo-Irish Catholic from north Wales and I had been brought up an abstemious Methodist in the flat lands of eastern England. But we were brought together by our love of the ski and mountaineering possibilities that our new environment offered.

One of our first adventures was to build an igloo on Rochers de Naye (2042m), which rose up steeply behind the school. John assumed the role of foreman and at the end of two or three hours we had a respectable snow house. The students returned to school and we spent the night in the igloo. We were cold and unprepared but got up early the next day and with skis and *peaux de phoques* (seal skins) set off for Chateau d'Oex. So started John's *randonnée* adventures, which remained his preferred Alpine activity.

John Monks in Ladakh at 5,800m in 1977.

For 55 years until his death in August 2017 John lived around the shores of Lake Geneva teaching French and German to International Baccalaureate level. He was over 30 years at the International School of Geneva where he was head of modern manguages. Apart from a three-year stint in the personnel department of Nestlé in Vevey, John remained a teacher for over 40 years. This gave him the opportunity to climb a number of Alpine peaks both on foot and on skis in the Alps. He was also able to climb mountains further afield such as in the Jotunheim in southern Norway, Mt Athabasca in Canada and two peaks of 5,800m in Ladakh.

My most memorable Alpine trip with John was when we crossed the Bernese Oberland on skis from the Jungfraujoch to the Grimsel pass on the 1 to 3 June 1974. On day three we left the Oberaarjochhütte (3258m) very early. It had snowed in the night leaving fresh powder. John was in his element and left an immaculate signature in the snow as we descended to the Grimsel.

We went twice to the Andes together. In 1971 we joined a London University graduate group for six weeks of exploratory mountaineering in the Cordillera Urubamba of Peru. John loved travelling with the pack animals and did many negotiations in Spanish as we sought to acquire animals. Several virgin peaks were climbed and John completed one of them, which we called Naranja, about 4,600m. (The rock was orange.)

In 1969 with a group of friends we went to Ecuador where John made several attempts on some of the world's highest volcanoes including Chimborazo and Cotopaxi. If we were not always successful we had a lot of fun, deepened friendships, and learned more about the Andes and its people. John was tough and was not badly affected by altitude and in later years reached 5,600m in Nepal aged 66.

John loved conversation, had a sharp wit and a gift for repartee and one-liners. He loved to argue and I believe sometimes so for the sake of it. In another life he might have been a lawyer. After teaching for a year in Vienna I asked him how my German was, hoping for some encouragement. As quick as a flash John replied, 'Tony, my boy, you speak fluent bad German!' Coming from John I took his remark as a compliment but with the passage of time he was probably being too generous.

John organised and led numerous student ski weeks and was heavily involved with field trips to many European locations. In retirement he became director of academic studies for several years at Le Rosey International Summer School as well as working as a translator for various commercial enterprises. He also wrote a children's book, *A Tale of Tea* (Pegasus, 2017), which was beautifully illustrated by his daughter Rosie.

He is survived by his daughter and son and by their mother Alison.

*Tony Welling*

## Elisabeth Parry
## 1921 - 2017

Only one member of the Alpine Club, past or present, has sung as a soloist at Glyndebourne; been a Middle East Forces Sweetheart during the Second World War; collaborated closely with Benjamin Britten and founded her own opera company. Elisabeth Parry did all these things before taking up serious mountaineering in early middle age and embarking on a wide range of ambitious climbs including the *Innominata* and *Peuterey Ridges* and the Weisshorn traverse.

Elisabeth was born in Aberdeen. Her mother Mhari Forbes was Scottish with a trace of French, her father, Arthur Haydn Parry, was Welsh. Music was in the blood. Not only was her father a talented pianist, her grandfather Joseph Parry was the composer of the famous hymn 'Aberystwyth', the tune popularly associated with Wesley's hymn 'Jesus, Lover of My Soul', and the first opera in the Welsh language. Although he was once described as Wales' greatest composer Elisabeth only discovered her Welsh musical heritage late in life. She adored her father, an outstanding scholar and musician at Cambridge, who after being seriously wounded in the First World War became a junior permanent secretary to Churchill. After the war, his career as a City stockbroker prospered and enabled the family to enjoy a leisured life in Kensington with holidays in Scotland and skiing in the Alps. This charmed life changed abruptly in 1929 when the stock-market crash ended both Arthur Parry's career and his marriage.

When her mother subsequently remarried her childhood sweetheart, Elisabeth's life resumed a semblance of normality. Her English boarding school education was polished at an avant-garde Paris finishing school, which closed its term with a visit to the Folies Bergère. Elisabeth's musical and academic talents, already evident at school, helped her secure a place at Lady Margaret Hall, Oxford to read French and German literature. However, when her 18th birthday coincided with the outbreak of the Second World War on

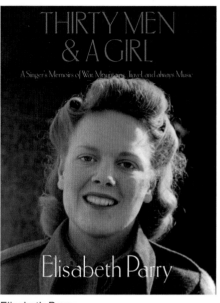

Elisabeth Parry

3 September 1939, she had no hesitation in forsaking academe's ivory towers to join the Red Cross as an ambulance driver instead.

In the autumn of 1940 she successfully auditioned for the Staff Band of the Royal Army Medical Corps as a soprano soloist and for the next three years gave musical shows and broadcasts for Forces programmes and the BBC's *Workers' Playtime*, interspersed with professional singing lessons. In November 1943, she was invited to join the Staff Band's tour of the Middle East as its sole female singer and for the next hectic year entertained British forces in Egypt, Palestine, Iraq, Persia, Syria and the Canal Zone. The tour involved 20,000 miles of travel, rough living and 200 official performances. At the end of it all, Elisabeth was voted British Forces' Sweetheart in the Middle East. She recorded this epic of wartime service and adventure in her autobiography *Thirty Men and a Girl* (Allegra, 2010) earning plaudits from Dame Vera Lynn and a host of other admirers.

After the war, Elisabeth launched herself into a full-time singing career with a classical repertoire that ranged from Mozart, Verdi and Rossini to Britten. Recitals at the Wigmore Hall led to engagements at Glyndebourne and a close involvement with Britten's newly formed English Opera Group where she sang the title role in his *Rape of Lucretia* and toured Britain with artists such as Kathleen Ferrier, Joan Cross and Peter Pears.

In 1950, Elisabeth established her own opera company, the London Opera Players, which, for the next 56 years, became the mainspring of her professional, artistic and social life both as its director and regular performer. The LOP was to stage 3,585 touring performances of 39 different operas employing 360 soloists, 13 conductors and a supporting staff of well over a hundred to bring the best of live opera to many thousands in Britain who would otherwise never have heard a note of it. The LPO was undoubtedly Elisabeth's greatest achievement and the Parry Trust, which she established to promote young singers and which is now administered by the Welsh National Opera, remains a lasting legacy.

Mountains had played an important part in Elisabeth's life from the time when she became the youngest member of the Ski Club of Great Britain. For many years she accompanied her mother and stepfather on successive family summer holidays to Zermatt, where they invariably stayed at the Monte Rosa Hotel when it was de rigueur to change for dinner. She had been captivated by the Pyrenees during a pre-war visit, but it was at Zermatt in 1950 that she met a young English mountaineer, Sidney Nowill, who encouraged her to climb and give free rein to her mountaineering imagination.

After Sidney's introduction to some easy routes on the Riffelhorn and Trifthorn, Elisabeth joined the Mountaineering Association in London for weekend excursions to North Wales and the Lakes. Back in Zermatt she engaged Willi Truffer as her guide to realise a long ambition not simply to climb the Matterhorn by the normal route but complete the traverse to Italy, yet be back in time for dinner at the Monte Rosa the following night. Another favourite guide was Celso Degasper with whom she did several Dolomite classics.

In 1961, her 40th year, Elisabeth engaged as her guide Gilles Josserand, a sophisticated Parisian who later became a top instructor at the École Nationale in Chamonix and a lifelong friend. On the Aiguille de l'M, Gilles lost patience with a slow-moving party in front of them, deliberately went off-route and then came off when a handhold broke. Elisabeth managed to check what would otherwise have been a fatal fall. The following year, she joined Sidney Nowill in the Bernina and after surviving an avalanche on the Piz Roseg went on to tackle Piz Palü before moving on to Chamonix for the *Rochefort Ridge*, the Aiguille Noire de Peuterey, the Chardonnet and the Purtscheller.

In 1963, Elisabeth was a member of Sidney Nowill's month-long expedition to the Turkish Ala Dağ where, during a 30-hour epic on its highest peak, the Demirkazık, she led the ice-encrusted crux in the *Hodgkin-Peck* couloir to make theirs the mountain's second British ascent. Driving back to England in her beat-up Morris Minor, Elisabeth and Nigella Blandy (Hall) stopped off at Chamonix to pick up Gilles and finish that summer with an ascent of the Grépon, a crossing of the col de Dolent into Italy and a traverse of Mont Blanc by the *Innominata Ridge*.

If 1963 had been a vintage year, 1966 was Elisabeth's most outstanding. During another of Sidney Nowill's pioneering Turkish expeditions to Hakkiari, and despite being robbed by armed Kurdish bandits, they still managed to climb Hendevade (3725m), the highest peak in the Sat range and several others. On returning to Europe, Elisabeth joined Sidney, Dorothea Gravina and Sylvia Yates and, with three guides led by Michel Vaucher and Gilles Josserand, embarked on a traverse of Mont Blanc by the *Peuterey*

*Ridge*. After an uncomfortable bivouac below the Aiguille Blanche, Vaucher took a chance on the weather, which deteriorated progressively the higher they climbed. In storm and whiteout, they unknowingly passed two climbers who had died in their tracks. Vaucher later described a seemingly endless ice pitch as longer and more difficult than anything on the Eigerwand. At the close of their third day, they staggered into the Vallot just as it got dark. Elisabeth had completed the traverse despite having her period and suffering from diarrhoea throughout. As a finale to their season, Elisabeth and Dorothea Gravina traversed the Weisshorn by the *Schalligrat* and north ridge, supported by Willi Truffer and his son Bernard.

This tempo had slackened somewhat by the 1970s, but Elisabeth managed to fit in a couple of Pyrenean seasons with Dorothea Gravina as well as joining Sidney Nowill for one of his three visits to Turkey's Kaçkar mountains where bad weather frustrated their attempts to climb Kaçkar Daği (3937m) itself. In 1983, her last serious expedition was an incident-packed, month-long journey through Zanskar. Even so, her zest for adventure remained unquenchable with subsequent treks in Iceland and Svalbard, a journey along the Silk Road when she was 84 and a trip to Patagonia when aged 86.

Elisabeth Parry's was an exceptional life of service to her country, her muse and the opera company she created to inspire and nurture six generations of young singers. Her charm and the warmth of her personality made her friendships life-long and unforgettable. In the epitaph she dedicated to Sidney Nowill she wrote: 'My dream of perfect dying is at the foot of some great mountain ... to step fearless and joyful into the Unknown'.

*J G R Harding*

## Royal Robbins
## 1935 - 2017

'Rock-climbing is a man's sport in England, somewhat like bullfighting.' So wrote Royal Robbins after his first visit to Britain in 1966. It was intended as a compliment for he had been climbing with the likes of Brown, Whillans and Patey and had taken part in the BBC TV live climbing 'spectacular' – teamed with Patey – from South Stack at Holyhead; thus the British climbing public first met the already famous Californian whose unforgettable name was already synonymous with the legendary Yosemite Valley.

At the time Royal was working at the American School in Leysin, mostly ski instructing but finding time to climb out of season. The previous year he'd put up the impressive *American Direct* on the Dru's west face in five days with fellow countryman John Harlin, subsequently killed so tragically on the *Eiger Direct*. During his first Alpine foray in 1962, despite feeling rather overawed by the unfamiliar objective dangers, he'd climbed several first-rate rock routes including a new west face variation on the Dru with his old acquaintance Gary Hemming, and the Grand Capucin with Bev Clark, climbs that marked the start of a period of serious Alpine achievements by visiting

Left: Royal Robbins, exhausted after the arduous eight-day first ascent of Tis-sa-ack in October 1969, rests during the descent from Half Dome. *(Glen Denny)*

Above: Royal Robbins with his daughter Tamara in the Lake District in 1976. *(John Cleare)*

Americans. Hemming advised him to visit Britain to sharpen up his free climbing.

It was in Chamonix in 1963 that I first met Royal, sitting with the 'Blonde God' Harlin in the Bar Le National. Later at his Leysin base I was struck by his cool, calm demeanour, measured speech and an apparent straight-faced seriousness that concealed wry stabs of humour when his horn-rimmed spectacles set off an occasional disarming smile. I might have described him as a gentle, if athletic, academic.

The following spring, while planning the BBC's South Stack 'circus', I suggested that repartee, acting even, might be as important as climbing ability, and that Royal would make a perfect foil for the ebullient irreverence of Tom Patey. Keen on any export dimension, the BBC readily agreed, and I invited Mr Robbins to join us. The sequel has passed into folklore: the final pitch on Red Wall involved aid climbing and Royal had swung up through the overhangs with his usual effortless ease, where Tom, a brilliant ice climber but not enamoured with 'mere gadgets', had followed, fought and suffered. As Tom emerged on the cliff-top, Royal glanced at his raw and bleeding hands.

'Back home in the Valley,' he observed, 'they say you can tell a good aid-man by his hands.'

'Lots of scars?' Tom said hopefully. Royal shook his head sadly.

'No scars.'

Robbins hailed from West Virginia where Royal had been his father's first name, but after two divorces and a rather traumatic childhood, by the time he was 10 he was living with his devoted mother Beulah in fairly restrained circumstances in the Los Angeles area. Independent and self-sufficient from the start and uninterested in conventional sports, he loved classical music and books and, inspired by James Ramsey Ullman's *High Conquest*, yearned to be a professional adventurer. It was with the Boy Scouts that young Royal discovered rock, mountains and Yosemite and first became conscious of the physical delight he found in overcoming a difficult move on a boulder or outcrop.

Leaving school at 16 he found a winter job at a ski area in the nearby San Gabriel mountains, retrospectively a wise move for skiing was to play an important part in his life. Co-ordination, control and determination he had in abundance, and by his second winter he was representing California in the Junior National Ski Championships. Nevertheless, a proper job eventually became imperative and he joined the Union Bank in Los Angeles as a bookkeeper. But he also started to climb seriously on nearby Tahquitz Rock, where encouraged by experienced local climbers he soon discovered his natural ability; indeed, within two years he had put up America's first 5.9 route on the 'Rock', eschewing any form of direct aid, which was the norm in those days. It proved a psychological breakthrough in American climbing.

He was just 22 when together with Jerry Gallwas and Mike Sherrick, he climbed the imposing, virgin and plumb vertical 2,000ft north-west face of Half Dome, which dominates the head of the Yosemite Valley. It took five days and was the first Grade VI route in America and now a world classic on anyone's tick list. Suddenly Royal Robbins was famous.

In 1958 the US Army caught up with Royal and he found himself posted as a clerk to Fort Bliss in Texas. Here he was able to forge weekend passes and beg frequent Friday night rides on military aircraft to California to climb at Tahquitz or even Yosemite, before hitchhiking the 800 miles back to camp. Needless to say there were several close shaves with AWOL charges. On demob in 1960 Royal returned to the Union Bank, this time in Berkeley, but his ideas had crystallised in the army and he knew that banking would not further his ambitions; after six months he quit to commence a hand-to-mouth existence as a winter ski instructor and summer climbing bum. As his fame spread, he found himself delivering lectures, running climbing clinics and operating a seasonal climbing school; for several years he part-timed as climbing editor of *Summit*, the first US climbing magazine. In 1971 and 1973 respectively, his two *Rockcraft* how-to-do-it volumes were published and become international bestsellers. In time he matured into a fine writer, well known for his philosophical and wry observations on climbers and climbing.

It's unnecessary to list here all Royal Robbins great climbs and myriad first ascents. Suffice to say that on his election in 1974 to the Club, he listed just fifteen of what he considered his most significant climbs up to 1969. Starting with the Half Dome route of 1957, it continues with his nine-day first ascent of El Capitan's south-west face in 1962, the second ascent of Yosemite's Leaning Tower, a four-day solo effort in 1964, and in 1968 the second ascent of *Muir Wall* on El Cap, once again soloed, in 10 epic days. Not to be dismissed as a mere Yosemite rock-jock, Royal also included, besides his Chamonix exploits, several mountaineering routes: a four-day first ascent on Mount Proboscis in Canada's Logans, the four-day first ascent of Mount Hooker's north face in the Wind Rivers, and in the Canadian Rockies the three-day first ascent of the north face of Mount Geikie and the third ascent, but first solo, of Mount Edith Cavell's daunting north face. In Alaska he bagged a clutch of new summits among Alaska's fabled Kichatna Spires. The form leaves so much unlisted and 50 years on it is still a formidable list by any standard.

Style for Robbins merged with ethics in the planning and execution of his great climbs; 'clean climbing' involved using only the reasonable minimum of rope, gear, food, water and time. There was little chance of retreat and none of rescue on many of these serious routes. 'What was the point,' he asked, 'in sieging a new route via a bolt ladder? What fun is there is a game when the odds are 100 to 1 in your favour?' His ethos did arouse controversy; he was accused of self-righteousness and seen as a bolt-chopper – which was true, although he later apologised, admitting that a minimum of bolts were sometime necessary in Yosemite.

As a brilliant technician and master of aid climbing, he especially admired the unwritten rules of climbing practised in Britain, and was the first exponent in the USA to advocate, import and popularise the use of nuts, for many years distrusted by peg-happy American pundits. Introspective, always self-trusting and hating rules, Royal even disabled the seat-belt warning in his car, refusing to allow a machine to dictate his personal safety. Thus it is not surprising that he enjoyed solo climbing and developed efficient safety systems to do so. 'A solo climb is like a big mirror,' he wrote. 'You're looking at yourself all the way up,' but added pointedly: 'the fullest expression of the climbing egoist.'

By 1963 Royal was established enough to get married and in due course set up home with Liz in Modesto, where her family owned a business, within easy reach of Yosemite. While working in Europe he'd designed a specialist rock boot for Galibier, the highly successful blue suede 'RR', which he distributed himself in America. Other outdoor lines followed and in 1970 they opened a retail store called Mountain Paraphernalia in Modesto, and later a second store in Fresno, both beautifully designed and tastefully fitted-out by Liz. Though successful, the firm was eventually sued by a client who had suffered an accident while using gear it had sold; it was not the first such incident in US climbing history, Chouinard having suffered badly in a similar case. Though finally emerging unscathed, they warily dropped the equipment business and decided to concentrate on clothing under the name Royal Robbins. Liz proved a talented, innovative and very successful designer. Many of her knitwear creations were made in the Lake District and the business is still going strong, though now under different ownership. Indeed, over the years Royal and Liz made frequent visits to Britain for both pleasure and later for business; they had many British friends and Royal always made the excuse that he had come over 'to recharge his batteries.'

Now a well-to-do businessman, Royal was only 43 when severe arthritis struck; frequently completely incapacitated, it spelt the end of his big wall climbing, although when in remission he could manage short, straightforward routes. However, he'd always been attracted to kayaking and now he took it up seriously. There were excellent white water rivers nearby and with Liz and friends old and new, Royal set out to make expeditionary first descents of many of the difficult wild rivers not only in the US but also as far afield as Chile and Siberia.

Tragically, some thirty years later, other symptoms gradually appeared and no longer in control of the situation, Royal was diagnosed with progressive supranuclear palsy, a rare degenerative neurological disorder with no known cure. Wheelchair bound and needing full-time care, his physical capacities gradually slipped away and he died on 1 March 2017. He left his devoted Liz and their now adult children, Tamara and Damon, both deeply committed to the wild country adventures with which they were brought up. As the master of big-wall climbing, the legacy of Royal Robbins is not only his bold routes but also his influence on the philosophy of American – and perhaps even world mountaineering. He wrote: 'Good things don't necessarily lead to a positive attitude. But a positive attitude leads to good things.'

*John Cleare*

## Allan Stuart
## 1923 - 2018

Not many climbers, on their first visit to the Alps, manage to get up five big mountains – the Aiguille de la Tsa, Tête Blanche, Dent Blanche, Matterhorn and Zinal Rothorn – all in a two-week holiday. Of those energetic characters who have done so, I suspect that even fewer will have spent their summer holiday fortnights for the next 33 years trying to better, in terms of quantity or quality, that very good score.

Yet that was the annual routine of Allan Stuart, who died in April at the age of 95. The Alps were, for Allan, the ultimate in climbing enjoyment. Opportunities to climb in the greater ranges came his way but he always took the view that the ratio of time likely to be engaged in actual climbing, as opposed to travelling, trudging or waiting for the weather, was ridiculously small. The Alps, by contrast, were just the right size to provide as much challenge as anyone could wish and they came already supplied with a network of huts, which solved all possible problems of logistics.

Of course, that routine still left the remaining 50 weeks of each year to be filled but Allan was no slouch at domestic climbing either. As a Liverpudlian by adoption – he trained in structural engineering there and worked for the city council for 40 years – he joined the senior local club, the Wayfarers', in 1953 and soon became one of that club's leading lights. He was a very versatile climber, enjoying the challenge of a Diff in the rain as much as a VS or HVS on dry rock, and was particularly attracted by Scottish winter climbing. So it was that during the 1950, 1960s and 1970s he accumulated an extraordinary success list, including all the classic rock routes on Cloggy and Scafell and all the best classic ridges and gullies of Glen Coe and Ben Nevis. He was president of the Wayfarers' during 1970-1 and a key member of the team which organised the extension of Robertson Lamb hut in Langdale, as a memorial to the custodian for 40 years, Harry Spilsbury.

Most of us know that it is not always easy to find just the right climbing partner available at the right time, especially when planning for the Alps. When Allan occasionally ran out of partners he would go anyway and either solo the easier routes or find someone in a hut. In that way in 1960 he met Kate Woods, an adventurous climber from what was then Rhodesia. They shared a further four Alpine holidays together and Allan was clearly smitten. But as she would not settle in England and he would not go to Africa the romance came to nought and Allan remained a bachelor.

In such a long climbing career it would be tedious to list all Allan's successes and all his many friends but fellow AC companions were Oliver Turnbull, George Lee, George Bintley and Ben Stroude. In various combinations, though always with Allan, they traversed the Weisshorn, Matterhorn, the Meije, the Drus, the Charmoz-Grépon and got up the north ridge of the Peigne and the north face of the Obergabelhorn, among many other good routes.

On retirement Allan moved to a bungalow on the edge of Keswick and continued climbing, mostly with another Lakeland retiree, John Ramsden, but also alone on a formidable selection of party pieces in Borrowdale. He was, in addition, introduced by a neighbour, Dennis Evans, to downhill skiing: an unlikely pursuit for one who had previously scorned skiers as the 'peacock parade of plankers'. But so enthusiastic did Allan become that he spent three or four ski holidays each winter from the age of 60 until he reached 80, when insurance became difficult. He continued walking on the local fells until his late eighties and to the Keswick shops and back until his nineties.

To this writer and to many others Allan was a wonderful companion and mentor on the hills, and a loyal friend anywhere. He will be greatly missed.

*Ben Stroude*

## Walt Unsworth
## 1928 - 2017

Walter Unsworth first came to the attention of the climbing public in 1964 with *The English Outcrops*, published by Gollancz at 30/-, or £1.50 in today's money. This was a narrative compendium, illustrated with photographs and sketch maps, broken down by rock-type and pointing climbers at crags

Walt Unsworth in 1976 in the Dolomites.    Walt Unsworth in 1990.

and quarries from the Wainstones and Malham to Stanage, Harrison's, Swanage, Bosigran and dozens of so-called outcrops in between. The book had required considerable research and a lot of climbing, arriving at the right moment in history. As Jack Longland wrote in his introduction: 'This is a very useful book.'

Walt was a Manchester schoolmaster who had started hill walking in his teens, progressing after the Second World War into rock climbing to become one of the weekend denizens at the famous Wall End Barn in Langdale. An early foray in the Jotenheim, some gorge exploration in the Libyan desert during National Service, and a hiking trip in the Maritime Alps had broadened his horizons, but after training in Chester he became a science teacher in Wolverhampton and got married. Though he rock climbed and mountaineered assiduously throughout the British Isles – climbing routes such as *Kaisergebirge Wall* and *Central Buttress* – he didn't revisit the big mountains for some years. However, by the time Chris Bonington proposed him for the Club in 1968, Walt had a further eight alpine seasons under his belt. He'd climbed in both the Eastern and Western Alps and led ascents of many of the classic peaks including the Matterhorn, the Zinal Rothorn and the Grand Charmoz. In due course he became head of physics at a large Manchester school where he encouraged pupils to hill walk and climb and introduced one of the earliest Duke of Edinburgh Award schemes.

But Walt had always aspired to write full time, and encouraged by selling a story to *Girl* comic in 1961, he wrote climbing guides to two crags where he'd been closely involved in the development: Anglezarke Quarry and

Pontesford Rocks. *The English Outcrops* followed to considerable acclaim, so the next year, more ambitiously, he published a biography of Whymper – *Matterhorn Man* – and then in 1967 *Tiger in the Snow*, a biography of Mummery. It was a time when public interest in the outdoors, in hill walking, climbing and mountaineering, was expanding rapidly, and in partnership with Brian Evans, a leading if rather younger Lancashire climber who was a professional artist and book designer, Walt set up Cicerone Press, initially to publish independent climbing guides to the Lakes for which there was, they thought, a gap in the market. The business soon took off, talented authors were located, encouraged and contracted, and Cicerone expanded into a whole library of hiking, cycling and climbing guides to Britain, to Europe and eventually to more distant places as diverse as Jordan and the Himalaya.

In the 1960s there was only one, hardly authoritative, monthly magazine devoted to mountain and hill-walking interests, and when the editor retired, the publishers invited Walt to replace him, and the re-hung publication, entitled *Climber & Rambler*, went from strength to strength under his knowledgeable and energetic editorship. It catered for the softer end of the outdoor market that the newly emergent and elitist *Mountain* failed to cover, and soon achieved a large circulation. In due course as editorial adviser to the publishers, Holmes McDougall, he launched the dedicated hill walking magazine *The Great Outdoors*, still publishing as *TGO*.

By now Walt had abandoned the world of chalk and blackboards in favour of the pen, quietly working away in his garage office in suburban Worsley. His three historical novels for teenagers became recommended reading for the national curriculum and a regular output of outdoor-oriented books followed, eventually totalling over 30 titles. Particularly highly acclaimed was *Everest: The Mountaineering History*, first published in 1981 and updated regularly thereafter, which won the first prize for mountain literature at the 1992 Trento Festival. Among other well-known titles are the useful *Encyclopaedia of Mountaineering* (1975) and *Hold the Heights: The Foundations of Mountaineering* (1993) while *Peaks, Passes & Glaciers* (1981) is a wide-ranging anthology of articles from the *Alpine Journal*.

Meanwhile he was masterminding, with Brian Evans, the ever-expanding Cicerone publishing empire. Soon proper premises were needed, there was warehousing to consider and staff to employ. Cicerone moved to the Old Police Station in Milnthorpe on the southern outskirts of the Lake District, and the Unsworth family, his wife Dorothy and two children, did likewise, into an old Georgian sea captain's house close by.

From the beginning Walt was always supportive of young or aspiring writers, giving many their first break into print. His kindly, avuncular encouragement started several now well-known guidebook writers and magazine journalists on their careers, and it is entirely fitting that he has been dubbed the 'father' of outdoor writing. Indeed in 1980 Walt was a founder member and first president of the nascent Outdoor Writers Guild (OWG), originally a small group of outdoor media professionals who came together at the annual outdoor and mountain equipment trade fair at Harrogate. The OWG soon expanded to encompass photographers, film-makers, broadcasters, publishers, designers and public relations folk, all experts in outdoor and wilderness activities, several other AC members among them. Walt proved an excellent and resourceful president and by the time he retired from the post in 2001 the OWG was recognised through-out the national and international media and membership had reached over 200; it is now the Outdoor Writers & Photographers Guild.

Although he had given up serious technical climbing, Walt never lost his enthusiasm for the mountains and wild places. Once time and circum-stances permitted, he trekked and travelled widely, often on journalistic as-signments for the national media, and visited mountain areas all over the world, from New Zealand to Patagonia, from Canada to China, where he was often able to make ascents of such important non-technical peaks as Kilimanjaro and Kinabalu.

Cicerone Press was sold as a going concern in 1999 on Walt's retirement from business, and now, 18 years later, continues to thrive with a list of over 250 titles 'for walkers and climbers, written and produced by walkers and climbers.' It is a worthy legacy. There will be few Alpine Club members without at least one of Walt's titles, or at least one Cicerone guide in their bookcase.

*John Cleare*

*Kev Reynolds writes:* In the mid-1970s Walt Unsworth changed my life with a phone call during which he invited me to write a guide to the Pyrenees for his newly-founded Cicerone Press, then just five or six years old. I'd never even looked at a guidebook before, but Walt's call polished my ego and I said yes.

Forty years on, *Walks & Climbs in the Pyrenees* has been joined by dozens of other titles for Cicerone, most of them inspired and mentored by Walt, who took me under his wing and nurtured my career by sending me off to explore distant mountain regions and report back with a manuscript of routes, a clutch of maps and scores of photographs to be transformed into another of his pocket-sized guides.

Knowing how difficult it is to make a living from such a precarious occu-pation, in the early days he'd set me a challenge by saying he had a gap in his production schedules, and could I let him have my next project six months (or so) before the contract deadline. That way he kept me on my toes and increased my workload. For a time I was producing two and sometimes three books a year for him, and he even gave me the freedom to develop a series of guides under the Cicerone imprint that enriched my career.

He was a generous man. If he had a compilation to write for a different publisher, he'd draw me in to contribute a chapter or two for him. And he would introduce me to rival publishers and magazine editors if he thought I'd benefit.

Walt's mountain knowledge was encyclopaedic, and planning new projects with him was always a joy. One day his by now instantly recognised voice came over the phone. 'Do you know Hubert Walker's *Walking in the Alps*? It's long out of date and we'd like to publish an updated version with greater coverage. We'd like you to do it.'

Of course, I knew Walker's book. Published in 1951 it had become my Alpine bible. But it only covered eight districts in the Alps. Walt wanted more. We haggled. He won, the result being that I embarked on a four-year crusade to cover the whole Alpine range in 19 chapters. Our version of *Walking in the Alps* appeared in 1998, 20 years after that first Pyrenean guide came into print. It was to be the last of my books that Walt published, for the following year he retired and sold Cicerone Press to Jonathan and Lesley Williams who share both Walt's vision and his love of mountains.

To my regret, I never had a single day on the hill with him. All our meetings were in Harrogate, Milnthorpe or at the London Book Fair, where we'd chew the cud, discuss mountains and mountaineering and, inevitably, signs contracts for yet another guide. With his death I've lost a mentor and a friend, whose phone call four decades ago, changed my life for the better. Of that there is no doubt.

## Mark Vallance
## 1944 - 2018

Mark Vallance on top of the *Nose*.

Mark Vallance died on 19 April at the age of 73. He had been suffering from the progressively debilitating Parkinson's disease for 19 years. His many climbing achievements and contributions to the sport are well documented in his autobiography *Wild Country* (Vertebrate, 2016) but he will always be remembered first and foremost as the maker of 'Friends'. In view of his book, what follows is more a record based on our friendship.

Mark arrived at Abbotsholme School in Derbyshire aged 14 a year before me. We were in the same class and soon discovered a mutual interest in climbing. As well as from my father, encouragement came from the headmaster, Robin Hodgkin, a respected rock climber and mountaineer. One of our early objectives was the breaking of the school rule that said: 'Thou shall not lead anything above V Diff.' And were we keen! Even the school buildings were fair game, the most alarming route being the outside traverse of a high chapel window, on 45° sloping footholds and pinch grips for hands. On a Duke of Edinburgh Award 30-mile hike over two days in North Wales we unofficially included three routes on Bochlwyd Buttress, *Munich Climb* on Tryfan, *Flying Buttress* with a new variation final pitch, *Main Wall* on

Cyrn Las and *Lockwood's Chimney*. We were in fact given a lot of freedom and both living within cycling distance of the grit edges of Birchen, Gardoms and Froggatt we began a long and steady apprenticeship on rock. It took us two years before we were comfortable on VS. We progressed more rapidly thereafter and remarkably our climbing standard remained the same. We were competitive but not fiercely so and we both wanted to lead everything. If Mark did a notable route I would repeat it within, at most, a few weeks, and vice versa, though I remember being somewhat daunted when Mark, then 16, reported that he had just soloed *Brown's Eliminate* in gym shoes. A year later we both managed to lead *Cenotaph Corner* the same day. Back in Bakewell my father treated us to a celebratory drink in his local pub causing a few of his bemused friends to think Mark and I had been vandalising a monument in Whitehall.

After leaving school we went our separate ways, Mark to study physical education at Goldsmiths College. We did meet up for a trip to the Alps in 1965, borrowing Mark's father's Mini for the six-week holiday. The car was grossly overloaded with Mark's brother Steven, Rick Johnson and me, plus all our gear. Unsurprisingly the suspension gave way in Italy. This was after Mark had a narrow squeak on the traverse of the Piz Palü. Crossing a steep snow slope to avoid a cornice a foothold broke beneath his rope-mate, who began to slide towards the abyss. A shout alerted Mark who was in front and he was able to turn and brace himself against the only knob of rock poking through the snow and hold the fall. It was a chastened but wiser team that returned to the hut. The car's broken suspension eventually severed the brake cable and we ended up in someone's garden near Bolzano with a stoved-in headlight: my fault as I, as front seat passenger, was in charge of the handbrake. After makeshift repairs, and good climbing in the Dolomites, the car finally gave up 10 miles from home in Matlock. Mark's father was remarkably sanguine about his wrecked vehicle.

After Goldsmiths, Mark joined the British Antarctic Survey as a general dogsbody mountaineer based at Halley Bay. He became base commander in his second year and on his return married Jan whom he had met whilst at college and who was then teaching in the Falkland Islands. They returned via the US where Mark met Ray Jardine, the inventor of Friends for the first time and climbed in Yosemite. Mark loved the Valley granite and returned years later to climb The Nose on El Cap with Hugh Banner. Back in the UK he got a job with the Peak District National Park Authority and it was whilst working as volunteers officer that Ray asked him if he would consider manuacturing and marketing Friends in the UK. Mark, having climbed with Ray previously and been shown the secret prototypes in action immediately realised their potential and despite having no engineering or business background seized his chance and, on a very steep learning curve, set up Wild Country. Any climber who saw Mark on the TV programme *Tomorrow's World* taking a leader fall onto a Friend from *Dexterity*, a crack climb at Millstone Edge, must have realised that here was a seriously effective piece of climbing protection. As well as opening up the possibility of giving some protection on routes deemed too bold to be justifiable it enabled many of the more timid of us to try climbs we had only dreamt about. Friends could be used on almost any climb of any grade that had a crack.

The business thrived but Mark was essentially an ideas man with, more significantly, the ability and impetus to transform his ideas into products. 'Rocks' followed Friends and were entirely his own invention. I still have a bunch of weird and wonderfully shaped prototypes he gave me to try out. Later, when president of the BMC, he designed and launched the plastic tear-proof and waterproof British Mountain Maps. Unable to persuade a recalcitrant Ordnance Survey to take any interest they were eventually produced by Harvey Maps with great success. He also knew a good idea of someone else's when he saw it. He negotiated with Boreal to market the sticky rubber-soled Firé rock boots and brought Dick Turnbull's 'Quasar' tent design under the Wild Country flag.

Mark's next project was inspired by a visit to an outdoor retailer in New England called L L Bean. He wanted to create something similar in the UK and 'Outside' was the result with its large retail space mini climbing wall and inside upstairs eating area. Mark knew I was interested in catering; we had had memorable meals in the Auberge de Loube near Buoux and at Philippos in Courmayeur and had noted the ease with which French cafés added a check tablecloth and morphed into a restaurant for the evenings. Mark wanted to try the same idea at Outside and asked if I would run it as an independent concern. He very generously provided all the capital, as I had none, and after a sticky patch early on, the café side, if not the restaurant, worked well.

We climbed a lot together in the mid 1980s with several trips to the Alps. He dragged me, an ice-climbing novice with gear borrowed from him, up the *Swiss Route* on Les Courtes. On another occasion after a trade show in Munich where our mettle was tested by our German hosts with a spell of bridge jumping on climbing ropes beneath an autobahn viaduct, we climbed *Bavarian Dream* on the Schusselkarspitze in the Wetterstein: a long hard climb by our standards but what impressed me most, descending in pitch darkness without a torch, was Mark's uncanny ability to see in the dark. I would have sat the night out but he was able to spot traces of the path and guide us down as it wound tortuously on through the woods.

Mark became president of the Climbers' Club shortly before its centenary. I once had a slide taken on a timer setting showing four grinning teenagers sitting on top of the Hound's Head Pinnacle at Tremadog. The pinnacle was dynamited a few years later. Of the four of us, one served as CC secretary, one on the committee and one, Mark, became its president. Ideal, I thought, for inclusion in the centenary journal though maybe I should have a copy made first in case it went astray. It did. I received a slide and a print back from Kodak showing the Taj Mahal and when I complained, the offer of a free film!

In 1990 Mark fulfilled an ambition to climb an 8,000er. Having had his first taste of high altitude on Himalchuli a year earlier, he ascended

Shishapangma. In 2002 he became a reforming president of the BMC pushing through a future policy review, updating the articles of association and persuading the BMC to abolish the club block vote.

My last climb with Mark was, in 2006, the Old Man of Hoy. By then he had coped with Parkinson's Disease for eight years and its effects were becoming more pronounced. He could no longer trust his feet on footholds through lack of sensation and his balance was not as good. He found the wide crack pitch on the original route strenuous but managed it fine. After a pill break we pushed on to the top from where it was decided that Mark, being the most experienced of us, would take charge and get us safely down the abseils, especially the diagonal one back to the first stance. He had brought a long length of tape to back up some dubious abseil tat for just such a purpose.

Remarkably for such an active person I never once heard Mark complain about his ill luck in contracting the disease and his sense of humour never deserted him. Before I saw him for the last time at his care home, where he was, at best, able to shuffle along using a Zimmer frame and, at worst, needed help to put a pill in his mouth, I phoned to see if a visit was possible. 'Yes' he replied, 'I'm not planning to go to the gym this morning.'

For a time Mark had a sticker on his car saying 'Just Do It'. This was his philosophy, right to the end.

*Nick Longland*

## Joe Walmsley
## 1924 - 2017

Joe Walmsley, who passed away on 1 February 2017, was one of a group of very active climbers in the YMCA Mountaineering Club with Ted Courtenay, Dave Briggs, Ken Davidson and my dad Alex Ferguson, who all became lifelong members of the Rucksack Club. Joe was just 22 when he joined in March 1947 and the comprehensive record in his application is very impressive: a list of 'notable' climbs such as *Deer Bield Crack* in the Lakes, climbs on Skye and many long walks. My dad proposed Joe for membership and in his letter to the president mentions Joe's enthusiasm: carrying a full hemp rope on a YMCA Marsden to Hayfield walk just in case there was time for a quick route on Laddow. 'Joe's interests in the hills will last throughout his life I feel sure, but perhaps one of his strongest references for membership of the club is his own good nature.' How true on both counts.

In the post-war years travel was limited so there was a focus on climbing in Wales and the Lakes. Langdale was a favourite with the hub being the Old Dungeon Ghyll Hotel (ODG), run for many years by well-known climbers and good friends of the Rucksack Club, Sid and Jammy Cross. Joe met Maureen his wife-to-be during a meet at the ODG at Christmas 1957. Maureen was working there over the holiday and says: 'Where else

Above: Joe Walmsley, pictured left, in Kathmandu ahead of the expedition he led to Nuptse that made the first ascent in 1961. Jim Lovelock, base camp manager, is standing next to him, then Trevor Jones, John Streetly and behind him Les Brown.
*(Chris Bonington Photo Library)*

Right: Joe Walmsley climbing on Nuptse. The route can be considered the first high-altitude wall climbed in the Himalaya, a precursor to the immense achievement of the south face of Annapurna in 1970.

would a mountaineer expect to meet his wife.' They had two daughters, Joanna and Susan.

Joe's considerable mountaineering ability was evident at home and in the Alps and it led to him being at the forefront of Himalayan climbing in the 1950s and 1960s. In 1957 Joe was the leader of the Masherbrum expedition when along with Ted Dance and Geoff Smith had to survive some appalling weather conditions. The expedition was struck by tragedy with the sad death of Bob Downes through illness. Joe, with a youthful Don Whillans, reached the high point on Masherbrum a few hundred feet below the summit only to be forced back by difficult conditions. In Joe's words, 'we suffered discomforts and hardships but there was always the one purpose in mind – to climb the mountain.' In 1961 Joe led the team that made the first ascent of Nuptse (7864m), a major achievement in the history of mountaineering. These were both ground-breaking and demanding expeditions: the time away from home and family for many months; the long overland journey through countries it is now difficult to visit; the exploratory nature of the expeditions to very remote areas; the adverse weather conditions and the hard nature of the climbing.

The 1963 *Rucksack Club Journal* has two enthralling articles on the Nuptse expedition by James Lovelock and Dennis Davis. The overland journey to Kathmandu in two Vanguard estate cars was an epic in itself. An official

The team photographed walking out from base camp. Left to right: Trevor Jones, Les Brown, Jim Swallow, Joe Walmsley, Jim Lovelock, Chris Bonington, Prabhakar Shamsher Rana (?), Tashi Sherpa, Dennis Davis. *(Betty Milledge/Chris Bonington Photo Library)*

send off by the mayor of Manchester then on through Europe into Turkey and through Iran. High passes, mechanical problems, running off the road and freezing weather conditions were all part of a journey navigated using an AA route map. In those days, you could ring the AA and ask for a route map from say Stockport to Fort William, or in this case, Manchester to Kathmandu. The map that arrived in the post was, I suppose, the forerunner of todays sat nav. James Lovelock remembered: 'It was a proud moment when the two battered cars crested the Tribhuvan Rajpath at 8,162ft and started the twisting, winding run down to Kathmandu. The overland party of the Nuptse expedition arrived there, exactly five weeks after leaving Britain having covered 8,336 miles from Manchester Town Hall.'

The climbing on Nuptse was technically difficult and extremely challenging and the route they took is considered to be one of the first technical 'big walls' in the Himalaya. It was a classic siege, following a tricky rightward slanting central ridge on the south face to a large snow field, then a long leftward traverse along these snow slopes and over a difficult rock barrier to reach a couloir breaking through to the summit arête. After establishing eight camps Dennis Davis and Tashi Sherpa reached the summit, followed a day later by Chris Bonington, Les Brown, Jim Swallow and Pemba Sherpa.

Their accounts capture the extreme nature of living and climbing on the Nuptse face: 'one final section of the hardest ice yet at 70 degrees barred our way. Cautiously we moved up it, balancing on tiny footholds and chipping out handholds.' This was in an era long before modern gear: 'we had worn our vests, shirts, pullovers, two pairs of long underpants, down trousers and jackets, gloves and down bootees in our double sleeping bags.

Over all of this we pulled our windproof suits. Our boots had as usual frozen up overnight.'

What is apparent from speaking with Joe's contemporaries is that without his drive, determination and sometimes much-needed calm temperament, the Nuptse expedition would not have enjoyed the success it did. The Masherbrum and Nuptse expeditions were the true forerunners of the great Himalayan expeditions of the 1970s.

Joe was born and grew up in Salford. He worked at Metro Vickers, later AEI, where he qualified as a member of the Institution of Mechanical Engineers. Then in 1968, Joe and Maureen and their family moved to New Zealand for three years where he worked on the Manapouri Hydro Electric Power station on South Island. Joe embraced the climbing community down under, joining the New Zealand Alpine Club and serving as treasurer and then warden of the NZAC hut at the bottom of South Island. When they came home in 1970, Joe joined National Nuclear Power and worked for them until he retired in 1989.

He remained throughout his life a dedicated servant of the Rucksack Club. John Allen fondly recalls Joe's Easter meets in the early 1960s, camping below Wallabarrow crag in the Duddon valley. These meets led to the discovery and purchase of High Moss, the club's hut nearby. Among the many posts he filled for the club, he served as president from 1966. Joe was closely involved in the early days of the British Mountaineering Council, making an invaluable contribution to its Technical Committee and holding the office of president in 1979-82. He was also the Mountain Rescue Committee's equipment officer for 18 years.

I have very fond memories of Joe. I remember when I was a young teenager being somewhat in awe of his Himalayan achievements, and then over the years, getting to know him on meets such as the famous High Moss family meets or at our home, and seeing for myself that friendly and good nature to which my dad referred.

*Rob Ferguson*

*A longer version of this obituary first appeared in the Rucksack Club Journal and is reproduced here with kind permission.*

# Alpine Club Notes

Capt R E Thompson (d1918), Hampshire Regiment,
died in the powerful German offensive of spring 1918 that sent the
Allies reeling, prompting Haig to demand a desperate defence.

# LINDSAY GRIFFIN

# President's Valedictory Address

Read before the Alpine Club on 26 November, 2016[1]

It might be worth starting by reminding you of the obvious. The purpose of the AC is to facilitate its members with their interest in, and love of, alpine mountains (and I use the word 'alpine' loosely). Our members comprise active and committed mountaineers, not so active or retired mountaineers but people who have done their time, and those who have a deep interest in the mountain environment through art, history or science. And like any other active club, one of the AC's main missions should be getting its members together: climbing, networking, exchanging information, socialising and also preserving and facilitating access to our heritage. I think it was Tom Price who said 'mountaineering is an activity that brings a lot of loners together.' We do all this through our climbing meets, our events, our communications, our exhibitions and our information dissemination: our encouragement.

We also believe we have a responsibility for preserving the values of mountaineering for future generations. I came across another quote recently, this one by a flourishing businessman. I'm sure it's not original, and I'm also sure he didn't have climbing in mind, but he said 'success in life is more or less a question of hanging on, when others have let go.' If you are at school and serious about your athletics, the holy grail would be to represent your country in the Olympics, to be a Usain Bolt. Nearly all climbers now come into the activity through indoor walls and with the acceptance of competition climbing as an Olympic sport, many young wall climbers will now see competitions as the natural extension. And being ever an optimist I don't see any problem with that myself, as long as the guardians of our broad activity don't become side tracked to the extent that the other important work carried out for the wider mountaineering community becomes neglected.

Why are we in the prime position to preserve the values of climbing and mountaineering? Over the last term AC members have put up a wealth of new routes: at the very blue end of the spectrum, on modest sea cliffs in Ireland, through bigger stuff in the UK and Africa, to major new Alpine lines in the Mont Blanc massif, and, well into the red end of the spectrum, hard technical first ascents on 6,000m and 7,000m peaks. I look at all the major new routes at altitude that have been achieved by British climbers in the Greater Ranges so far this year and all were done by expeditions that included AC members, many supported by the new Montane Alpine Club Climbing Fund. During my term the AC has supported around two dozen

[1]. This is an edited amalgamation of two speeches the president gave at the 2016 AGM and the annual dinner that evening.

expeditions all with the aim of making first ascents in excellent style in Alaska, South America, Greenland, Kyrgyzstan, Tajikistan, China, India, Pakistan and Nepal.

It's true these have involved a relatively small percentage of our members, but have greatly enhanced the prestige of the Club, especially internationally. Many more of our members have been involved in our own meets. Over the three-year term we have expanded our meets programme considerably. When I started, someone took me aside and reminded me that presidents have a notorious reputation for never going on meets, so I was determined to rectify that. I failed. I think I've managed six altogether. Even I can do the simple arithmetic; that's on average only two a year. But large or small, they were all good. The AC ran well over 30. We've created more diversity, explored new venues both at home and abroad, more meets for those relatively new to the game, slightly more in the way of joint events with foreign climbers. I'd hoped to do better with that; it may come, and similarly joint meets with other clubs.

I came in keen to improve both our public face and our voice and it is great that we now have an attractive and ever developing website. It not only publicises all our up-coming events and meets, but contains reports on the latter, news, an increasing number of English descriptions for climbs of all disciplines within a reasonable distance of the Chamonix valley, a regularly updated Mont Blanc weather report, and information on our books, photographs and archives. We should shortly have every expedition report in the library digitised and online, all 1,100 of them, thanks to David Kinniburgh and the IT team; we currently have all the *AJ*s back to 1930 online and are continuing the digitisation of the earlier volumes. We also hope to have a strong community aspect, and to introduce a section on members' activities.

Let's turn again to the international stage and particularly the Piolets d'Or, in which we are heavily involved, and have helped to evolve into a more informal event that celebrates all that is great and good about progressive modern alpinism. In the last three years each of the Lifetime Achievement Awards, presented by the Piolets d'Or, has gone to three of our members, while again in the same timespan three of the ascents awarded Piolets d'Or have also involved our members. As either part of the organization, or as a speaker, or a recipient, 13 of our members took part in this year's event in La Grave.

In Italy this year two of our members were presented with the Karl Unterkircher Award, an Italian-based biennial award to a team or teams that have demonstrated great climbing skills or carried out extreme expeditions in alpine style. Like the ethos of the Piolets, it tries not to be competitive but is an award for fair play. It's also worth adding that our members sometimes excel in other quarters; one was recently awarded the Nobel Prize for physics.

We are supporting the developing online Alpine route database Camp-Camp, and the app MountaiNow, a crowd-sourcing initiative that aims to share the current mountain conditions on any day of the year. We're directly represented at the UIAA and on its Mountain Protection Commission. Various other commissions also have delegates and post holders who are

AC members. We have reorganized the Spirit of Mountaineering, the AC's commendation of those, of any nationality, who in the true spirit of mountaineering have unselfishly given exceptional assistance to those in need of help in the mountains. By inaugurating an international panel, we have had a much greater voice on important affairs both at home and abroad: several of our statements have been taken, translated, and publicised by foreign alpine organisations.

This period has obviously been one of the busiest for the AC Library, with our crucial involvement in the celebrations to mark the 150th anniversary of the Golden Age of alpinism. Many of our paintings, engravings, artefacts and scans of a number of our historic photographs became the exhibition 'The Treasures of the Alpine Club and Alpinism in the 19th Century'. It formed the key part of the display in Chamonix's Alpine Museum. This exhibition, with changing content, was visible to the public all through the 2015 summer, and over last winter up until May. Work continues to have this displayed to a greater or lesser extent at venues throughout the UK. The first of these will be a relatively small show at the Frenchay Village Museum in Bristol, running from January to March next year. And over the last year or so there has been significant liaison with the BMC's newly inaugurated digital archive of historic mountaineering images. I hope we will continue to increase our involvement with, and representation on, events of international importance, because continuing to raise our already high profile abroad will in turn raise it within the UK. New leaflets and a discounted subscription aimed at the under 25s, student liaison, and a fledgling university mentoring system are promoting the club to the young.

When I began my term the property sub-committee had been asked to investigate the potential for redevelopment of the clubhouse. It's been a long road and Victor has outlined the current situation, where planning application for a two-storey extension has been turned down, but permission given for a set-back single story, and then if and how we should maximise use for the club. Fortunately, the top floors of Charlotte Road continue to be attractive for rental, with Shoreditch having become a desirable residence for small businesses. Rental income from Charlotte Road has grown considerably over the last few years, making rents our largest source of income, greater than subscriptions.

One of the great success stories, in my humble opinion, is taking partnership with ABMSAC of the George Starkey hut in Patterdale. The AC at last has a climbing hut, a venue outside London where members can meet and climb together. It is also an asset that may help us in the future negotiate reciprocal rights. I would like to thank all those who took part in the on-line consultation. There was a large response, with more than 90% supporting the proposal that the AC should purchase a share in the building. We now have a board of directors and a management committee that are already discussing improvements and ways to make it more accessible to members. We hope to have an easy to use on-line booking system in place by early next year. And there is its potential use for events – we've recently endorsed a meeting of top young alpinists there over a weekend in December, and an AC alpine training weekend will be held there next year. It's a good hut in a good location: let's use it.

Talking of the hut and our members reminds me that membership now stands at a little over 1,500: full members 75%; aspirants 20%; associates 4%. I'm going to talk a little more about this later, but it is noticeable that rather more climbers now enter the club as aspirant members and then progress within the club to become full members, than come straight in as full members. We should be encouraging their progression. For example we elected 11 new members in the month of October, plus two more who had gained the experience to change their status from aspirant to full. Nine of those new members came in as aspirants, two as full. The overall number of members is, in itself, arguably less important than having that constant influx of committed young climbers.

Another of my goals was to improve on the gender balance, and while we've had partial success, with significantly more women in key posts, this still needs more work, though the percentage of female members in the AC, currently 11%, compares very favourably with other major climbing clubs in the UK. You can slant statistics to say anything, as politicians know, but of those accepted for new membership in October 18% were women. But if you look at those accepted as full members, it was 50%! On the most recent meet 30% were women.

So, in order to make all I've talked about, and more, happen, much committee time has been spent over the term in making considerable improvements to our operating procedures, management structure, regulations, rules, documentation, and administration. All this might seem a bit tedious to the outsider, and to be quite honest, sometimes it is, but by getting the club operating efficiently and smoothly, we free up a lot more time to be devoted towards fundamental goals, such as facilitating climbing and augmenting member benefits. We took the step of bringing in a professional manager for the office, and for most of the term our administration and office management have been largely in the hands of Ursula and Iwonna. Ursula, amongst a number of achievements made great progress with our website, social media and advertising, while Iwonna has always been primarily involved with looking after our membership. Both have now left us, and we wish them well for the future.

Nearly three years ago we came up with a new, brief vision statement, which is in the front of this handbook, and followed that with what we quickly realised was perhaps an overly ambitious mission statement outlining how we were going to implement it. Many of the things we set out to do have become reality. I'm pleased about that. Some we only partially achieved to my satisfaction, and one or two we didn't make much progress at all. However, apart from a couple of items, not fully completing a project was not really due to meeting insuperable problems, it was simply due to lack of resources, suitable 'person-power'. As a club we are certainly not alone in this. It's a perennial problem with voluntary organisations. There are always too few people trying to do far too much work. Yet volunteering is a great way of having your say, putting something back into the club, and back into mountaineering. From time to time we send out Alpinet messages, advertising for people who can lend a hand with a current, specific project, a project that can often require no more than a few hours a month. So spread the word, and we can spread the workload. It is your club, and a club is only the sum of its members.

A few years ago, I was climbing in Italy and attended a lecture given by a friend of mine. He introduced the concept that climbing could be defined by the four 'As': *avventura*, *ambiente*, *amici* and *agonismo* or adventure, the environment, friendship, and competitive spirit.

I'm going to shuffle them around because the mix you come up with, the various priorities, will determine your outlook and motivation when it comes to climbing. It will be different from one individual to the next and it will be different in various stages of your climbing career. For instance, when you're 23 or 24 the order of importance will be as follows: first, competitive spirit, then adventure, environment and lastly friendship. I can relate to that. But even before you get to my age that order has completely reversed. I think that as time goes by routes are still important, summits are still important, but increasingly so are the people you meet along the way. As we all know, climbing can bring enduring friendships. I thought about this earlier in the year when I had two great days on the crag, full of banter, with people whom I first climbed with in 1972. I'm not going to name them, as they might not want it known they are quite that old.

I think the Alpine Club will cater for any mix; a climbing club should be all about getting its members together. We each climb for very different reasons, and I believe our activity should be big enough to accept these. For me, exploring new ground, looking around the corner, has been, I suppose, the aspect that has always given me the biggest buzz, from my first new route in the Mont Blanc massif when I was a difficult-to-manage whippersnapper of 20, right up to this year which has only resulted in some extremely modest new rock routes at various locations, home and abroad. We can all have escapades to different degrees: even on a short, new, trad rock route.

Adventure. People will always push the limits of our activity, and a number of climbers who have been considered amongst the best mountaineers of their respective generations have died this year in the mountains. But generally, and it is a generalisation, climbing is becoming more risk averse. Alpinism is seeing a marked decline all over Europe. You know, 30 years ago in mountaineering it was much easier to be experienced than it was to be technically accomplished. Now it is exactly the reverse.

There are contributing issues to this decline. For instance, students now have a hard time, both financially and with the need to find internships out of term time, so in the UK we have lost most of the university expeditions we saw in the past and numbers on alpine meets have dwindled. I've come across a couple of universities where nowadays the university 'mountaineering club' is largely a bouldering club. There are exceptions, of course:

one of our guests here tonight is Francis Tochter from Coventry University Mountaineering Society, which over the last few years has run a very successful Alpine programme during the summer vacation, with 20 or 30 participants. Most young, committed mountaineers now also have careers, you know that proper job thing, and are limited to 20 or 25 days per year. And as we live in a world where everything appears to be judged by success, and the number of likes on your Facebook page, quite understandably there is a growing trend to opt for venues that, for a quick hit, can tip the odds in their favour, like Alaska and Patagonia.

This isn't meant to be negative, as I still see alpinism as being in a good state. For a start I don't see us returning to, for example, the situation in the 1980s when there was a very high death toll, notably amongst Polish mountaineers who were top of the tree in that decade. There simply wasn't then the communal knowledge we have today; there was also an expectation to up the anti on each successive ascent. Some of the greatest high-altitude, out-on-a-limb ascents during the 1980s have only recently been surpassed, or indeed equalled.

I'm optimistic too when it comes to style and ethics. Many more mountaineers appear to be openly honest about what they achieve. Technology improves all the time and most of us embrace it, though I think there are few here today tweeting from the summit. In recent years I think the single event that has really impacted on climbing, certainly in more hostile terrain, has been the ability to receive up-to-date and accurate weather forecasts in the field, or indeed on the climb. Taking that sort of communication is definitely a personal choice, and we should never allow it to become mandatory. However, the majority of expedition reports I encounter these days imply that the teams have been working from received weather reports, enabling them to plan their ascent at the right time, to go more lightweight and consequently faster.

Equipment has obviously got lighter for the same strength and warmth. And then elapsed time, the growth in communal experience, the ease of access to information, Google Earth, even the use of drones to scope your route have all gone a long way to making the outcome more certain. As Hansjörg Auer said: 'If I want to make a difficult ascent on a little known mountain I have to be prepared to work for it, and that can sometimes take several years. If I want to go to a familiar peak, all I need to do is Google it.'

So in order to keep the fundamental raison d'être of our activity alive, that necessary uncertainty that is key to adventure, alpinists will just add more into the mix. For a start they have got a whole lot better. As with other sports, people now train much harder, they are fitter, stronger. Then there is the greater knowledge of nutrition, hydration, diet: it's called progress. I believe more and more people will climb in better style and it's happening already. They'll climb free, whereas in the past they aided, and they will have less negative impact on the environment. On the majority of mountains, certainly not all by a long way, but on the majority of mountains, getting up at all costs will become a thing of the past.

And the Alpine Club should, indeed I hope will, be playing a significant part in all this. I look at all the major new routes at altitude that have been achieved by British climbers in the Greater Ranges so far this year and all were done by expeditions that included AC members. In order to preserve our activity, and its values, they and more importantly their eventual successors, need the support of this Club.

That starts with our aspirant members, and its great to see we have a whole table full of new aspirants here tonight; I appreciate you coming. For some of the reasons I've outlined earlier, our statistics show that these days rather more climbers enter the club as aspirants and then progress within the club to become full members. Most will go on to have some fine adventures in the Alps, or further afield in the Greater Ranges, and it's our role to facilitate this. In X years time, some of these will be the role models for another generation, and maybe one of the Aspirants on that table tonight will, in the future, be delivering this speech.

As I outlined earlier, we've greatly expanded our activity in the last few years. There is a long list of people who made this work and I want to thank them. If I started to name individuals, not only would it take all evening, but it would also sound like an Oscars speech. So I will be brief and say a huge thanks to all those on our IT, communications and publication teams, all those involved with our properties, those who do such sterling work in the library with our books, photographs, paintings, reports, the displays and exhibitions, making all our material so much more accessible. And I certainly won't forget all those involved with our regional events, dinners, our lecture series and organising our meets. I think it is appropriate to mention key players we are going to lose at the end of this year, who have done so much for the club over the last three years on the committee: outgoing vice president Malcolm Bass, chair of finance Kimball Morrison, Susan Jensen Charlie Burbridge and Jerry Lovatt. As you'll know Jerry is stepping down from his position of honorary librarian, and will take emeritus status from the start of next year. He's been in post for more than 25 years. We know that a certain George Yeld edited the *Alpine Journal* from around 1896 to 1926: that's a remarkable 30 years. But, to paraphrase this year's Nobel Laureate for Literature, the times they have changed. 25 years in this day and age is a really remarkable contribution. Jerry is unable to be with us today, but we'll be thanking him more formally later.

Despite some of our meetings being, inevitably, fraught at times, I've had a lot of help from committee members, and others. So, I'm now completely going to break the rule I made a minute ago by saying a big, big thanks to someone who isn't actually leaving, and that's been my right-hand woman Anna Lawford. When Anna does eventually stand down from the post of hon secretary, she's going to be an almost impossible act to follow.

It now remains to hand the torch onto John Porter. There were many times when I found myself thinking that having just a climber as a president leaves much to be desired: what you really need is an ex company director. Well, now you've got both, and I'm confident the Club will progress in the right direction, at least the sort of direction we have guided it over the last three years. I suspect John should cover his ears for the next bit. Personally, I'm entering the de-mob happy period, really looking forward to gaining an extra 30 hours a week for many weeks of next year, so I'll hopefully be getting back to earning a living, and doing a lot more sorely needed climbing. I've certainly found it challenging and very time consuming, and while I very definitely couldn't put my hand on my heart and say I enjoyed every minute, I have learnt a lot; for instance I can now recite perfectly the North Wales to London timetable. I do have a nice sense of satisfaction that we made a lot of progress. Above all, I'm deeply honoured that I had the privilege of being your president. Thank you.

*Lindsay Griffin*

## Spirits of the Dolomites

The discovery of instructions for Alpine Club thermometer No325, positioned near the summit of Marmolada in 1860, was like finding a holy relic from the early days of mountaineering in the Dolomites. It happened when my sister Susan and I were in Cortina researching our book, *Spirits of the Dolomites*, where we retrace Amelia Edwards' pioneering journey through the Dolomites in 1872, which she recorded in *Untrodden Peaks and Unfrequented Valleys*.

John Ball, first Alpine Club president, and John Birkbeck, accompanied by their guide Victor Tiarriz from Chamonix, left Val di Fassa on 31 August 1860 to climb Marmolada, the highest peak in the Dolomites. They chose to climb Punta Rocca, which turned out to be the second-highest summit, but strong winds hindered their climb. Nevertheless, they left the minimum thermometer No325, with its instructions, a few feet below the top, at the time the highest point anyone had reached on Marmolada. Here is John Ball's account, from his personal diary, of how they fixed the thermometer:

*The account of Amelia Edwards' pioneering Dolomites journey, Untrodden Peaks and Unfrequented Valleys.*

B. [Birkbeck] very miserable, shivering from the cold and altogether unhappy. The lunch over, I set to work, with Victor's assistance, to fix the minimum thermometer to the rock behind us. He attached a slip of pine wood, which I had prepared, with a couple of strong nails, to which I added a third, and, behind the board, attached the thermometer with string! Not having wire; the wind meanwhile so piercing that, though the temperature was 5.6 = 42 Fahrenheit, my fingers were quite benumbed. I asked B. to fill up the form to be left in the glass tube. He swore bravely at the d----d thermometer, but filled up the paper tant bien que mal, which I attached. I fear the winter – or perhaps sooner – will see them all set loose from the rock: the best chance is that the snow will reach this place soon.[1]

1. *Alpine Journal* XVIII, p386.

Left: Giuseppe Ghedina, Amelia Edwards' guide in 1872. Right: Stella d'Oro Hotel, Cortina, 1890.

No, we didn't find the instructions on top of Marmolada! Here's the story of our serendipitous discovery.

We met mountaineering historian Carlo Gandini, now in his 70s, and one of the famous *Scoiattoli* (Cortina Squirrels) in his youth – amateur climbers dedicated to climbing the *diretissima*. Carlo's eyes lit up when he heard that we were following Amelia Edwards and invited us to his home, next to the Olympic ice stadium, where he generously shared his vast archive of photographs and documents about the first local guides who led their illustrious clients on most first ascents in the Dolomites. He gave us a photograph of Giuseppe Ghedina, Amelia's guide, and arranged for us to meet Giuseppe's great-granddaughter Cinzia Ghedina; the family still lives in Cortina. Carlo also went out of his way to fix-up a meeting with another old-timer, Marco Menardi.

Marco is related through his father's family to Francesco 'Checo' Lacedelli, the oldest Dolomite mountain guide, who was favoured by the Austrian climber Paul Grohmann; Checo and Grohmann made the first ascents of four of the top ten Dolomite peaks during 1863-4, when Checo was 68 years old. Marco's uncle, Lino Lacedelli, made the first ascent of K2 in 1954. Marco's maternal family owned the famous Stella d'Oro, one of the first hotels in Cortina.

Although the hotel closed and was turned into the Cassa Rurale ed Artigiana bank in 1973, Marco has preserved the guest books from when the inn opened in 1844. He invited us to his home to look at the books and see if we could find anything of interest. By then, we knew that Amelia stayed at the Aquila Nera Hotel while she was in Cortina, coincidentally at the same time William Edward Utterson Kelso was a guest when he made the first ascent of Becco di Mezzodì with his guide Santo Siorpaes.[2] So our interest was more general than specific to Amelia Edwards.

2. *Alpine Journal* VI, p201

Marco is a quiet, unassuming person and a gracious host who made us feel welcome without any fuss. His kindness and generosity were appreciated as we carefully turned the pages of the Stella d'Oro guest books and travelled back in time. If we had been digging for gold then this was the biggest nugget in town; these crumpled pages contain the fading signatures of most Alpine pioneers of the Victorian era and many more who visited later.

We found Gilbert and Churchill, with and without their wives, Francis Fox Tuckett, with and without his sisters, Rev T G Bonney and all the usual suspects including the flamboyant signature of the artist Elijah Walton. Marco pointed out the page from 6 September 1860 where we made our surprising discovery. John Ball and John Birkbeck signed in on their way from Val di Fassa to Longarone, after they had climbed Rocca di Marmolada. And on the facing page, sometime later, somebody had attached with sealing wax the instructions for the Alpine Club minimum thermometer No325 that Ball and Birkbeck struggled with, hampered by wind-chill, on top of Punta Rocca.

Readers who studied O-level physics will remember that a minimum thermometer uses pure alcohol which freezes at -114°C. The glass index, a thin rod about 10mm long with a disc at each end, is inside the colourless liquid and it is pulled down the bore of the thermometer by surface tension as the temperature drops. When the temperature increases, the alcohol moves past the index as it rises up the thermometer, leaving the end of the index at the lowest temperature that the thermometer recorded. The use of this piece of scientific equipment reminds us that the original members of the Alpine Club were interested in recording scientific observations as well as climbing mountains and this research tradition continues today. A barometer was another essential accoutrement for John Ball which he used to estimate the height of the peaks he climbed.

Some contextual information may help readers unfamiliar with the early exploration of the Dolomites to appreciate its significance. Mountaineering was unknown in these valleys until 1857 when John Ball reached the summit of Pelmo and wrote about his climb.[3] This was the first recorded ascent of any Dolomite peak, although we now know that Ball probably made the third ascent of Pelmo; the earliest was claimed by local chamois hunter Belli Battista Vecchio who found a human skeleton near the summit in 1824.[4] Word soon spread among Alpine Club members, through the pages of this journal, about these unclimbed, spectacular peaks and many accomplished alpinists like Francis Fox Tuckett, Leslie Stephen, Douglas Freshfield, Charles Comyns Tucker and Edward Robson Whitwell all claimed first ascents in the Dolomites during the 1860s and 1870s.

The mystery of how these instructions ended up sealed into the Stella d'Oro guestbook fascinated me. Marco Menardi is not sure what happened, but clearly somebody removed them from Punta Rocca and took them to Cortina. Our first suspect was Anthon von Ruthner, one of the founders

3. J Ball, *Guide to the Eastern Alps*, Longmans, 1869, p525 & *Alpine Journal* XVII, p381.
4. F Torchio & R Decarli, *Ad Est Del Romanticismo: 1786-1901 Alpinisti vittoriani sulle dolomiti*, New-Book, 2014, p383.

Instructions for the Alpine Club thermometer. *(Alan Boyle)*

---

ALPINE CLUB
NOTICE TO TRAVELLERS

Minimum thermometer marked "Alpine Club No. 325" has been placed by *Messrs Ball & Birkbeck on the Marmolata – highest ridge about 150 feet below the topmost rocks & east of the same, attached to a rock facing N. West*

Any person finding the same is requested not to touch or disturb the instrument, but to note the lowest temperature, as indicated on the scale of the Thermometer by the end of the glass index farthest from the bulb. A memorandum of the measurement should be made in the column headed "Minimum" at the back of this paper (a duplicate of which will be found enclosed in a glass tube near the instrument), and an entry inserted of the hour, day, month, year, and observer's name in their respective columns. Next, observe the 'actual temperature' and enter it in the corresponding column. Travellers are also requested to preserve a written record, *made on the spot*, of the temperatures so observed, as well as of those previously registered, and the number of the instrument, enter a copy of them on the back of the paper, and transmit a duplicate to F.F. Tuckett, 10 Baldwin Street, Bristol, England. Provided with a good ordinary Thermometer, it would be well to observe if the 'actual temperatures' indicated by the 'Minimum Thermometer' agree; and, if not, to note the amount of discrepancy, together with any other matter of interest, in the column headed 'Remarks'. The paper should then be carefully replaced, and the tube securely closed.

A previously unpublished sketch by Amelia B Edwards of Becco di Mezzodì & Croda da Lago. *(Griffith Institute, University of Oxford)*

of the Austrian Alpine Club, who made the second ascent of Punta Rocca in 1861. However, Paul Grohmann reported that he found the thermometer and instructions when he made the third ascent in 1862.[5] Next on the spot was Johan Jakob Weilenmann who made the fourth ascent in 1862. There is an outside chance that the thermometer survived long enough to be picked up by one of the British party consisting of the Bryce brothers, Lee Warner, Nettleship and Oxenham who made the next ascent in 1863, although they record that the whole route was covered with soft, deep snow.[6] By then, they all realised that Punta Rocca was lower than Punta Penìa and Grohmann was the first to reach that summit, the highest point on Marmolada, in 1864 with the guides Angelo and Fulgenzio Dimai from Cortina. After that, climbers were more interested in reaching the highest peak. My guess is Paul Grohmann brought the instructions back to Cortina, but I'd be delighted to hear from any readers with more information.

Apart from illuminating the adventures of these pioneers, the incident added something more valuable to our research. In *Spirits of the Dolomites* we set out to discover what has changed and what, if anything, remains the same since Amelia Edwards' journey at the dawn of mountaineering and tourism in the region. We visited the same places that Edwards passed through and made contact with relatives of people she met. The humble wooden chalets and small wayside inns that Edwards wrote about have been replaced by modern apartments and swish five-star wellness centres; rough bridle paths and footpaths are now smooth highways, so changes are obvious. What remains the same is more intriguing.

From *Untrodden Peaks and Unfrequented Valleys* we recognise the special appeal of these mountains and the emotional effect they had on Edwards, revealed through her fervent pen portraits. Unsurprisingly, these mountains have the same profound effect on our feelings and we attribute this to something we call the mountain spirits of the Dolomites. Amelia Edwards also wrote heart-warming accounts of incidents on her journey describing the honesty, natural humility, openness, welcoming charm and authentic

5. *Alpine Journal* XVII, p384.
6. *Alpine Journal* I, p201.

care shown by the ordinary people she met by chance on her travels. And what we discover from our research is that these behaviours and attitudes of genuine humanity have passed through generations because they are the same today, exemplified by Carlo Gandini, Marco Menardi and almost everyone we met, as they were in Amelia's time. We call them the human spirits of the Dolomites.

*Alan Boyle*

### Boardman Tasker Award 2017

The 2017 Boardman Tasker event, held once again at the Kendal Mountain Festival, was a great success. There was a big demand for tickets and five of the six shortlisted authors were able to attend. Andy Perkins welcomed everyone to KMF with Martin Wragg, chair of the BT Charitable Trust, welcoming everyone to the shortlisted authors' event before handing over to Stephen Venables to interview authors present.

Stephen began by talking to **Tommy Caldwell**, author of *The Push*. This is a candid, bold and compelling book about climbing at the very top level. The book gives a fascinating insight into big-wall free climbing and the complex challenges that characterise a life in the sport. A gripping read by one of the modern masters of rock climbing. Next up, Stephen talked to **Rob Collister**, author of *Days to Remember*. This is a thoughtful, varied and highly literate book, describing journeys in mountain landscapes that are solitary, but seldom lonely. There is a fine sense of honesty and humility in Rob's prose and his reflections on life as a mountain guide. It is a very fine, quiet and contemplative book expressing a deep love of the mountain environment.

The third writer on stage was **Ed Douglas**, author of *The Magician's Glass*. This is a very fine collection of essays exploring climbing controversies, failures and the impact of mountaineering on local communities. A superb example of intelligent mountaineering journalism, it tackles moral issues in particular with great skill and observation. The next author on stage was **Bernadette McDonald**, author of *Art of Freedom*. Her new book is a very accomplished biography of one of the greatest alpinists of all time Voytek Kurtyka. Lucidly and economically written, the book succeeds in making extreme mountaineering accessible to the lay reader and records a life of great adventure.

The final writer to be interviewed was **Christopher Nicholson**, author of *Among the Summer Snows*. Lyrical and tender, this is a fascinating account of the remaining snows of the Scottish highlands. A work of great originality and charm, it offers an unusual view of the relationship between humans and the natural world. The sixth book shortlisted was *Night Naked* by **Erhard Loretan** and **Jean Ammann**, was unrepresented on the day. This first-hand account of the well-known high-altitude Swiss alpinist Erhard Loretan's achievements, now translated into English, is well paced and characterised by a lively vocabulary and self-deprecating humour. In particular, accounts of adventures in the Himalaya, notably on Gasherbrum II are deeply rewarding.

The chair of judges for 2017 was the well-known poet Helen Mort and the other two judges were Peter Gillman, chair for 2018, and former *Alpine Journal* assistant editor Catherine Moorehead. Helen gave an excellent, informative and humorous speech, again outlining the panel's experience of dealing with well over thirty entries. She explained the difficulties of dealing with one of the BT's outstanding shortlists. After full deliberation, they decided that the winner of the 2017 Boardman Tasker Award for Mountain Literature was *Art of Freedom* by Bernadette McDonald. In her speech Helen outlined the impact this outstanding biography had, and touched on a sharp expression of Voytek's character in his steadfast refusal to accept the Piolet d'Or:

*Voytek maintained that alpinism was far too complex to rank and compare. There were so many facets: aesthetic, physical, metaphysical, logistical, imaginative. And there was so much suffering. How could you measure the suffering of climbers?*

• The 2018 Boardman Tasker event is at Kendal Mountain Festival on Friday 16 November 2018.

*Steve Dean*

**Performing Mountains**
Full of surprises, creativity and interdisciplinary conversations from an experienced and varied range of participants, this was the final event of an Arts and Humanities Research Council funded project led by Jonathan Pitches, professor of theatre and performance at the University of Leeds. This 18-month project is partnered with Kendal Mountain Festival and will result in a book, *Performing Landscapes: Mountains* from Palgrave Macmillan. A series of seminars bringing together climbers, artists and academics – the 'Mountainsides' conversations – had already taken place on the themes 'Risk', 'Training', 'Light', and 'Composition'. They can be viewed on the project website: *https://performing-mountains.leeds.ac.uk//mountainsides-talks/*. Another earlier outcome from the project was a 15-minute film of a performance at Leeds in November 2017, 'Black Rock', that arose out of collaboration with Johnny Dawes and explored the research question: how can the experience of climbing be translated to an audience on the ground? Its director and designer, the Performing Mountains project's post-doctoral fellow David Shearing, showed this film at the symposium and gave a talk on how practice-led research in performance can contribute to mountain studies through 'translating mountain experience'.

When I asked the Welsh artist, Dave Ball, about the positive aims underlying his amusingly subversive presentation, his reply might stand for the achievement of the whole symposium: 'expanding the spectrum of response to mountains.' His talk, on searching for the national mountain of Wales – 'the perfect Welsh hill' – was, of course, a critique of the whole idea. He had made an exhibition of careful line drawings of candidates, which were subverted by the accompanying bland text of data about them. Ball showed a hilarious video of his walking all day trying to avoid actually looking at a mountain. His current PhD project at Winchester School of Art is on how the approach of 'tactical absurdity' might reveal what is taken for granted in our response to mountains. Sharing this panel were Richard Gough's account of taking a two-person Welsh dragon for a walk in the Brecon Beacons with no audience whatsoever (until a military patrol suddenly had it surrounded for serious questioning) and scenographer (set-designer to you and me) Susannah Henry taking a tiny model of herself for a walk to be photographed out of scale. She was exploring something about 'seeing a place and remembering when you were there' which she called 'remi-instance', I think. The subversive tone of this first evening was followed by a play in which a geared-up 'Gary' attempted to walk to and fro for an hour along a line in a simulation of covering the distance up Everest whilst a commentary from his partner simulated an academic paper of 60 chapters of dry facts about Everest, about Gary and about the play group which had loaned the blow-up paddling pool filled with polystyrene snow in which he was sitting. This performance was 'On Everest' by Lone Twin.

Actually there were academic papers, on 'Mountain Time and Ritual', 'Performing Mountain Archives', 'Mountain Histories', 'Mountain Identity and Gender', 'Mountain Bodies and Movement', and 'Mountain Architectures' in which buildering and 'walking arts practice' in Tate Modern's Turbine Hall featured. There was also poetry, photography, fine art, storytelling, improvisation, and dance in which a sub-discipline of 'vertical dance' has been developing over the last twenty years. For many participants the most moving presentation of the symposium was called 'Roped Together', devised by Kate Lawrence Vertical Dance and performed by Kate and her partner, Simon. Simple in conception – two harnessed climbers tied into a rope that passed over a pulley in the roof - this piece was subtle in suggesting the effects of one partner's movements upon the other when roped together. When we entered the space one climber was prone on the ground and the other standing above her, apparently on the phone. The rescue narrative included her climbing the rope above him, bringing him to her level, then her climbing onto his shoulders and falling backwards. The tension (real and dramatic) between them somehow expressed their caring for each other and concluded in an enfolding of each other that was both emotional and pragmatic. Their grey hair belied their experience and the profound maturity they had communicated demonstrated what can be achieved in 'performing mountains'.

The event opened with Doug Scott and the poet Helen Mort who had been asked to speak 'On Exposure'. Doug talked about making decisions in exposed situations as the essence of climbing and confessed to having been excited by the decisions ahead when he and his companions were faced with getting him down the Ogre with two broken legs. Helen gave us a new poem, specially commissioned for the symposium, printed opposite.

*Terry Gifford*

## The Exposed
*after Wilfred Owen*

We were high, but this was more than just the drag of height –
I saw the known world shelve away from us
and found no name for it. Dawn was a brief chaos of light.
I kept our camera shuttered, hidden in plain sight.
        You could say nothing happened.

We were not unsafe. We were rarely unkind.
The ledge was suitable; exactly coffin-wide
and sturdy, stable, table-flat. I put my axes to one side,
breathed in – a salted sharpness keen as lemon rind.
        You could say nothing happened.

We were young – it matters now – and competent.
Our feet were shaped for niches, smoothness, grit and dust.
We thought that friction was the same as trust.
We built good anchors, gripped with granite confidence.
        You could say nothing happened.

When stonefall scalded through our silence
we were not afraid. It was always somewhere else.
We climbed until we clambered right outside ourselves –
I moved with all my father's subtle violence.
        You could say nothing happened.

At camp, you'd shown me how your camera worked:
the shutter speed, lens aperture, the light reaching the film
and touching it, light fixing everything – the valley's rim,
the morning and the undone route. *Exposure.* One word.
        You could say nothing happened.

I kept it stashed down in my rucksack half the time,
wrapped in a thermarest, swaddled like a lame bird.
I took no shots. It angered you. You couldn't find the words
and if you had, I'd have replied *what's yours is mine.*
        You could say nothing happened.

Our coldest night, your babbled visions of the news:
our faces beaming from a breakfast TV show.
*A test, a triumph…and they said it wouldn't go!*
You reckoned fame was something you could choose.
        I said nothing would happen.

There's something private about falling snow.
I ducked their questions afterwards. Exposed.
I keep your name, a single label from your clothes.
Your heart was weak. How could I know?
     I told them nothing happened.

And nothing is repeated every day,
it breaks across closed eyelids, over sleeping chests
and fills the careful places where we planned to rest,
until it finds us, holds us, folds us carefully away.
     Now say it – slowly. Nothing happens.

*Helen Mort*

### Alpine Club Library Report 2017

Our new honorary librarian, Barbara Grigor-Taylor, had a first important task: to engage a new professional librarian as after eight years with us, Tadeusz 'Tad' Hudowski left in the spring. Nigel Buckley was appointed in the autumn of 2017. Nigel has an MA from Newcastle University, has librarian experience with Kingston University, and is just completing his second MA, in library collection management, at University College, London.

At the Frenchay Village Museum, Bristol, January to March, we showed a 'Golden Age of Alpinism' exhibition. This was a success being visited by many local AC members and others; 120 people attended our related evening lecture. For the Mountain Heritage Trust, Glyn Hughes attended to provide several exhibits for the 'British Women Climb' exhibition at Keswick Museum and Art Gallery from September 2017 until September of this year. These included the AC painting, 'The Fee Glacier and the Allalinhorn' by Hilda Heckle. At the AC, we exhibited paintings by Rowan Huntley, Neil Pittaway and Tim Pollard with each collection on show for around two months.

Barbara, Nigel, and Peter Rowland gave illustrated presentations to visiting groups from Hoe Bridge School, Woking; the London College of Communications; David Coral; Climbing Club of Equador; and others. Project topics included the Eiger, Everest, South American peaks, and the history of mountain photography.

The Alpine Club Collections are cared for by the library team. These comprise mountaineering books, journals, MEF reports, tracts, archives, artefacts, photographs, paintings, and the Himalayan Index, which lists key ascents over 6,000m and is maintained by Sally Russell. In all, this comprises around 100,000 items. The AC owns the great majority, a few are owned by the ACL, a registered charity, and a few are held in trust for owners. Together, these form one of the most significant assemblies of mountain material in the world. Members can visit the library on Tuesdays, Wednesdays, and Thursdays (except during August and the week of Christmas and the New Year. Some items can only be viewed by appointment so please telephone or email to check if travelling from afar. Catalogues of our books, archives and the Himalayan Index are on the AC website.

The book catalogue now holds 27,404 volumes; with tracts, pamphlets and maps, the overall total is well over 30,000 items. Barbara and Jerry completed the mammoth task of making a new valuation of the books so we have up-to-date figures for insurance. At the same time the shelving was cleaned and improved. Peter Payne and Philip Meredith created further book space by building extra shelving. Digitisation of Mount Everest Foundation (MEF) expedition reports (nearly 1,300 to date) continues and this should be completed soon. Digitised editions of the *Alpine Journal* from 1930 to

Above: Nigel Buckley, new AC librarian and mixologist.

2014 are now on our website and 1911 to 1929 are due to be added soon. Our High Asia maps, e.g. Tian Shan and the Karakoram, are popular for reference and some can be digitized.

We are always grateful for donations of second-hand mountaineering books. We retain some to expand the collections, e.g. good condition volumes, or as extra loan copies, and we offer others for sale to members, providing an opportunity to purchase classic books at reasonable prices. Barbara and Gordon Turner circulate these duplicate lists. This generates funds that go directly to the upkeep of the library stock. Duplicate books have also been donated to the George Starkey hut, Somerhill School, Tonbridge, and the Climbers' Club huts.

The year has been very fruitful for archive acquisitions, particularly diaries. Donated by his son Tony, the Frank Smythe archive includes his diaries from Kamet, Everest and the Rockies, and photographs that survived a conflagration. The Charles Marriott archive, passed on to us by our member John Atherton, includes accounts of climbs with Eric Shipton and Denise Evans, but also two voyages with Tilman. Colin Kirkus' diary from Gangotri came by a circuitous route from his brother. This diary makes an interesting companion – and contrast – to Charles Warren's diary of the same expedition, already in the archives. Over several visits, we had been helping Susan to sort George Band's books and records. Searches for George's diary of his first ascent of Kangchenjunga in 1955 failed. However, a visit by Glyn located this at last and now we are scanning it to make it readily available for study.

Our honorary keeper of the photographs Peter Rowland, and his able deputy Bernie Ingrams have continued to search the photo collection boxes, quantify what we have, and scan many at high resolution. Examination

'The Fee Glacier and the Allalinhorn' by Hilda Heckle.

of 51 albums in 26 boxes, acquired as the Basil Goodfellow collection, found some important photos of people. For many photos, thumbnail images have been added to the catalogue in Capture software; currently, this stands at around 3,500 images. Overall, it is estimated that the entire collections contain 35,000 images, including George Band's slides, so there is still a lot to do. As photo sales manager, Sue Hare has continued to gain one-use reproduction fees for photos to appear in magazines, publicity and journals: always an important source of income to the library.

During 2017, the BMC started a mountain photo collection for viewing on their website. We prepared 100 of our historic photos for the BMC website. Work is also in progress to digitise 1,500 slides of the Himalaya donated by Harish Kapadia, including transferring these into a better archival environment.

Also amongst treasures in the Alpine Club Photo Library are 192 stereoscopic slides from AC member Albert Hackett (c1860-1910). We have now digitised and electronically cleaned these; they are a treasure and represent the great popularity of stereo pictures during the late Victoria era. We presented a large framed print of a photo of Joseph Biner to the Lauber family at the Bahnhof in Zermatt in June. The daughter of the Biner family of famous guides has married into the Lauber family of guides who now own and run the Bahnhof. The traditional link with the Club has been continued.

Peter organised the new AC Photographic Competition, with John Cleare as the chief judge, and the winners were announced at the annual dinner in November. The superb award-winning photos are in the AC Calendar, published for 2018.

John Fairley, our honorary keeper of the paintings, has completed a catalogue and database of 740 paintings and works of art, each with a thumbnail digitised photo for identification. Now we are running trials of this catalogue, 'The Painting Collection Revealed', on our visitor desk, so all visitors can browse the Club's paintings.

We have been delighted to receive two large bequests: from Alan Lyall, our late member known for his definitive book *The Descent of the Matterhorn*; and from Lord Roger Chorley, renowned climber when younger with the ACG, and AC president 1983-85. The trustees are applying these to specific projects to improve the AC collections for future generations of mountaineers.

In March, with great regret, we learned of the death of Peter Mallalieu, who had been our keeper of the paintings for around 20 years. Peter com-

Ben Tibbetts' winning photograph 'Innominata Ridge, Mont Blanc' in the AC Photo Competition 2017.

Setting up the Alpine Club exhibition at Frenchay Village Museum, Bristol. Alan Freke, curator, greets Tony Westcott, who is inspecting the ice axe used by Dr Raymond Greene on Everest 1933.

piled *The Artists of the Alpine Club*, an important biographical dictionary recording the many artists represented in the AC collections.

Every member can, and should, be proud of the continuing tradition of care and access provided by the library team. All our thanks are due to the many volunteers who have provided their time an expertise so effectively.

*Hywel Lloyd*
*Chair of the Alpine Club Library Council*

# Contributors

**MALCOLM BASS** has always been fascinated by exploration. At first he focused on caving and cave diving, but his head was turned by a winter trip to Ben Nevis and since then he has been absorbed by the process of trying to climbing new routes in Scotland, Alaska, Pakistan, India and China. He and Paul Figg were nominated for a *Piolet d'Or* for their ascent of the west face of Vasuki Parbat in 2010.

**ANTONIO GÓMEZ BOHÓRQUEZ** is a librarian and information scientist and lives in Murcia, Spain. He has climbed since 1967 and specialises in ascents in the north Peruvian ranges. He has written two books: *La Cordillera Blanca de los Andes, selección de ascensiones, excursiones y escaladas* and Cordrillera Blanca, Escaladas, Parte Norte.

**MARK CAREY** is a professor of environmental history and the history of science at the University of Oregon. He studies the societal dimensions of glaciers, icebergs, and climate change, working in the Andes and more recently in the Arctic and Antarctic. Before that he was a climber and ranger at Glacier, Rainier, and Yosemite national parks.

**GEORGE CAVE** works for much of the year as a design engineer in Warwick. In search of more adventurous peaks he developed in interest in planning expeditions abroad, particularly to central Asia. In recent years he has climbed or skied in Kyrgyzstan, Iran, Morocco and Russia.

**JOHN CLEARE** has been a freelance professional photographer for over 50 years but a climber for rather longer. Business and many expeditions have taken him all over the world, while he has several dozen books, several films and live TV broadcasts, more than a few new routes and several virgin summits to his credit. An ex-vice president of the AC and an ex-president of the Alpine Ski Club, he lives in remote Wiltshire.

**MICK CONEFREY** is a filmmaker and writer, specialising in exploration and mountaineering. He's the author of *Everest 1953* and *The Ghosts of K2*. His film on the first ascent of K2 won several international awards. He is currently at work on a history of the first ascent of Kangchenjunga.

**TARQUIN COOPER** is a freelance journalist who writes everything from obituaries for the *Daily Telegraph* to travel features for the *Financial Times* to content for outdoor clients like GORE-TEX, Suunto and Land Rover. Until recently he was based in Salzburg where he worked for Red Bull as an editor, presenter and race reporter – and discovered an enthusiasm (if not ability) for ski-mountaineering races.

**LINDSAY ELMS** lives on Vancouver Island and has climbed or travelled on all seven continents including ascents of Mt Logan, Mt Waddington and numerous peaks throughout South America. He has also written two books about the history of mountaineering and exploration on Vancouver Island.

**PAUL EVANS** is an artist and climber based in Sheffield. He is the recipient of a number of prestigious awards including the Eyestorm Gallery Award for painting. Recent exhibitions include 'Confluence' at Herrick Gallery, Mayfair. Evans often collaborates with leading writers, including the ongoing The Seven Wonders | De Mirabilibus Pecci poetry and painting project *www.seven-wonders.org.*

**PETER FOSTER** is a retired consultant physician. He has been a member of the Alpine Club since 1975. His biography of T Graham Brown is to be published by Vertebrate in January 2019.

**RODNEY GARRARD** is a geologist, climber and photographer and sometimes ends up mixing the three together. His PhD dissertation at the University of Bern, Switzerland, explored landscape dynamics in the Everest region in Nepal. He has also conducted research in the mountains of Peru, Switzerland and Eastern Africa.

**TERRY GIFFORD** was director of the annual International Festival of Mountaineering Literature for 21 years. Former chair of the Mountain Heritage Trust, he is the author of *The Joy of Climbing* (Whittles, 2004) and *Al Otro Lado del Aguilar* (Oversteps Books, 2011). Visiting professor at Bath Spa University's Centre for Writing and Environment and *profesor honorífico* at the University of Alicante, he celebrated his 70th birthday appropriately on *Wreckers' Slab.*

**DENNIS GRAY** started climbing on Yorkshire gritstone in 1947. Secretary of the ACG, first national officer, then general secretary of the BMC, Dennis has visited over 60 countries, most recently travelling widely in China. He has written two autobiographies, two books of stories, a novel and a volume of poetry, plays the banjo and sings on three CDs of climbing themed songs.

**JIM GREGSON** has climbed widely in the Alps since 1972. He is also a telemark ski mountaineer who makes regular trips to Norway. He first visited the Arctic in1991 and has returned many times, often as an expedition leader, and is one of Britain's leading Arctic mountaineers. His book *Exploring Greenland* documents many of his trips and showcases his photography.

**LINDSAY GRIFFIN** lives in North Wales, from where he continues to report on developments in world mountaineering. An enthusiastic mind still tries to coax a less than enthusiastic body up pleasant bits of rock and ice, both at home and abroad. He recently completed his term of office as president of the Alpine Club.

**LEO HOULDING** is one of the UK's top climbers, best known for his hard technical routes on big walls around the world, including his 10-year odyssey to climb The Prophet at Yosemite. He climbed Everest for a documentary about Mallory and Irvine and made groundbreaking films in the Arctic and Antarctic.

**GLYN HUGHES** is a some-time hon secretary of the Alpine Club, but now carries out the equally important roles of hon archivist and barman: or as the AC quaintly puts it, 'chairman of the Wine Committee'. In 2014 he took on the near-impossible task of following Bill Ruthven as hon secretary of the Mount Everest Foundation.

**TOM LIVINGSTONE** is a 26-year-old climber and writer based in north Wales. He has a penchant for trad, winter and alpine climbing: the bigger and harder the better. Among his recent successes are ascents of *Divine Providence* (ED3), and a winter ascent of the *Walker Spur* (ED3), but he's still hungry for more. He works as an outdoor instructor, holding the Mountain Leader and Single Pitch Award, and as a rope access technician.

**BRUCE NORMAND** is a research consultant at the Neutrons and Muons Research Division at the Paul Scherrer Institut in Switzerland, after spending five years as a professor of theoretical physics at Renmin University in Beijing. He has made over 40 first ascents on 6,000m peaks in Nepal, Pakistan, India and China. In 2007 he climbed K2, the first Scotsman to have done so. He won a Piolet d'Or in 2010 and was nominated for a second in 2011.

**DONALD ORR** is a member of the Scottish Mountaineering Club and recently retired from a career in theology and fine art, which does beg questions. He now spends his time climbing and writing, and being irresponsible with his grandsons. His writings on mountaineering and the mountain environment have contributed over the years to the *Scottish Mountaineering Club Journal*.

**SIMON RICHARDSON** lives in Aberdeen. Experience gained in the Alps, Andes, Patagonia, Canada, the Himalaya, Caucasus, Alaska and the Yukon is put to good use most winter weekends whilst exploring and climbing in the Scottish Highlands.

**C A RUSSELL**, who formerly worked with a City bank, devotes much of his time to mountaineering and related activities. He has climbed in many regions of the Alps, in the Pyrenees, East Africa, North America and the Himalaya.

**VICTOR SAUNDERS** was born in Lossiemouth and grew up in Peninsular Malaysia. He began climbing in the Alps in 1978 and has since climbed in the Andes, Antarctica, Papua, Rockies, Caucasus and across the Himalaya and Karakoram. Formerly a London-based architect, he is now an IFMGA guide based in Chamonix. His first book, *Elusive Summits*, won the Boardman Tasker Prize. In 2007 he received an honorary MA from the University of Stirling for services to Scottish mountaineering.

**MARCELO SCANU** is an Argentine climber who lives in Buenos Aires. He specialises in ascending virgin mountains and volcanoes in the Central Andes. His articles and photographs about alpinism, trekking, and mountain history, archaeology and ecology appear in prominent magazines in Europe and America. When not climbing, he works for a workers' union.

**MIKE SEARLE** has been on over 30 expeditions, starting in Patagonia, Peru and Ecuagdor, and progressing to the Himalaya in Ladakh, Zanskar, Garhwal and throughout Nepal and Bhutan. In the Karakoram he has climbed on K2, Masherbrum, Biale, Trango and on granite spires in the Baltoro, Biafo and Hushe regions. He has also rock climbed in Jordan and Oman and is now professor of earth sciences at the University of Oxford.

**BEN SILVESTRE** is a North Yorkshire-born climber, now based in Sheffield. Working as an industrial abseiler allows him a lot of freedom for going climbing, and although he loves the small Peak District outcrops, he tries to spend as much time travelling to, and climbing in new and adventurous locations, whether that means British sea cliffs, or distant mountains.

**RODERICK SMITH** is an emeritus research professor at Imperial College London. He has climbed and travelled in mountain areas in many parts of the world over the last 60 years but still enjoys returning to where he started, the Pennines and the Lake District, despite traffic problems en route, which he failed to solve while chief scientist at the Department for Transport.

**BEN TIBBETTS** is a photographer, artist and IFMGA guide based in Chamonix and the UK. He studied Fine Art to postgraduate level and spent almost two years working in the Antarctic and over four months in Greenland. In Europe he is usually preoccupied with climbing long Alpine routes of different styles and difficulty or looking for interesting lines to ski. Over the last few years he has been working on a large format photographic guidebook on the finest routes on the 4,000m peaks of the Alps.

**KOEN VAN LOCKE** finished his studies at the University of Ghent in 2012. After working as a ski instructor in Switzerland, he returned to Belgium to work as a history teacher and study for a PhD on participation in mountaineering at the University of Leuven. In his spare time he tries to be outdoors as much as possible, cycling or climbing, or mountaineering and skiing in the holidays.

**IAN WALL** worked at Plas-y-Brenin in the 1960s. Since then he has climbed extensively throughout the UK, the Alps and in Norway. He was involved with the first round of the Kendal Mountain Film Festival in 1980. He has led treks in Africa, Ladakh, Tibet and Nepal, where he now lives and acts as an advisor to the Kathmandu International Mountain Film Festival, Kathmandu Environmental Education Project and in developing and training the Nepal Mountain Leader programme working closely with the Nepal Mountaineering Association.

**JONATHAN WESTAWAY** is a research fellow in history at the University of Central Lancashire, examining the history of mountaineering, exploration and the outdoor movement, part of a wider interest in the intersections of liberalism, modernity, masculinity, physical culture and imperialism in the late 19th and early 20th century. His research on Eric Shipton's mountain travel writing while in the pay of the British Indian imperial security state, 'That undisclosed world: Eric Shipton's *Mountains of Tartary* (1950)', appears in *Studies in Travel Writing*, vol 18, No4, pp357-373.

**RICHARD ZÖLLNER** is a German writer and mountaineer. He is drawn to remote places and has developed a love affair with the mountains of Iran and its people.

# NOTES FOR CONTRIBUTORS

The *Alpine Journal* records all aspects of mountains and mountaineering, including expeditions, exploration, art, literature, geography, history, geology, medicine, ethics and the mountain environment.

**Articles** Contributions in English are invited. They should be sent to the Hon Editor *The Alpine Journal*, Alpine Club, 55 Charlotte Road, London EC2A 3QF, UK. (**journal.editor@alpine-club.org.uk**) Articles, including images, can be sent as an email attachment, on a disk or memory stick. File-sharing services are also acceptable, by prior arrangement with the editor. With files created in Microsoft Word please confine formatting to italics and bold. A typical article is 2,500 words **and may be edited or shortened at their discretion.** Longer pieces should be discussed with the editor.

*The Alpine Journal* is unable to offer a fee for articles published, but authors who are not AC members receive a copy of the issue of the *Journal* in which their article appears.

**Maps and diagrams** These should be well researched, accurate and show the most important place-names mentioned in the text. If submitted electronically, maps and route diagrams should be originated as CMYK .eps files in Adobe Illustrator, Freehand or similar ensuring embedded images are at 300dpi resolution and CMYK. Hard copy should be scanned as a Photoshop compatible 300dpi tiff at A4 finished size. This can be arranged through the editor if required.

**Photographs** Image files should have unique names or serial numbers **that correspond to the list of captions** appended to the article, as a separate document, or in an email. They should be large jpgs or tiff files. Captions must include the photographer's name. Colour transparencies should be originals. Pre-scanned images should be **300dpi** Greyscale or RGB, tiffs or maximum quality jpegs at A4 final size or larger.

**Copyright** It is the author's responsibility to obtain copyright clearance for text, photographs, digital images and maps, to pay any fees involved and to ensure acknowledgements are in the form required by the copyright owner.

**Summaries** A brief summary, listing team members, dates, objectives attempted and achieved, should be included at the end of expedition articles.

**Biographies** Authors are asked to provide a short autobiography of about 50 words, listing noteworthy highlights in their climbing career and anything else they wish to mention.

**Deadline** Copy and photographs should reach the editor by **1 February** of the year of publication.

# Index 2018